MW00861239

THE RISE OF
NEWPORT'S CATHOLICS

THE RISE OF
NEWPORT'S CATHOLICS

*From Colonial Outcasts
to Gilded Age Leaders*

JOHN F. QUINN

University of Massachusetts Press
AMHERST AND BOSTON

Copyright © 2024 by University of Massachusetts Press
All rights reserved
Printed in the United States of America

ISBN 978-1-62534-797-8 (paper); 798-5 (hardcover)

Designed by Sally Nichols
Set in Adobe Garamond
Printed and bound by Books International, Inc.

Cover design by adam b. bohannon
Cover art: A color postcard of St. Mary's Church, Spring Street.
Title on postcard reads *C9768-St. Mary's church, Newport, R.I.*, c. 1910.
Courtesy of Newport Historical Society.

Library of Congress Cataloging-in-Publication Data

Names: Quinn, John F., 1964– author.
Title: The rise of Newport's Catholics : from colonial outcasts to gilded
age leaders / John F. Quinn.
Description: Amherst : University of Massachusetts Press, [2024] | Includes
bibliographical references and index. |
Identifiers: LCCN 2023046508 (print) | LCCN 2023046509 (ebook) | ISBN
9781625347978 (paperback) | ISBN 9781625347985 (hardcover) | ISBN
9781685750718 (ebook)
Subjects: LCSH: Catholics—Rhode Island—Newport—History. | Newport
(R.I.)—Church history.
Classification: LCC BX1418.N59 Q56 2024 (print) | LCC BX1418.N59 (ebook)
| DDC 282/.7457—dc23/eng/20240213
LC record available at https://lccn.loc.gov/2023046508
LC ebook record available at https://lccn.loc.gov/2023046509

British Library Cataloguing-in-Publication Data

A catalog record for this book is available from the British Library.

Chapter 2 was previously published as "From Dangerous Threat to 'Illustrious Ally': Changing Perceptions in Eighteenth-Century Newport," in
Rhode Island History 75 (Summer–Fall 2017): 56–79; republished with
permission of the Rhode Island Historical Society. Portions of chapters 4
and 5 were previously published as "'Where Religious Freedom Runs in
the Streams': Catholic Expansion in Newport, 1780–1855," *Newport History*
80, no. 264 (Spring 2011): 1–29; republished by permission of the Newport
Historical Society.

To Marguerite, Michael, Kathleen, and Stephen

CONTENTS

ILLUSTRATIONS

ACKNOWLEDGMENTS

Having worked on this project for a dozen or so years, I have accumulated a host of debts that I am happy to acknowledge now. I have to begin with George Antone, a former colleague, who encouraged me to take up the project and has remained supportive as I have slowly progressed with it. Father Robert Hayman, the archivist of the Providence diocese, has also been a great help to me. I found his diocesan histories indispensable and greatly appreciate the warm welcome he gave to me on my many visits to the diocesan archives. Patrick Murphy, the Newport city historian, has a wealth of knowledge about Newport, and he has repeatedly shared helpful materials with me, including indexes he painstakingly completed of the city's newspapers. My home institution, Salve Regina University, provided me with critical help as well, awarding me two sabbaticals that made it possible for me to complete my research and writing. I have also received generous financial support from the University provost, Nancy Schreiber, and from the John E. McGinty Fund at Salve Regina.

I am grateful to have had the opportunity to present portions of my research to the Newport Historical Society, the American Catholic Historical Association, the Historic Deerfield Conference, and the Irish Cultural Association of Rhode Island. Most of all, though, I am deeply appreciative of the welcome that I have received from the Museum of Newport Irish History, especially from the late Vince Arnold, as well as from Mike Slein, Ann Arnold, Deanna Conheeny, and Steve Marino. On several occasions, I have presented papers or served on panels where I had the chance to address issues related to Newport's Catholics.

Many archivists and librarians have helped me with my research, including Robert Johnson-Lally and Thomas Lester at the Boston Archdiocesan Archives; Maria Medina at the Hartford Archdiocesan

Archives; the late Sister Eleanor Little, R.S.M., and Elizabeth Johnson of the Mercy Heritage Center; the staffs of the National Archives in Waltham, Massachusetts; the archives of the Sisters of Saint Joseph of Springfield, Massachusetts; the Massachusetts Historical Society; the Rhode Island Historical Society; the College of the Holy Cross Archives; and Georgetown University's Special Collections. In Newport, I would like to thank Bertram Lippincott III, Ingrid Peters, Kaela Bleho and Molly Patterson of the Newport Historical Society, Patrick Crowley and Michelle Farias of the Redwood Library, Nicole Markham and Katie Harnett of the International Tennis Hall of Fame Archives, and the staff of the Newport Public Library.

It has been a pleasure working with the University of Massachusetts Press. Matt Becker, the editor-in-chief; Sally Nichols, the editorial, design, and publishing manager; Rachael DeShano, the former managing editor; and copyeditor Dawn Potter have helped me to improve the manuscript in a variety of ways. Several colleagues at Salve Regina have also aided and encouraged me along the way: James Yarnall, Barbara Kathe, Sarah Littlefield, John Rok, Tim Neary, Bill Leeman, Sister Madeleine Gregoire, D.H.S., Donna Harrington-Lueker, John Parrillo, Tom Svogun, Clark Merrill, Peter Colosi, and two departed friends: Sister Eugena Poulin, R.S.M., and Frank Maguire. I am also thankful to Kurt Schlichting, Paul Harpin, the late Philip Gleason, Elizabeth Stevens, Bill Issel, Robert Hayman, Steve Marino, David Carlin, Timothy Meagher, Eve Sterne, and my wife, Marguerite Quinn, for reading some or all of my manuscript and offering many helpful suggestions. I am especially grateful to my brother Bill, who provided a close and insightful reading of my chapter drafts. For help with statistical analysis, Kurt Schlichting and my son Michael Quinn were indispensable. I want to mention as well Paul O'Malley, the late Syd Williams, Victoria Johnson, Lew Keen, the late Kevin McGrath, O.P., Don Deignan, Raymond Roy, the late Sister Marie Hennessy, my sister Maryann Quinn, and my late brother Peter Quinn. I am grateful as well to Makenzie Sadler, an undergraduate history major at Salve Regina, for proofreading my chapters with an eagle eye. Finally, I want to thank my Salve Regina colleague and Newport authority Dan Titus for his help with my many technology questions and for sharing his wonderful collection of Newport postcards with me. Several of the images in the book come from Dan's holdings.

THE RISE OF
NEWPORT'S CATHOLICS

INTRODUCTION

When a mob set fire to the Charlestown Convent near Boston in the summer of 1834, many New England newspapers reacted with indignation to the "outrage."[1] A Newport newspaper, however, went a step further. The *Rhode-Island Republican* urged the nuns to move their convent and school to Newport:

> We would recommend to the Ursulines, if they should revive their institution . . . to turn their attention to this Island, to this healthy and delightful spot, to which scholars may be sent with the greatest expedition and facility. Here they may avail themselves not only of the free political institutions of Rhode Island, but also of the more liberal standard of public opinion where religious freedom runs in the streams and floats in the breeze. . . . The Catholics have recently built a handsome new Church in this town, and are a large society well received by this community, and who have the good wishes of all.[2]

A group of Newport residents picked up on the *Rhode-Island Republican*'s proposal and invited the bishop of Boston, Benedict Fenwick, to relocate the sisters to Newport and reestablish the school. The bishop and the sisters must have considered the invitation seriously because the bishop's own newspaper, *The Jesuit*, noted that "the attention of the Catholic Bishop has been drawn toward Newport . . . where the well known liberality and generous feelings of the inhabitants, would always be a guarantee or safeguard from an infatuated or infuriated mob."[3] In the end, the Charlestown community decided to disband. The sisters had sought compensation for their lost property, but the Massachusetts legislature rejected their appeal. Lacking the funds to rebuild, the sisters dispersed, moving to convents in Canada and Louisiana.[4]

Three years later, Father John Corry, the pastor of Newport's Catholic chapel, received word from Bishop Fenwick of his coming transfer to Providence. Disappointed at the news, Corry confided to his friend, Reverend Arthur Ross, whose Baptist church was located close to the Catholic chapel, "I have never seen a town in the United States, among whose inhabitants there is less intolerance and religious bigotry. I have for six years, been more or less among them, and during that time period, none have denied me the common civilities of life, because I was a Catholic priest, but always treated me with the greatest respect."[5]

Newport's Uniqueness

This book seeks to explain why Newport was so welcoming to Catholics. Most of New England in the nineteenth century was inhospitable territory for Catholics, to say the least. A convent of the Sisters of Mercy in Providence was surrounded and nearly attacked, a Jesuit priest in Maine was tarred and feathered and left for dead by his assailants, Know Nothings were elected governors of Rhode Island and Massachusetts, and "No Irish Need Apply" notices were commonplace in newspapers and store windows throughout the region. These nativist episodes have been ably addressed by a number of scholars: Ray Allen Billington, George Potter, John McGreevy, Nancy Lusignan Schultz, Thomas O'Connor, Timothy Meagher, Evelyn Savidge Sterne, Robert Hayman, Paula Kane, Patrick Conley, and Matthew Smith.[6] However, no historian has yet looked at Newport and tried to explain why the Catholics' experience there was so different.

First, it is important to note that Newport was not always so welcoming. In the colonial era, Catholics were very scarce and were viewed with suspicion. In the years leading up to the revolution, Newporters celebrated Guy Fawkes Day with as much gusto as the people of Boston did. Effigies of the pope were paraded down Thames Street and then were burned in a great bonfire to mark the anniversary of the 1605 Gunpowder Plot, in which Fawkes and several other Catholic conspirators planned to kill England's King James I. Newport ministers such as the Congregationalist Ezra Stiles warned about the dangers of Popery, and the editor of the *Newport Mercury* used his press to produce anti-Catholic pamphlets.

During the American Revolution, however, thousands of French soldiers and sailors landed in Newport and stayed there for almost a year. Top officers such as the Comte de Rochambeau and Admiral Charles de Ternay took up residence in Newport's finest homes, and the Colony House was transformed into both a hospital for ill soldiers and a Catholic chapel. While waiting for military instructions, the French rebuilt much of the city, which the British had damaged during their occupation. They also socialized with the residents, dancing and dining with them and charming them thoroughly. The French officers and priests were learned and refined, not at all what the people of Newport had expected. By the time the French departed to set out on the Yorktown campaign, one of their officers noted, "There was now a universal sigh of regret."[7] The people of Newport were going to miss their congenial occupiers.

Newport had long been a religiously diverse seaport. While much of New England was dominated by Puritans, Newport had Quakers, Jews, Congregationalists, Episcopalians, and several varieties of Baptists living and working together. When Newporters finally encountered Catholics in the form of these French troops, they were willing to accept them just as they had accepted the other religious minorities in their midst. While almost all of the French left Newport in 1781, they made a lasting impression on the residents of Newport. When Irish Catholics started arriving in Newport in the 1820s to work on Fort Adams, they were received well. They had no trouble establishing a Catholic chapel, Rhode Island's first, in 1828. The Fort Adams laborers were a hard-drinking lot and got into brawls from time to time. Still, the local press downplayed problems at the fort, with one paper declaring that the Fort Adams workers had "proved themselves, with few exceptions, respectable in their vocations, and peaceable and respectful in their demeanor."[8]

In the years following, Newporters would repeatedly come to the aid of the Catholics in their community. During the Civil War, Newport's newspapers paid tribute to the city's Irish immigrants, who fought and, in some cases, died for the Union. In 1864, the *Newport Mercury* hailed the courage of the city's Irish soldiers who "marched shoulder to shoulder with those who in former years wanted to deprive them of the rights of citizenship."[9]

Gilded Age Gains

After the war, Newport emerged as the nation's leading summer destination for wealthy tourists.[10] Attracted by the city's fine beaches and mild climate, some visitors stayed for weeks at one of its grand hotels. Others who wanted to avoid the crowded hotels chose to build luxurious homes of their own. These hotels and summer cottages provided numerous opportunities for Newport's Irish residents. While the Irish in many New England cities toiled in mills and fought the owners for better wages, in Newport a number of Irish prospered by catering to the needs and wants of the summer colonists. Thomas Galvin, for example, operated a successful nursery, Michael Butler ran a profitable floral business, and Michael McCormick was a highly regarded builder. By the end of the century, Newport's Catholics were no longer an Irish monolith; Italian and Portuguese immigrants began arriving in the city in the 1880s and were also able to find jobs supporting the summer colonists.

Newport's Catholics received considerable help as well from their Protestant neighbors, especially from Episcopalians, who were closer to them theologically than were the other Protestant denominations. George Downing, a prominent black Episcopalian in Newport, led the efforts in the 1880s to help immigrants obtain the vote in the state. In the 1890s, when the pastor of Saint Joseph's, a new parish, was trying to establish a parochial school, George Babcock Hazard, a wealthy Episcopalian, stepped forward and funded it. To express his gratitude, the pastor named the school for Hazard. Twenty years later, another wealthy Episcopalian, George Gordon King, donated parcels of land when Saint Augustin's parish was being established in Newport's heavily Irish Fifth Ward. At the same time, still another well-heeled Episcopalian and former mayor, Frederick Garrettson, helped the Daughters of the Holy Ghost establish Saint Clare's Home for elderly women and a daycare center for young children in the center of Newport.

By the end of the nineteenth century, Patrick Boyle, an Irish Catholic, had become mayor of Newport and would hold the office for sixteen years. Boyle worked well with the Vanderbilts, Astors, and other summer colonists while not neglecting the needs of the city's year-round residents. After World War I, the Gilded Age came to a close. The summer colonists, burdened by increasing taxes and frustrated by Prohibition, were no longer entertaining lavishly. Many were eager to dispose of their properties, and several donated them to communities of nuns or brothers, who then turned the mansions into residences or schools. By 1930, Catholics had established a remarkable infrastructure in Newport. In a city of just 25,000, there were four Catholic parishes, three grammar schools, two high schools, a retreat center, a cloistered convent, an orphanage, two homes for the elderly, and a daycare center for the children of working parents. Catholics' place had clearly changed dramatically over the decades. No longer suspect, Catholics had gained influence in all aspects of the city's life.

Chapter 1

"WE KNOW OF NONE AMONG US"

The Specter of Catholics in Colonial Newport

I believe there never was held such a variety of religions together on so small a spot of ground as have been in that colony. It has been a colluvies of Antinomians, Familists, Anabaptists, Anti-sabbatarians, Arminians, Socinians, Quakers, Ranters, everything in the world but Roman Catholicks, and real Christians. . . . The condition of the rising generation upon that island, is indeed exceeding[ly] lamentable.

—Cotton Mather, *Magnalia Christi Americana* (1702)

From the time of its establishment in 1636, Rhode Island was known as a safe haven for religious minorities.[1] It was especially appealing to those in neighboring Massachusetts and Connecticut who could not accept orthodox Puritan doctrines. Some dissenters joined Roger Williams in Providence, and a number followed Anne Hutchinson, who settled for a time in Portsmouth.[2] However, Newport, founded in 1639, would be the Rhode Island town that attracted and accepted the widest variety of faiths. In the 1650s, Newporters allowed Quakers into their town while Massachusetts was strictly forbidding their entrance on pain of death.[3] Likewise, Jews settled in Newport without incident in the seventeenth century when anti-Semitism was widespread in much of New England.[4] Newport was home as well to Congregationalists, Anglicans, a variety of Baptist factions, and eventually even a contingent of Moravian Brethren.[5] Yet few, if any, Catholics chose to settle in Newport in the colonial era. For a time Newporters might have accepted them as they accepted Quakers and Jews, but England's two major conflicts with

6

Catholic forces—the Glorious Revolution of 1688 and the French and Indian War—sparked intense distrust of Catholics throughout New England. As a consequence, most colonial Newporters, who were otherwise quite tolerant, feared and disliked Catholics.

Rhode Island's Charters

By the 1640s, Roger Williams recognized that Rhode Island needed a charter to give it legitimacy and protect it from neighbors eager for additional territory. In England, he met with his friend Oliver Cromwell, who helped him secure a charter from the Puritan-controlled Parliament in 1643.[6] The document stressed liberty of conscience, and scholars agree that Williams wanted this doctrine to extend to Catholics.[7] However, by 1660 the Puritans were out of power; Cromwell's son Richard had been deposed and the Stuart monarch, Charles II, had been restored. One of the new king's first moves was to annul all acts of the Puritan Parliament, including Williams's charter. On hearing this news, Rhode Island's leading citizens contacted John Clarke, a Baptist minister and physician from Newport, who was then in England. Instructed to obtain a new charter, Clarke drew up a detailed document that stressed religious freedom for all Christians and made no provision for an established church. Charles II, who sympathized with England's tiny Catholic population and would join the Catholic church shortly before his death, was generally of the same mind as Clarke on church-state matters.[8] He was also deeply pained by the persecution that the Quakers were enduring in New England.[9] In 1663, he signed Clarke's charter, which called for "full liberty in religious concernments," declaring

> that true piety rightly grounded upon gospel principles, will give the best and greatest security to sovereignty, and will lay in the hearts of men the strongest obligations to true loyalty. . . . [O]ur royal will and pleasure is, that no person within the said colony, at any time hereafter, shall be any way molested, punished, disquieted, or called in question, for any differences of opinion in matters of religion, [that] . . . do not actually disturb the civil peace of our said colony.[10]

While the Charter was presumably meant to include Catholics, it is not clear that any Catholics resided in Rhode Island in the seventeenth century. In 1680, Rhode Island's governor, Peleg Sanford, remarked, "As for Papists, we know of none among us."[11] Yet, while lacking Catholics, Newport was populated by a host of other faiths. In the 1660s and 1670s, increasing numbers of Quakers and Baptists settled in Newport along with a group of fifteen Sephardic Jewish families.[12] Writing in the 1690s, the Puritan divine Cotton Mather declared Rhode Island to be the "sewer of New England," a pagan land inhabited by "serpents."[13]

Newport's residents did not appear to share Mather's concerns. These disparate peoples worked well with each other and prospered, raising sheep, pigs, and horses and exporting their surplus to markets in the South and the Caribbean.[14] By 1700, Newport's population was approaching 3,000, and the town was emerging as a center of agriculture and trade.[15]

The Glorious Revolution and Its Effect on Catholics

By 1700 any Catholics inclined to move to Rhode Island, given its reputation for tolerance, would have recognized that a mood of suspicion toward Catholicism had taken hold in the colony. Events in England had triggered the shift. When Charles II died in 1685, he was succeeded by his younger brother, James II, the duke of York. Like Charles, James had Catholic sympathies, but he was not as discreet about them. James had converted to Catholicism in 1672 and had surrounded himself with Catholic laymen and a Jesuit priest as his advisors.[16] In the colonies, too, he made sweeping changes, consolidating Massachusetts, Connecticut, Rhode Island, New Hampshire, New York, and New Jersey into the Dominion of New England under an unpopular appointee, Sir Edmund Andros.[17]

After the death of his first wife, Anne, James married an Italian Catholic noblewoman, Mary of Modena, who was twenty-five years younger than him.[18] When she gave birth to a boy in 1688, England's parliamentary leaders recognized that they were facing the prospect of a Catholic dynasty. To avert this danger, they invited James's Anglican daughter, Mary, and her Dutch husband, William of Orange, to seize power.[19] The couple agreed and sailed to England in November. James fled England before they arrived, but then fought William in Ireland, hoping its Catholics would help him regain the throne. After being defeated at the Boyne River in 1690, he sought refuge with Louis XIV in France and made no further effort to challenge William and Mary. But his supporters, the Jacobites, did not give up so easily.[20] In 1715, they tried to place James's son, who styled himself James III, on the throne; and, in 1745, they fought alongside James II's grandson, Bonnie Prince Charlie, in his bid for power.[21]

In the aftermath of what became known as the Glorious Revolution, Catholics suffered grievously for having supported James, while Anglicans benefited from the favor of the new sovereigns. In England and Ireland, a new set of penal laws forbade Catholics from holding office, voting, practicing law, or worshipping publicly.[22] In Maryland, which was home to the majority of the colonies' Catholics, a series of penal laws was enacted against them in the early eighteenth century, and Anglicanism was made the established church. Catholics lost the right to vote, practice law, or worship publicly, and additional taxes were imposed on Catholics of Irish ancestry.[23] In North Carolina, Anglicanism was established, and a 1696 statute promised "all Christians (Papists only exempted) . . . full liberty of conscience."[24] South Carolina passed similar legislation, promising religious liberty to Jews as well as to all Protestants. In 1716, South Carolina prohibited the importation of Irish Catholic servants into the colony.[25]

Massachusetts, which had long been a Puritan stronghold, retained its Congregationalist establishment in its 1691 charter but promised to tolerate Anglicans and other Protestant denominations: "liberty of conscience allowed in the worship of God to all Christians (Papists excepted)."[26] Catholics, on the other hand, faced additional punitive legislation because they were suspected of harboring French sympathies. In 1700, the Massachusetts General Court forbade any Catholic clergyman from entering the colony. A priest crossing into Massachusetts would be "accounted an incendiary and disturber of the public peace and safety, and an enemy of the true Christian religion."[27] First-time violators would face life imprisonment, while repeat offenders would be subject to the death penalty.[28]

Rhode Island, too, moved to accept Anglicans while restricting the rights of Catholics. In 1698, Anglicans in Newport founded Trinity Church and established additional parishes soon after in Wickford, Bristol, and Providence.[29] In 1719, Rhode Island's General Assembly passed a bill stating that "all men professing Christianity . . . who acknowledge and are obedient to the civil magistrate, though of different judgments in religious affairs (Roman Catholics only excepted) shall be admitted freemen and shall have liberty to choose and be chosen officers in the colony."[30]

This measure has long been a source of controversy for historians of Rhode Island. In the late nineteenth century, an influential historian, Sidney S. Rider, argued that the law had been published in error in 1719 and then reprinted in subsequent years.[31] One modern scholar, William McLoughlin, a Brown University professor who was a leading expert on the history of Rhode Island, saw this legislation as so out of keeping with Rhode Island's traditions that he, like Rider, wondered if it were mistakenly recorded.[32] However, another scholar of the colonial era, Mary Augustina Ray, notes that this anti-Catholic statute was renewed five times in the years following without any debate in the Rhode Island legislature.[33] Furthermore, as it was the practice throughout the colonies to deny Catholics their rights at this time, it seems likely that Rhode Island was following the example set by other legislatures.

Rendering to God and Caesar

In the first decades of the eighteenth century, Newport rose to become one of the top five colonial seaports, standing with New York, Philadelphia, Boston, and Charleston, and its population grew to 4,600 by 1730.[34] The town attracted southern visitors, especially in the summer months, and became a center for trading spermaceti candles, rum, furniture, and, not least, slaves. Indeed, the historian Elaine Crane points out that the slave trade played a crucial part in Newport's booming economy. She notes that, by 1770, "well over 70%" of the slave ships leaving the colonies were departing from Newport.[35] Jay Coughtry, an authority on the slave trade, found records of 934 slave ships leaving Rhode Island for Africa over the course of the eighteenth century and noted that most sailed out of Newport, with lesser numbers departing from Bristol and Providence.[36] Even workers not directly involved in Newport's slave trade often contributed to it. Carpenters and caulkers repaired the ships, coopers made barrels to hold the rum that would be exchanged for slaves, and clerks kept detailed account books for the shipowners.[37]

At the same time, however, Newport was becoming recognized as an intellectual center. In 1730, the philosopher George Berkeley helped to establish a literary and philosophical society in the town. Berkeley returned to Ireland in 1731, but the society continued to meet for discussions and debates in the years following.[38] In the 1740s, two members of the group, Abraham Redwood, a Quaker, and Henry Collins, an Anglican, decided to establish a library. Founded in 1747, the library was named for Redwood because he had contributed £500 for the purchase of the first books.[39] From its earliest years, the library was truly an ecumenical enterprise, with Aaron Lopez and several other Jewish merchants in Newport providing generous support.[40]

While Newport was flourishing economically and culturally, the religious enthusiasm that had been so evident in many of its residents in the seventeenth century was fading.[41] In 1740, George Whitefield, the famed Great Awakening evangelist, arrived in Newport after a highly successful tour of Georgia. Whitefield had attracted enthusiastic crowds throughout most of New England with his emotional, open-air preaching, but he was disappointed in Newport.[42] After three days of delivering twice-a-day speeches before sizable congregations at Trinity Church, he remarked in his journal, "All I fear, place the Kingdom of God too much in meat and drink, and have an ill name abroad for running of goods." He concluded his entry with a prayer for the people of Newport: "Lord Jesus give them to know thee, and the power of thy resurrection, and teach them to render to Caesar the things that are Caesar's, and to God the things that are God's."[43]

Whitefield's discouraging experience can be better understood by a study of Newport's demographics in these years. Ezra Stiles, a learned Congregational minister who directed the Redwood Library and later served as president of Yale College, tried to estimate the religious makeup of the city in 1760 and again in 1770. The city's population had grown to 8,000 by this time, almost double what it had been thirty years earlier.[44] In his survey of the residents, Stiles found a sizable number of Congregationalists, Baptists and Anglicans and a handful of Jews and Moravian Brethren, but the largest group comprised "nothingarians"— people with no religious affiliation. A meticulous recordkeeper, Stiles calculated that approximately 42 percent of Newporters were not associated with any denomination in 1770.[45]

Burning Tax Collectors and Popes

Newport's drift towards nothingarianism did not lead to any greater acceptance of Catholics. In fact, the French and Indian War of the 1750s and 1760s sparked a new wave of anti-Catholicism throughout the colonies. The struggle against Catholic France and their Catholic Native allies led Pennsylvania, New York, and Maryland to enact additional restrictions on the Catholics in their colonies and provoked ministers such as John Burt of the First Congregational Church in Bristol, Rhode Island, to employ apocalyptic imagery to denounce the French.[46] The French were to be seen as the children of the "Scarlet Whore, that Mother of Harlots, who is rightly the Abomination of the Earth. . . . Their religion, repugnant to the Religion of Jesus Christ, divests them of all Humanity."[47] Newporters would likely have been familiar with Burt's pronouncements on the French and the Catholic church because his sermon was published in Newport by James Franklin Jr., the editor of the *Newport Mercury*.[48]

After the war's end in 1763, the British government sought to recoup some of its debts by imposing taxes on colonists via the Sugar Act and the Stamp Act. Although the duties were light, angry colonists resisted these measures strenuously, especially in the port cities of Boston, Newport, New York, Philadelphia, and Charleston.[49] Both opponents and defenders of the taxes often drew on anti-Catholic images to express their political views. Martin Howard, Jr., a leader of an influential group of Tories known as the Newport Junto, used anti-Catholic allusions in his defense of Parliament's authority over the colonies.[50] In February 1765, Howard published in Newport *A Letter from a Gentleman at Halifax, to His Friend in Rhode-Island*, in which he sharply criticized many of his fellow colonists for their disdainful attitude to the British Crown:

> It gives me great pain to see so much ingratitude in the colonies to the mother country, whose arms and money so lately rescued them from a *French* government. I have been told, that some have gone so far to say, that they would, as things are, prefer such a government to an *English* one. . . . I ardently wish that these spurious, unworthy sons of *Britain* could feel the iron rod of a *Spanish* inquisitor. . . . [I]t would indeed be a punishment suited to their ingratitude.[51]

Howard's inflammatory letter sparked a pamphlet war in the weeks following. Rhode Island's governor, Stephen Hopkins, and a Boston politician, James Otis, Jr., wrote lengthy rejoinders. After Howard answered them dismissively, Otis followed with a savage attack on the junto, referring to Howard as "Martinus Scriblerus" and his associate, Dr. Thomas Moffat, as "Dr. Small-brain" and "Dr. Murphy." Otis claimed that Howard and his friends had sympathized with the French in the late war: "[T]hey were in hopes to join *Te Deum* with their French Catholic Brethren in the churches, chapels and meeting-houses of Boston, New-York and Newport. Upon all occasions during the war, they manifested their joy and exultation at any little success of the French—but kept vigils and severe fasts when they were drubbed."[52] Otis then accused them of being Jacobites as well:

> [Howard] is at no loss any ev'ning to find some *of his old gang*, who . . . have cracked many a bottle of true sterling to the health of J___m__y S____t. . . . Such is the little, dirty, drinking, drabbing, contaminated knot of thieves, beggars and transports . . . and made up of Turks, Jews and other Infidels, with a few renegado Christians & Catholics, and altogether formed into a club of scarce a dozen, at N___p____t.[53]

In August, the conflict over the Stamp Act turned violent. In Boston, effigies of the city's stamp commissioner, Andrew Oliver, and of other officials were paraded around town by a large, unruly crowd. Eventually the effigies were consigned to the flames, to the delight of the crowd. Before the night was over, Oliver's home and one of his commercial properties had been ransacked.[54] A little more than a week later, an angry, drunken group of Newporters took to the streets in a similar fashion. Effigies of Howard, Moffat, and Augustus Johnston, the city's stamp commissioner, were paraded, then hung from a gallows before being set on fire. No doubt inspired by Otis's tracts, the rioters attached to Moffat's effigy a placard describing him as that "infamous . . . Jacobite Doctor Murphy."[55] By labeling Moffatt a Jacobite and giving him an Irish surname, the Newport protestors, like Otis, were attempting to tie him to Catholicism.[56]

On the following night, the rioters, now armed with axes, attacked Howard's home: they "broke the Windows and Doors all to Pieces, damaged the Partitions of the House and ruined such Furniture as was left in it."[57] They then stormed Moffat's house, slashing paintings and destroying his library and scientific equipment. Fearing for their lives, Howard and Moffat boarded a British ship in Newport's harbor. Neither ever returned to Newport.[58]

The Stamp Act riots had much in common with the raucous and sometimes violent demonstrations that occurred in Newport each year on November 5 to mark Pope's Day.[59] On that night, a sizable gang of men and boys would carry effigies of the pope and usually one of the devil and eventually throw them into a great bonfire constructed for the occasion. As I mentioned in the introduction, this was a commemoration of the 1605 Gunpowder Plot, when Guy Fawkes and several other Catholics attempted to blow up the House of Lords, kill King James I, and replace him with a Catholic sovereign.[60] In addition, the revels celebrated William of Orange's landing in England, which had occurred on November 5.[61]

While Boston had more elaborate Pope's Day events, Newporters also commemorated the date with enthusiasm.[62] Its celebrations had begun in the 1730s and, by the mid-1760s, had become elaborate affairs, no doubt in response to the French and Indian War.[63] In the 1860s, the *Newport Mercury* published a detailed description of the city's seventeenth-century revels:

FIGURE 1. Broadside depicting Pope's Day festivities in Boston, 1768. Library of Congress.

A great bonfire was established on the lower end of the main street. . . . Soon after dark, a rude stage . . . placed on wheels and drawn by horses, made its appearance, on which was seated . . . an effigy of the pope, hideously painted, and behind him stood another representing the Devil. . . . Two men with masks on their faces and fantastically attired, attended the grotesque figures. . . . One of these men was furnished with a pole, at the end of which a little basket was suspended in which to receive contributions for drinking the King's health, and the other man carried a small bell; the whole was surrounded with lanterns, and a crowd of men and boys sung the following:

From Rome! From Rome the Pope has come,
All in 10,000 fears,
With fiery serpents all around
His head, nose, eyes and ears.

This is the treacherous dog that did contrive
To burn our King and Parliament alive;
God by His grace did this prevent,
And saved the King and Parliament

Now if you will a little money give
No longer shall the treacherous creature live
We'll burn his body from his head
And then we'll say the old dog's dead

Don't you hear my little bell go chink-chink-chink?
Give us a little money to buy a little drink.

According to the article, the entourage would go to the homes of the wealthy, ring the doorbell, and, dangling their basket from a pole, ask for a contribution. If the owner did not donate, "the end of the pole was driven through the [window] glass and the pageant proceeded to some other house amid the shouts and uproar of the crowd." When the parade ended, the pope's effigy was then thrown on the bonfire to great cheering. The article concluded, "It was a night of great license to the lower orders . . . and the more sober citizens were heartily glad when it was over."[64]

"The Nature and Danger of Popery in this Land"

While some Newporters sought to burn imaginary popes, one prominent member of the community, Solomon Southwick, attacked the papacy in print. Southwick, who had purchased the *Newport Mercury* from the Franklin family in 1764, decided to reprint an anti-Catholic polemic, *A Master Key to Popery*, written in the 1720s by Antonio Gavin, a Spanish priest who had become a Protestant minister in England and Ireland.[65] In June 1773, Southwick announced that he was republishing the tract, which combined attacks on Catholic teachings with tales of nuns' and priests' lecherous behavior.[66] He assured his readers that he was reprinting Gavin's treatise "as fast as the nature of the work will possibly admit."[67] By October, he reported that it was available for purchase for four shillings.[68] Southwick urged his readers to buy the book, promising that it would

> give a more clear, full and true account of the horrid oppressions
> and infernal practices of the Romish Priests, Friars and Inquisitors,
> than any thing ever published before in this country; and ought to
> be read by people of all ranks and conditions, for what has happened
> to other countries may, possibly, happen to this, and therefore it
> behoves everyone to be on his guard against POPERY.[69]

Perhaps Southwick's tracts were making an impression in the colony. John O'Kelly, an Irish Catholic immigrant who had settled in Warren, Rhode Island, seemed very aware that his background made him suspect. In an October 1773 business letter to the Newport merchant Christopher Champlin, he assured the merchant that, if he were "loath to trust an Irish man," O'Kelly would understand and not take offense.[70]

By the end of 1773, all of New England was astir over the Boston Tea Party, which had sent £10,000 worth of tea into Boston Harbor. While some prominent colonists such as George Washington were disturbed by the incident, both of Rhode Island's newspapers vigorously defended the actions of the rebellious merchants.[71] In late December, Southwick noted that "more than three hundred families in this town have lately abandoned the use of that noxious WEED."[72] A week later, he reported that an association had been formed in Newport "against the use of India TEA, which we hope will effectually extirpate that pestilential herb from every habitation in this colony."[73]

With Newport and other New England towns rallying against tea, the British government considered how to respond to what it took to be Boston's wanton destruction of private property. Parliament enacted four Coercive Acts to punish the Massachusetts Bay Colony. The most notable was the Boston Port Act, which closed the city to all shipping until the cost of the tea had been repaid. Angry colonists nicknamed these laws the "Intolerable Acts" and called for a meeting of a congress of all colonies to determine an appropriate response to Parliament.[74]

In 1774, tensions with the British reached even higher levels throughout the colonies, a response to the Quebec Act, enacted by Parliament in June to conciliate the 80,000 French Catholics in Canada. This legislation recognized the Catholic church's prerogatives, including its right to receive tithes. It also allowed Canadians to keep the governmental system established by the French, which had no provision for an elected assembly. For many colonists, especially those in New England, this measure proved as upsetting as the "Intolerable Acts."[75] Parliament was expressly encouraging the spread of popery on their northern and western borders.[76]

In Newport, Southwick responded with new notices about his exposé on popery. This time his advertisement in the *Newport Mercury* included a swipe at Parliament. Gavin's book, he wrote, was

> highly necessary to be kept in every protestant family in this country; that they may see to what a miserable state the people are reduced in all arbitrary and tyrannical governments, and be thereby excited to stand on their guard against the infernal machinations of the British ministry and their vast *host* of tools, emissaries, etc. etc. sent hither to propagate the principles of popery and slavery, which go hand in hand, as inseparable companions.[77]

In July, Southwick began reporting on the debate over the Quebec Act and ran a steady series of stories and critical commentaries through December.[78]

In late August, the paper announced that the House of Commons had approved the bill after a "warm debate" and quoted at length from one of the dissenters, Thomas Townshend, who declared:

> Little did I think, that a country as large as half [of] Europe and within the dominions of the crown of Great Britain, was going to have the Romish religion established in it as the religion of the state. Little did I think, that so many thousand men, entitled and born to the rights of Englishmen . . . should . . . contrary to every idea of the constitution, be subjected to French papists and French laws.[79]

In October, the *Newport Mercury* reported that an Englishman returning from Quebec had sworn that the Protestants were forced "to exercise their religion in secret for fear of the resentment of the Roman Catholics."[80]

Ezra Stiles, already an outspoken critic of the British Crown, was just as exercised on the matter. He wrote in his diary:

> The King has signed the Quebec Act, extending that Province to the Ohio and Mississippi and comprehending nearly Two Thirds of English America, and established the Romish Church & IDOLATRY over all that space; in this Act all the bishops concurred. Astonishing that Kings, L[or]ds and Commons, a whole protestant parliament should expressly establish popery over three Quarters of their Empire.[81]

In November, Newporters, still angry about the Quebec Act, staged an unusually large Pope's Day commemoration, this time focusing not only on the pope but on their Tory foes as well. Stiles noted that, on the afternoon of November 5, "three popes etc. paraded thro' the streets, & in the Evening they were consumed in a bonfire as usual—among others were Lord North, Gov. Hutchinson & Gen. Gage."[82] At the end of the month, Stiles mentioned the act in a sermon at Newport's Second Congregational Church. Drawing on Saint Paul's Second Letter to the Thessalonians— which alludes to the coming of the Antichrist—he preached "on the Nature and Danger of Popery in this Land, from the Operation of the Quebec Bill for the Establishment of the Romish Religion over Two

Thirds of the British Empire."[83] Southwick, too, was stirred into further action by the legislation. By January 1775, he was again hawking his edition of *A Master Key to Popery*, pointing out that the book was "very proper for all those who would thoroughly understand what the present *popish* Administration would be at."[84]

Newport's Pope's Day celebrations and Southwick's and Stiles's fulminations against popery illustrated many colonists' deep-seated fear of Catholics. Yet no more than a handful of Catholics had ever lived in Newport before the American Revolution, meaning that most residents had never met a Catholic of any sort, much less a priest or a bishop.[85] When Stiles calculated Newport's religious composition in 1760 and again in 1770, he did not come across a single Catholic residing in the city at either time. Nonetheless, most Newporters harbored suspicions towards them. Elaine Crane notes that, when a Frenchman, Francis Vandale, established a French language school in Newport in October 1774—in the midst of the Quebec Act furor—he took out a notice in the *Newport Mercury* making clear that he was not a Catholic: "[He] will readily attend any young ladies and gentlemen at their dwellings; and as he is a Protestant, he doubts not he shall meet with encouragement equal to his abilities."[86] Such anecdotes suggest that most Newport residents, while willing to live and work with Jews, Quakers, Baptists, Congregationalists, and Anglicans, were no more accepting of Catholics than were the people of Boston or any other New England city. Their anti-Catholic inclinations would be put to the test in 1780, when thousands of French Catholic soldiers and sailors arrived in Newport, giving the citizens ample opportunity to determine what they really thought of Catholics and the Church of Rome.

Chapter 2

THE FRENCH EFFECT

Newporters' Changing Perspective toward Catholics

The arrival of the Fleet and Army hath given new life to the Town.
—William Channing, letter to Ezra Stiles, August 6, 1780

In the fall of 1774, as tensions worsened between the colonies and the Crown, many colonial leaders seemed to be of a mind with Ezra Stiles and Solomon Southwick in seeing popery and British tyranny as twin threats.[1] Six months later, the American Revolution began in Massachusetts with skirmishes in Lexington and Concord. Yet over the next six years of war, many of the rebels, who were greatly aided by France, came to reconsider their views of Catholicism. Newport's opinions were particularly subject to change. Thousands of French troops spent almost a year in the town, meaning that its residents had more contact with Catholics than did any other townspeople in America. By the war's end, most Newporters had grown accustomed to and tolerant of Catholics.

The Coming of War

In September 1774, fifty-five delegates representing twelve of the colonies gathered in Philadelphia to respond to Parliament's "Intolerable Acts."[2] Rhode Island sent two representatives to the First Continental Congress: Samuel Ward from Newport and Stephen Hopkins from Providence.[3] On the Congress's first day in session, Paul Revere rode into Philadelphia with the Suffolk Resolves, Boston's response to Parliament's measures. The document sternly condemned the Coercive Acts that had closed the port of Boston and shut down the colonial government of Massachusetts. It also denounced the Quebec Act "as dangerous in an extreme degree to the Protestant religion and to the civil and religious liberties of all America."[4] The Congress approved the resolves unanimously.[5]

During the next month the delegates focused on economic matters and eventually approved a total boycott on English goods: the colonies would not import any items from Britain after December 1 and would stop exports in September 1775 unless the Coercive Acts were repealed.[6] Delegates did not forget about popery, however. In October they sent a letter to the people of Great Britain expressing their outrage at the Quebec Act:

> [B]eing extremely dangerous to our liberty and quiet, we cannot forbear complaining of it, as hostile to British America. . . . Nor can we suppress our astonishment, that a British Parliament should ever consent to establish in that country a religion that has deluged your island with blood, and dispersed impiety, bigotry, persecution, murder and rebellion through every part of the world.[7]

In more measured language, they also wrote to King George III expressing their unhappiness with the Quebec Act. At the same time, they sent a letter to the residents of Quebec, assuring them of America's friendship and downplaying any religious divisions:

> We are too well acquainted with the liberality of sentiment distinguishing your nation, to imagine, that difference of religion will prejudice you against a hearty amity with us. . . . The Swiss Cantons . . . [are] composed of Roman Catholic and Protestant states, living in the utmost concord and peace with one another, and thereby enabled, ever since they bravely vindicated their freedom, to defy and defeat every tyrant that has invaded them.[8]

Clearly, colonial leaders were willing to be more accommodating toward Catholics when they felt that political or military concerns warranted it.

Although the delegates had taken defiant steps at the First Continental Congress, probably none had anticipated—or desired—war with England. However, in April 1775, General Thomas Gage, who had been appointed military governor of Massachusetts, sent troops to clear out the munitions that colonists were rumored to be storing outside of Boston. At Lexington and Concord, the British fought colonial militiamen and suffered three hundred casualties to the colonists' one hundred. After returning to Boston, the British found themselves surrounded by a ring of colonial troops: the siege of Boston had begun.

In May, when the Second Continental Congress convened, many of the delegates were more agitated than they had been in the fall. They readily accepted John Adams's proposal that George Washington be appointed commander-in-chief of the colonial army and directed him to go to Massachusetts to oversee the troops. Before he reached Boston, more fighting had broken out; and, in June, the British dislodged colonial forces from Bunker Hill (also known as Breed's Hill), but only after suffering heavy casualties.

In spite of the escalating violence, only a few radicals in the Congress were calling for war. In July, moderates led by John Dickinson of Pennsylvania drafted the Olive Branch Petition to the king, asking him to repeal the Coercive Acts and promising him their loyalty. Their hopes were dashed when the king dismissed their appeal out of hand and declared the colonies to be in a state of rebellion.

In the fall, General Benedict Arnold led an invasion into Canada, hopeful that the Canadians would rally to the colonists' cause. However, the bishop of Quebec, Jean-Olivier Briand, was unsympathetic. He was well aware of the American outcry against the Quebec Act and had concluded that the colonists were anti-Catholic, and most of the priests in Canada shared his perspective.[9] Yet by the end of 1775, even as the Canadian offensive was failing, the colonists' prospects in Boston were brightening. As Washington contemplated an attack on Boston, he learned that his troops planned to commemorate Guy Fawkes Day on November 5. Still hoping for aid from the French Canadians and anxious not to alienate the Catholics serving in his army, Washington was not about to tolerate such an event.[10] From his headquarters in Cambridge, he issued a stern warning:

> [Having been told] of a design form'd for the observance of that ridiculous and childish custom of burning the Effigy of the pope—He cannot help expressing his surprise that there should be Officers and Soldiers in this army so void of common sense, as not to see the

impropriety of such a step at this Juncture; at a time when we are soliciting, and have really obtain'd, the friendship and alliance of the people of Canada.[11]

The Continental Congress shared Washington's hope that the Canadians might yet be persuaded to join the American cause. To that end, members decided in February 1776 to dispatch a three-man delegation to visit Canada. Charles Carroll, the most prominent Catholic political leader in the colonies, was appointed to accompany Benjamin Franklin and Samuel Chase of Maryland on the mission. John Adams then lobbied to have Father John Carroll—Charles Carroll's cousin—join them. Though Adams had often written derisively of Catholics, he spoke admiringly of Carroll as a "Roman Catholic priest, a Jesuit and a gentleman of learning and Abilities."[12] In April, the group reached Montreal, where they received a cool reception. While the Carrolls sought to assure the Canadians that they would enjoy complete religious freedom if they were to join the war against England, they had trouble explaining why the Quebec Act had caused such anger in the colonies. By May, the delegates headed home, recognizing that their mission had been a failure.[13] Six months later, however, Franklin would set sail for Paris, hoping that the French would be more supportive of the American cause.[14]

Although frustrated in their attempt to secure Canadian aid, the colonists advanced in Massachusetts. Washington maintained his siege on Boston; and, in March 1776, the British and their Tory sympathizers evacuated and set sail for Halifax, Nova Scotia. The Continental Army then marched triumphantly into the city.[15] With the conflict escalating, the Continental Congress directed Thomas Jefferson to draft an official declaration of war. By the end of June, the document was complete. Jefferson argued that the king's "repeated injuries and usurpations" had left the colonists no choice but to rebel. In his list of charges against the king, he included taxing the colonists without their consent, quartering English troops in the colonies, hiring Hessian soldiers to police the colonies, and encouraging attacks by "merciless Indian savages." Jefferson also criticized the Quebec Act for "abolishing the free system of English laws" in Canada but was careful to avoid any reference to popery. After three days of debate, the document, shorn of any criticisms of slavery and the slave trade, was approved.

Rhode Island's delegates strongly supported the Declaration of Independence, once references to the slave trade were excised.[16] Indeed, Rhode Island was, in the historian William McLoughlin's words, part of the "vanguard of revolution."[17] In 1774, the colony supplied food to the people of Boston and, in the spring of 1775, sent the besieged town £225.[18] In May 1775, 1,000 Rhode Island troops arrived in Boston to support the siege, and 150 Rhode Island men took part in Benedict Arnold's failed attack on Quebec.[19] In May 1776, the Rhode Island General Assembly declared its separation from the king, using language similar to what Jefferson would later use.[20]

Still, when the war came to Rhode Island a few months later, inhabitants reacted more cautiously. In December 1776, General William Howe, who had been routing Washington's forces in and around New York, dispatched Lieutenant General Henry Clinton, 7,100 English and Hessian troops, and more than seventy ships to Aquidneck Island in Narragansett Bay, home to the towns of Portsmouth, Middletown, and Newport. Clinton planned to establish his winter quarters in Newport, and, at sight of the fleet, residents put up no resistance.[21] In McLoughlin's words, the town "fell without a shot."[22]

Newport's Protestant denominations, which had gotten along so well for decades, split bitterly over the war.[23] Most Congregationalists and Presbyterians, who favored the patriots, fled the island before the British and Hessians arrived. Ezra Stiles, for example, resigned his Congregational pastorate in February 1776 and moved to Dighton, Massachusetts.[24] On the other hand, most Anglicans, who favored the Tories, and most Quakers, who were neutral because of their pacifism, stayed on the island.

Thus, roughly 5,000 people were on hand when the British and Hessians arrived, and some were quite pleased to see them.[25] Indeed, Newport's leading Tories escorted the British officers to the Colony House. In the following days, the British settled themselves in Newport's finest houses, made use of the Redwood Library, and established their own Loyalist newspaper, the *Newport Gazette*.[26] Then they bided their time, waiting for orders.

In the summer of 1777, General John Burgoyne planned to travel from Canada to New York and join General Howe. According to this plan, their two armies would be met by a smaller contingent under Colonel Barry St. Leger, coming from western New York, and these forces would cut off New England from the rest of the colonies. But the plan was bungled from the start. Howe chose to take his troops to Philadelphia, St. Leger was pinned in western New York, and no effort was made to use the troops in Newport. In the end, Burgoyne found himself cornered in Saratoga and running low on supplies. He and five other generals and almost 6,000 British and Hessian soldiers surrendered to General Horatio Gates, who arranged to have them all shipped back to England.[27]

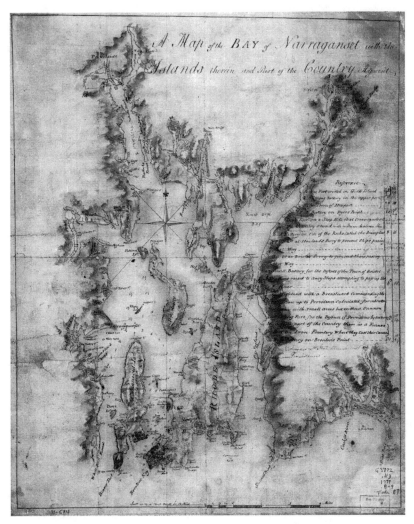

FIGURE 2. Charles Blaskowitz, map of Narragansett Bay, c. 1777. Library of Congress.

The French Alliance

As news of the great American victory at Saratoga reached France, Benjamin Franklin, the American representative, was at last able to argue that the rebels were a serious fighting force poised to defeat the British. In February 1778, impressed by the American triumph and eager to exact revenge for the French and Indian War, King Louis XVI agreed to an alliance with the Americans and promised that ships and soldiers would be forthcoming.[28]

In July, the Comte Jean Baptiste D'Estaing arrived in Sandy Hook, New Jersey, at the head of a formidable fleet.[29] D'Estaing was unwilling to attack the British in New York City, fearing that the harbor was too shallow for his ships, so Washington directed him to work with General John Sullivan, who hoped to expel the British forces from Newport and possibly end the war. Sullivan had 8,000 troops under his command and, with the support of the Marquis de Lafayette and his 2,000 soldiers and D'Estaing's ships and his 4,000 men, hoped to overwhelm the 3,000 British soldiers stationed in Newport.[30] Sullivan's troops quickly moved to occupy British redoubts in the neighboring communities of Portsmouth and Middletown and began shelling British positions. The plans went awry, however. Rather than stay in Narragansett Bay, D'Estaing decided to pursue Admiral Richard Howe's fleet, which appeared to be heading to New York. During the chase, the French ships were badly damaged in a hurricane, so D'Estaing brought the fleet to Boston for repairs. Sullivan was frustrated: not only had D'Estaing abandoned him, but many of his own troops were deserting.[31] Fearful that the British would send reinforcements to Newport, he pulled back to Portsmouth, at the northern end of Aquidneck Island. On August 29, Sullivan's troops engaged British and Hessian forces there in what would become known as the Battle of Rhode Island. After several hours of intense fighting, Sullivan and his men managed an orderly retreat from the island.[32]

Meanwhile, D'Estaing and his troops settled in Boston for two months and waited for their ships to be repaired. Over the course of their stay, the French received a decidedly mixed response from the residents. While D'Estaing and other top officers were welcomed into the homes of city leaders such as John Hancock, lower-ranking sailors were treated more coolly and even occasionally attacked. Indeed, two of D'Estaing's aides were assaulted and one, the Chevalier de Saint-Saveur, was killed by a mob of fifty club-wielding dockworkers when they came ashore seeking food for their crew.[33]

On the whole, the French sailors were not harassed or abused; they were just left alone. Still, some citizens took an interest in them. Abigail Adams, who entertained several officers while her husband was in Paris assisting Franklin, was charmed by the French.[34] Yet she lamented that "they have been neglected in the town of Boston. [V]ery few if any, private families have any acquaintance with them."[35] Even the interactions that did take place were short-lived as, in November, D'Estaing set sail for the West Indies and Lafayette returned to France to lobby for additional forces.[36] Americans would have to wait another year and a half for more French aid.

In March 1779, as the war dragged on with no end in sight, the Continental Congress sought divine aid, calling on the states to establish a day of "Fasting, Humiliation and Prayer." In April, Rhode Island's governor, William Greene, complied, issuing a proclamation asking for prayer to

> Almighty God that he be pleased to avert those Impending Calamities, which we have but too well deserved. . . . That he will be a Father to the fatherless children, who weep over the Barbarities of a Savage Enemy. . . . That he will bestow on our Great Ally all those blessings which may enable him to be gloriously instrumental in protecting the Rights of Mankind.[37]

Greene set aside the first Thursday in May for Rhode Islanders to pray and fast on behalf of themselves and their French benefactors.

The British, too, were getting discouraged. In June, Spain's decision to enter the conflict meant that England was now fighting on multiple fronts, struggling to defend its holdings in India, Gibraltar, and the West Indies. Due to these pressures, British commanders decided to concentrate their forces in the southern colonies, where Loyalists were thought to be more numerous. Thus, in October 1779, the troops in Newport, along with about fifty Tory families, headed to the British stronghold of Halifax.[38]

Although no battles had taken place in Newport, it had still suffered much during the British occupation. In search of burnable fuel, troops had chopped down trees all over the island, torn up many wharves, and demolished more than two hundred homes.[39] William Ellery, a signer of the Declaration of Independence, returned to Newport a month after the evacuation and described it as "a barren city, with shuttered houses, a pillaged library, books burned and commerce practically at a standstill."[40]

In May 1780, another fleet of French forces set sail for the colonies. This time they headed straight to Newport, knowing that it had been evacuated but probably unaware of its dilapidated state. Led by Comte Jean Baptiste Rochambeau and Admiral Charles de Ternay, the force included forty-four ships and almost 6,000 soldiers. Most were French, but there were also some troops of Irish descent.[41] As they prepared to land in July, the commanders had misgivings, for they saw Newport as a Tory stronghold and a center of corruption.[42] Newporters, too, were uneasy about the prospect of a second occupation.

When Rochambeau arrived in the town, he found the streets deserted and no one there to greet him. The next day, however, General William Heath arrived from Providence and arranged a formal welcome. Candles were placed in most Newporters' windows and guns were shot to salute the French. Ezra Stiles reported that the "town was beautifully illuminated . . . & 13 grand rockets were fired in the Front of the Statehouse."[43] Relations between the French and the townspeople improved as it became clear that Rochambeau was prepared to pay in cash for anything his troops required and that he would maintain strict discipline over his men at all times.[44]

After these initial meetings with the colonists, Rochambeau set to work. His sick men, who numbered about 1,700, were in need of immediate treatment, so primitive hospitals were established at Colony House and at several of the churches in town, including Stiles's old meetinghouse.[45] Several hundred were also sent to Bristol and Providence to recuperate.[46] Houses in the town center that had been seriously damaged during the British occupation were repaired, and French officers moved into them. Some officers took over vacated properties, while others boarded with Newport families.[47] Rochambeau, for instance, occupied the stately Vernon House, but the Comte de Noailles resided with the Robinsons, a Quaker family on Water Street.[48] In total, Rochambeau paid 100,000 francs to make the homes into comfortable residences for his officers.[49]

Along with soldiers and sailors, the French brought along twelve chaplains, at least two of whom were Irish.[50] The priests established a makeshift chapel in a room of the Colony House and celebrated Masses there. Yet the

FIGURE 3. Samuel King, portrait of Reverend Ezra Stiles, c. 1770. Stiles is sitting in the Redwood Library. Courtesy of Yale University Art Gallery. Bequest of Dr. Charles Jenkins Foote, B.A. 1883, M.D. 1890.

city's residents, who had been suspicious of popery before the war, were unperturbed. They now openly welcomed the French and their priests. Stiles, who had assumed the presidency of Yale College in 1778, returned to Newport for a visit in August and enjoyed socializing with the French officers. On one evening he dined with Rochambeau and conversed with him in Latin. He especially appreciated the Marquis de Chastellux, who was a top aide to Rochambeau and a member of the French Academy. Stiles noted in his diary that he had dined at Chastellux's grand home on Spring Street "in a splendid manner on 35 dishes. He is a capital Literary Character . . . the Glory of the Army."[51] Stiles must have spent time with one of the French chaplains as well because he received a letter from Abbé Colin de Sepvigny a few weeks after his return to New Haven. Writing in Latin, the priest assured Stiles of his friendship, despite their religious differences.[52] Stiles had even warmed to King Louis XVI, hailing him as "his Most Christian Majesty, the illustrious ally of the States."[53] Louis XVI's feast day, August 25, was celebrated by the Continental Congress and by many churches throughout the colonies. In Newport, the king's feast day was marked by a parade by the French forces and a review by Generals Rochambeau and Heath, followed by fireworks in the harbor.[54] As the historian Lee Kennett has noted, "Protestant America thus joined in the feast of Saint Louis."[55]

Concerned that the British navy might attempt to retake Newport, Rochambeau ordered his able-bodied men to build defenses around Aquidneck Island. Within a few weeks, however, he changed his mind and turned his focus to helping Washington end the war. In September, the two met in Hartford, Connecticut, and discussed Washington's plans for an attack on New York. Because Rochambeau was expecting as many as 10,000 additional troops from France, he and Washington agreed to put off any offensive until the spring.[56] In the meantime, he sent his son to Paris to ascertain how many ships and soldiers would be coming to America.

Catholic Rites in Protestant Newport

At the end of August, a group of twenty Native leaders traveled from Canada to visit Rochambeau and Admiral de Ternay. The trip had been arranged by General Philip Schuyler, who was troubled by the pro-English sentiments of many of the tribes in the Mohawk Valley. When the chieftains arrived in Newport, the French commanders held a grand dinner in their honor and bestowed blankets and other gifts on them.[57] Then, at the visitors' request, a Mass was celebrated in an open field, with most of the French troops in attendance. No doubt, many Newporters also observed the ceremonies.[58]

Four months later, in December, a large number of Newporters witnessed their first Catholic funeral after de Ternay died of typhus at the age of fifty-eight. He had not been especially popular with officers or enlisted men; Lafayette described him as "ill-tempered and stubborn, but firm, clear sighted and intelligent."[59] Still, in recognition of his high rank, his funeral rites were elaborate: a nineteenth-century historian described the event as the "most imposing funeral scene ever witnessed in the town."[60] An eyewitness, Thomas Hornsby, recalled that the casket was escorted through the town by Rochambeau and a long line of other officers, all in dress uniforms. He noted that the townspeople were very curious: "Every eligible place was used by the people to witness the scene; every window and housetop was crowded along the way."[61] As there were no Catholic chapels in Newport, the procession wound its way to the Anglicans' Trinity Church in the center of town. Officiating were "twelve Priests . . . with lighted torches in their hands. Around the grave they chanted the Roman Catholic service, and performed all the customary rites of the Catholic Church, with a genuine feeling of sadness."[62] According to Hornsby, "[T]he people were deeply impressed by this strange, fascinating and mournful scene. They seemed to feel for a moment that the pomp of death had a sublime reality, and that the grand ceremony they had witnessed was not the vain thing which their education had taught them to believe."[63]

De Ternay's funeral was markedly different from the Chevalier de Saint-Saveur's, who had died two years earlier in Boston. Although the Massachusetts General Court had issued a formal apology for his death, and Governor John Hancock had offered to arrange the funeral, D'Estaing worried that a public Mass might provoke hostile reactions among Bostonians.[64] Consequently, he ordered a private, discreet ceremony, conducted by a Franciscan friar, Father de Borda, late one night in a crypt of King's Chapel, an Anglican church.[65] Apparently, the French saw the people of Boston as more antagonistic to Catholicism than the Newporters were.

The Soldiers in Newport

As the French troops awaited reinforcements from their homeland, they had weeks of free time. While virtually all would have been baptized Catholics, Austin Dowling, a late nineteenth-century church historian, believed that "religion sat lightly on them."[66] He claimed that many of the troops were skeptics influenced by the Enlightenment and that a number were involved with Freemasonry.[67] Two prominent officers neatly fit that description: Lafayette, who was an active Mason, and Chastellux, who was friendly with *philosophes* such as Voltaire and Denis Diderot.[68] While both men socialized with local dignitaries such as Stiles, most of their comrades spent their time riding around Aquidneck Island, playing cards, and pursuing young women (single and married) at dinner parties and dances.[69]

Though many of the officers were not particularly observant, some were curious about the Protestant milieu in which they had found themselves. One of them, Jean-Francois-Louis Clermont-Crevecoeur, recorded his observations in his diary:

> The town of Newport has many Protestant churches, nearly all built of wood, without ornament and regular in shape, for the practice of the different religions that are all tolerated in this country. The predominant religion is Anglican. Much of the town . . . is inhabited by Quakers. These men are extremely grave in their dress and manner and very temperate. They speak little . . . and "thee and thou" everyone. . . . Their form of worshipping the Supreme Being seems rather bizarre. . . . It often happens that they leave the meetinghouse without having uttered a word.[70]

Another officer, Louis Berthier, observed that the townspeople saw religion as a private matter: "[They] practice their various religions without dissension or discussion."[71] Still another, Jean Baptiste Antoine Verger, thought that the Newporters were mostly secular Presbyterians and Baptists: "[T]he people in general are very little attached to their religion, and each child has the right to practice his religious duties or not."[72] Despite these contrasting impressions of Protestants, all of the French officers agreed that there were no native Catholics in their midst.

The COLONY·HOUSE 1739·1776 : The STATE·HOUSE 1776·1900 : NEWPORT, R·I·

FIGURE 4. Edith Ballinger Price, woodcut of the Colony House, c. 1940. Colony House served as a hospital and Catholic chapel during the French occupation of Newport. Collection of Daniel P. Titus.

"A Universal Sigh of Regret"

In March 1781, Washington paid a weeklong visit to Rochambeau in Newport, and the commander of the Continental Army was greeted with great fanfare by the French and the Newporters alike. Parades, receptions, and a formal ball were held in his honor. No strategic decisions were made, however, because Rochambeau still did not know how many reinforcements he would receive and when they would arrive.

In May, Rochambeau's son finally returned from France, bringing additional funds but also the news that no more men or ships were forthcoming. The king's top advisors were disturbed by Benedict Arnold's defection to the British and worried about Europe's stability in the wake of the death of the Holy Roman empress, Maria Theresa.[73] Consequently, they were unwilling to send any more regiments to America. Rochambeau now realized that he could not accede to Washington's plan to attack the British stronghold in New York; he simply did not have enough troops. He concluded—and Washington reluctantly agreed—that they would instead have to bypass New York and pursue Lord Cornwallis's smaller forces in the South.

In early June, almost all of the French troops were packed and ready to leave Newport for Providence and then points south.[74] According to Louis Berthier, both the soldiers and the citizens were sad about the departure:

> The whole army had spent a delightful winter in Newport, and as each man got the word and prepared to leave, the pleasures ceased and gave way to regrets in which the whole town joined, especially the women.
>
> Although Newport is largely inhabited by Tories . . . there was now a universal sigh of regret. Everyone's feelings had changed so much that each officer was like a member of his host's family.[75]

Samuel Vernon, whose family home had served as Rochambeau's head-quarters, wrote dejectedly to his father in August, "We are at present very dull and defenceless."[76]

But not all Newporters regretted the French departure. Jonathan Easton, in a report to the tax assessors, noted that the British had burned down three of his houses, cut down his orchard, and stolen his farm animals. Yet the incoming French had also been troublesome: "[they] encamped in the medow . . . [and] kept there cows and horses in the medow the whole time they stayed."[77] Silas Cooke complained about more serious problems: "The French had my still house, store, stabel and two men quartered upon me and will not pay any rent."[78] Nonetheless, it is clear that the French brought new life to the battered town and that many Newporters enjoyed their company and were sorry to see them leave.[79]

As the French troops marched southward, ships under the command of Comte François Joseph de Grasse in the West Indies and Comte Jacques-Melchior de Barras in Newport headed for Chesapeake Bay.[80] Meanwhile, Cornwallis, who had been battling the rebels in the Carolinas with mixed results, led his men into Virginia. There he hoped to meet up with Benedict Arnold's forces and connect with the British fleet in the Chesapeake. Cornwallis settled in at Yorktown and waited for rein-forcements. In September, Admiral Thomas Graves tried to come to his aid but was blocked by the combined fleets of de Grasse and Barras. In October, a superior French-American army laid siege to Cornwallis and forced him to surrender his 8,000 troops.

While Yorktown would be the final campaign of the war, it was not immediately apparent that the Americans had won. The British had heavily fortified New York City and controlled Charleston, Savannah, and Wilmington, North Carolina. As peace negotiations were held in France, sporadic fighting continued throughout 1782. At last, in September 1783, the Treaty of Paris was signed, giving America its independence and ending England's struggle with its European foes.

During those negotiations, the Rhode Island legislature decided to revisit its policies towards Catholics. In February 1783, the General Assembly amended its 1719 law and recognized that "all the rights and privileges of the Protestant citizens of this state . . . are hereby, fully extended to Roman Catholic citizens."[81] It would be a mistake to attribute Rhode Island's shift entirely to the presence of French troops in Newport; certainly, a movement was afoot in several colonies to expand Catholics' rights, at least to some degree. Pennsylvania and Maryland both guaranteed Catholics complete religious freedom in the fall of 1776, and New York approved liberty of conscience for Catholics in 1777, though it refused to allow foreign-born Catholics to gain citizenship.[82] In its 1780 constitution, Massachusetts guaranteed Catholics freedom of worship but did not grant them the right to hold office and maintained Congregationalism as the established religion.[83] However, Newport was surely affected in a unique way by its encounter with the French, who had made a positive impression on its residents and eased their apprehensions about Catholicism.[84] Thus, while the Revolutionary War sowed ill will and division among Newport's Protestants, it helped usher in a more tolerant attitude toward Catholics. Although the town probably had few Catholics at this time, the changed atmosphere would make it more appealing to them in years to come.

Chapter 3
SHELTER FROM THE STORM

Catholic Refugees in Post-Revolutionary Newport

The city of Newport . . . exhibits a melancholy picture of declining
commerce and population. . . . Its former prosperity was chiefly
owing to its extensive employment in the African slave trade,
of which some remnants continue to support it. The town is
large, but many of the houses, and the most elegant of them, are
altogether out of repair, and for want of painting make a dismal
appearance; the streets are dull, and the wharves appear more
frequented by idlers than by men of business.

John Quincy Adams, diary entry, September 14, 1789

With the Revolution finally over, Newporters set about trying to
rebuild their badly damaged town. Although the British had
occupied several cities during the war, Newport suffered much more
than the others did and would face greater challenges in the years to
come.[1] But even as the town struggled to regain its pre-revolution status, the first influx of Catholics began arriving—mostly French refugees
fleeing revolution in the Caribbean—and Newport accepted them, as it
had accepted Jews and Quakers before them. Despite this welcome, the
émigrés rarely stayed for long. With the town reeling, first from Thomas
Jefferson's restrictive trade policies and then from the War of 1812, they
found few opportunities, and most soon headed to more prosperous cities
such as Boston and New York.

A New Government

By the mid-1780s, it was clear to most members of the U.S. Congress that
the Articles of Confederation, which had come into effect in 1781, needed

36

to be strengthened. Under the Articles, the national government had the authority to establish a post office, coin money, and fix standards for weights and measurements, but it had no power to levy taxes. Amending these weak articles was a cumbersome process that required approval from all thirteen states, and George Washington, James Madison, and Alexander Hamilton pressed for a convention to revise them.[2] In February 1787, Congress agreed and invited each state to send representatives to Philadelphia in May for a constitutional convention. All of the states sent delegates, except for Rhode Island, which, as the historian Samuel Eliot Morison noted, "sulkily declined the invitation."[3] Afraid of being dominated by a powerful national government, Rhode Island wanted to be free to pursue its own policies, especially in financial matters. In fact, to resolve its war debts, Rhode Island had printed its own paper money and was forcing creditors to accept it as payment, though it was worth much less than silver and gold currency.

By September 1787, the delegates had completed their work, drafting the U.S. Constitution to take the place of the Articles. The new document granted the federal government considerably more authority, including the power to tax, and could be amended more easily than the articles could. While most of the states quickly ratified the Constitution, Rhode Island rejected it again and again. In the view of its critics, the state was proving itself to be "Rogue's Island."[4] A Boston newspaper declared that it should "be dropped out of the Union or apportioned to the different States which surround her."[5]

George Washington was equally impatient with Rhode Island. After his inauguration in April 1789, he undertook a triumphal tour of the New England states, visiting sixty cities and towns in Connecticut, Massachusetts, and New Hampshire, including New Haven, Hartford, Boston, Salem, and Portsmouth. He pointedly avoided Rhode Island as its status in the new republic was uncertain.[6] In 1790, however, Rhode Island at last agreed to hold a convention to consider the Constitution, after having rejected thirteen prior proposals. After weeks of bitter debate, its delegates approved the Constitution by a thirty-four to thirty-two vote, making Rhode Island the last of the thirteen states to ratify it.[7]

Washington Returns to Newport

Washington was so pleased by Rhode Island's decision that he decided to make up for having avoided it during his previous tour. In August, accompanied by Secretary of State Thomas Jefferson and several other officials, he set off from New York to visit the state. When the party arrived in Newport, town leaders welcomed them, and a group of eighty Newporters dined with them at the Colony House. After dinner, they all marched in procession to the visitors' accommodations on Thames and Mary Streets.[8] On the following morning, Washington was greeted at the Colony House by representatives of four groups: town officials, the Protestant clergy, a spokesman for Touro Synagogue, and the Masons. The town leaders apologized to the president, explaining "that the present circumstances of this Town forbid some of those demonstrations of gratitude and respect which the citizens of our sister States have displayed on a similar occasion." Still, they expressed confidence that "our languishing Commerce shall revive and our losses be repaired." The clergy, representing the Baptists, the Episcopalians, the Congregationalists, and the Moravian Brethren, assured Washington that "Divine Providence hath raised you up" and prayed that, during his presidency, America would experience "peace and prosperity, with all the blessings attendant on civil and religious liberty."[9] The final welcomes were both offered by Moses Seixas, who was warden of the synagogue and master of the King David Lodge of Masons. Speaking on behalf of Touro, he expressed the congregation's gratitude to the "Ancient of Days" that the new American government "to bigotry gives no sanction, to persecution no assistance."[10] Speaking for the Masons, he hailed Washington as an "illustrious Brother" with a "heart worthy of possessing the ancient mysteries of our Craft."[11]

Before departing for Providence, Washington replied in writing to each of these welcomes. In his stirring response to the Hebrew Congregation, he quoted from Seixas's speech and the Old Testament:

> It is now no more that toleration is spoken of, as if it was by the indulgence of one class of people that another enjoyed the exercise of their inherent rights. For happily the Government of the United States, which gives bigotry no sanction, to persecution no assistance requires only that they who live under its protection should demean

themselves as good citizens in giving it on all occasions their effectual support. . . . May the Children of the Stock of Abraham, who dwell in this land, continue to merit and enjoy the good will of the other Inhabitants, while every one shall sit in safety under his own vine and fig-tree, and there shall be none to make him afraid.[12]

Organizing a Church

Considering the wide variety of people who welcomed Washington to Newport—from a Moravian Brethren minister to a Jewish Mason—it seems likely that the Catholics would also have been free to offer greetings, if they had had a community of any note in the city.[13] Yet while Catholics were scarce in Newport in 1790, the church was beginning to establish itself in other parts of the country. In 1789, Father John Carroll had been appointed bishop of Baltimore and was given jurisdiction over all of the Catholics in the country. With just twenty-four priests to assist him, he tried to spread them out as much as possible. To Boston, he first sent a French naval chaplain, Father Claude de la Poterie, who celebrated Masses in a former Protestant church for the fifty or sixty French and Irish Catholics in the city.[14] De la Poterie had had a checkered career before coming to Boston and soon was quarrelling with Carroll. Before the end of 1789, the bishop suspended de la Poterie's priestly faculties and replaced him with another French émigré, Father Louis de Rousselot.[15] Although Rousselot was more responsible than his predecessor, several English-speaking Catholics were eagerly anticipating the arrival of a celebrated Yankee priest, Father John Thayer. Born in Boston and educated at Yale, Thayer had been ordained a Congregational minister. When visiting Rome in the early 1780s, he had had a dramatic conversion experience, which he described in a widely circulated book.[16] After being received into the Catholic church and studying at a seminary in Paris, he was ordained in 1787 and set sail for America two years later. Thayer was anxious to return to Boston, intent on bringing the city and all of New England into the Catholic fold. He was learned and articulate but could also be combative and polarizing. Nonetheless, many people came to Thayer's masses and public lectures, where he sought to explain and defend Catholic doctrines.[17] Some, including Father Rousselot and his French followers, were put off by Thayer's zeal. Soon relations between the two priests deteriorated to such an extent that each offered Masses at separate locations and refused to communicate with one another.

Uncertain of his position in Boston, Thayer spent some of 1790 traveling to other towns to administer the sacraments to the Catholics there. He made three visits to Salem that summer, and a prominent church historian, Father John E. Sexton, believes that he probably also visited towns south of Boston, including Newport.[18] Thayer was certainly in Newport in February 1791, where he baptized an African American boy, Joseph Deane.[19] After briefly returning to Boston, he headed south again, this time traveling to Philadelphia. Stopping off in Hartford, he visited with his old Yale classmate, Noah Webster, and celebrated a Mass that Webster attended. From Hartford, Thayer went to New Haven, where he had an unfriendly encounter with Ezra Stiles, Yale's president. Stiles noted in his diary that he had been "visited by Mr. Thayer the Romish Priest; born at Boston a Protestant . . . went to France & Italy, became a Proselyte to that Chh. . . . Of haughty insolent & insidious Talents."[20] Yet Stiles must have been intrigued by his brash former student because he went twice over the following days to hear Thayer preach in a local Congregational church.[21]

In the summer Bishop Carroll made an extended visit to Boston to sort out the feud between the Thayer and Rousselot factions and bring about a reconciliation. But in the fall, after receiving a lengthy complaint about Thayer from a group of Catholics, Carroll directed him to leave Boston for a time.[22] Thayer obeyed and headed back to Newport, arriving in late October. This time he baptized two members of the Gouffranc family, whose father had fled Saint-Domingue, soon to be known as Haiti.[23] Thayer could not have stayed long in Newport because he had to be in Baltimore in early November to attend a synod convened by Carroll.

By the beginning of 1792, Carroll had decided that another priest needed to be sent to Boston to heal divisions among the Catholic factions. So in August, Father Francis Matignon, newly arrived from revolution-torn France, was sent to the city. Carroll informed Thayer that he would be transferred to Virginia, and the priest accepted the decision gracefully and left for Norfolk. Rousselot likewise agreed to depart and set off for the island of Guadeloupe.[24]

Fleeing the Revolution

By 1793, the French Revolution, which at first seemed so similar to the American Revolution, had taken a much more radical turn. Louis XVI had been guillotined by the militant Jacobins, and Marie Antoinette was languishing in prison, awaiting trial. The revolutionaries' harsh treatment of the royal family horrified most European heads of state and drew England, Prussia, Austria, Spain, and Holland into war with France. But the aristocratic officers who had played such a critical role in the American victory would not lead France in this war. A year earlier, Lafayette, who had exultantly sent Washington the key to the Bastille prison at the start of the French Revolution, had fled to Austria, fearing for his life.[25] Since then, the revolutionaries had beheaded admirals D'Estaing and de Grasse, and General Rochambeau had been imprisoned and sentenced to death.[26]

The upheaval in France had dramatic repercussions in its wealthy, sugar-producing colonies in the Caribbean. After the French government ordered the enfranchisement of the mixed-race population of Saint-Domingue, the white planters resisted, and then hundreds of slaves rose up, destroying plantations and killing whites in the northern province. In June 1793, Saint-Domingue's main city, Cap-Français, was in flames as an army of former slaves took revenge on the planters, setting fire to their grand homes. In one night alone, one hundred ships laden with desperate refugees set sail for America, landing in Philadelphia, Charleston, New York, New Orleans, and Newport.[27]

Rhode Island newspapers detailed the horrors of Cap-Français:

> [A]n indiscriminate massacre of both sexes took place—men, women and children were cut to pieces, to the number of between 8 and 10 thousand; numbers took refuge in the mountains, where it is supposed they have shared a similar fate with their brethren ere this; those who were more fortunate escaped on board the shipping, with what little cloaths they had on; the wretches then began to plunder the town, after which they set fire to it, and on the 23rd [of June] . . . there were not more than 50 houses standing.[28]

The papers also noted that ships were starting to reach Newport: "Capt. Hicks, in a Brig, arrived there on Wednesday from Cape-Francois [*sic*].

He sailed in company with a large fleet of merchantmen, bound for various ports of the United States, under convoy of two French Ships of the Line and five frigates. . . . He brought a number of French passengers."[29]

Many of these French refugees were probably Catholics, though records about them are scarce. Often their names have been lost, yet hints remain. For instance, in November 1793, one refugee placed the following advertisement in the *Newport Mercury*:

> A young married gentleman, obliged to seek for a safe asylum from the horrid crimes and the consequences attending the conflagration of the town of Cape Francois [*sic*] arrived in this town the 1st of October. . . . Deprived like many other unfortunate inhabitants of the same place of sufficient means to maintain himself and lady in the character becoming them, [he] proposes to make use of the talents he acquired through his education.
>
> He therefore offers to wait upon any young ladies and gentlemen, who are desirous to learn DANCING at their houses; flattering himself with the expeditious improvement of his pupils.[30]

The refugee dance instructor did not include his name in the notice; he only mentioned that he was staying at "Mr. Rivera's house on Easton's Point." However, it is possible that he was Monsieur Carpentier, whom George Gibbs Channing recalled in his memoir of childhood in 1790s Newport: "[A] dancing-school was kept in . . . Church Lane by Monsieur Carpentier, where lads and lasses were taught graceful motion. Although the teacher was lame, he was wonderfully successful in his art. Monsieur Carpentier was also employed in many families as an instructor of the French language."[31] In 1802, Carpentier did advertise in the *Newport Mercury* under his own name, offering dancing and French language classes "for six dollars a quarter for each scholar."[32]

Channing's memoir also mentions Julius Auboyneau, a clerk who worked at the family shipping company, Gibbs and Channing, as well as Pascal Faisneau, a barber in town.[33] Like Carpentier, Faisneau advertised in the *Newport Mercury*, announcing that he and his partner, Perry Cornell, had "commenced the Hair-Dressing business . . . at the large and commodious shop opposite Mr. John Hadwen's, Thames Street, where they carry on the above business in its various branches. They have a small supply of the best French Perfumery."[34] Though Carpentier, Auboyneau, and Faisneau probably had Catholic backgrounds, it impossible to know for certain. Diocesan records for the period list only the names of the baptized, so Catholics who were single, widowed, or beyond childbearing age did not appear on church rosters.

The Gouffrancs, baptized by Father Thayer, do appear in the registers, as do members of four other French Caribbean families whose children were baptized in Newport during these years: the Dugars, the Arcambals, the Giberts, and the Mehes. All were from Saint-Domingue or the violence-wracked islands of Guadeloupe and Martinique.[35] One of the women, Catherine Gibert, was married to an Italian, John Nicolai, and they had at least five children together. George Champlin Mason, who was born in 1820, remembered Nicolai:

> When I first knew him he was an old man, a widower with three maiden daughters and two or more sons. On the front of the building there were two stores. . . . In one of the stores Miss Eliza taught school. . . . The other sisters were Catherine, the eldest, and Emily, the youngest. . . . They were all intelligent . . . and the lives of all three sisters were adorned with the Christian graces.[36]

The most prominent members of Newport's small Catholic community were Joseph and Catharine Wiseman, who arrived in 1795. "Don Josef," as he was styled, was a Spaniard of Irish descent who served as vice consul for the Spanish Crown. He concerned himself with ships in Spanish ports and the privateers who made shipping so perilous. Wiseman was in regular contact with Don Juan Stoughton, the Spanish consul in Boston, and hosted both Stoughton and Don Carlos Martinez de Iruja, the Spanish minister to America, at his home in Newport. After the minister's visit, Stoughton assured Wiseman that Martinez de Iruja was "much pleased with the enchanting prospects and views of your little island."[37] Catholic clergy in Boston also took an interest in Wiseman. Father Jean de Cheverus, another French exile, even planned to make a "collecting visit" to the Wisemans in Newport but was called away to other business.[38]

It was notable that Wiseman was stationed in Newport rather than Providence; clearly, despite the damage it had suffered during the American Revolution, the town was still a place of significance in the 1790s. Channing's memoir supports that view. He depicts Newport as a bustling if not overly prosperous town. Certainly, his family's shipping company was thriving, thanks to its involvement in Far East ventures and the African slave trade.[39] It reported $90,000 worth of property in 1798 and $100,000 in 1801.[40]

Newport was also important strategically, and in the late 1790s the federal government began construction on a fort to protect its harbor against invaders. The project was overseen by a French engineer, Major Louis de Tousard, who, on July 4, 1799, presided over the opening of Fort Adams, named in honor of President John Adams. According to the *Newport Mercury*, after Tousard's speech, the "whole assembly . . . passed under the arches of the entrance gates, [and] three guns were fired from the battery, which ended a ceremony worthy [of] the great occasion."[41]

Father Thayer Returns

In the summer of 1798, Father Thayer was preparing to leave Boston for the last time. Since departing in 1792, at Bishop Carroll's request, he had ministered for a few years in Alexandria, Virginia, but had quarreled with a leading member of his congregation. From there, he had traveled to Quebec, serving in a parish for a time, but the bishop did not ask him to stay. So he returned to Boston in 1797, spending a year there before accepting an invitation to serve in Kentucky.[42]

That May, Thayer decided to deliver an address in Boston's Catholic parish, choosing the day that President Adams had set aside for prayer and fasting. His subject was France because, at this time, America was on the verge of going to war with the French over the XYZ Affair, a scandal involving three French officials who had demanded $250,000 before they would receive America's representatives.[43] In his lecture, Thayer denounced the French Revolution, mourning the thousands of priests and laypeople who had been murdered by the radicals, and concluded with a rousing call to arms: "France is the great oppressor of the universe; and, therefore, opposition to her is the *common cause of the human race* against their tyrants, plunderers and murderers. . . . [I]t is your cause; it is my cause; it is every honest man's cause."[44] The speech made a power-ful impression: Father Cheverus said he "was moved to tears by it," and Thayer arranged to have it published as a pamphlet.[45]

In June, as Thayer began his trek to Kentucky, the press was still hail-ing his hard-hitting address.[46] In early July, he stopped at Newport, his first visit in almost seven years. During his stay, he baptized four chil-dren: Louis Dugar, Susanna Arcambal, Catherine Wiseman, and a slave girl named Marie who was owned by Marguerita La Paiaux.[47] He also found time to deliver a public lecture at the Colony House. On July 3, the *Newport Mercury* ran an advertisement for a "federal discourse," which Thayer would give that evening in "the Court-House in Newport."[48] The talk was probably similar to his Boston address, but there are no reports in the press of its contents or of Newporters' reactions to it. Soon afterward, Thayer left town and continued his journey south.

"I Was Taught to Hate Popery"

Despite the activities of luminaries such as Father Thayer and Joseph Wiseman, most residents remained uncomfortable about Catholicism. Channing's memoir depicts Newport in 1800 as a staunchly Protestant town. It fondly recalls the ministers linked to the various denominations—Episcopalians, Seventh-Day Baptists, Congregationalists, Methodists, Moravian Brethren. Channing remembered that the Yearly Meeting of the New England Society of Friends, held in Newport, lasted a full week and drew "immense" crowds.[49] As a boy, he wrote, he had enjoyed walk-ing inside Trinity Church, but he "could not bear the crown and the mitre on top of the organ. I was taught to hate popery,—I did not know why; and these signs of man-worship were too significant for my par-ents' spiritual digestion."[50] He recalled that the gathering places of the Congregationalists and Baptists were invariably referred to as "meeting houses." To speak of them as "churches" would have been thought a "con-cession to Romanism."[51]

It is notable that John Nicolai's three daughters, Catharine, Emily, and Eliza, were attractive and accomplished, yet none of them married.[52] There would have been few, if any, eligible Catholic men in Newport. Just as the Nicolai sisters may have remained single because they would not consider marrying Protestants, Protestant men would not have been interested in converting to Catholicism in order to marry the sisters.

The Catholic Community Scatters

A few more Catholic clerics visited Newport after Father Thayer's 1798 stay. In the summer of 1802, Father Matignon came to town and baptized William Gibert, and in the following summer Father John Tisserant, another French exile, baptized the Nicolais' son John. In the fall of 1803, Bishop Carroll, returning to Baltimore after a trip to Boston, was forced to land in Newport because of unfavorable winds. He ended up staying for two weeks and, during that time, baptized two sons of Joseph and Louise Mehe.

But not long after Carroll's impromptu visit, the Catholic community started to disappear. In 1805, Joseph Wiseman died of yellow fever at the age of forty-six.[53] The *Newport Mercury* lauded him in an obituary:

> During a residence of nine years in Newport, a correctness and faithfulness in discharging the duties of his office marked his public [life], as did his urbanity and pleasing manners [and] his private character, and gained him general esteem—a widow and three children lament an irreparable loss. The number of very respectable citizens who attended his funeral ... evinced the sense they entertained of his worth, while living, and their regret at his death.[54]

Shortly afterward, his widow, Catharine, sold some of their possessions and moved her family to Philadelphia.[55] Meanwhile, the French Caribbean refugees were also dispersing.[56] The Giberts moved to Brooklyn in 1804 or 1805.[57] The Audinets, who were related to the Giberts, moved to Boston in about 1805. When Mary Catharine Audinet died in 1807, the *Newport Mercury* reported that Father Matignon had presided over her funeral in Boston and noted that she had spent twelve years in Newport and had received the "esteem of all who knew her."[58]

The refugees may have left because of Newport's growing economic troubles. George Gibbs Channing believed that the Embargo Act of 1807 was to blame. Before its passage, "no place of the size of Newport, on the seaboard, was more distinguished for commercial activity than 'little Rhody.'"[59] President Thomas Jefferson had enacted the embargo in response to Great Britain's seizure of the *USS Chesapeake*, which had left three American sailors dead and four impressed into the English navy. The new law closed all American ports to imports and exports and was extraordinarily destructive to local economies. The historian Gordon Wood writes, "Perhaps never in history has a trading nation of America's size engaged in such an act of self-immolation."[60] He points out that the act's effects were especially severe in New England, which was extremely dependent on trade.

"A Ruinous and Unnecessary War"

In response to Jefferson's legislation, many Newporters tried to find new sources of income away from the water. Coal seemed to be a promising possibility. In 1808, coal veins had been discovered in Portsmouth, and some of Newport's leading citizens invested in mines, supporting a lottery to raise funds for a new firm, the Aquidneck Coal Company.[61] The *Newport Mercury*'s editors hoped that it would "counteract the baleful influence of the Embargo."[62] Yet the coal proved to be difficult to burn; and although the mines would operate intermittently for decades, they never turned a substantial profit.[63]

In 1809, as Jefferson was leaving office, he relaxed the Embargo Act, replacing it with the Non-Intercourse Act, which allowed Americans to trade with countries other than England or France. Newport and other trading centers might have been able to adapt to these regulations, but escalating conflict with England stymied them. In 1812, President James Madison declared war on Great Britain over its continued seizure and impressment of American sailors. While many in the South and the Midwest were "war hawks," eager to wrest control of Canada from the British, most New Englanders dreaded the prospect. In Providence, church bells tolled, flags were lowered to half-mast, and "regret and consternation were depicted on every countenance."[64] In Newport, Stephen Gould, a tax assessor, noted grimly that the town's wealthier residents were "face[d] with ruin" and the poorer ones risked "starvation, for want of business to procure food to eat."[65] The *Newport Mercury*'s editors declared themselves unable to fathom "the folly and madness which has plunged this country into a ruinous and unnecessary war; and this, too, in opposition to the feelings and wishes of a vast majority of the people of the northern states."[66]

American military forays into Canada during the War of 1812 all ended in failure. However, the nation's fortunes brightened considerably in 1813, thanks to the leadership of Lieutenant Oliver Hazard Perry at the Battle of Lake Erie. A twenty-eight-year-old Newport resident, Perry continued to battle the British even after his own flagship was destroyed.[67] Momentum in the war shifted again in the summer of 1814, when British forces chased Madison out of Washington and then sacked and burned the White House and the Capitol.[68] The British then contemplated an attack on Rhode Island—four ships of the Royal Navy had just attacked Stonington, Connecticut—but sailed instead into Baltimore's harbor and shelled Fort McHenry.[69]

In response, Rhode Island's governor, William Jones, sent troops to Fort Adams, and the Rhode Island legislature dispatched four delegates to the Hartford Convention, a closed-door meeting of New England representatives called to discuss the war.[70] Rumors spread that the New England states were planning to secede from the Union or to sign a separate peace with the British. In the end, however, the convention's delegates made no radical pronouncements, and no shots were fired on Fort Adams. On Christmas Eve 1814, Secretary of State John Quincy Adams helped to broker the Treaty of Ghent, which ended the fighting but did not resolve any of the underlying causes of the war, such as the impressment of American sailors.

While Newport had not been bombarded or burned, it nonetheless suffered grievously during the War of 1812. According to the economic historian Peter Coleman, many residents were afraid that the British would occupy Aquidneck Island, so a considerable number of the town's wealthiest citizens fled and never returned.[71] The historian Rockwell Stensrud argues that Jefferson's embargo, the war, and a powerful hurricane known as the "Great Gale of 1815" were the "knockout punches" that destroyed Newport's standing as a leading seaport.[72]

Many of the town's key organizations folded during these years. The First Congregationalist Church, which had proudly traced its roots to 1695, struggled to pay its minister's salary after 1815; and when the "Great

Gale" hit, the church was unable to repair its damaged steeple for two years. Trinity Church's wardens had to sell stock and lease some of its land-holdings to support its rector.[73] Touro Synagogue was faltering as well. Most of its members migrated to New York City after 1800, including Moses Seixas, the warden who had welcomed Washington to Newport in 1790.[74]

The Redwood Library was also struggling. Occupied by the British during the revolution and stripped of many of its books, the building was in such disrepair that, in 1790, a letter in a Newport newspaper described it as "totally neglected and moulding into ruin."[75] George Champlin Mason, who chronicled the Redwood's first decades, noted that its directors complained in 1807 about the difficulty of attracting new members. Two years later, the library did not have enough members to hold its annual meeting.[76]

Until the Embargo Act, priests from Boston had continued to visit Newport annually. Father Tisserant had visited in the summer of 1804 and baptized a Gibert baby; Father Matignon had come in the fall of 1805 and 1806 and baptized a total of three babies; and Father Tisserant had returned in the fall of 1807 and baptized three more.[77] But by about 1810, the clerics' visits shifted into other parts of Rhode Island. Another decade would pass before the Boston clergy would take note of Newport again. By then, a new group of Catholics—Irish immigrants—had taken the place of the long-departed French refugees.

Chapter 4

"RESPECTABLE IN THEIR VOCATIONS"

Irish Labor at Newport's New Fort

> On his return he [the bishop] learns from the Rev'd Mr. Byrne
> that he found at Newport Rhode Island working on the fortifica-
> tions a greater number of Catholics than he had anticipated—that
> he had confessed and given communion to about 150 persons . . .
> & to about twenty or thirty at the coal pit.
>
> —Bishop Benedict Fenwick, journal, February 2, 1827

Unlike Baltimore and Washington, Newport had not been bombed or burned during the War of 1812, but its already weak economy had been further damaged by the conflict.[1] The town suffered a sharp decline in trade because so few ships could enter its harbor or set sail from it during the war. But after the war, Newport slowly rebounded, thanks to the construction of a new Fort Adams as well as the arrival of summer visitors, who were beginning to recognize the town's many charms. For years, hundreds of Irish Catholics worked on the Fort Adams project, and they formed the nucleus of Rhode Island's first Catholic congregation. Established in 1828, the chapel on Mount Vernon and Barney Streets served the Irish laborers along with a handful of wealthy Catholics such as Catherine and Emily Harper, a mother and daughter who were among the growing number of summer colonists descending on Newport.

Monroe's Grand Tour

In 1816, with his second term drawing to a close, President James Madison backed fellow Virginian James Monroe to succeed him as the Democratic-

Republican nominee. Monroe had served as secretary of state since 1811 and, for a time, as secretary of war. He had played a key role in directing the war efforts, especially during the British assault on Washington. Monroe was a veteran of the Revolutionary War who could boast that he had crossed the Delaware with Washington, and he had no trouble defeating his Federalist opponent.[2]

In his inaugural, Monroe praised the "heroic efforts" of the nation's military forces during the recent war. However, he warned that further attacks might be coming and argued that America's "coasts and inland frontiers should be fortified." This undertaking would be "attended with expense," but he urged people to remember that the "work when finished will be permanent." Much of the address was optimistic. Monroe was pleased with the nation's general prosperity and impressed by its new roads and canals. Most of all, he was excited about the "increased harmony of opinion which pervades our Union." He assured his listeners that promoting this harmony would be the object of his "constant and zealous exertions."[3]

To foster harmony among the citizenry, Monroe decided to tour the northern states, much as Washington had done in 1789. Accompanied by General Joseph Swift of the Army Corps of Engineers, the new president embarked on a sixteen-week trip that would take him from Baltimore to Portland, Maine, and as far west as Detroit. He especially wanted to visit New England to show his good will toward the region that had opposed the War of 1812 so adamantly.[4]

As he moved up the East Coast, Monroe took time to visit every existing fortification to see if it could withstand future attacks. He arrived in Newport on a steamboat in late June and was greeted by Oliver Hazard Perry and a committee of town leaders. Monroe's escorts took him to see Fort Adams and also to Fort Wolcott, which stood on Goat Island in Newport's harbor. On Sunday, Monroe tried to be ecumenical: he worshiped at Trinity Church in the morning, then attended a second service at the Second Congregational meetinghouse and a third at the Baptists' meetinghouse. He also took time to visit with eighty-nine-year-old William Ellery, one of the last surviving signers of the Declaration of Independence. After leaving Newport, Monroe stopped briefly in Bristol before sailing on to Providence and Pawtucket. The *Newport Mercury*'s editors admitted that their town could not provide "the magnificence and splendor of more wealthy and populous Cities" but affirmed that Newport's citizens had demonstrated "our sincere attachment to the union of the States, our high respect for the Supreme Executive of the Nation, and . . . our cordial esteem for . . . our present Chief Magistrate."[5]

In early July, Monroe reached Boston, where he inspected its harbor forts, climbed Bunker Hill, and dined with John Adams.[6] A Boston Federalist newspaper concluded that an "era of good feelings had begun."[7] From Boston, the weary president soldiered on to Maine, then headed to New York and finally to Ohio to see the site of Perry's great naval victory. By the time he returned to Washington, Monroe had traveled 3,000 miles by boat, carriage, and horse.[8]

Newport's and Providence's Changing Fortunes

While Newporters were probably flattered that the president had spent three days in their midst, Monroe's visit did not lead to any immediate relief for the town. Eventually, federal funds would be allocated to rebuild Fort Adams and a string of other fortifications on the eastern seaboard.[9] However, several years would pass before any monies would be made available. In the meantime, the townspeople continued to invest in other enterprises, including coal mining.

While Newport struggled to adapt to the steep decline in maritime trade, Providence, Pawtucket, and other towns in the northern portion of the state grew steadily and prospered. These towns had established their first textile mills before the embargo, and they rapidly increased the number of mills during the war.[10] Newport, by contrast, did not establish any mills at this time, and no Newporters invested in the factories upstate.[11] As William McLoughlin notes, "[s]eaports like Newport, Bristol, Warren, Wickford, and Westerly faded into quaint backwater towns, while . . . [c]rowded, smoky cities in the northern half of the state became the center of enterprise, prosperity, and power."[12]

This is borne out by the towns' changing demographics. In 1820, Newport's population stood at 7,300, a 7 percent drop from 1810 and a 20 percent decline from its peak population in 1770. Providence, on the other hand, had nearly 12,000 residents in 1820, almost triple the number of people who lived there in the 1770s.[13] According to Rockwell Stensrud, Newport "hit its nadir" in about 1820, and there is much evidence to support this claim.[14] In the winter of 1821, the British abolitionist Adam Hodgson visited Newport as part of a nationwide fact-finding tour.[15] He was shocked by what he saw:

> The morning after my arrival in Newport . . . I strolled about the town; and a more desolate place I have seldom seen, or one which exhibited more evident symptoms of decay. The wooden houses had either never been painted, or had lost their paint and were going to ruin. A decent house, here and there, seemed to indicate, that some residents of respectability still lingered behind; but the close habitations, with their small windows, and the narrow, dirty and irregular streets, exhibited no trace of the attractions which once rendered this a summer resort for the planters from the South.[16]

One of these decayed buildings was the venerable Touro Synagogue. By the War of 1812, most of the town's remaining Jews had departed. The last Jewish resident, Moses Lopez, left in 1822 and entrusted the keys of the synagogue to a Quaker caretaker.[17] George Channing recalled that the shuttered building then went to "the bats and moles, and to the occasional invasion . . . of boys, who took great pleasure in examining the furniture scattered about."[18]

Forgotten by Boston?

The Catholic population of Newport must have dwindled as well because Boston priests devoted their energies to other Rhode Island towns. In 1812, Cheverus, now the bishop of Boston, came to Portsmouth to minister to the Irish miners and their families.[19] During his visit, the bishop confirmed three children. A week later, he was in Bristol, confirming a French girl. In the beginning of 1813, he returned to Portsmouth, confirming another youngster.[20] But he did not go to Newport.

Bishop Cheverus continued to visit Bristol and Portsmouth on a regular basis throughout the 1810s. In 1815, Father Matignon visited Providence, Portsmouth, and Bristol, and Cheverus spent two weeks in the state.[21]

If the bishop were going to New York or Baltimore, he would make a point of stopping for a few days in Rhode Island on his way back. In 1817, Cheverus spent several days visiting the Portsmouth coal mines and celebrated Mass there.[22] From there he went to Bristol, where he baptized the baby of a French family. In Bristol, Cheverus made the acquaintance of Alexander Griswold, Episcopal bishop of the Eastern Diocese.[23] Griswold was taken with Cheverus and invited him to preach from the pulpit of Saint Michael's Church, then serving as the Episcopal cathedral. Cheverus agreed, and a large crowd listened to him with great curiosity.[24]

While continuing to visit Catholic communities from Maine to Connecticut, Cheverus began focusing on a project closer to home: establishing a convent next door to Boston's cathedral. The foundation was the idea of Father Thayer, the convert priest who had served in Massachusetts and Rhode Island in the 1790s. At the time of his death in 1815, Thayer was trying to establish a house for Ursuline sisters in Ireland. In his will, he left more than $10,000 to Father Matignon to continue this work in Boston. When Matignon died three years later, he bequeathed his own funds and Thayer's money to Cheverus.[25]

By the summer of 1820, the convent was finished, and Cheverus traveled to Montreal to escort four Ursuline sisters back to Boston.[26] Soon the community would receive new candidates, including Catherine Wiseman, whose father had been the Spanish consul in Newport.[27] The convent's school for girls opened in the fall and was immediately popular with both Protestant and Catholic families.

By 1822, Cheverus had grown weary of Boston and decided to return to France.[28] In 1823, over the loud protests of many of Boston's leading citizens, he accepted the offer of a bishopric in southern France from Louis XVIII, the Bourbon king who had gained power after Napoleon's fall. Meanwhile, the diocese of Boston would be without a bishop for two years as officials in Rome tried to find a suitable replacement for Cheverus.

Missing the Marquis

The Marquis de Lafayette's 1824 tour of America provided a clear indication of Newport's irrelevancy. The marquis, who had never been enthusiastic about monarchy, was unhappy with Louis XVIII's policies; so, in

1823, he wrote to Monroe to broach the idea of a visit.[29] The president was well aware of Lafayette's exalted status as the last living general of the Revolutionary War and responded enthusiastically. In February 1824, he sent Lafayette a resolution, which Congress had approved unanimously, welcoming him as "the Nation's Guest."[30]

Americans eagerly anticipated his arrival, and the editors of Newport's newspapers were confident that the general would want to return to the town.[31] The *Rhode-Island Republican* was especially sanguine:

> Newport is one of the places rendered memorable by the events of the revolutionary war, and Lafayette once commanded the army stationed on this Island; it is therefore highly probable the veteran General will pay us a visit—and it is to be hoped that suitable measures will be adopted to evince our respect and gratitude to this great benefactor of America.[32]

In August, Lafayette set sail for New York City, accompanied by his son George as well as his secretary and his valet.[33] On arrival, the party was greeted by the mayor and 80,000 well-wishers. A week later they rode into Boston, where the governor and a huge crowd waited to greet the marquis with fireworks and church bells.[34] Learning that Lafayette planned to stay in Boston for several days, a committee of Newport's leading citizens drew up an invitation and directed William Vernon, Jr., and Robert Rogers to present it to him.[35] On August 25, the pair was able to secure a brief meeting with him in Cambridge at the house of the Harvard College president, Reverend John Kirkland. In their letter, the Newport leaders expressed their "hope [that] it may not be inconvenient to you to revisit this Island,—one of the early scenes of your glorious life; in that case they flatter themselves, that the inclination to do it, will not be wanting. . . . Please, Sir, to inform us, if we may expect of you this favor; and if so at what time."[36] Lafayette received them politely but told them that he was unable to visit Newport now, due to the press of other invitations. He assured them that he would try to get there at a later date.

Over the next twelve months, Lafayette crisscrossed the country, visiting the White House, stopping at Mount Vernon to pay his respects at Washington's tomb, going to Monticello to confer with Jefferson, traveling up and down the Mississippi, and even venturing to Niagara Falls.[37] In June 1825, he returned to Boston at the invitation of the Freemasons to lay the cornerstone for the Bunker Hill monument.[38] In September, his triumphal tour came to an end at last. He had visited dozens of cities and towns throughout the country, including Providence and Pawtucket, but he had never found time to go to Newport.[39]

Newport's New Fort

After years of stagnation, Newport's fortunes at last began to improve with the building of a new Fort Adams. In 1816, Congress had established a Fortifications Board, which, in 1821, recommended that Fort Adams be given top priority for funding.[40] The board believed that the fort would not only protect Newport but also serve as the linchpin for defenses in Narragansett Bay.[41] In 1824, Congress allocated $50,000 to commence the work.

The supervising engineers needed a few skilled masons and hundreds of laborers to assist them. Most of these unskilled workers would be Irish immigrants. Irish workmen played a key role in virtually all of the nation's public works projects in the first half of the nineteenth century, from the Erie Canal and the Blackstone Canal in the North to the Savannah railroads and Lake Pontchartrain's canal in the South.[42] When touring America in 1842, Charles Dickens took note of the Irish and their shanties. He was not surprised: in his journal, he noted, "[W]ho else would dig and delve . . . and make canals and roads, and execute great lines of Internal Improvement!"[43] Some Irish laborers were recruited in Great Britain by agents sent over by the canal companies, who were unable to find enough Americans to do the work. Others learned of job openings through want ads in Irish newspapers or announcements posted by American consuls in Ireland.[44] Many Irish were eager for jobs of any sort. Since Napoleon's defeat in 1815, farm earnings had plummeted in Ireland, even as the population was steadily climbing.[45] There were not many prospects at home for young Irishmen and women.

In America, the Irish quickly gained a reputation as hard workers, willing to toil in bad weather and dangerous conditions for as long as the jobs lasted. Many were also hard drinkers, relying on shots of whiskey to get through their workdays.[46] They could be quick to anger and were suspicious of laborers from other Irish counties. Faction fighting between natives of County Cork and County Longford was a recurring problem and, on at least one occasion, led to fatalities.[47]

It is not clear if any Irish workers at Fort Adams were recruited in Ireland, but in other respects their experience paralleled that of other Irish laborers in the United States. They, too, were hard-working and courageous, with several suffering major injuries and at least two dying on the job.[48] Some would drink to excess, and some were prone to violence. In 1826, dozens of Irish from the fort battled one other in what the newspapers termed a "riot" but may really have been a faction fight, and between twenty and thirty of them were sent to jail.[49] In the following year, Irish laborers were involved in another pitched battle, this time with Newport locals. The conflict resulted in the death of one Irishman, who fell off the roof of his boardinghouse, where he had gone seeking slates to hurl at his foes.[50]

At Fort Adams, the first task for the workmen was to demolish all of the original fort, which, because of its small size, had been deemed "worse than useless" in an 1820 engineering report.[51] Serving under Lieutenant Andrew Talcott, "upwards of a hundred laborers" made quick work of the task.[52] By the fall of 1824, all that was left of the old fort was its name.

In the spring of 1825, the *Newport Mercury* announced that Lieutenant Colonel Joseph Totten, a key member of the Fortification Board, would be coming up from Washington to oversee the building of the new pentagon-shaped fort.[53] When Totten arrived in Newport in August, he determined that the job would require ten skilled masons. To secure them, he ran advertisements in Rhode Island newspapers for a month, seeking "first rate MASONS, [who] are masters of the business."[54] As the fort would be one of the largest constructed during this era, Totten required massive quantities of building materials. In 1826, he ran notices looking for bids for 600,000 bricks, 6,000 perches of building stone, and 15,000 bushels of sand for mortar.[55] He continued to advertise for skilled workers in 1826, now seeking twenty or thirty skilled stonemasons and six or eight brick masons. To find them, he placed notices in newspapers throughout the region, reaching as far south as New York.[56]

Commemorating the Glorious Fourth

In 1826, as the nation prepared to celebrate fifty years of independence, Newport's leaders appointed a committee to organize a program. While only $100 was made available to them, the committee was nevertheless able to arrange an impressive series of events for the day. The *Newport Mercury* reported the "ringing of Bells, and the roar of cannon, announced at dawn . . . the fiftieth anniversary of our country's birthday."[57] Later that morning, a great parade made its way through the town. The procession was headed by the town's clergymen, followed by boys carrying banners representing every state of the Union. At the Colony House, John Handy, a seventy-year-old veteran of the revolution, read aloud the Declaration of Independence, just as he had done as a young officer fifty years earlier.[58]

Soon after the festivities ended, Americans were stunned to learn that two of their former presidents—John Adams and Thomas Jefferson—had died within hours of each other on the Fourth of July.[59] When President John Quincy Adams learned of his father's death, he left the White House and returned to Massachusetts. For the next few weeks he worked to settle his father's complex estate and attended numerous memorial services for him throughout the state.[60] He also met with a steady stream of clergymen and civic leaders who wanted to offer their condolences.[61]

In October, the president was finally ready to head back to Washington. However, he had a number of stops to make along the way, and one of them was in Newport to examine the progress of the new fort. A strong proponent of internal improvements, Adams supported federal funding for forts and major roadways and even backed a national university and national observatory.[62] When he arrived in Newport, he was given a tour of the Redwood Library and the Colony House and was then rowed over to Fort Adams in the company of Colonel Totten. The colonel showed the president what had been built and then gave him a thorough account of what still needed to be completed. Adams later noted that the plans for the fort "appeared to me excellent."[63]

Bishop Fenwick's Initiatives

Boston's new bishop, Benedict Fenwick, was one of the few Massachusetts clergymen who did not seek a meeting with the president, no doubt because he was tending to the needs of his diocese, which stretched from Maine to Connecticut. A Jesuit from Maryland, Fenwick had been serving as president of Georgetown College when he accepted his appointment as Cheverus's successor.[64] Arriving in Boston at the end of November 1825, he found that only three priests were available to assist him in ministering to approximately 7,000 Catholics in the diocese.[65] Undaunted, Fenwick sent them all into the field, where they offered the sacraments to any Catholics they could find.

FIGURE 5. Portrait of Bishop Benedict Fenwick of Boston, c. 1830. Fenwick established Newport's first Catholic church. Courtesy of the Archives of the Archdiocese of Boston.

In 1826, Fenwick dispatched Father Patrick Byrne, a young Irish-born missionary, to visit Rhode Island.[66] Byrne traveled first to Woonsocket in the northern part of the state; a few months later, he made trips to Providence and then to Portsmouth to visit the coal miners.[67] In early 1827, Fenwick, having heard that Catholics were working on the fort, directed Byrne to visit Newport as well. A week later, Byrne returned to Boston, informing the bishop that he had heard the confessions of 150 people, had distributed communion to them, and had baptized six babies. At the coal mines, he had baptized three infants and had confessed and given communion to twenty or thirty people.[68]

Fenwick was encouraged by this report. He wanted to increase the church's presence in Rhode Island, but for the moment he needed Byrne's assistance at the cathedral. He would have to bide his time until he had a priest to spare. Meanwhile, the bishop turned his attention to the Ursuline sisters, lodged next door to the cathedral. Because the community had been plagued with illness and had recently lost three of its members, he decided, in 1826, to relocate it to a ten-acre farm in Charlestown, north of Boston.[69] On a hill, named Mount Benedict in honor of the bishop, an elegant brick building was constructed as a residence for the sisters and their boarding students. It was surrounded by terraced gardens and orchards, and on the edge of the property a chaplain's cottage was built for Fenwick. The bishop would celebrate Mass regularly for the sisters and, whenever possible, would spend time reading in the cottage or strolling around the grounds.

1828: An Auspicious Year

On New Year's Day, the bishop, accompanied by newly ordained Father James Fitton and Deacon William Tyler, traveled to Charlestown to bless the completed convent and celebrate a solemn high Mass.[70] Good tidings awaited Fenwick when he returned to Boston: Robert Woodley, a student at Georgetown during Fenwick's presidency, had become a priest and was hoping to serve in the Boston diocese. Though he had been assigned to serve in Charleston, South Carolina, Woodley told Fenwick that he could not abide the summers and presented the bishop with a letter from Bishop John England releasing him to serve in the North.

After pondering Woodley's proposal, Fenwick decided to send him to Rhode Island to consider the feasibility of establishing a congregation in Pawtucket or Providence. Residents of those cities had already written to Fenwick requesting a priest and promising to build a small church for him.[71] Woodley, a former Methodist, took up his assignment with a convert's proverbial zeal, traveling all over Rhode Island and southeastern Massachusetts. While Fenwick had directed Woodley to spend most of his time around Providence, Woodley went further afield. In March, he wrote to the bishop from Newport, informing him of a "beautiful Schoolhouse in a central situation in the town capable of holding four or five hundred people conveniently, now offered for sale." Having been assured that the building would "answer all the purposes of a decent church," Fenwick gave Woodley permission to buy the property for $1,100.[72]

The schoolhouse had been built in 1809 by Elezear Trevett, who had used it as a private school for more than a decade. By the mid-1820s, however, Newport had begun to establish its public school system, and Trevett's enrollment declined.[73] By 1828, he was leasing the building to the Democratic Party's Tammany Society for its meetings.[74]

In April, Woodley informed the bishop that the sale had gone through. Fenwick was pleased, noting in his diary, "This is the first Catholic church established in that State."[75] The Rhode Island press was similarly enthusiastic. The *Newport Mercury* reported on April 12 that "Roman Catholic services were observed at the Academy, on Sunday last, for the first time," adding that "many of our Irish population attended." The *Providence Patriot* speculated that the new church would be "capable of containing nearly a thousand persons."[76]

Though Fenwick was happy about the Newport church, he still saw Providence as a higher priority and wanted Woodley to concentrate his attention there, so the priest rented quarters in Providence and continued to look for a possible church in the area. In August, he was able to report that David Wilkinson, a Protestant millowner in Pawtucket, had donated a sizable tract of land to the diocese. Soon Rhode Island would have a second Catholic church.

Although Woodley spent the bulk of his time in Providence and Pawtucket, he was able to visit Newport about once a month. During the week before his arrival, Woodley would place notices in the town newspapers alerting his parishioners to his upcoming visit.[77] While there, he would celebrate Mass, perform baptisms, and occasionally officiate at weddings.

In late October 1828, Bishop Fenwick traveled to Newport to administer confirmation and view Woodley's new chapel. After celebrating early morning Mass there, he admitted that he was "greatly disappointed" with the property.[78] The bishop was frustrated that so much money had been spent on the building, for "with eleven hundred dollars (especially in Newport where in the declining state of this city Lots are so cheap) a much more eligible & much larger Lot could have been purchased & a far more decent Building could have been erected on it."[79] The only solution, in his view, was "to recommend the purchase, as early as possible, of the Lot next to it, that a sufficient space might be obtained for a future Church."[80] Still, on November 2, he confirmed eleven parishioners in a chapel that "was crowded to excess." When he returned that afternoon to deliver a sermon, he was happy to see a "large concourse of People" who included many "strangers and Protestants."[81] Despite his irritation about the building, the bishop left Newport feeling optimistic about the state of Catholicism in the town.

More than a year passed before Woodley was able to carry out Fenwick's directive. For much of 1829, he was occupied with the construction of Saint Mary's Church in Pawtucket, which opened on Christmas Day. Fenwick was happy to hear about the new church, but Woodley was in financial straits. He owed money to the carpenters, and they were soon pressing the bishop for payment. Finally, in May 1830, the young priest was able to turn his attention to Newport. He had his eye on the lot adjoining the Barney Street chapel, but to purchase it, he had to deal with Trevett, who had bought the land in 1828, right after selling the schoolhouse. Once again, Trevett took advantage of Woodley, charging him $100, though he had bought the property for $70.[82]

In the fall, Woodley's financial troubles worsened, forcing him to sell off a lot he had acquired in Providence. Then, in November, Father Thomas O'Flaherty, Fenwick's vicar-general, recalled Woodley to Boston and replaced him with Father John Corry, a newly ordained Irish priest who had received his seminary training in Maryland. The reasons for Woodley's transfer are unclear. Perhaps O'Flaherty was frustrated with his money-management issues. Or maybe he thought an Irish priest would relate better to the immigrant communities.[83] But the abrupt removal unsettled Woodley, who decided he did not want to remain in the diocese. With Fenwick's permission, he left Boston in 1831 and returned to Georgetown to join the Jesuits.[84]

Corry Attempts a Church

Like Woodley, Corry was initially entrusted with all of Rhode Island as well as nearby Taunton, Massachusetts. After settling into residence in Taunton, Corry set about building a small church there, which he dedicated as Saint Mary's in 1832. In the fall of that year, however, Fenwick sent another priest to oversee Providence and Pawtucket, and Corry's responsibilities were reduced to Taunton and Newport. In February 1833, he met with the bishop, and they agreed that a new church needed to be built on Barney Street. Fenwick urged Corry to acquire the corner lot before attempting to build. Because Corry was not an American citizen, he could not buy land; so Loughlin Dowling, one of his parishioners, purchased the lot for him for $195 and then resold it to Fenwick for the same price.[85]

Corry wanted to build a small Gothic church, and he asked the bishop to design one for him. Though Fenwick did not draw up any plans, he did visit Newport in May to consult with Corry—his first trip there in almost five years. After celebrating Mass and confirming seventeen people, Fenwick examined the lots and concluded they would be an excellent site for the new church.

Twenty-two supporters came to Corry's first meeting about the new church, and Fenwick and Corry hoped that construction could be completed in a few months.[86] Progress was slow, however. At the end of 1833, the bishop noted in his journal that the building would not be "entirely completed until next year."[87] In fact, the church would take another three and a half years to finish. Much of the delay centered around the difficulty of paying for labor and materials. Corry had been counting on his Irish parishioners from Fort Adams to provide most of the $4,000 in construction costs and much of the labor to build it.[88] But the four hundred or so laborers were each paid only about $1 a day, meaning that it would be challenging for Corry even under the best of circumstances to raise that sum.[89]

When Corry began the project, the fort seemed to be a stable source of employment for laborers. The government still seemed to be committed to its completion; for, in February 1833, the *Newport Mercury* reported

that Congress had appropriated another $100,000 for fort construction.[90]
Then, in June 1833, President Andrew Jackson, who was touring the northern states, stopped in Newport to visit Fort Adams. The *Newport Mercury*
reported that he "expressed himself highly gratified with the appearance
of that extensive Fortification."[91] In fact, however, Jackson was ambivalent
about using federal funds for public works. While he supported these
projects in principle, he worried about the federal deficit and generally
preferred to have states or private organizations pay for them. In 1830,
he had vetoed an appropriation for the Maysville section of the National
Road in Kentucky, arguing that it should be funded at the state level.
In the weeks following, he had vetoed bills providing monies for canals,
roadways, and lighthouses.[92]

Although Jackson declared that all defense-related works should be
supported by the federal government, forts struggled to secure funding
during his presidency. In March 1834, the Newport newspapers reported
that Congress had adjourned; as a result, the Fortifications Bill, which
would have given another $100,000 to Fort Adams for the coming year,
was never enacted.[93] The *Newport Mercury* explained that construction
had thus been "necessarily suspended for want of funds. All the workmen employed at Fort Adams were discharged . . . and in consequence,
there are now several hundred Irish laborers wandering about our streets,
destitute of employment."[94]

Although sharp divisions existed in Congress over whether to fund
public works, the most pressing matter in Washington in 1834 was the
Bank of the United States. Jackson had vetoed its recharter in 1832 and
had ordered the Treasury Department to start transferring money from
the federal bank to the state banks. These actions worried legislators and
became the overriding concern of the congressional "Panic Session" of
1833–34.[95] No resolution was reached in the bitter standoff between the
bank's defenders and detractors; but, in June, Congress reconvened and
approved a Fortifications Bill and a number of other measures that had
been left unsettled in the spring. Though some items were stripped from
the original version of the bill, Fort Adams once again received $100,000.[96]
In July, the *Newport Mercury* noted approvingly that "near 400 laborers
are now daily employed."[97]

The "Outrage of Charlestown"

Fenwick must have been pleased that the Irish were back to work at Fort Adams, but his thoughts were focused on a crisis closer to home.[98] In August, tensions flared at the Charlestown convent after one of the nuns, Sister Mary John Harrison, left in an agitated state and went to stay with friends. After meeting with Fenwick, the sister decided to return to the cloister, but her erratic behavior raised suspicions among the townspeople. Concerned that the bishop may have pressured her to return, a group of town leaders asked to visit Harrison inside the convent. Although the superior allowed them to meet with her, trouble continued to brew. On the night of August, a group of torch-wielding men surrounded the convent. The superior defied the mob, which reacted by setting fire to the convent and Fenwick's cottage, forcing the sisters and their fifty students to flee. Some of the rioters returned the following night, laying waste to gardens and groves and ransacking the sisters' cemetery. While none of the sisters or students was killed, the fire gutted the buildings, causing $50,000 in damage.[99]

Many of Boston's leading citizens were appalled by the attack. The mayor, Theodore Lyman, convened a meeting at Faneuil Hall, where he denounced the mob as "cowardly and unlawful." Many regional newspapers expressed anger as well. The *New-Bedford Mercury* declared that the destruction of the convent "has called forth the liveliest feelings of indignation against the authors of the outrage and of sympathy for the sufferers."[100] The Newport newspapers were equally upset. In its August 16 issue, the *Newport Mercury* reprinted three articles from Boston papers that offered detailed accounts of the "Disgraceful Outrage."[101] The *Rhode-Island Republican* ran a lengthy editorial on the attack, taking direct aim at the history of religious intolerance in Massachusetts: "The same spirit which hung the Quakers . . . and the same fanaticism which condemned and executed innocent and unoffending people for supposed witchcraft, has, in this enlightened age, broken out in the shape of Mobocracy, and wreaked its persecuting and barbarous tyranny on defenseless women and children":

> We would recommend to the Ursulines, if they should revive their
> institution . . . to turn their attention to this Island, to this healthy
> and delightful spot, to which scholars may be sent with the greatest
> expedition and facility. Here they may avail themselves not only of

the free political institutions of Rhode Island, but also of the more liberal standard of public opinion . . .—where religious freedom runs in the streams and floats in the breeze. . . .

The Catholic population of Newport have nearly all been introduced since the work on Fort Adams commenced, and principally consists of Irish, who have conducted themselves . . . in a manner to do away with any prejudice against that people, if it ever existed. They have proved themselves, with few exceptions, respectable in their vocations, and peaceable and respectful in their demeanor. . . . The Catholics have recently built a handsome new Church in this town, and are a large society well received by this community, and who have the good wishes of all.[102]

After the attack, the Ursuline sisters moved in with the Sisters of Charity, who had recently established themselves in Boston. Then they rented an estate in Roxbury, hoping to reestablish their school there. But when Fenwick arrived in mid-October to inspect the premises, he was not impressed. He thought the building was too small to serve as a convent and a school.[103]

At about this time, a group of Newport residents picked up on the *Rhode-Island Republican*'s proposal and invited Fenwick to relocate the sisters to Newport. Newspapers in Newport, Providence, and Baltimore soon reported that the bishop would be establishing a convent in Newport "to supply the place of the one recently destroyed at Charlestown, Mass."[104] Most striking was the appearance of an October article in *The Jesuit*, a Boston Catholic paper that Fenwick himself had founded. *The Jesuit* reprinted a piece from the *Providence Herald* stating that the "attention of the Catholic Bishop has been drawn toward Newport . . . where the well known liberality and generous feelings of the inhabitants, would always be a guarantee or safeguard from an infatuated or infuriated mob."[105]

Fenwick may well have been interested in the proposal; but to act on it, he first needed to be compensated for the property lost in Charlestown. In February 1835, the Massachusetts legislature took up the matter, and, in March, its lower house resoundingly defeated a bill that would have provided state funds to the sisters. A few days later, the press reported that the Ursulines had "abandoned the thought of rebuilding anywhere in New England."[106] The community disbanded soon after, and its members joined Ursuline communities in Quebec and Louisiana.[107]

FIGURE 6. Engraving of Fort Adams, 1888. From Richard Bayles, *History of Newport County* (New York: Preston and Company, 1888). Reprinted courtesy of Salve Regina University, Newport, RI.

Funding for the Fort

Although deeply pained by both the attack on the convent and its aftermath, Fenwick pressed on, continuing to build churches and schools across his vast diocese. In August 1836, Corry let him know that new churches in Fall River and Newport were "in a fair way of being finished shortly." In reality, the Fall River church was much closer to completion, though it had been started later, because the Newport construction remained dependent on the Irish presence at Fort Adams. While funding for the fort had been restored in the summer of 1834, Congress again failed to pass a Fortification Bill in the spring of 1835. This time the issue involved different versions of the bill in the House and the Senate, which could not be reconciled before the session ended.[108] Colonel Totten was apparently caught off guard by the funding gap for in January and February, he had been running notices seeking 1 million bricks and 50,000 bushels of sand.[109] However, as soon as he learned of Congress's inaction, he dismissed all of the laborers at the fort. With fewer Catholics now residing in Newport, Corry visited the town less often. In 1834, he had split his time between Taunton and Newport. But by 1835 and 1836, the *Catholic Almanac* was reporting that Corry resided full time in Taunton, visiting Newport only every third week.[110]

In the spring of 1836, the local press began to publicly wonder if funding would ever be restored. One Newport newspaper, the *Herald of the Times*, ran a dire headline in May: "Fortifying of Newport to be Abandoned." The paper noted that Secretary of War Lewis Cass had informed Jackson in his annual report that Fort Adams was already too large and that he could "not foresee the existence of any circumstances which call for a fortress of this magnitude now in the heart of New England."[111] Fortunately for Newport, Cass soon left the War Department to become minister to France, and Congress appears to have entirely disregarded the outgoing secretary's recommendation. In July, it not only approved funding for the fort but allocated $200,000 to make up for the previous year's gap.[112] Almost immediately, many Irish laborers returned to Newport. In mid-July, the *Newport Mercury* estimated that two hundred to three hundred were at work and, by the end of the month, the *Providence Journal* claimed that the number had risen above five hundred.[113]

"Evil Passions" at the Fort

Though Fort Adams was once again a hive of activity, all was not well there. While Totten and the other supervising officers resided in more comfortable quarters in the town, many laborers lived in boardinghouses at the fort.[114] When not working, some whiled away the hours drinking and gambling.[115] On a Saturday night in November 1836, an Irishwoman named Catherine Conners had the misfortune to step inside a boardinghouse operated by John McCarty. She had come to the fort from Newport in search of her husband, Dennis, who worked there.

Conners claimed that she had been invited into the boardinghouse by McCarty and his wife. But, she said, later that evening she was raped and severely beaten by McCarty and two other men, all of whom were drunk. Initial testimony was taken at the Newport jail, and the case received widespread coverage in Rhode Island and Massachusetts.[116] One resident of McCarty's boardinghouse acknowledged that more than a quart of rum had been consumed that night in the kitchen, but he was sure that McCarty had gone to bed early. A resident of a neighboring boardinghouse said that he had "heard a noise—heard a woman crying for mercy." John C. Murphy, the laborer who found Conners the next morning near a haystack, said her "face was bloody and her eyes were black" and at first he could not tell if she was "dead or alive."[117]

A grand jury in Providence brought indictments against McCarty and James McCroly, a laborer at the fort. Given Conners's uncertainty about the identity of her assailants, jury members did not charge a third man. The case was heard in December by Roger Taney, the newly installed Chief Justice of the U.S. Supreme Court. In the end, however, the prosecution was unable to demonstrate that McCarty and McCroly were the guilty parties, so both men were acquitted.

Although he had not obtained a conviction, the state's district attorney, Richard Greene, decided to write to U.S. Secretary of State John Forsyth and inform him of the disturbing activities at the fort. Greene enclosed a report from the jurors that noted the "existence of houses or shantees for the sale of ardent spirits located immediately without the lines of said fort. . . . They believe the evil practices here . . . were instrumental in strengthening and stimulating the evil passions (which commonly accompany a depraved heart) to action and on this occasion to one the most inhuman and wicked." The jurors concluded with a plea to make it a criminal offense for "any one knowingly to sell ardent spirits to any artificer or laborer employed on the public works."[118]

For Corry, these events must surely have been disturbing. Because he knew many of the laborers at the fort, he was called to testify at the trial.[119] He no doubt agreed with the recommendations put forth by Greene and the grand jurors about alcohol at the fort, for, in the years following, he became an outspoken temperance advocate.[120]

Saint Joseph Church

In the weeks after the court case, Corry at last had good news to report to the bishop: the new church, which Fenwick had been calling for since his first visit to Newport in 1828, was complete. The building, measuring sixty-five by forty feet, would be dedicated to Saint Joseph, and Fenwick would preside over the dedication in August. To raise money for the church and "prevent the blackguards of the town from rushing in & occupying the best seats," Corry published notices announcing that entry tickets would cost $1 and be required for admission to the ceremony.[121] Even with the fee, the church was reasonably crowded, and the congregation included some Protestants. After blessing the church, Fenwick confirmed nine children.

The bishop was pleased with the new structure, noting in his diary that "it [is] agreeably situated and sufficiently well finished. . . . Stands on the high ground of Newport in the middle of a good Lot of ground."[122] As the bishop's remarks make no reference to Woodley's schoolhouse chapel, it is likely that Corry sold it and had it removed from the property before construction began on the new church. On this visit, Fenwick had a chance to explore Newport for the first time, taking an afternoon stroll to the beach with Corry and Father Constantine Lee, an Irish priest then serving in Providence.[123] The three walked "to the Sea shore, & were greatly pleased with it," not returning from their "truly agreeable" walk until eight o'clock.[124]

Three days later, Fenwick summoned Corry and Lee to Boston and informed them he was switching their assignments. Because Lee was running into debt in his efforts to build a church in Providence and was clashing with parishioners, Fenwick decided to replace him with Corry. Given that Corry had managed to build and pay for churches in Taunton, Fall River, and Newport, the bishop no doubt hoped he would be able to fix the problems in Providence. For his part, Lee would take over Corry's brand-new church in Newport and assume responsibility for churches in the Massachusetts towns of New Bedford, Wareham, and Sandwich. However, neither priest prospered in his new position. In March 1839, Lee, perhaps feeling overextended, would leave the Boston diocese for Illinois; and, in September 1843, Corry, after a quarrel with Fenwick, would leave the diocese for mission work in the West.[125]

Corry appears to have been disappointed about his transfer. Shortly before being reassigned, he wrote a letter to Reverend Arthur Ross, whose First Baptist Church was located a couple of blocks from Saint's Joseph's. In it, Corry had nothing but praise for Newport: "I have never seen a town in the United States, among whose inhabitants there is less intolerance and religious bigotry. I have for six years, been more or less among them, and during that time period, none have denied me the common civilities of life, because I was a Catholic priest, but always treated me with the greatest respect."[126] Ross, who was compiling a lengthy discourse on religious freedom to mark Newport's bicentennial, included Corry's letter to show that Catholics were fully accepted members of the community. In his section on Catholics, Ross concluded:

> [Newporters] studiously avoid all interference with and uniformly respect the rights of all denominations. . . . And this feeling toward the Catholics, so far as I have been able to ascertain, is mutual, and reciprocated by every sect of Protestant Christian in the town, demonstrating that the great principle of religious toleration and liberty of conscience, established on this Island two hundred years ago as the basis of the Colony of Rhode-Island have come down to us unimpaired.[127]

Ross was probably right to declare that Catholics were accepted in Newport. Likewise, the *Rhode-Island Republican* had probably been right in 1834 to point out that anti-Irish prejudice in Newport was nonexistent. Nonetheless, the Irish were seen as distinct from the rest of the Newport community. When covering news events, the local papers would indicate in parentheses if the persons involved were Irish. For example, regarding the Conners case, the *Newport Mercury* reported the "trial of John McCarty and John M. Croly (Irishmen) for a rape committed at Fort Adams."[128] Perhaps the clearest indication of Irish otherness appeared in the notices that the postmaster placed each month in the papers. In his "List of Letters," he provided an alphabetized roster of all Newport residents with mail waiting for them. Listed below the Newporters were people from Middletown, Portsmouth, Jamestown, and sometimes New Shoreham.[129] At the very bottom was the heading "Irish," followed by several unalphabetized names. These notices appeared through the end of the 1830s.[130]

The Summer Colonists Arrival

In the mid- and late 1830s, Newport's prospects at last seemed to be brightening. While the national economy was foundering—the Bank War had helped to trigger the Panic of 1837, which would be followed by another panic two years later—Newport was beginning to prosper.[131] For the first time in years, carpenters and masons were at work on multiple large structures: Zion Episcopal Church (1834), the Newport Artillery Company building (1836), and a stately home for Alexander McGregor, Fort Adams's Scottish-born master mason (1835). All were in the Greek Revival style, which was then in fashion.[132]

Much of Newport's growth was driven by tourism. With the advent of steamboats, people could travel in comfort from New York to Newport in just a few hours. And ever-increasing numbers found their way to the town.[133] In the summer of 1836, a young Julia Ward reported to her grandfather, "Newport is quite full, visitors flocking from every direction to cool themselves in its breezes, fogs, waves. The houses swarm with straw hats and canes; the beach with . . . bathing dresses. . . . There are sailing parties, walking parties, fishing parties, riding parties, dancing parties."[134]

To accommodate these growing numbers, hotels were built in the center of town, and demand increased for carpenters, caterers, chambermaids, grocers, florists, jewelers, restauranteurs, and other workers. The town's burgeoning tourist industry, along with two newly established cotton mills and an iron foundry, made Newport's economy more robust than it had been in decades.[135] Along with visitors from New York and Boston, sizable numbers of wealthy planters, anxious to escape the South's oppressive heat, took steamboats from Savannah or Charleston to New York and then another boat to Newport.[136] While most of the southern visitors were Episcopalians who worshiped at Trinity Church, Catherine Harper was a prominent exception.[137] She was the widow of Robert Goodloe Harper, a Federalist senator and congressman from Maryland. She herself was descended from the Carrolls, the leading Catholic family in Maryland: her father was Charles Carroll, the only Catholic signer of the Declaration of Independence. Catherine and her daughter Emily enjoyed Newport so much that they built a home at the intersection of Bellevue and Narragansett Avenues in 1839.[138]

When Bishop Fenwick visited Newport in the summer of 1840, he stayed with the town's new pastor, Father James O'Reilly. Like Corry, O'Reilly was Irish-born, but he had trained for the priesthood in the United States and had been sent to Newport in August 1839, shortly after his ordination. When celebrating Mass at Saint Joseph's, the bishop was dismayed to learn that O'Reilly had no candidates to put forward for confirmation. Nonetheless, he was pleased to see "a pretty numerous congregation," which included Catherine Harper, her daughter Emily, and her foster daughter Catherine Seton, as well as "a number of other respectable southerners." Seton, the daughter of Mother Elizabeth Ann Seton, had grown up in the Harper household after her mother became a nun.[139]

Himself a member of an old Maryland Catholic family, Fenwick knew the Carrolls quite well.[140] So after the Mass, when Catherine Harper invited him to stay at her new summer home, he agreed and spent a relaxing and enjoyable week with the three women. On one evening, he recalled, the Harpers hosted a party "at which most of the Southerners, amounting to 30 or 40 attended." Fenwick spent a day exploring the town on his own and another day with O'Reilly, who took him out to see Fort Adams.[141]

In years to come, the Harpers would continue to visit Newport regularly and were always on friendly terms with the bishop and the local clergy. As the Catholic population in the town grew, the Harpers began pressing for a larger and grander church to take the place of Saint Joseph's. They made clear that they would be willing to contribute generously to help pay for it.

Chapter 5

"A VALUABLE ORNAMENT TO THE TOWN"

Our Lady of the Isle Church

This church is a splendid specimen of architecture, and reflects the highest credit upon the taste and unwearied efforts of our excellent and esteemed friend, the Rev. James Fitton, the Pastor.

Newport Daily News, July 26, 1852

In the 1840s, Newport's Irish Catholics were coming together to raise funds for Irish famine relief and support Irish nationalist leader Daniel O'Connell's political campaigns. The community's top priority, though, was a new church. Although Saint Joseph Church had been recently completed and approved by the bishop, the town's new pastor, Father James Fitton, and Newport's Catholic summer colonists already wanted to replace it. The Harpers and other influential visitors pressed for a larger, sturdier church in a more central location. Their financial backing, combined with the labor donated by the Irish workers at Fort Adams, made it possible to construct a grand new church designed by a highly regarded Irish-born architect, Patrick Keely. The Holy Name of Mary, Our Lady of the Isle would be dedicated in 1852, to the great satisfaction of the entire community, both Protestants and Catholics. Two years later, a group of Mercy sisters would arrive to oversee the parish school. The completion of this imposing building and the coming of the nuns signaled a new era for Newport's growing Catholic community.

"Our Much-Beloved Pastor"

While Bishop Fenwick enjoyed his stay with the Harpers in 1840, he was apparently unsatisfied with the overall condition of the parish.

Immediately after the bishop's departure, Father James O'Reilly placed notices in all three local newspapers indicating that he would be giving a lecture at Saint Joseph's on a point of Catholic doctrine.[1] He did not specify his subject, but it may have concerned the sacrament of confirmation, for we know that his lack of candidates had disturbed Fenwick. Two days after the lecture, O'Reilly went to Boston to visit the bishop, and no doubt he spoke about his presentation and his parishioners' response.[2] Over the next several months, O'Reilly kept in regular contact with the bishop, visiting him three more times.[3]

In June 1841, one of O'Reilly's parishioners wrote a letter cataloguing all that had been recently accomplished in the Newport parish and submitted it to the *Boston Pilot*, the leading Irish paper in New England.[4]

> The Catholic Church here is greatly improved. Few, very few indeed, ever entertained the idea that such would, or could be the case, considering the circumstances of this place. But, thanks to the wise and zealous exertions of our much-beloved pastor, not forgetting at the same time the liberality of the poor, but moral and industrious Irishmen of Newport, our church is at present as neat and respectable as any in the New England states. Heretofore, it looked like a place that had no owner and that was totally forgotten and neglected. But it seems that we now live in a new era— that the transgressions and omissions of others are consigned to oblivion—that peace and unity have taken the place of discord and disunion—and that all persons rival one another in supporting their Church and their pastor.[5]

The author, who identified himself as "J.H.," was probably James Hennessy, an Irishman who was active in the congregation.[6] He clearly felt that the parish had gone through difficult times under O'Reilly's predecessor, Constantine Lee. A few weeks later, O'Reilly again visited Boston and gave a more measured account than "J.H." had, reporting to Fenwick that Saint Joseph's was "in a good state of repair and that everything now looks decent."[7]

A week later the bishop and his vicar-general, Thomas O'Flaherty, traveled down to Newport. On the night they arrived, the two, along with

O'Reilly, went "to pay [their] respects" to Catherine Harper and her sister, Mrs. Richard Caton.[8] After taking tea with them, O'Flaherty returned with O'Reilly to his lodgings near Saint Joseph's, and the bishop stayed with the Harpers for two nights. Two weeks later, Fenwick was again in Newport, this time for a weeklong stay with the Harpers. On a Sunday, he preached to a crowded audience that included many Protestants, and he confirmed seventeen parishioners, a dramatic change from the prior summer. During the week, he read and relaxed and took a walk one evening on the beach with O'Reilly and another priest, which he found "delightful." He twice spent time with Dr. William Ellery Channing, a well-known Unitarian minister with roots in Newport, whose Boston church was next door to the Catholic cathedral. Although Channing was a sharp critic of Catholicism, he had been a close friend of Bishop Cheverus and sympathized greatly with Fenwick over the Charlestown convent attack.[9]

In September, Fenwick visited Newport once more, this time in the company of his brother George, who was also a Jesuit priest. Learning from Emily Harper that his friend and fellow Marylander, John Chance, the bishop of Natchez, Mississippi, was in town, Fenwick met up with him and brought him to see the Harpers. Over the next few days, the two bishops visited with Dr. Channing; with William Gibbs, a former governor of Rhode Island; and with Hugh Legaré, the newly appointed U.S. attorney general.[10]

When Fenwick returned to Boston, he undoubtedly saw a letter from O'Reilly in the *Pilot*, warning that an anti-Catholic lecturer would be coming to Newport from New York to speak about confession, American Catholics' alleged loyalty to the pope over their homeland, and Catholic opposition to religious liberty.[11] Because O'Reilly sent this letter to the *Pilot* rather than to the *Newport Mercury*, he was likely trying to get the attention of the bishop and make it clear that he was working to safeguard the faith of his parishioners.

Toasting Saint Patrick and Irish Causes

In the beginning of 1842, O'Reilly delivered a temperance lecture at Saint Joseph's.[12] He probably knew about the drinking issues among the Irish at Fort Adams and the Portsmouth coal mines (where workers were given whiskey on the job). Their behavior often got out of hand, so much so that several Irishmen and women—including Patrick Kennedy, Patrick Farley,

Ellen Rice, and James Riley—had been consigned to Newport's asylum on Coaster's Island as punishment for drunkenness.[13] But O'Reilly's lecture was also a nod to Fenwick and other American bishops, who were strongly promoting the temperance movement and the work of Father Theobald Mathew, who was having extraordinary success in administering the total abstinence pledge in Ireland.[14]

In March, the bishop stopped briefly in Newport on his way to New York City. So as not to trouble O'Reilly about lodgings, he took a room in a Newport hotel but nonetheless spent two full days visiting with the parish priest.[15] Then, one week later, on March 17, O'Reilly staged an ambitious event for the parish: working in conjunction with the Newport Catholic Temperance Society, he organized the town's first ever Saint Patrick's Day parade.[16] In the morning, he celebrated a Mass at Saint Joseph's and preached on temperance. Afterward, the congregation marched behind a grand marshal and a band "through the principal streets" of Newport. They finished at the Masonic Hall on School Street, where they dined together. During the meal, both the parishioners and their distinguished guest, Dutee Pearce, a former Democratic congressman, offered toasts, presumably not with alcohol.[17] The speakers praised Saint Patrick, Father Mathew and the Irish temperance movement, Daniel O'Connell's campaigns for Irish freedom, and the United States, which they hailed as the "asylum of the oppressed of all nations." Finally, they offered an effusive toast to O'Reilly, "to whose zeal and exertions we are indebted for the blessings of being a united, temperate, moral people. May he continue for a long time to preside over his congregation with the same talent and ability as he has since he came amongst us."[18]

O'Reilly then took the floor and repeated some of the tributes that others had offered to Mathew and O'Connell. He also took the opportunity to denounce the British government's policies regarding Ireland and predict that God "in his justice is now about to visit England for her injustice, her crimes and abominations. . . . Yes, England shall fall by her own power, by her own right hand, and Ireland shall again be free."[19] While clearly advocating Irish independence, he was careful not to weigh in on American politics. Neither O'Reilly nor Pearce nor any of the other speakers said a word about the controversy that was then raging in Rhode Island over state legislator Thomas Dorr's efforts to replace the state's 1663 Charter with a more democratic document.

Dorr's War

Dorr, a Harvard-educated lawyer, was first elected to the Rhode Island assembly in 1834 and then immediately joined the newly established Constitution Party, which was seeking to draft a new state charter. The existing one had no provision for reapportioning seats in the assembly according to population shifts. As a result, small farm communities had more seats than did the new mill towns in the northern part of the state. The state also continued to tie voting to land ownership: only men with at least $134 worth of real estate could go to the polls.

Throughout the 1830s, Dorr and other leaders of the Constitution Party pressed for changes but were repeatedly stymied by opponents in the assembly. So, in 1841, he and his allies took to the streets, staging mass demonstrations in Providence and Newport. Although orderly, the rallies were clearly meant to intimidate. In Providence, workers carried a banner that read, "War Forever Against the Tyrannical Government of Rhode Island," and, in Newport, some of the marchers were armed.[20]

As appeasement, the Rhode Island assembly called for a constitutional convention in November 1841, but the Dorrites doubted that it would accomplish much. Instead, they organized a people's convention in October and drew up their own constitution. Known as the People's Constitution, it would have enfranchised all white men, including immigrants, and would have redistricted the assembly to take into account the growing urban areas.[21] Dorr's constitution was supported by more than 14,000 Rhode Islanders, including large numbers of Irish immigrants. But, in the meantime, delegates at a rival convention were drawing up their own document, the Landholders' Constitution, which would have enfranchised all native-born Rhode Island men, including Black residents, but only those immigrants who owned property.[22] This second constitution was scheduled to come to a statewide vote in the week after O'Reilly's Saint Patrick's Day parade.

Some backers of the Landholders' Constitution engaged in Catholic baiting, warning that public schools would be in jeopardy under the People's Constitution as ever increasing numbers of Irish demanded aid for parochial schools.[23] One of the severest critics of the People's Constitution was Henry B. Anthony, the editor of the *Providence Journal*.[24] A nativist,

Anthony ran an editorial on the eve of the vote, warning that, under Dorr, the balance of power would be "among 2,500 foreigners and the hundreds more who will be imported. They will league and band together. . . . Their priests and leaders will say . . . give us by law every opportunity to per-petuate our spiritual despotism. At the feet of these men will you lay down your freedom."[25]

Despite the *Providence Journal*'s determined efforts, the Landholders' Constitution was narrowly defeated. Emboldened, Dorr and his associ-ates called an election and chose Dorr as Rhode Island's new governor. Over the strenuous objections of the sitting governor, Samuel Ward King, Dorr was inaugurated in an empty warehouse in Providence, and eighty members of the People's Legislature assumed their seats.

To break the standoff between the two governments, Dorr resorted to force. On an evening in May, he assembled about three hundred armed supporters and tried to capture the Providence armory. But the Dorrites' cannons would not fire, and the aggressors quickly dispersed.[26]

One might assume that Dorr's forces were filled with Irishmen, given the immigrant voting rights enshrined in the People's Constitution and the anti-Catholic and anti-immigrant tenor of Anthony and the landholder faction. Yet only a handful of Irish took part in Dorr's raid.[27] Many surely recognized that taking up arms with him would have been rash. Moreover, the priests then serving in Providence, John Corry and William Wiley, were adamant that no Catholics should become involved.[28] According to Erik Chaput, Dorr's biographer, Fenwick himself was monitoring events in Providence and did not want Catholics to take part in any way.[29]

After the attack on the armory, Dorr fled the state but then returned to Rhode Island a month later to make a final and even more quixotic stand. Headquartering himself in Chepachet, a village in western Rhode Island, he began trying to amass an army. His supporters spread through the state in search of soldiers. In Newport, they were rumored to be organizing the Irish at Fort Adams. Apparently, the plan was to group the laborers into two companies that would prevent the artillery company and other forces loyal to Governor King from leaving Aquidneck Island.[30] Yet the orga-nizing effort, if it even existed, was ineffectual. Instead, sizable numbers of militia from Newport, Middletown, and Portsmouth converged on Chepachet and helped to rout Dorr and his two hundred backers. Before the skirmish ended, Dorr again took flight, and this time he remained out of the state for more than a year. On his return, he was tried in Newport and received a life sentence for his role in the insurrection. He was released from prison after just a year, but his goal of suffrage for immigrants had been thwarted.[31]

In July, about a month after the events in Chepachet, O'Reilly published another notice in the newspapers, this time indicating that he would be lecturing at Saint Joseph's on Catholic doctrine.[32] It is possible that the Dorr Rebellion had motivated him to speak about citizens' rights and duties toward their rulers. A day before the scheduled lecture, however, the *Newport Mercury* reported that the "work on this important Fortress, now so nearly completed, has been suspended by orders from Washington."[33] This was worrisome news for O'Reilly. A month later, he went to Boston and informed the bishop that he was "unable to live there [in Newport] any longer, his income from the church being only about $20 per quarter—that the people employed about the fort who had hitherto proved his chief supporters, had all left it."[34] Fenwick temporarily moved O'Reilly to a parish in Boston and told him he would consider where to send him next.

Finishing the Fort?

Although Fort Adams had received continuous funding since 1836, Colonel Totten and the other engineers were constantly worried that the money would run dry. In 1837, Congress again failed to pass a Fortification Bill, but work continued because Totten still had $70,000 left from the prior year.[35] In 1838, Congress allocated $100,000, but that figure was reduced in 1839 to only $10,000.[36] Again, Totten had $60,000 from the previous year so was able to continue without interruption.[37] Still, he was anxious that he would not have enough money to pay all of the Irish workers, so, in February 1839, he wrote to Benjamin Howland, the secretary of the Newport asylum, announcing that he was setting up an account at a local bank to support laborers in need of funds.[38]

In 1840, Congress approved an $80,000 grant for Fort Adams, but Totten, who had by now returned to Washington to serve as chief engineer of the U.S. Army, did not like the wording of the bill.[39] He told his deputy in Newport, Lieutenant James Mason, that the money was "tied to the condition of the Treasury."[40] Totten was concerned about the state of the nation's finances under President Martin Van Buren: the Depression of 1837 had shown no signs of easing, and the president's critics were deriding him as "Martin Van Ruin."[41] With the economy tottering, the colonel wrote to Mason in July and ordered him to shut down operations at Fort Adams. In August, however, Totten had second thoughts and modified his directive. If Mason could obtain favorable terms from the laborers and could reduce the size of the work force, then the work could proceed.

By October, Newport's Whig paper, the *Herald of the Times*, had learned about pay cuts at the fort and decided to use the situation as a way to criticize Van Buren, the Democrats, and its Democratic rival, the *Rhode-Island Republican*:

> [T]he poor laborers on Fort Adams were told some two months since . . . that if they would shovel dirt for 75 cents per day and take Treasury orders, payable in April next, for that miserable pittance, they might keep to work, or otherwise look for employment elsewhere. A number of them being encumbered with families, which they could not move . . . were finally obliged to go to work on the terms proposed. . . . These *facts* the writers in the *R.I. Republican knew* and might have known also that the last *cash* payment these poor laborers received, which was more than two months ago, was in French gold. . . . And yet they are endeavoring to hold up Martin Van Buren . . . as the *sincere friend of the laboring class.*[42]

Mason replied in the following day's issue of the *Newport Mercury*, doing his best to show that the claims made in the *Herald of the Times* were exaggerated. He noted that no laborer at the fort was getting seventy-five cents a day. Thirteen people were being paid ninety-two cents a day, and the other seventy were receiving eighty-four cents. He acknowledged that these wages were lower than they had been but attributed the reduction to the "low market price of labor in the vicinity" and made no reference to the directives that he had received from Totten.[43]

By the following spring, things at the fort seemed to be returning to normal. Congress approved a $35,000 grant, and, thanks to Mason's economies, $62,000 remained from the prior year. The *Newport Mercury* reported approvingly that "the completion of this important work . . . is now progressing with great rapidity. Upwards of three hundred mechanics, laborers, etc. are daily employed on this extensive fortress."[44] But Totten, still fretting about money, warned Mason to be prepared for the "contingency of no appropriation being granted at the next session of Congress."[45]

By the summer of 1841, General Winfield Scott, who had just been appointed commanding general of the army, determined that Fort Adams was complete enough to be garrisoned. Totten had apparently not been consulted, and he was far from enthusiastic. Writing to Mason, he called the decision "extraordinary but I suppose there may be some good reason for it unknown to me."[46] In late August, two New York artillery companies, under the command of a major, moved into the fort.[47]

Though the fort was now occupied, construction continued on various buildings. Work was halted for lack of money in August 1842, but just as O'Reilly was leaving Newport, a new appropriations bill passed, and construction quickly resumed.[48] So after spending only a few days in Boston, the priest returned to Saint Joseph's, apparently with the bishop's approval.[49] By the end of October, the *Newport Mercury* was able to report that a large brick stable with a slated roof had just been completed at the fort.[50]

"Rhode Island is for Repeal!"

In 1843 Newport's Irish community was large enough to stage a successful rally for Daniel O'Connell, who was gaining momentum in his nationalist campaign in Ireland. In 1840, he had launched the Repeal movement, which sought to undo the Act of Union of 1801 that tied Ireland to England. Repealing the act would give Ireland its own legislature in Dublin and enable the Irish to control most of their domestic matters. O'Connell had been advocating Repeal in 1840 and 1841; but, in 1842, he solemnly predicted that 1843 would be the "Repeal Year."[51] As a consequence, his meetings grew larger and larger, on some occasions drawing hundreds of thousands of supporters.[52]

As soon as O'Connell launched his movement, societies supporting Repeal sprang up in cities throughout the United States. Boston established the first Repeal organization in October 1840, and Philadelphia and New York City soon followed.[53] Dozens of other cities and towns with Irish populations set up their own Repeal organizations and began holding meetings and forwarding money to support O'Connell. Many Democratic politicians, eager to criticize the British government and attract Irish voters to their ranks, were vocal supporters as well.[54] Chapters were soon set up in Pottsville, Pennsylvania; Utica, New York; and Frankfort, Kentucky; they also sprang up St. Louis, Natchez, Detroit, Savannah, and a host of other towns around the country.[55] The Providence Repealers established themselves in 1841 under the leadership of Father Corry and sent contributions to O'Connell on several occasions.[56]

Newport's Irish community was slow to sign on to Repeal. Perhaps the funding hiccups at the fort had distracted it from the cause. Moreover, by August 1843, when the Newport Repealers gathered to hold their first meeting, O'Connell was embroiled in controversy. In London, the prime minister, Sir Robert Peel, had warned Parliament that he would go to war, if necessary, to prevent "the dismemberment of the Empire."[57] In the United States, pro-slavery Repealers increasingly resented O'Connell's efforts to tie the American abolition movement to his campaign. To him, the link was obvious: both movements sought to liberate people from enslavement.[58] But to Repealers in Savannah, Charleston, and Natchez and in many northern cities as well, O'Connell seemed to be foolishly meddling in American politics. In June, after he had delivered a fiery speech denouncing slaveholders and anyone who cooperated with them, the Charleston and Natchez Repeal chapters had announced they would dissolve. While other branches continued to support Repeal, they sharply disagreed with O'Connell about slavery.[59] Only a handful of Irish Americans expressed support for his position.[60] Most were too worried about job competition from free Black workers and too insecure about their own standing in American society to countenance abolition.[61]

When the Repealers convened in Newport's town hall, they carefully avoided any discussion of slavery. There was no chance that they would endorse O'Connell's stand: the meeting was chaired by Dutee Pearce, an outspoken opponent of abolition; and the anti-slavery activist William Lloyd Garrison had already decried the town as the "Charleston or New Orleans of New-England."[62] Still, attendees did not publicly challenge O'Connell's abolitionism. Instead, they listened intently to a speech by eighteen-year-old Thomas D'Arcy McGee of Boston, then an agent for the *Boston Pilot* and soon to be its editor.[63] In the days following the meeting, he published a glowing report of the proceedings in the *Pilot*:

> Last Thursday evening, for the first time in the history of our American agitation, has the cause of Ireland been canvassed in this ancient town. . . . The Town Hall . . . was thronged to its utmost capacity; a large portion of the audience being ladies, and several persons from the southern cities of the Union, who come here plentifully during the summer season. . . . [T]he most unanimous enthusiasm prevailed from the opening to the adjournment. The handsome amount of SEVENTY SEVEN dollars was received during the evening. . . . Now truly we may exclaim, "Rhode Island is for Repeal!" Honor to the Independent and Irish-hearted men of Newport, and hurrah for Repeal.[64]

In September, McGee returned to Newport to speak at another sizable Repeal meeting and then headed to New York City to participate in the National Repeal Convention.[65] He attended as the representative of Newport and also of New London and New Haven, Connecticut. The four hundred delegates established a national committee that would lead the cause in America and took pains to avoid any quarrels over slavery.[66]

In Ireland, however, O'Connell was facing a succession of difficulties. In October, he planned to hold his largest Repeal rally yet: a mass meeting at Clontarf, site of an Irish victory over Viking invaders during the Middle Ages. But Prime Minister Peel, exasperated by these "monster meetings," banned it just twenty-four hours before it was scheduled, and O'Connell acquiesced.[67] A few days later, Peel had O'Connell arrested for sedition. In 1844, O'Connell was convicted by a packed jury and sentenced to a year in prison. The verdict was overturned, and he was released after only three months. Nonetheless, his time in jail had an ill-effect on him. He emerged in September 1844 less sure of himself and seemingly less committed to Repeal. A vague and meandering speech to his supporters left many of them confused and discouraged.[68]

As the movement faltered in Ireland, it likewise started to decline in America. But in the first months of 1844, it remained vibrant. On Saint

Patrick's Day, President John Tyler, hoping to secure the Democratic nomination in the fall, sent a friendly note to the Repealers of Washington, D.C.[69] In the summer, Boston's Repealers sent O'Connell £1000, and the Charleston Repealers, who had reconstituted themselves after O'Connell's arrest, sent in two smaller contributions.[70] In September, McGee was back in Newport and again joined forces with Dutee Pearce: first, running a temperance meeting at Fort Adams, then a Repeal rally on the following evening at the town hall. McGee spoke for an hour and a half about English policy toward Ireland, and took up a collection that netted $61 for the cause.[71] Neither McGee nor Pearce mentioned the presidential race between the Democrat, James K. Polk, and the Whig, Henry Clay. Nor did they touch on the issue that was then riling the local Irish community: the recent conviction of John Gordon, a twenty-nine-year-old Irish immigrant, for the murder of a wealthy mill owner, Amasa Sprague, in Cranston, a town near Providence.[72] In the weeks before his death, Sprague had clashed with Gordon's brother Nicholas over a liquor store he operated near Sprague's mill. An all-Protestant jury had convicted John Gordon of the crime and sentenced him to death, but Gordon was petitioning the Rhode Island Supreme Court for a new hearing.[73]

McGee and Pearce's September Repeal meeting would be the last one held in Newport. By October, word of O'Connell's missteps had reached America, and the movement began to unravel. In November, the *Truth Teller*, a leading Irish-American paper, lamented, "All is idle with Repeal now except for Boston and New York City."[74]

Dividing the Diocese

One notable absent from the Newport Repeal meetings was Father O'Reilly. It is possible that he was out of town in August 1843 because he was also responsible for a mission in New Bedford.[75] However, it is likely that he did not think priests should be involved in political movements. In this, he differed from Corry.

When he returned to Newport in the fall of 1842, O'Reilly was still facing financial challenges. In January 1843, frustrated that one of his parishioners, Samuel Goddard, was far behind with his pew rents, the priest directed the sexton and three other men to forcibly remove Goddard from

Saint Joseph's. Goddard was so incensed that he filed suit against O'Reilly for $1,000 in the Court of Common Pleas.[76] Although the suit was eventually withdrawn, the case attracted negative publicity to O'Reilly and probably convinced Fenwick that he needed to transfer him.[77]

But the bishop's main concern in 1843 was a much larger issue: splitting the Diocese of Boston to make it more manageable. Since his appointment as bishop eighteen years earlier, the number of Catholics in the diocese had expanded almost tenfold, from 7,000 to 68,000, largely a result of Irish immigration.[78] In late 1841, Fenwick, who was not yet sixty, had confided to Samuel Eccleston, the archbishop of Baltimore, that he was "getting both old and feeble" and thus needed a smaller diocese and a coadjutor bishop to help him carry out his duties.[79] Now, two years later, change was afoot. In May 1843, the bishops at the Fifth Provincial Council approved both of Fenwick's proposals. A new Diocese of Hartford would be established under Reverend William Tyler to cover all of Connecticut and Rhode Island, and a coadjutor bishop, John Fitzpatrick, would assist Fenwick in administering the Boston diocese.[80] Fitzpatrick, ordained a priest in 1840, was then only thirty, but he had Fenwick's complete confidence.[81]

Although the American bishops had ratified Fenwick's requests, Rome needed to approve them before he could proceed. In the meantime, he remained responsible for Connecticut and Rhode Island. In September, he removed Corry from Saints Peter and Paul in Providence over concerns about his handling of the parish's finances.[82] To the dismay of many of his parishioners, Corry then left the diocese and headed to Arkansas to work as a missionary.[83] In Corry's place, Fenwick appointed Father James Fitton, a Boston-born priest of English descent who had served with great success in Worcester and had established an academy there that would develop into the College of the Holy Cross. Fenwick also decided to move O'Reilly from Newport to Fall River, Massachusetts, where he would live with Father Edward Murphy, the pastor of Saint John the Baptist Church, and visit Newport from time to time.[84] Apparently the bishop believed this assignment would help resolve O'Reilly's financial problems in Newport.[85]

In February 1844, Fenwick received letters from Rome approving the establishment of the new diocese and the appointment of a coadjutor bishop. On St. Patrick's Day, he ordained Tyler as bishop of Hartford in the Baltimore Cathedral.[86] The thirty-eight-year-old Tyler was a convert and a longtime protégé of Fenwick, but he was often in frail health.

One of the new bishop's first acts was to assist Fenwick with the ordination of Fitzpatrick, which took place a week later in Visitation Chapel in Washington, D.C., and was witnessed by many of the Jesuits from Georgetown College as well as by the Visitation sisters.[87]

Although he had been appointed bishop of Hartford, Tyler chose to live in Providence because the Catholic population in that city was considerably larger than Hartford's.[88] Initially, he had only three priests to assist him in Rhode Island. Two of them, James Fitton and William Wiley, had studied with him in the seminary and were stationed in Providence; the third, William Ivers, lived in Pawtucket. Fitton's first task was to assuage Corry's supporters, who were irked at Fenwick for removing him. But by the summer of 1844, Tyler had given Fitton a new assignment: he was to visit all of the Rhode Island Catholic communities outside of Providence: Pawtucket, Woonsocket, Warwick, and Newport.

Saint Joseph's Found Wanting

With such a large region to cover, Fitton was unable to travel to Newport more than once a month in 1844 and 1845.[89] As a consequence, Saint Joseph's began to deteriorate. In the summer of 1844, an anonymous letter writer complained to the *Newport Mercury* about conditions in the graveyard next door to the church: graves were filled with more than one coffin, and corpses from Fall River were being dropped off in the churchyard and left unburied for hours.[90] Several months later, the *Newport Mercury* reported that the church had been burglarized and "ransacked in every part."[91]

By the fall of 1846, Tyler had acquired a few additional priests, so he was able to assign Fitton to Newport full time. By now, it had been three years since a priest had resided in Newport; and the church building, though it was less than ten years old, was in poor shape. Fitton recalled in his memoir that it was "far from being safe"; due to poor workmanship, it was "in a very shaky condition."[92] As he examined Saint Joseph's, Fitton was no doubt remembering the tragedy he had witnessed in New Haven in 1834, when he had accompanied Fenwick to the dedication of Christ Church. At the start of the ceremony, the gallery had collapsed, killing two people and seriously injuring seven.[93] And he would have heard the story of Holy Trinity, the church for Boston's German Catholics, whose tower had collapsed in 1843.[94]

To prevent any such occurrence in Newport, Fitton wanted to build a new, sturdier church for the town's Catholic population, which he estimated at about 375 people. Though he would have been perfectly satisfied with a small church, his wealthier parishioners were more ambitious. He noted in his memoir that the Harpers "encouraged the building of a more substantial edifice . . . that would be a credit to the religion they dearly loved" and would impress the townspeople.[95] When Catherine Harper offered to help pay for this grand new church, Fitton moved quickly to carry out her wish. In January 1847, just two months after his arrival in Newport, he purchased the former Newcomb estate on Spring Street with $4,000 from the Harpers.[96] The property was ideally situated, located near the harbor and Bellevue Avenue, which was becoming fashionable with the summer colonists.

Relief for the Irish Famine

Just days after Fitton's purchase, his attention—and the rest of the nation's—shifted to the terrible news coming from Ireland. Two years earlier, in the fall of 1845, blight had damaged the potato crop on which much of Ireland's population depended. Then, in the fall of 1846, the blight struck again, destroying virtually the entire crop.[97] Conditions in Ireland became dire. As reports of the famine reached America, a Pittsburgh paper urged Irish-Americans to take action: "[H]undreds of thousands of Irishmen are pining in hunger, and dying. . . . Thousands of dollars were raised a few years ago for Repeal. Can nothing be raised for bread?"[98] Over the next few months, the Irish in America responded generously. John Fitzpatrick, who, in August, had become bishop of Boston after Fenwick's death, issued a pastoral letter on the famine and preached on the subject with great emotion: "[Ireland] bewails her sons and daughters, and her little children suffering, starving and dead. The loud cry of her anguish has gone through the world. She calls upon all, she calls upon you especially . . . to look upon her sufferings with eyes of compassion."[99]

In February 1847, U.S. Vice President Alexander Dallas presided over a mass meeting in Washington, D.C., in which he called on every American, whatever their ancestral roots or religion, to help the suffering Irish.[100] The response was immediate. Contributors included West Point cadets, the congregation of a New York City synagogue, Boston abolitionists, southern plantation owners, leaders of the Choctaw Nation, and temperance advocates in Cincinnati.[101] Charity balls and concerts were held, and plays were staged to raise money. At Boston's Faneuil Hall, Mayor Josiah Quincy Jr. organized a plan to send a warship loaded with food and clothing to the suffering Irish; and, in April, the USS *Jamestown* embarked from Boston to Cork, laden with eight hundred tons of supplies.[102] According to the historian Helen Hatton, the American response was "overwhelming."[103]

The response in Rhode Island was equally prompt and open-handed. Meetings were organized in Providence, Bristol, Woonsocket, Pawtucket, Newport, and elsewhere.[104] Nonetheless, the editor of the *Newport Daily News* was not sanguine about what the people of Newport would be able to accomplish at their March 1847 meeting on the matter: "Business is so limited in Newport, that it cannot be expected that we shall do a great deal; still, it is our power to offer our mite, whatever it may be, and heaven will reward us even for that."[105] He would probably have been more optimistic if the gathering had taken place in the summer months, when the town was full of well-heeled visitors.

In the end, however, the editors of both the *Daily News* and the *Mercury* were pleased by what was achieved at the meeting. In attendance were town leaders such as Congressman Robert Cranston, an anti-Dorrite; Dutee Pearce, Dorr's close associate; Reverend Charles T. Brooks, the pastor of Newport's Unitarian church; and Alexander MacGregor, the supervisor at Fort Adams. The *Daily News* editor noted that the town hall was "well filled with ladies and gentlemen, among whom we noticed quite a number of the sons and daughters of the Emerald Isle." A committee of thirty men—none from the Emerald Isle—was organized to collect money from each of the town's five wards. The funds would be sent to the Dublin Central Committee via a Philadelphia Quaker group that was spearheading relief efforts.[106]

Fitton did not attend the meeting, nor did he coordinate with the committee in the weeks following. Like many other priests during this period, he preferred to work through Catholic channels.[107] In March 1847, he took up a collection at Saint Joseph's, which raised $100.[108] He sent that money and possibly additional funds as well to Bishop Tyler, who forwarded a total of $3,600 to the Irish bishops.[109]

The town relief committee's leaders did not seem troubled by Fitton's stance. In May, they reported that they had sent $289 to the Quakers, who would use it to buy meal that they would then ship to the Dublin Central Committee. The relief committee's report noted that Newporters had donated $1,654.75, "without reference to the amount forwarded by the Catholic Church and by those amongst us having friends in that country, which is said to be considerable."[110]

A Church for the Summer Colonists

By the end of 1847, Fitton had established himself in the house on the former Newcomb estate and had erected a schoolhouse on a parcel of land west of Spring Street. It became the home of the parochial school he had founded in January 1846, under the direction of a lay teacher. Fitton celebrated daily Mass in his house but continued to use Saint Joseph's for Mass on Sundays and holy days. On Christmas Eve 1847, the *Newport Daily News* reported that the "two Episcopal churches and the Catholic chapel in this town have been beautifully dressed with evergreens for Christmas; they will be opened for public worship to-morrow, as usual, in celebration of the holy festival of the birth of the savior of the world."[111]

In 1848, Catherine Harper contributed another $3,000 to the new church's building fund, and Patrick Charles Keely, a young architect who specialized in Gothic designs, drew up the plans.[112] Lieutenant William Rosecrans, a West Point–trained engineer who was now supervising the remaining building projects at Fort Adams, offered his services as well.[113] Rosecrans was a zealous young convert, and he assisted eagerly with the work, which began in August.[114] In the evenings, he would bring over Irish laborers from the fort to dig trenches and lay the foundation.[115]

By June 1849, Fitton was ready to lay the cornerstone for the new brownstone church. Its formal name would be Holy Name of Mary, Our Lady of the Isle, but it would be known as Saint Mary's. Fitton had planned to ask Bishop Tyler to preside at the cornerstone ceremony and Father Charles Constantine Pise, a well-known priest from New York, to deliver the sermon.[116] However, Tyler was gravely ill with rheumatic fever that summer, and Pise did not want to travel because of a cholera outbreak in New York. Consequently, Bishop Fitzpatrick took Tyler's place, and a Boston priest, Nicholas O'Brien, filled in for Pise.

In his diary, Fitzpatrick noted that an immense number of people, both Catholics and Protestants, were in attendance and that the Protestants' "demeanor . . . [was] very becoming and respectful."[117] The crowd watched as the acolytes, the clergy, and the Fort Adams band marched in procession from Levin Street to the church.[118] After Fitzpatrick blessed the cornerstone and hammered it into place with a wooden mallet, Father O'Brien delivered the sermon. Reminding his listeners that the Cross had been planted "by the valiant sons of France" in Newport during the American Revolution, he declared that it was "here planted again this day." He said, "This is a noble monument which you are rearing; those who come after you will bless your memory and offer prayers for your souls." The editor of the *Daily News* predicted that "this building will be the most beautiful in Rhode Island and will be a valuable ornament to the town."[119]

After the ceremonies, Bishop Fitzpatrick accepted the "invitation of Lieut. Rosecranz [sic] a very pious convert" to visit Fort Adams and "examine the place in detail." That night the bishop stayed with Mr. and Mrs. Albert Sumner at Rockry Hall, their new cottage on Bellevue Avenue, which faced the Harpers' home. A guidebook described the Sumner mansion as an "Elizabethan building of considerable architectural merit."[120] Mrs. Sumner was a recent convert to Catholicism. Her husband was a Protestant but, in the bishop's view, "seem[ed] well disposed."[121]

The next day, Fitzpatrick took a steamboat to Providence, traveling amid a group of Quakers who had been in Newport for their annual meeting. When he reached Tyler's residence, he saw that the bishop of Hartford was "much worse" and administered last rites.[122] Three days later, the forty-three-year-old Tyler died, and Father William Wiley was appointed administrator of the diocese until a new bishop could be selected. In March 1850, Wiley brought Fitton to Providence to run the cathedral parish, Saints Peter and Paul, and sent a recently ordained priest, James Gibson, to take Fitton's place in Newport. In November, Bernard O'Reilly, an Irish-born priest, was appointed as second bishop of Hartford. Like Tyler, he chose to live in Providence. Now, with O'Reilly in the cathedral, Fitton was able to return to Newport, and Gibson became pastor of Saint Mary's in Warwick, Rhode Island.[123]

Fitton's long absence surely slowed progress on the new church, but as soon as he returned, he set to work on fundraising. He sent an appeal to the *Boston Pilot* and then began a tour of New England churches, seeking support.[124] By the summer of 1852, Fitton felt that sufficient money had been raised; and though the church was still missing its bell tower, the organ, and pews, it was complete enough to dedicate. He invited bishops O'Reilly and Fitzpatrick to preside at the ceremonies, and attendees would be required to buy tickets at $1 apiece. Even the local newspaper editors invited to "chronicle the event" would need to buy tickets if they wished to be present.[125] Ticket sales would support the building fund, for the church would ultimately cost about $42,500 to complete—roughly ten times the price of Saint Joseph's.[126]

Interest in the new church was widespread throughout Rhode Island. In the week before the dedication, a Providence newspaper informed readers that they could obtain tickets at the Catholic bookstore on Westminster Street and would be able to take a steamboat down to and back from Newport on the day of the ceremony.[127] The event apparently came off without difficulty. The *Daily News* reported that the "ceremonies were very imposing and impressive, and . . . in keeping with the grandeur of the church," and the editor noted that the church was crowded and included many strangers. He thought Bishop O'Reilly's sermon was "able and appropriate" and said that the music of the Fort Adams band was "excellent."[128]

"A Favorite Resort for Rank, Fashion and Beauty"

The dedication of Saint Mary's was just one indication that Newport was in the midst of a revival in the 1850s. Bellevue Avenue was being extended south at this time, and Alfred Smith, a shrewd and prescient developer, was dividing up parcels of land on the street.[129] A new and exclusive social club for men, the Reading Room, was established in 1853.[130] And political leaders had altered Newport's charter, making it a city rather than a town, though its year-round population was still not quite 10,000.[131]

John Ross Dix, who produced the first guidebook to Newport in 1852, remarked that "an air of prosperity seems to pervade the place generally—but in 'the season' all is hurry and drive."[132] His book listed six leading hotels and five boardinghouses where visitors might want to stay. Two of the hotels on Bellevue Avenue, the Ocean House and the Atlantic House, were especially impressive. The original Ocean House had burned down in 1845 but had been rebuilt and expanded in 1846 in order to accommodate six hundred guests.[133] Atlantic House, perched on a hill, offered wonderful views.[134] Across the street was the luxurious Sea Girt Hotel, established in 1854 by the African American businessman George Downing.[135] There were many activities to keep guests busy: they could bowl in one of the fourteen alleys in town, bathe at Easton's Beach, or take a boat ride to Fort Adams. Dix noted that, on Tuesdays and Fridays, there was a "review in the great square of the Fort."[136]

Getting to Newport had become easier since the establishment of the Fall River Line in 1847. Every day, passengers could travel on a luxurious steamboat from New York to Newport to Fall River. From there they could take a train to Boston.[137] Often described as "floating hotels," the steamboats were outfitted with chandeliers, lace curtains, and fine carpets and were managed by a staff of African American stewards and waiters.[138] Hundreds of New Yorkers and Bostonians used the Fall River Line for their Newport holidays.

Edmund Quincy, Jr., scion of a prominent Boston family, took a steamboat to Newport in August 1852 to visit relatives and celebrate his eighteenth birthday, and he kept a detailed record of his visit.[139] Quincy stayed at the Ocean House and wrote of bowling, visiting Fort Adams, horseback riding, and swimming at Easton's Beach. It was "quite an amusing sight," he said, "to see some 500 people dressed like demons floundering about in the briny ocean."[140] In the evenings, he dressed for dinner at the hotel, then listened to a concert by a German band or promenaded through town with female acquaintances.[141]

While Newport was especially attractive to New Yorkers and Bostonians, it drew visitors from farther afield as well. In August 1850, Senator Henry Clay, who had been laboring for months on slavery-related legislation that would come to be known as the Compromise of 1850, visited from Washington.[142] During the following August, President Millard Fillmore's wife, Abigail, stayed at the Bellevue House with their son and daughter.[143] Fillmore joined his family in September and met with the town's leaders.[144] The next summer, Franklin Pierce, the Democratic nominee for president, stayed in Newport while mapping out his successful campaign.[145]

Every summer, the *New York Times* ran articles describing the major events of the Newport season.[146] Leading magazines such as *Harper's* and *The Atlantic* also covered Newport, sometimes comparing it to Saratoga Springs. But George W. Curtis, writing for *Harper's*, thought there was no contest between the two: "[Saratoga's] unique hotels, its throng, its music, its dancing, its bowling, its smoking, its drinking, its flirting, its drives to dinners, and sunsets at the Lake, are not enough to equal the claims of Newport, which has most of these and more. Saratoga is a hotel, Newport is a realm."[147]

Keeping the Know Nothings at Bay

While the residents of Newport were prosperous and congenial, tensions were flaring between native-born American Protestants and immigrant Catholics, both in other Rhode Island communities and around the nation. Questions about Bible reading in public schools and funding for parochial schools were especially divisive. In Philadelphia, riots had broken out in May and July 1844 over nativist fears that Catholics were trying to eliminate Bible reading from the public schools.[148] By the early 1850s, nativists had become even more vocal, alarmed by the waves of unskilled and often illiterate Irish coming to America to escape the famine.[149] Between 1845 and 1855, close to 1.5 million Irish emigrated to the United States.[150] Most settled in cities in the Northeast, but some went to Chicago or further west to Butte and San Francisco.[151] By 1850, Manhattan and Brooklyn had 134,000 Irish immigrants and Boston had 35,000.[152] In 1854, there were 10,000 Irish in Providence, and they constituted 20 percent of the state's population.[153]

In the 1852 presidential election, many observers declared that Pierce owed his victory to the Irish, who tended to vote as a bloc for the Democrats. Pierce's decision to appoint an Irish Catholic, James Campbell, to the coveted Postmaster-General position led many to conclude that the president was in league with the Irish.[154] In response, disaffected Whigs joined with nativists to form a secret political party that would come to be known as the Know Nothings.

With nativism surging, Rome decided, in the summer of 1853, to send an Italian archbishop, Gaetano Bedini, to visit the United States. He was directed to resolve disputes over church property between bishops and lay trustees and report to the pope about the state of the church in America.[155] When nativists learned of Bedini's trip, they circulated charges that he had ordered executions of rebels during a recent uprising in the Papal States.[156] Derided as the "Butcher of Bologna," the archbishop was heckled and burned in effigy in several midwestern cities.[157] According to Bishop Fitzpatrick, when Bedini reached Boston at the end of September, he was in fear for his life. To calm Bedini's nerves, the Boston bishop, accompanied by Bishop O'Reilly of the Hartford diocese, quietly took him to Newport, where Catherine Harper hosted the three men for two nights. On their return to Boston, Fitzpatrick introduced the archbishop to some of the city's leading citizens, including the celebrated intellectual and Catholic convert, Orestes Brownson.[158] Nonetheless, after leaving Boston, Bedini encountered more menacing protesters, and Archbishop John Hughes of New York City had to sneak him onto a boat on Staten Island so that he could safely return to Rome.[159]

FIGURE 7. Thomas Sully, portrait of Emily Harper, 1853. Harper was a generous supporter of the Catholic church in Newport. From Ann C. Van Devanter, *"Anywhere So Long as There be Freedom": Charles Carroll of Carrollton, His Family, and His Maryland: An Exhibition and Catalogue* (Baltimore: Baltimore Museum of Art, 1975). Reprinted by permission.

A Convent in the "Eden of America"

More clashes with nativists occurred in 1854. In Massachusetts, a Know Nothing was elected governor; in Rhode Island, party members would soon gain numerous seats in the legislature; and in Maine, a Jesuit priest was tarred and feathered because of his opposition to requiring Catholic children to read the King James Bible in the public schools.[160] Newport, however, remained largely free from this strife, so Fitton was able to focus his energies on improvements to his parish.[161]

Though the church was still not entirely finished, he turned his attention to the school, contacting the Sisters of Mercy and inviting them to take charge of it. This initiative, too, was tied to the Harpers, who were friendly with the sisters. The Mercy community, founded by Mother Catherine McAuley in Dublin in 1831, had sent its first group of sisters to America in 1843, at the request of the Irish-born bishop of Pittsburgh, Michael O'Connor. Emily Harper had met with the group's superior, Mother Frances Xavier Warde, and her three companions when they stopped in Philadelphia on their way to Pittsburgh.[162] She and Mother Xavier would remain friends for the rest of their lives. She was also still close to her foster sister Catherine Seton, who had joined the Mercy sisters in New York in 1846.[163]

In March 1851, Bishop O'Reilly, on the recommendation of Bishop O'Connor, had invited the sisters to Providence.[164] Almost as soon as they arrived in Rhode Island, the sisters began to think about setting up a second foundation in Newport. In October, Mother Xavier had told Dr. Patrick Moriarity, who was administering the Hartford diocese in O'Reilly's absence:

> Next May we propose having a local house at NewPort, the second city in this state. We will have a fine free school there. The climate there is so delightful that it is called the "Eden of America." A fine benevolent lady of high rank and good fortune, Miss Harper of Baltimore will assist in getting up that establishment. Her mother has a beautiful summer residence there.[165]

In fact, Mother Xavier would have to wait longer than expected, for Fitton was not initially enthusiastic about the idea.[166] He was probably worried about the expenses associated with a convent; for, by the end of 1852, he had spent $30,000 on the church and had taken in only $17,700 in donations.[167]

MOTHER MARY XAVIER WARDE
American Foundress

FIGURE 8. Photograph of Mother Frances Xavier Warde, R.S.M., c. 1880. The founder of the Sisters of Mercy in America, she brought the first nuns to Newport in 1854. Collection of the Sisters of Mercy of the Americas, Mercy Heritage Center, Belmont, North Carolina. Reprinted by permission.

In May 1854, Mother Xavier and four sisters sailed from Providence to Newport. For the time being, the sisters would have to live in a portion of the convent and operate the school in another section of the building. After getting them situated, Mother Xavier returned to Providence and left Sister Gertrude Bradley in charge. With the help of Emily Harper, the sisters made much needed improvements to the property and started classes for the girls of the parish, leaving the boys' education to the lay teacher.[168] The *Catholic Almanac* for 1854 took note of the new school: "St. Maria's of the Isle, Newport. The Sisters of Mercy in this city have charge of the Female Free School, attended by 160 children. The institution is only in its commencement."[169]

In March 1855, however, Mother Xavier and her community in Providence found themselves in a crisis. Similar to the rumors that had circulated in 1834, charging that a nun was being held against her will at the Charlestown convent, reports in the *Providence Tribune* charged that a young novice, Rebecca Newell, was being held in the Mercy convent against her will. The story was groundless and was even refuted by Henry Anthony, the editor of the *Providence Journal*. Nonetheless, the Know Nothings seized upon it.[170] A crowd of 2,000 people gathered in front of the convent and demanded Newell's release. Through the combined efforts of Bishop O'Reilly, a sizable detachment of police, and Mayor Edward Knowles, the crowd was eventually persuaded to disperse. Fortunately, the Mercy sisters did not suffer the same fate as the Ursulines in Charlestown.[171]

In Newport, the Mercy sisters faced no such hostility. In fact, in July, when the sisters received two young women as postulants, the *Daily News* reported that the event drew "an immense crowd" to the ceremony at Saint Mary's, "mostly Protestants." The reporter was awed by the ritual, noting the beauty of the church with "its gilded altars, adorned with statuary," and was impressed by the candidates, who were "in bride's attire, pure white with lace streaming down their heads." He concluded, "It was a very solemn and imposing occasion and one which will not soon be forgotten."[172]

A month later, Fitton left Newport and the Diocese of Hartford to accept an appointment to a parish in East Boston. The late Father Wiley, who had been its pastor, had, as his last request, asked that his friend and classmate, Father Fitton, succeed him.[173] Though Fitton had spent nine years in Newport, he had not yet put a spire on Saint Mary's or provided a suitable convent or school for the sisters, and he had left the church with a debt of $11,000. His successor, Father William O'Reilly, the brother of Bishop O'Reilly, would have to reckon with these loose ends. Still, Fitton had accomplished a great deal for his Irish parishioners and had maintained good relations with the town's non-Catholics. The editors of the *Daily News* expressed deep sadness at the prospect of his departure: "Mr. Fitton has . . . accomplished a vast deal of good. As all are aware, he has been the means of building that noble edifice . . . which is an ornament to the city. As pastor he is unceasing in his labors, as a Christian he is devoted to the great cause, and as a gentleman he is esteemed by all who know him."[174]

Chapter 6

FIGHTING FOR THE BLUE AND THE GREEN

Newport's Civil War Irish

As officer Carpenter was distributing notices to drafted men, yesterday, about a dozen Irish women set upon him when in Holland street, which is one of the worst localities in the city, inflicting some severe injuries. They struck him with clubs, spattered him with mud and stoned him in true Irish style.

—*Providence Journal*, July 20, 1863

Saint Mary's new pastor, Father William O'Reilly, was anxious to complete the church building and erect a school for his growing congregation. Irish immigrants were continuing to settle in Newport, drawn by the city's tourist economy. By the late 1850s, however, everyone's attention had turned to the looming national crisis. Many Newporters had some sympathy with the South and wanted to avoid a war at all costs. But when the conflict came, they volunteered without hesitation to defend the Union and served with distinction in the first campaigns of the Civil War. By 1863, most had grown weary of the conflict and were troubled by the North's increasing emphasis on abolition. Still, many Irish fought till the war's end, determined to prove their loyalty to America and, in some cases, hoping to use their military experience to free their homeland from British rule.

Tragedy at Sea

When Father Fitton left Newport, the Hartford diocese was short of priests, so Bishop O'Reilly decided to go outside of it to find a replacement. He contacted the bishop of Buffalo, John Timon, and asked if he would loan out Father William O'Reilly, his own younger brother. Timon agreed to release the priest for two years, and Father O'Reilly came to Newport in September 1855.[1] Soon after his arrival, the bishop gave him additional responsibilities, making him administrator of the diocese while the bishop sailed for Europe to raise funds and recruit priests and religious brothers to serve in the diocese.

In December 1855, Bishop O'Reilly set off on a journey that would take him to France, Belgium, and Ireland. In January, he met with the director of the Propagation of the Faith in Paris and asked for his financial backing. In his record of the meeting, the bishop noted that between 55,000 and 65,000 Catholics lived in Connecticut and Rhode Island, most them working in factories. The diocese now included thirty-seven parishes and thirty schools, several of which were staffed by the Sisters of Mercy. Yet the overall tone of his notes was bleak:

> This part of New England . . . has an ingrained hatred for the Catholics. . . . The "Know Nothings" tried to destroy the convent of the Sisters of Mercy in Providence. Four thousand of the cutthroats surrounded the house of the good sisters but the presence of the authorities which I had called and also the presence of several hundred well armed Catholics made them disperse without doing any harm. . . . I believe that my diocese, its population considered, is the poorest of all our dioceses. . . . I ask nothing for myself, nor for a cathedral, even though my cathedral is quite miserable, but for the . . . triumph of our Holy Religion.[2]

A week later O'Reilly boarded the wooden steamer *Pacific* in Liverpool for his return voyage to New York. In early February, however, the *Providence Journal* reported that the *Pacific* had had a difficult crossing from New York and had lost one of its lifeboats en route.[3] A few days later, another Providence newspaper carried a report from Sandy Hook, New Jersey, indicating that the *Pacific* had not yet been sighted and that there were "great masses of ice" in the area.[4]

For the rest of the month, the *Providence Journal* reiterated, "No news of the *Pacific*."[5] In early March, it reported that the "highly esteemed" bishop was thought to have been a passenger but, at the beginning of April, declared that O'Reilly had not boarded the ship after all: "Many persons, besides those under the spiritual charge of the Bishop, will rejoice at the news of his safety."[6] Three weeks later, this optimistic report was retracted. The bishop had, in fact, been on the doomed ship.[7] Church leaders held out hope for a few weeks longer; but, in June, Archbishop John Hughes offered a requiem Mass for him in Saint Patrick's Cathedral in New York.[8]

The weeks of uncertainty about Bishop O'Reilly's fate must have been an intense strain on his brother.[9] Still, Father O'Reilly carried on, dutifully administering the diocese. In September 1856, reports appeared in the *Newport Mercury* and other papers that Father Francis McFarland of Utica, New York, had been selected as the new bishop of Hartford.[10] However, another eighteen months would pass before his ordination and installation.[11] During the interim, O'Reilly purchased land and established new parishes in Providence and Cranston.[12] He also continued to attend to Saint Mary's, working to finish it and pay off its debt. Fortunately, Newport was attracting more and more wealthy summer visitors, so there were many opportunities to fundraise during the season.

Newport's Building Boom

In the mid-1850s, Newport's economy continued to flourish, though its industrial base was unsteady. The Coddington Manufacturing Company closed its doors in 1856 after several sluggish years, and the Perry Mill reopened after being sold at auction in 1855.[13] Still, the city's strong tourist economy more than compensated for its industrial weakness. Shortly after Saint Mary's dedication, Episcopalians from Trinity Church laid the cornerstone for Emmanuel Church, a wooden building of Gothic design that would serve as their mission to the mill workers on the south side of Newport.[14] At the same time, the Congregationalists moved their plain wooden church across town, where it was rechristened Aquidneck Hall and opened to the public for meetings and lectures. In place of the old church, the Congregationalists built a sandstone Romanesque edifice topped by towers of unequal height.[15] One observer referred to it as a "noble and commanding pile."[16]

The city's hotels were being remodeled and expanded as well. A writer for the *Mercury* noted:

[T]he work on the Bellevue and Fillmore Houses is rapidly progressing. . . . The other hotels are preparing to compete by adding
such improvements as experience points out as most needed; and
there has been no lack of new paint, incessant cleaning, scrubbing
and polishing. The number of rooms engaged for the season was
never larger, and we see no reason why we may not expect a crowd
here during the summer.[17]

More significant were the new summer homes that were going up
on and around Bellevue Avenue—among them, William Wetmore's
Chateau-sur-Mer and Mrs. Andrew Ritchie's Fairlawn.[18] When Catherine
Harper had built her home in 1839, it was one of the few summer cottages
in Newport. Even as late as 1852 only twelve summer colonists were listed
on the tax rolls. Over the next two years, however, sixty additional houses
were completed; and, by 1857, *Boyd's Newport City Directory* listed 174
summer colonists, mostly from New York and Boston but including a few
southerners as well.[19]

Newport's hotels were not disappearing, but a shift was underway. The
historian Jon Sterngass characterizes it as the "privatization of leisure."[20]
Wealthy summer visitors were choosing to spend their time in their own
cottages, holding dances and dinner parties at home when they felt like
socializing. They were spending less time in Newport's downtown or on
its public beach, where they would have to rub elbows with strangers. A
correspondent for a Boston newspaper noticed the change in Newport
in the summer of 1856: "[S]o many *habitues*, weary of hotel life, have this
year, resorted to cottages and private dwellings. If the number of equi-
pages arrayed on the beach, and rolling through the streets, or the list
of names on the club registers be any test, Newport is more crowded
than ever; but the evening gatherings at the hotels, have, thus far, been
sparse."[21]

Sterngass notes that there were many good reasons for abandoning big
hotels such as the Ocean House and the Atlantic House. While they had
elegant public rooms and verandas and attractive grounds, the bedrooms
were small and poorly ventilated and almost never had their own baths.
The meals likewise were of mixed quality as the hotels struggled to feed
hundreds of guests at the same time.[22]

FIGURE 9. Engraving of Galvin's Gardens, 1888. Galvin's was a successful nursery on Spring Street and catered to many of Newport's summer colonists. From Richard Bayles, *History of Newport County* (New York: Preston and Company, 1888). Reprinted courtesy of Salve Regina University, Newport, RI.

The bustling town offered a host of employment opportunities for the city's Irish population, which had grown to about 1,500 by 1858.[23] According to that year's *Boyd's Newport City Directory*, a handful of Irish owned their own businesses: Patrick Conroy had a grocery store, William Ahearn had a bakery, and Thomas Galvin and his son ran a thriving nursery on Spring Street. There were also a few craftsmen: Edward Finerty was a shoemaker, James Costello was a stonecutter, and John Lyons and Honora Flanagan were blacksmiths. Several of those listed were clearly employed in serving the summer colonists: Joseph Curran, Thomas Kenney, and William Lanagan were waiters; and Michael Butler, Richard Lynch, and John Kennedy were gardeners.[24]

The majority of Irishmen, however, listed themselves as "laborers" in the *Directory*.[25] Most were not employed at Fort Adams, where construction had largely wrapped up.[26] Instead, they were probably working in town on the renovation or expansion of hotels, the extension of Bellevue Avenue and other roads, or the construction of cottages that were going up all over the city. Some also would have been working at local textile mills.[27]

Many of the Irishwomen would have been at home, raising large families. However, a considerable number of young Irish and Irish American women were living in the homes of affluent Newporters. For example, Charles Brooks, a Unitarian minister and scholar, lived on Thames Street with his wife and two children and their nineteen-year-old Irish-born servant, Sarah Cooney. William Swinburne lived next door to the Brooks family with his wife and daughter and their twenty-five-year-old Irish-born servant, Bridget Gillroy.[28] Three doors down lived another minister and his family and their two servants, one Irish and one Irish American.[29] Other Irishwomen, such as Mary Quin and Celinda Kelley, ran laundries out of their own homes.[30]

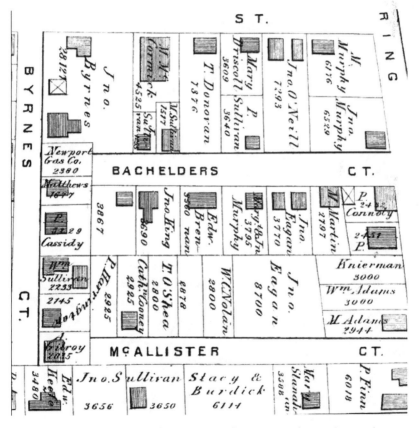

FIGURE 10. Map detail of Newport's Fifth Ward, 1876. In these cross streets between Spring and Thames Streets, most of the residents were Irish. From *Atlas of Newport, Rhode Island* (Philadelphia, 1876), plate 14.

Newport's Irish population was not concentrated in a single neighborhood at this time. Some lived on or near the wharves, while others lived a little further from the water in the cross streets between Thames and Spring streets. Pockets of Irish resided on Prospect Hill; on Perry, Pope, and Holland streets; and on Byrnes Court and Lee Avenue in the city's Fifth Ward. Another pocket lived on the northern side of the city near Tanner Street (later known as West Broadway and now called Dr. Marcus Wheatland Boulevard).[31] This enclave, which would be called Kerry Hill in the 1870s, was bounded on its northern side by Warner Street. The neighborhood was attractive to recent Irish arrivals and to African Americans because of its affordable prices.[32]

Finishing Saint Mary's

Before his transfer to Boston in 1855, Father Fitton had been working to raise funds to complete the church. At the end of July, the *Providence Journal* had reported that Madame LaGrange, a highly regarded French opera singer, would be performing at Saint Mary's to raise money for the organ.[33] The *Daily News* assured its readers that it would be "a brilliant affair" with music "that has never before been heard in this city." The author stressed that tickets, which cost $1 apiece, had to be purchased in advance.[34] At the same time, Saint Mary's was sponsoring a three-day fair at the Masonic Hall. The *Daily News* reporter noted that there was a "large attendance of the summer visitors" at the fair and that "sales were extensive."[35]

In the summer of 1856, Father O'Reilly continued Fitton's initiatives. In August, Madame LaGrange and her troupe returned to "chant the service at the Catholic Church, in which a new organ has recently been placed. You will remember that, last season, she gave a concert at the same place, in behalf of this object."[36] Two weeks later, the *Providence Journal* reported that a member of the troupe had sung in the church to help defray the cost of the new organ. On the following day, the singers took part in a high Mass celebrated in Bishop O'Reilly's memory.[37]

In 1857, the *Daily News* reported that the women of Saint Mary's were running a four-day Fancy Fair at Aquidneck Hall, the former Congregational church, raising funds for "the completion of the tower of their grand and beautiful church." The writer urged all readers to support it.[38] Each day the paper reported on the progress of the fair, which "[has] given the utmost gratification to every one who has been to it." In addition to offering a variety of sale items and refreshments, the organizers had hired a brass band from Providence to entertain the crowds.[39] After the fair ended, the *Boston Pilot* reported that they had succeeded in raising $2,100 for the parish.[40]

By the following July, the *Newport Mercury* was pleased to note that a "very fine-tuned bell was placed in the tower" of Saint Mary's: "[The] completion of the building is near at hand, and workmen are now engaged in putting up the porch and the tower will be run up in accord with the original plan."[41] The timing was propitious because, just three weeks later, Bishop McFarland, who had been ordained in March, would be making his first visit to Newport. On August 1, the new bishop confirmed eighty-two children and blessed the new bell. In his diary, he noted that 175 boys were attending the school run by William Delany, an Irish-born ex-seminarian whom Father O'Reilly had hired as the schoolmaster and church sexton.[42] The Mercy sisters' school was slightly smaller, with 150 girls. Both schools had just held exhibitions at Aquidneck Hall, where the top students were given awards for their accomplishments. Yet while he was pleased with the church and the schools, the bishop recorded that Saint Mary's was still $13,000 in debt.[43]

A month later, McFarland was back in Newport to officiate at the wedding of Fannie Carpenter and Henry Pitman at the Atlantic House. The bride's father was the late General Thomas Carpenter, a prominent lawyer and Catholic convert who had defended the Gordon brothers in the Sprague murder trial.[44] The *Newport Mercury* reported that a large party was present for the wedding, including Father O'Reilly and Father Edward O'Neill, who then serving as the assistant pastor of Saint Mary's.[45] Presumably, Pitman was not Catholic. Otherwise, the wedding would have taken place in the church rather than a hotel.

The Southerners Depart

For decades, southern visitors had been enjoying Newport's cool breezes and welcoming atmosphere. Some, such as John Calhoun, a senator from South Carolina who had twice served as vice president, had met their spouses there.[46] George Noble Jones, a Savannah planter, had also met his wife in Newport, and he had built a cottage—later known as Kingscote—on Bellevue Avenue near the Harpers' home.[47] At times, Jones and other planters would bring their slaves with them for the summer.[48] Though Newport also attracted staunch abolitionists such as William Ellery Channing, Sophia Little, and Charles Lenox Remond, the topic of slavery was apparently not broached at town social events during the 1830s and 1840s.[49]

By the early 1850s, however, southern visitors were recognizing that the mood in Newport had changed. In an 1851 letter, Emma Izard, whose family owned a large plantation in Charleston, told her cousin Eliza Middleton Fisher, "We shall end up at Newport if matters ever get right between the North and South, but not otherwise I am inclined to think."[50] Izard was right to be wary because matters were not in any way getting right.

During the decade, the North and the South became increasingly polarized over slavery. Two measures in particular alienated many northerners: the Fugitive Slave Act of 1850 and the Kansas-Nebraska Act of 1854. The first statute, which was part of Henry Clay's Compromise of 1850, required northerners to help slaveowners recapture slaves who had fled from them months, years, or even decades earlier.[51] The horror of this became real for many in 1854, when 2,000 troops—many of whom were Irish—marched Anthony Burns, a twenty-year-old store clerk, through the streets of Boston to a ship waiting to return him to slavery in Virginia.[52]

The Kansas-Nebraska Act was even more galling to northerners, including those who were not particularly sympathetic to abolitionism. According to the Civil War historian James McPherson, "[T]his law may have been the most important single event pushing the nation toward civil war. Kansas-Nebraska finished off the Whig party and gave birth to a new, entirely northern Republican party."[53] The act, which was the brainchild of Stephen Douglas, a Democratic senator from Illinois, left the question of slavery to the people who settled in those territories. What made Douglas's call for popular sovereignty in Kansas and Nebraska so upsetting was that this question had already been settled more than thirty years earlier. Under the Missouri Compromise of 1820, all states north of the 36° 30′ line (except for Missouri) were to be free, while those south of the line could have slaves. Given that Kansas and Nebraska were both above that line, they were supposed to be free states.

Although northerners were fuming, Douglas knew he could count on the support of President Franklin Pierce, a pro-slavery Democrat, and most of the southern senators and congressmen. But conflict was inevitable. As soon as the bill was approved, both slaveholders and abolitionists rushed to settle in the territories in order to influence the course of slavery there. In Kansas, the foes set up rival legislatures in Topeka and Lecompton and took up arms against one another. In 1856, Senator Charles Sumner of Massachusetts, a Republican and fervent abolitionist, spoke in the Senate about the "Crime against Kansas." His address included personal attacks on colleagues such as Senator Andrew Butler of South Carolina, whom Sumner felt was responsible for the act.[54] Sumner's inflammatory language outraged many southern legislators, including Butler's cousin, Preston Brooks, a congressman from South Carolina. Brooks took action, thrashing Sumner on the Senate floor with a gold-tipped cane. As a result of the attack, Sumner suffered a severe brain injury and had to retire from the Senate for three years to recuperate.

These expressions of southern militancy alienated all but the most pro-slavery northerners. Even in Newport, tolerance for the "peculiar institution" was fading. A week after the Sumner caning, the *Newport Mercury* printed a long editorial on slavery. The editors noted, "[I]t is not often that we have touched upon the vexed question of Slavery, for the reason that we have ever held that it was a local affair and that so long as it was kept within its original limits, it was a matter with which we of the North have very little to do." But recent events had changed their minds:

> The South has bullied and blustered long enough; its members of Congress have cut down unarmed men whom they could not bend to their purpose or awe into silence; the government has been shamefully vacillating till the inhabitants of Kansas have been murdered in cold blood. . . .
>
> Whatever may be the merits of the question of slavery within its old bounds, it is clearly the settled determination of the South to *force* it at all hazards into the new territories. . . . To be abused, upbraided and threatened, is bad enough; but to see citizens of a free territory shot down for entertaining sentiments of liberty, and the floors of Congress dyed with the blood of those who uphold them in their rights, is to place ourselves in a position to be continually subjected to every indignity a ruffian can conceive of.

The editors called on readers to take a bold stand: "Are we prepared to submit longer to the degrading influence of the slave power? Will any Northerner, calling himself a man, dare to abuse his trust by keeping silent on such an issue?"[55]

In the months following, many northerners saw signs that the pro-slavery powers were on the march. In November, James Buchanan, another pro-slavery Democrat, was elected president. His Republican opponent, John Frémont, had won all of the New England states and most of the rest of the North, but Buchanan's lock on the South had given him a narrow victory.[56] Just two days after Buchanan's inauguration, the southern-dominated Supreme Court weighed in on slavery with its *Dred Scott* decision. Scott, a Missouri slave, had sued for his freedom because his master, an army surgeon, had taken him for extended periods into a free state, Illinois, and a free territory, Wisconsin. Chief Justice Roger Taney, joined by six other justices, issued a sweeping ruling. As a black man, Scott was not considered a citizen under the Constitution and there-fore did not have standing to sue in federal court. Furthermore, Congress had no right to exclude slavery from the territories (as it had done with the Missouri Compromise). In passing such legislation, Congress was deny-ing citizens their constitutional rights to do with their property as they saw fit.[57]

While many southern partisans hailed the decision as a vindication, most northerners, even Democrats, were troubled by its radical implica-tions.[58] If Congress had no power to ban slavery in the territories, then what about the Kansas-Nebraska Act? Could the people of Kansas vote to outlaw it? And what about the northern states that had banned slavery decades earlier? Were they violating citizens' property rights? In Rhode Island, there was little enthusiasm about the *Dred Scott* decision. The *Newport Mercury* reported the majority's opinion in full without com-ment but also provided a detailed summary of the opinions of the two dissenting justices, William McLean and Benjamin Curtis.[59]

The *Providence Journal*'s editors also tried to be careful in their response, noting that they were "accustomed to speak with respect and with deference of the judgments of the courts." Yet this ruling so dis-turbed them that they found themselves unable to remain silent:

[T]he decision that a man born in this country, entitled to vote and eligible to political office in many of the States, is not a citizen, will strike the public with astonishment. . . . It cannot fail to greatly weaken the public confidence in this tribunal, which, till the feeling was shaken by the apprehension of this decision, has been looked to as removed above all partisan or sectional influence. . . . It is not so looked upon today.[60]

The *Dred Scott* decision would continue to reverberate in the months to come. In the spring of 1858, Republicans won seats easily in Rhode Island, Connecticut, and New Hampshire.[61] In the summer, Abraham Lincoln challenged Stephen Douglas to a series of debates in which he referred often to *Dred Scott* and the continuing bloodshed in Kansas. As Lincoln said, the nation was "a house divided." The *Charleston Mercury* was of the same mind, on that point at least: "On the subject of slavery, the North and South . . . are not only two Peoples, but they are rival, hostile Peoples."[62]

Still, there were indications that divisions between North and South might be bridgeable. In the summer of 1858, Senator Jefferson Davis of Mississippi was directed by his doctor to get some rest. Davis, his wife, and their two young children traveled to Portland, Maine, for several weeks of vacation. But on their way home, they had to stop in Boston because their infant son was dangerously ill with croup. The historian Thomas O'Connor notes that "never had Boston extended a more generous welcome to an out-of-town guest."[63] Concerned residents came to the Davises' hotel to help care for the baby and allow Mrs. Davis to get some sleep, and after a few days the family was able to continue their journey south. In Newport, too, southerners were still welcome visitors. That same summer, the Charleston planter Henry Middleton bought eight acres of land on Ochre Point and, in the winter of 1860, the Pringles of Charleston were building a new cottage for their summer stays.[64]

John Brown's "Mad Attempt" and Abraham Lincoln's Election

Soon it was southerners' turn to feel anger and apprehension. In October 1859, John Brown, a militant abolitionist, launched a raid on the U.S. armory at Harper's Ferry, Virginia. Three years earlier, he had led an attack on pro-slavery settlers in Kansas, kidnapping and killing five. This time, he hoped to spark a slave uprising, using weapons seized from the government. But within two days, Brown's twenty-two-man rebellion had been routed by a force of marines led by Colonel Robert E. Lee.

The immediate reaction, among all but the most radical abolitionists, was shock and revulsion. In an editorial published a few days after Brown's capture, the *Newport Mercury* expressed outrage at Brown's actions and blamed "[t]he leaders of a wide spread conspiracy of fanaticism in the Northern States . . . for the danger now existing of civil war, and of whatever loss of life and liberty may be incurred in the settlement of the tremendous question which they have raised."[65] Yet after Brown was sentenced to death, many opponents of slavery began to cast him as a martyr. The Transcendentalist author Henry David Thoreau was so taken by Brown's courage and zeal that he referred to him as a "saint." By November, the *Mercury*, too, began to soften its tone. While continuing to decry Brown's "mad attempt . . . to create an insurrection among the negroes at Harper's Ferry," the editors stressed the gravity of the slavery issue:

> As citizens of a nation—a part of whose constitution declares that it is made to secure the blessings of liberty—we cannot but feel that slavery is incompatible with that declaration; and, believing as we do, that freedom regulated by good and wholesome laws is preferable to slavery, we should be glad to see freedom prevail, if it can be obtained in such a manner as to be consistent with the welfare of all, and especially of our fellow-countrymen who are slaveholders.[66]

When Brown was hanged on December 2, church bells tolled in Boston and many other northern cities.[67] Gatherings were held in New York, Chicago, Providence, and elsewhere to raise money for his widow and other family members.[68] Newporters, however, did not make any notable effort to memorialize Brown. Instead, the *Newport Daily News* reported on "Union" rallies that were being organized by Democrats to reassure southerners.[69] Newport's Irish community was probably loath to pay tribute to Brown, considering its long-standing opposition to abolitionism. The *Boston Pilot* depicted him as a crazed fanatic and was pleased to point out that "no shadow of an Irish name" could be found among his forces.[70]

Still, as James McPherson aptly writes, "John Brown's ghost stalked the South as the election year of 1860 opened."[71] In the spring, the Democrats, holding their convention in Charleston, found themselves bitterly divided between supporters of Douglas's popular sovereignty doctrines and pro-slavery hardliners, who, like Roger Taney, believed there could be no restrictions of any kind on slavery in the territories. After a second dead-locked convention in Baltimore, most southern Democrats walked out and chose John Breckinridge of Kentucky as their nominee, while north-ern Democrats stuck by Douglas. Worse yet, from the southerners' point of view, was the Republicans' decision to select Lincoln, a personable and articulate proponent of a moderate antislavery position.

Lincoln would be a formidable standard bearer for the Republicans; and, with pro-slavery forces split three ways (John Bell, a Tennessee slave-holder was running on the Constitutional Union ticket), the Republicans looked poised to win. Knowing that he was an underdog, Douglas decided to break with tradition and campaign for himself. Having been advised that he could "carry Maine, New Hampshire, Rhode Island and Conn[ecticut]," he decided to take a New England tour in the summer.[72] After delivering an address at Harvard, Douglas visited his childhood home in Vermont and then, at the beginning of August, headed to Providence, where he was greeted by a large crowd. On the following day he went to Rocky Point, a popular waterside resort in Warwick, for a "mammoth clam bake" that drew a crowd of about 30,000.[73] Afterward, exhausted from his travels, Douglas and his wife went to Newport's Atlantic House for two weeks of vacation. On his arrival, salutes were fired, and marching bands escorted the couple to Touro Park, where Mayor William Cranston offered him a formal welcome.[74] The Douglases spent several days enjoying themselves at the beach and at balls. But before leaving, Douglas was visited by his finance chairman, August Belmont, a brash German-born banker who was also the American representative of the Rothschilds. Belmont had married a promi-nent Newporter, Caroline Perry, and was building a summer cottage on Bellevue Avenue that he would name By-the-Sea.[75] Now Belmont informed the senator that he was having great difficulty raising funds because most potential donors considered Lincoln to be a sure winner.[76]

In the end, Douglas's extensive campaign travels did not help him at all and probably contributed to his death in the following year. Although

Lincoln received just under 39 percent of the vote nationwide, he swept almost the entire North, winning a clear majority in the Electoral College. Douglas received only twelve electoral votes, winning Missouri and a portion of New Jersey's delegates. Lincoln easily captured Rhode Island, but Douglas ran almost even with him in Newport.[77] Of course, most Irish immigrants in the state were blocked from voting because they could not meet the property requirements.[78] In Newport, for example, the Rhode Island census of 1865 recorded almost 2,000 Irish-born men and women but only sixty-eight Irish voters.[79] Had the immigrants been allowed to vote, Douglas would have been a stronger candidate in the state.

Despite favoring Lincoln for president, Rhode Island voters chose a wealthy Democrat for governor: William Sprague III, who had drawn liberally on his family fortune in the campaign.[80] Just twenty-nine years old, the "boy governor" was the son of Amasa Sprague, whom the Gordon brothers had been charged with slaying in 1843. Although not an abolitionist, Sprague was a strong defender of the Union and had no sympathy for secessionists.

"For Union!!"

Within six weeks of Lincoln's election, the Deep South states started to secede. South Carolina was first, followed after the New Year by Mississippi, Florida, Alabama, Georgia, Louisiana, and Texas.[81] Meanwhile, both houses of Congress established committees in an effort to avert war between the Union and the new Confederacy. In February 1861, Virginia, a critical border state, invited all of the states to take part in a peace conference in Washington chaired by John Tyler, the former president. Twenty-one states, including Rhode Island, sent delegates to the meeting. Over the course of three weeks, they approved a series of resolutions on slavery intended to mollify both North and South. Nonetheless, Republicans in Congress thought that the measures conceded too much to the South so they voted them down just hours before Lincoln's inauguration.[82]

In his inaugural address, Lincoln tried to strike a conciliatory note toward the southern states, assuring them that they were "not enemies, but friends." At the same time, he warned that he would not relinquish any federal properties: though South Carolina had seceded, he was not about to turn over Fort Sumter in Charleston's harbor. After a month of deliberations and consultations, Lincoln sent food to the federal garrison in Charleston, using unarmed supply ships; but when the Confederacy's president, Jefferson Davis, learned of the incoming shipment, he and his cabinet decided to shell the fort before the ships arrived.

With the fall of Fort Sumter, war had begun. Lincoln called for 75,000 men to volunteer for ninety days to suppress the rebellion. For Virginia, North Carolina, Tennessee, and Arkansas, Lincoln's call for troops was the final provocation: they chose instead to follow the Deep South states out of the Union.[83] Throughout much of the North, however, both Democrats and Republicans rallied to the president. Stephen Douglas backed Lincoln wholeheartedly, telling a crowd in Chicago that there could be "no neutrals in this war, only *patriots* or *traitors*."[84] Newport summer resident August Belmont, who had also strongly opposed Lincoln, wrote to Lionel Rothschild after Sumter's surrender, saying that he was "convinced that the whole North, to a man, will stand by the administration in the present struggle."[85]

Still, there was not universal enthusiasm in Newport about the Union cause. According to Isaac Lawrence, a Democratic Party official in Providence, half of Newport's "taxable property belongs to Southern people, and one half of its summer population are from the South"; in his view, this meant that Newporters would naturally be interested in conciliating the South.[86] The *Mercury* was quick to correct Lawrence, pointing out that southerners were not nearly so prominent on the Newport tax rolls. Yet the editors themselves seemed ambivalent. When the war began, the paper ran a picture of an American flag under the heading "For Union!!" Then, underneath the picture, the editor posted a gloomy column that appeared to support Lawrence's claim: "Peace, contrary to the hopes of the friends of peace, seems about to depart from the length and breadth of the Union as it was; and war, horrid war, has already been inaugurated in its place." The editor clung to the belief that "the conflict in that harbor was chiefly at least of a local nature; and, it may be hoped, not necessarily involving the peace of the whole country."[87]

Newport's citizenry responded more positively to Lincoln's appeal for troops. In 1860, the town's population stood at 10,500, significantly smaller than Providence's, which had risen to approximately 50,000, and Providence County's, which had reached 107,000. Given such numbers, Newport would not be expected to provide a significant share of the state's quota, which Lincoln had set at 780 men.[88] But the townspeople stepped forward. Within two weeks, 1,040 members of Rhode Island's First Regiment had sailed down to Washington under the command of Colonel Ambrose Burnside.[89] They included slightly more than a hundred Newport men, a handful of whom were Irish: Francis Harrington, Thomas Keating, William Keating, Edwin Kelley, and Daniel McCann. All told, the First Regiment included forty-five Irish-born men.[90] Aware of the Catholic presence in the troops, Governor Sprague asked Bishop McFarland if a priest could be released to serve as a chaplain alongside a Baptist minister, Reverend Augustus Woodbury. McFarland agreed and allowed Father Thomas Quinn, an assistant pastor at the cathedral in Providence, to join the regiment.[91]

Just two weeks after his initial request for troops, Lincoln called for 60,000 more volunteers to serve in the Army and the Navy and asked them to commit for three years rather than three months. By June, Rhode Island had assembled its Second Regiment, which, like the first, numbered just over 1,000. Newport's company consisted of about eighty men, and the Irish were a notable presence. Two of its eight corporals—Timothy Sullivan and John Murphy—were Irish, as were about a quarter of the privates: John Barry, John Callahan, John Conly, Lawrence Connor, James Cooney, Dennis Corcoran, John Courtney, John Devlin, Martin Finn, Patrick Kilroy, John Higgins, John McCabe, William McCann, Patrick Mullen, John Murphy, John Riley, John Sullivan, and Patrick Sullivan.[92] The regiment, under the command of Colonel John Slocum, set sail for Washington to join Burnside's forces and Governor Sprague, who wanted to take part in the combat.[93]

Throughout the nation, both in the North and the South, the Irish responded in much the same way. More than 140,000 served for the Union, and roughly 30,000 joined the Confederates.[94] Most were no doubt attracted by bounties and the promise of a regular salary. Many enlisted to demonstrate their loyalty to the United States or the Confederate States, but some were more focused on their homeland. The most militant nationalists had aligned themselves with the Irish Republican Brotherhood, or Fenians, which had been established in 1858 and sought Irish independence "by means of physical force."[95] For them, the Civil War was a chance to become battle-tested, and they hoped to use their knowledge and skills to eventually help Ireland break free of British rule.[96]

Wartime Newport

In some respects, Newport in 1861 was a changed city. Roughly two hundred of its men had gone off to war, leaving their families behind. But when the U.S. Naval Academy moved from Annapolis to Newport in May, the city gained an equal number of midshipmen. George Bancroft, the academy's founder, had been worried about the secessionist leanings of many Marylanders. Because he had a summer home on Bellevue Avenue, he was familiar with Newport and thought it would be an ideal location for the academy during the war.[97] After he persuaded Congress to approve the move, faculty, staff, and students sailed into Fort Adams. The fort was already occupied by army troops that had arrived after Sumter's fall, but they made way for the academy arrivals and moved to Fort Wolcott on Goat Island.

Almost as soon as the naval personnel settled into the fort, officers began complaining about its damp and drafty conditions. So, in August, the navy moved the academy to the Atlantic House, which it rented for $5,500 per year.[98] With the middies regularly parading and drilling on Bellevue Avenue, Newporters were constantly reminded that the nation was in the midst of a war. In other respects, however, Newport seemed to be little affected by the war. In June, the *Mercury* urged its readers to attend the National Circus, which was coming to town. In July, it noted that General Tom Thumb, one of P. T. Barnum's star attractions, would be performing at Aquidneck Hall.[99] In August, the *Daily News* reprinted a letter from a New York newspaper about Newport's atmosphere:

> Notwithstanding the absence of "Southern Belles and Beaux," Bellevue Avenue presents as gay and brilliant an aspect . . . as it did in the days of "Auld Lang Syne." The Hotels are filling rapidly. . . . The feeling of sadness, and anxiety which pervades the whole community prevails to a certain extent here. . . . As we take our ease . . . and inhale the balmy ocean breeze, we heave a sigh of sympathy for the brave defenders of our country . . . and trust that ere long we shall welcome them back, and that with the returned allegiance of the South, the whole country, one and undivided, will under Divine Providence, take out a new lease of prosperity.[100]

For Newport's Catholics, life went on much as it had before. Father O'Reilly continued to attend to his parish duties; and, in February 1861, he brought in Bishop McFarland to speak.[101] It would be interesting to know if the bishop addressed the looming political crisis when he spoke at Saint Mary's. Certainly, it was on his mind. In the previous December, he had issued a pastoral letter "relating to the dangers that threaten the Union" and had called for "fervent prayer for the country."[102]

For Saint Patrick's Day, O'Reilly organized an evening of activities, including a lecture by the assistant pastor, Father M. T. Maguire. In July, the parish held its sixth annual exhibition at Aquidneck Hall, showcasing the work of the boys and girls at the schools.[103] In August, the bishop was back in Newport to confirm forty-four young people and consecrate the new parish cemetery on Spruce and Warner streets.[104]

Now that the church construction was finished, O'Reilly's top priority was to build a schoolhouse that would complement Saint Mary's. This would be an expensive undertaking, and the task of raising money had become more complicated since the death of Catherine Harper in February. In the words of the *Newport Mercury*, she had been "a devoted member of the Roman Catholic Church, and the society in this city, [had] on many occasions received the benefit of her charitable disposition."[105] With funding resources in question and the war underway, O'Reilly decided to hold off on the school for the time being.

The "Disastrous Result" at Bull Run

In late July, Union forces, prodded by an anxious president, set off from Washington under the command of General Irvin McDowell. They were headed first to Manassas Junction, or Bull Run, and then planned to take Richmond, the Confederate capital. The Union forces assumed that they would make quick work of the rebels, and their entourage of congressmen, wives, and journalists was eager to witness their triumph. The fighting was intense and lasted for an entire day. For a time, the battle seemed to be going McDowell's way, but the Confederates, especially those under the command of General Thomas "Stonewall" Jackson, stubbornly resisted. Eventually, the Confederates counterattacked, provoking a frantic retreat by the northern soldiers and their picnicking civilian supporters.

At first, some northern newspapers reported that the Union forces had won the battle, but it soon became clear that the Union had not only lost but been routed.[106] Rhode Island's lieutenant governor, Samuel Arnold, did not mince words in the statement he delivered two days after the battle: "All hearts are bowed in sorrow at the disastrous result . . . at Bull Run in Virginia."[107] All told, 625 Union soldiers died, 950 were wounded, and 1,200 were captured by the Confederates. For the South, 400 died, and 1,600 were wounded.[108]

Rhode Island's regiments were in the center of the action and suffered heavy losses. Governor Sprague, who had wanted so much to be in the fight, had his horse shot out from under him. The First Regiment lost thirteen soldiers, and another seventy were wounded or missing.[109] The Newport company in the First lost two soldiers: Francis Harrington, an immigrant from County Kerry, and John Peckham, a Newport native. Eleven members of the company were wounded, one of whom, T. Wheaton King, died a few months later from his injuries.[110]

The Second Regiment suffered even higher casualties. One member of the First, writing to his father in Newport, told him that "the 2d regiment is badly cut up."[111] The regiment lost its commander, Colonel Slocum, as well as three of its officers and twenty-three of its enlisted men. Another fifty-eight were wounded, and twenty were missing.[112] Several Irish from the Newport company were among the casualties. Patrick Mullen was killed, and William McCann was wounded and would die six days later.[113] John Barry and John Riley were wounded and missing. John Courtney, John Sullivan, and Patrick Kilroy were wounded, and John McCabe was missing.[114] Corporal Timothy Sullivan had been shot in the arm and captured by the Confederates. A Richmond surgeon would amputate his arm before sending him back to the Union lines in October.[115]

The day after the battle, Father Quinn sent a poignant letter to Bishop McFarland: "I am safe, thank God. I was alternately in the field and in the hospital,—the scene was awful. I anointed a great many not only of our own but of other Reg[imen]ts. I was hit in the leg by a rifle ball but it merely raised the skin. . . . There are not more than a half dozen Catholics killed and as many more wounded." He then added a postscript:

Mrs. McElroy's son on Federal Hill is safe.[116] Doherty is killed, and Harrington of Newport, and one or two others. The wounded are doing well, I have just seen young Gilroy of Newport. He got a ball through his side. The wound is not dangerous. He is cheerful and contented, and doing well.[117] Governor's Sprague's horse was killed under him and so was T. F. Meagher's.[118]

Stunned by the grim reports from Virginia, the state's political and religious leaders appeared together at an impromptu rally for the Union in Providence. Bishop McFarland joined the mayors of Providence and Newport and several other notables and offered some brief remarks. The *Providence Evening Press* reported that the bishop, "in a few telling sentences, pledged the audience that his efforts and prayers will not be wanting for the defence of the Union and the Flag." The correspondent added that McFarland was then "vociferously cheered."[119]

The *Newport Daily News* urged that a rally be organized in Newport, "the semi-Capital of the State, to follow close upon that had in Providence yesterday," but no one followed up on this recommendation.[120] Instead, the city prepared to welcome home the First Regiment's Newport company, which was about to disband at the end of its ninety-day term. The returning troops received a hero's welcome as they marched into Touro Park, and the town paid tribute to the two soldiers who had died on the field. The *Daily News* was especially effusive:

> [Harrington] was a native of Ireland, and left, if any, none but distant relatives in the United States. . . . With that fidelity so characteristic of the sons of Ireland, he promptly responded to the call of his new government, and as promptly laid down his life for it in its hour of necessity. . . . Mr. Harrington formerly worked in the Perry Mill, earned a good reputation as a citizen, and sealed it with a hero's death. He was about thirty years of age, and unmarried.[121]

With the First Regiment mustered out and the Second Regiment reduced in strength after Bull Run, Governor Sprague called for volunteers to form Third and Fourth regiments in August. Peter Sinnott, a politically active Irishman from Providence, had recruited a number of his countrymen for what he hoped would be an all-Irish regiment, and this group formed the nucleus of the Third.[122] In an effort to attract more

Irish volunteers, Sprague appointed Father Quinn chaplain of the regiment and assured the men that all veterans would hereafter be allowed to vote, whether immigrant or native-born.[123]

Quinn traveled around the state, trying to drum up enlistments for the new regiments. In early September, he was with Newport's mayor at Touro Park, speaking before a crowd of between 2,000 and 3,000 people.[124] While no newspaper summarized his remarks in Newport, the *Providence Journal* recounted his speech at the Cranston Print Works, given on the following day, which was probably similar to his Newport address. In Cranston, he strongly defended the efforts of the northern troops at Bull Run, especially the brave Irishmen in the ranks, and urged those who had already served to reenlist as they would be "better than raw recruits."[125] Quinn and the other speakers were cheered in both Cranston and Newport, yet listeners were not as quick to sign up as they had been in the spring. The *Daily News* tried to encourage men to go to the enlistment office on Thames Street, pointing out that the city would provide a $20 bounty to each volunteer, but even that incentive did not have much effect.[126]

FIGURE 11. Engraving of Lovell General Hospital at Portsmouth Grove, c. 1865. The hospital was established in 1862 and overlooked Narragansett Bay. Reprinted courtesy of James E. Garman.

The Hospital at Portsmouth Grove

For several months after the Battle of Bull Run, the Virginia front remained quiet. In November, Lincoln appointed a new general, George McClellan, to oversee the Union armies. McClellan was cautious and wanted to make sure that his troops were better prepared for combat than were those who had fought at Bull Run. In June 1862, he made several attempts to close in on Richmond but was outmaneuvered each time by the new southern commander, Robert E. Lee.

Meanwhile, in Rhode Island, Governor Sprague recognized that the military hospital in Providence was overwhelmed, and he consulted with the surgeon general, William Hammond, about setting up a new facility in the state. Sprague soon settled on a former resort in Portsmouth that had easy access to Narragansett Bay. The locale seems to have been chosen for the same reason that the Naval Academy had been moved to Newport: Aquidneck Island was a safe haven, far from the battlefields.

In July, just as Lovell General Hospital at Portsmouth Grove was opening, a ship arrived with more than 1,700 wounded and ill Union and Confederate soldiers. The hospital was not yet equipped to handle them, and several soldiers died while waiting to be treated.[127] Months would pass before all of the property's fifty-eight buildings were complete. Eventually the hospital would include wards for the sick, a mess hall, a bakery, a laundry, a chapel, a blacksmith shop, a stable, a residence for female nurses, and more.[128] During the hospital's three years in operation, more than 10,000 patients came to Portsmouth, and 300 were buried in its graveyard.[129]

The bishop entrusted Father O'Reilly and his rotating roster of assistant pastors with the task of caring for the Catholics at the hospital.[130] According to the *Catholic Directory*, the Saint Mary's priests were also responsible for the little chapel near the Portsmouth coalmines, which had reopened in 1850 after being closed intermittently in the 1830s and 1840s.[131] O'Reilly seems to have taken his responsibilities at the hospital seriously. After visiting Portsmouth Grove and anointing four Catholic soldiers who were near death, he wrote to ask if the bishop could send another priest to visit the hospital in the coming week, promising that "we will attend it afterwards."[132]

Draft Evasion, Desertion, and Death

With the hospital up and running, Sprague turned his attention once more to the North's urgent need for manpower. In July, in the wake of McClellan's failed attempt to take Richmond, the War Department had called on the states to provide 300,000 more troops for three years. Then, in August, it had called for another 300,000 soldiers for nine months.[133] According to James McPherson, these quota measures established a "quasi-draft."[134] If the states failed to meet their quotas, then a full-fledged draft would surely follow.

In August, a rally was held in Newport to stir up support for the North. Several speakers addressed the crowd, including Mayor Cranston and a senator from Illinois, Lyman Trumbull. Thomas Coggeshall, Jr., a Middletown resident, attended the meeting and heard speakers praise John Brown and call for the immediate emancipation of the slaves. Writing to a family member, he said that Newport had only been able to come up with 50 of the 125 men needed for its company in the Seventh Regiment. He added that "some people here are very much afraid of the draft" but that he was not worried about it.[135] In fact, soon after Coggeshall wrote his letter, the *Providence Post* reported that Newport had reached its quota.[136]

In September, the city's leaders joined with August Belmont in an effort to raise $15,000 for bounties that they hoped would attract another 135 men into the Eleventh and Twelfth regiments. They also assigned two or three people to canvass each ward and try to identify candidates. For the Fifth Ward, whose population was almost two-thirds Irish or Irish-American, the recruiters selected Belmont, who was well known as a Democratic Party leader. Assisting him was Thomas Galvin, Jr., then the most prominent Irish member of the community.[137] An immigrant, he ran a successful nursery business and had just begun a term on the City Council.[138]

Galvin and Belmont apparently had some success in their canvass of the Fifth Ward. In October, the *Mercury* published the names of the ninety-six members of the Twelfth Regiment's Newport company. Eleven Irishmen were on the list: Henry Brady, Pat Crimmin, John Dunn, William Doyle, John Harrington, George Kenney, John Mulvy, George Nolan, James Noonan, David O'Connell, and Jefferson O'Reilly. The *Mercury* also listed, without comment, the names of the latest deserters who had been rounded up. Of the six Newporters, three had Irish surnames: Michael Lynch and William Keating, who had deserted on the same day; and John Sullivan, who had deserted a few months earlier.[139] The men were not the first Irish Newporters to abandon their posts. At least three Irish members of the Second Regiment, who had signed on for three years of service in 1861, had disappeared by 1862: Dennis Corcoran, who had left in 1861; and John Conly and Lawrence Conner, who had deserted on the same day in 1862.[140] Aware of this problem, Governor Sprague soon assigned a War Department official the task of "arresting bounty jumpers and other deserters."[141]

In September, northern spirits were lifted by news that the Union forces had repulsed Lee's incursion into Maryland at Antietam. Lincoln, who had been waiting for a victory, decided that the time was right to issue the Emancipation Proclamation: as of January 1, 1863, all slaves in rebel-held territory would be free. The war, which had at first been fought to preserve the Union, was becoming a crusade to end slavery.

Lincoln had been hoping that a quick win would end the war, and he was frustrated by McClellan's deliberate pace. So in November 1862, he appointed Ambrose Burnside as the commander of the Army of the Potomac. Anxious to please the president, Burnside immediately attacked the Confederates at Fredericksburg. But the action was poorly planned and executed, and the battle was a major defeat for the North, resulting in the loss of more than 12,000 Union troops.[142]

As the new year dawned, Lincoln searched for a new top general, and Congress sought to replenish the Union forces. He soon settled on General Joseph Hooker, and Congress decided in the spring to enact a draft law that would take effect in July. All men between the ages of twenty and forty-five would be eligible for the draft, but draftees could be exempted if they paid $300. Many Irish were outraged by this measure: they saw themselves as targets because few, if any, would have the money to pay for substitutes.

Already, they were weary of the war. The Irish units, especially the famed New York–based Irish Brigade, had endured high casualties. In addition, many did not embrace the new emphasis on emancipating the slaves. As a result, several Irish communities violently resisted the imposition of the draft.[143] In New York City, angry Irish rioters took to the streets, attacking draft offices and setting fire to the Colored Orphan Asylum and several black churches. After three days of anarchy, Union troops were able to quell the chaos, but 105 people—mostly Irish—died in the melee.[144] In Boston, Irishwomen chased draft officers out of their neighborhood, and areas of the city erupted in violence. Several people were killed before state militias were able to gain control.[145] There were also disturbances in Troy and Staten Island, New York, and in Newark, New Jersey.[146]

Newport, too, had a dust up in the Fifth Ward. Apparently sensing trouble, the *Mercury* reported in early July that "the draft which has been so much dreaded by the citizens of this State, has at last been ordered and made." The paper reported that the names of 299 Newport men had been drawn; and the Fifth Ward, with eighty-six possible draftees, had the city's largest share.[147] Trouble started on July 16, two days after the Boston riot and in the same fashion. According to the *Daily News*, when Officer Carpenter went into Holland Street in the Fifth Ward to distribute draft notices, two dozen women gave him a "severe pelting of mud and stones" and forced him to withdraw. The *Mercury* noted that Carpenter had to "go home and bathe his wounds," and Mayor Cranston put military units in the city on alert. Both papers stressed that there were no further disturbances and that the Irish community should not be blamed for the day's events. The *Daily News* declared that it had no "apprehensions [of any further conflict], especially from our Irish citizens who as a class are a law-abiding and industrious set of men."[148] The *Mercury* concurred, noting that "[p]rominent men among the Irish are determined to discountenance every movement indicating rowdyism and we do not believe there are enough evil disposed persons in the whole city to create a disturbance."[149]

The *Providence Journal*, which had a nativist slant, offered a very different perspective. The paper's Newport correspondent titled his article "Almost a Riot" and depicted the events in a much darker light. He claimed that the women had assaulted Carpenter with clubs "in true Irish style." By evening, "it grew evident that certain parties were seeking an opportunity for an outbreak. Crowds collected along the streets without any seeming purpose." The correspondent believed that the mayor's prompt response and the prospect of calling in troops from Fort Adams or the Newport Artillery Company had frightened "the would-be mob, and probably this alone restrained the parties which were longing for an affray and for the plunder which such an occasion must place within their reach." While acknowledging that no further violence had occurred, he cautioned that an outbreak "may appear at any moment."[150]

The draft officers decided to wait a few weeks for tempers to cool before examining the candidates. In late August, the *Newport Mercury* was shocked to learn that only one Newport man had thus far entered the service as a result of the draft. Sixty-six had been exempted for health reasons, seventeen were deemed too young or too old, fifteen were sons of dependent widows, six did not meet the height or weight requirements, eight had purchased substitutes, and twenty-eight were not citizens and therefore not subject to the draft. Most of the non-citizens were Irishmen from the Fifth Ward.[151] By the time the draft was completed in September, the *Providence Post* was reporting that Rhode Island had been able to produce only 105 draftees, a fraction of the War Department's quota of 2,880 for the state.[152]

While the draft was deeply unpopular in many parts of the North and provided little benefit to the Union forces, the battlefield tide was finally turning in the North's favor. In July 1863, Lee suffered heavy losses at Gettysburg, and General Ulysses S. Grant captured the key port of Vicksburg for the Union. In the months following, the Union's army and navy would make further gains in much of the South, though Lee continued to frustrate the Union generals in Virginia. In 1864, Grant, who had by now been appointed commander of the Army of the Potomac, tried to grind down Lee with his superior numbers. Grant's tactics were eventually successful but came with significant casualties.

The Newport Irish were not spared. John Murphy and John Sullivan of the Second Regiment were wounded at the Battle of the Wilderness in May 1864, and John Kilroy, a Newporter from Roscommon serving in the Seventh Regiment, was killed at Petersburg in June.[153] The community's sacrifices did not pass unnoticed. In July 1864, the *Mercury*, noting the prominent part that marchers from Saint Mary's had taken in the city's Independence Day parade, stressed the patriotism that the Irish were demonstrating: "The present rebellion has shown that the foreign born is as anxious to enjoy the . . . rights guaranteed by our Constitution as the native born and have marched shoulder to shoulder with those who in former years were anxious to deprive them of the rights of citizenship."

In another column in the same issue, the paper reported that fifty-seven graduates of Saint Mary's School had served in the military and fourteen had given their lives.[154]

Fenian Feuds

During these years, the Fenian movement gained adherents rapidly as many Irish soldiers in both the Union and the Confederate forces vowed to fight for Ireland once the war in America was over.[155] In 1863, the Fenian Brotherhood held its first national convention in Chicago. Unlike their Irish compatriots, who were fearful of arrest or British infiltration, American Fenians typically operated in the open. Three hundred delegates joined the "head centre," Colonel John O'Mahony, for the three-day meeting.[156] The representatives agreed that their "young members [must] learn military tactics" and that conventions would be held each fall until Ireland gained its independence.[157]

Some bishops in America were suspicious of the Fenians. They were put off by what they took to be the Brotherhood's anticlerical posture and its emphasis on physical force rather than parliamentary initiatives. All would have known that Ireland's primate, Archbishop Paul Cullen, had denounced the Fenians as a secret society.[158] Chicago's bishop, James Duggan, was the first American prelate to condemn the group. Two other leading members of the hierarchy, James Wood of Philadelphia and Peter Kenrick of St. Louis, spoke out against them as well.[159] However, most bishops, including Hartford's Patrick McFarland, were worried about alienating their Irish parishioners, so they chose to keep any misgivings to themselves.[160]

After the war's end in April 1865, Fenian activists were able to devote themselves completely to the cause of Irish independence. In Rhode Island, the movement began to swell during the summer. In July, a Fenian organizer from Hartford held a meeting at Aquidneck Hall, seeking recruits. In the days following, William Delany, the schoolmaster of Saint Mary's, sent two letters to the *Daily News*, warning readers that the Fenians were a secret society condemned by Archbishop Cullen.[161] Father O'Reilly backed up Delany, condemning the Fenians from the pulpit of Saint Mary's on the following Sunday and warning that no Fenian would be allowed to receive the sacraments or a Catholic burial.[162]

The priest's stern admonition does not appear to have had much effect. In the week after O'Reilly's pronouncement, Fenian leaders in Hartford and Providence wrote to the *Daily News* and the *Providence Journal*, assuring readers that the brotherhood was not a secret society and dismissing the criticisms of the "ever officious" Archbishop Cullen.[163] In early August, the brotherhood began advertising a "grand excursion to Rocky Point" in the *Newport Daily News*. Excursionists could take a steamboat from Newport in the morning, enjoy music from various bands, and spend the day dancing and picnicking at the beach. They would also have the chance to hear two of the Fenians' national leaders, John O'Mahony and William Roberts. The editor of the *Daily News* thought that a "jovial good time" would be had by all. He added that "[t]hose who have only heard of the Brotherhood and wish to know their principles, will do well to attend the excursion, and they will hear the whole case stated."[164] The day proved to be a resounding success for the Rhode Island Fenians. The *Providence Journal* offered a long and appreciative account of the event, noting that the morning's overcast skies had quickly cleared, giving the excursionists a warm and sunny day: "[F]ive thousand was the estimate which we heard of the number on the ground, but it was very likely larger."[165]

A month later, the Newport chapter of the Fenians held a public meeting, inviting James McDermott, the national secretary, up from New York and inviting him to speak. The gathering, which drew two hundred men and women, was first addressed by William Hudson, the head centre of the Newport organization. McDermott then delivered a lecture cataloguing England's many misdeeds toward Ireland over the centuries.[166] A few days later, Bishop McFarland traveled to Newport for the day to meet with Father O'Reilly and the Mercy sisters. The bishop must have received an earful from O'Reilly about the meeting because he noted in his diary, "The Fenians have been rampant in Newport, denouncing the church, etc."[167]

Although O'Reilly and McFarland did not then know it, the Fenians had peaked and were starting to falter. At the time of McFarland's visit to Newport, the British were shutting down the Fenian newspaper in Dublin, *The Irish People*, and arresting key leaders of the brotherhood. In October, American Fenians held a convention in Philadelphia. This time the meeting was wracked by discord as William Roberts and his allies ousted John O'Mahony as head centre. Roberts and his supporters thought that the American wing of the brotherhood should launch an attack on Canada.

They were confident that a raid on Canada would divert British attention from Ireland, thereby strengthening the Fenians' prospects there. O'Mahony thought this was a foolish idea but was eventually persuaded by his supporters to approve a competing Canadian raid.[168]

In March 1866, Fenians were out in force in Newport, Providence, and a host of other cities, parading in honor of Saint Patrick.[169] Reports were widespread in the press that a Fenian assault on Canada was imminent. In April, O'Mahony's men made the first move, launching a few small sorties onto New Brunswick's Campobello Island before beating a retreat back to Maine.[170] Two months later, Colonel John O'Neill, an ally of William Roberts, crossed from Buffalo into Ontario with a better-organized force. Leading eight hundred Fenians, O'Neill defeated the Canadians at the Battle of Ridgeway. O'Neill's momentum was then stalled because the American government moved to block any more Fenians from crossing the border to reinforce him. Over the next few days, 7,000 would-be invaders were sent home, and the Canadian invasion was called off.[171]

The American factions, deeply suspicious of one another, were also increasingly frustrated by the vacillation of the Irish Fenians' leader, James Stephens. In the beginning of 1867, a Civil War veteran, Colonel Thomas Kelly, came from America to Ireland to take over the Brotherhood and lead the long-awaited uprising but found the Fenian forces in disarray, plagued by internal divisions and riddled with informers. When Kelly launched the rising in March, even the weather worked against him: rare snowstorms discouraged rebels from coming out and hampered communication among the Fenian operatives. In the end, the attempted rebellion fizzled out in a week, and many top Fenians were captured.[172]

The Fenians' failures in Canada and Ireland greatly weakened the movement in the United States. Meetings were held occasionally in Providence and other cities, and conventions were organized through the end of the decade; but for most Irish-Americans the movement had lost its luster.[173] In 1870, Colonel O'Neill attempted a raid into Canada from St. Alban's, Vermont, this time employing volunteers from Rhode Island, Massachusetts, and Vermont. Poorly organized, the attack failed miserably, and O'Neill was arrested by a U.S. marshal.[174] In reporting the news, the *Newport Mercury* expressed very different sentiments about the movement than it had a few years earlier: "The Fenian campaign has come to an end as pitiable as its course was brief and inglorious."[175] By this time, Bishop McFarland felt free to speak out as well, offering warnings about secret societies.[176] Although Fenianism had faded for the time being, interest in the Irish cause would remain strong in Rhode Island in the coming years.

Father O'Reilly's "Lasting Monument"

While irritated by the Fenian agitation, O'Reilly was not nearly as concerned about it as he was about the war.[177] Still, by 1864, as the conflict appeared to be winding down, he was able to turn his attention again to building a suitable school for the parish. Already, in the summer of 1863, he had auctioned off Saint Joseph's Church on Barney Street to raise money for the school, but the sale had netted only $250.[178] Michael Butler, the buyer and also a parishioner, dismantled the building in February 1864 to use the materials for tenements he was building on Perry Street.[179] In March, the *Mercury* reported that the parish had "long had in contemplation the building of a fine school house for the use of the increasing number of scholars who are now but poorly provided with proper accommodations." The paper noted that O'Reilly had commissioned Patrick Keely, the architect for the church, to design the schoolhouse.[180]

Another year would pass before O'Reilly would break ground on the school. Presumably he was waiting for the war to end. In late April, just days after Lee's surrender at Appomattox and Lincoln's assassination, the priest was in Providence discussing his plans with the bishop.[181] By the end of April, the *Mercury* was reporting that workmen under the direction of Michael McCormick and John McCormick were "rapidly progressing with their new building," which the reporter said was expected to cost about $25,000.[182] The *Daily News* added that $3,000 had been raised on the day of the groundbreaking.[183]

As soon as construction started, O'Reilly thought of almost nothing else. In June, he wrote to the bishop asking if he could put off the collection the bishop wanted for diocesan orphanages because he would be taking up a special collection for the school. O'Reilly said that construction was moving along quickly, and he hoped that the bishop would "do us the favor" of laying the cornerstone and "saying something on the occasion."[184] McFarland agreed and fulfilled O'Reilly's request in a dramatic fashion. Following a line of twenty-eight acolytes and six priests, the bishop, clad in his episcopal garb, solemnly processed to the school building, blessed it, and put the cornerstone in place. He then delivered an address that traced the growth of Catholicism in the diocese. The *Mercury*'s reporter was impressed, calling it "a historical day in the annals of the Catholic parish of St. Mary's."[185]

To finish the grand building, however, O'Reilly would need considerably more funds. By the time construction was complete, the school would cost $80,000, more than three times the original estimate. Inflation, which was rising after the war, was responsible for some of the additional expenses, but O'Reilly's decisions had played a part as well. He had hired a prominent architect and chosen expensive building materials—Rocky Farm stone trimmed with granite.

In August 1865, O'Reilly wrote to the bishop again. This time he wanted to avoid attending the annual clergy retreat because he and his assistant were then "so much occupied in collections for the new school house." He added, "It is absolutely necessary, that we should attend to matters, if we expect to . . . have the building enclosed in this season."[186] Construction continued for the next several months; and by the summer of 1866, the three-story building was more or less complete. The lower floors would house the boys' and girls' schools, and the top floor was intended for meetings.

O'Reilly brought the bishop down in July for a tour of the building and a visit to the beach.[187] With construction mostly finished, he then decided to hold a fair on the top floor to raise more funds. In August, a number of parish women ran the two-week event, and the *Mercury* reporter estimated that it had drawn thousands of attendees.[188] Finally, in the spring of 1867, the building was ready to be used by the schools' 250 boys and 250 girls.[189]

For the Mercy sisters, who had been teaching the girls out of rooms in their convent, the opening of the school must have been a great relief. It also enabled them to expand their academic offerings. In October 1867, they opened Saint Mary's Academy, a coeducational high school, in the convent classrooms. The first class had just twenty-eight students, but enrollments would increase gradually in the years following.[190]

O'Reilly, too, must have pleased. After all, he had completed Saint Mary's Church and built the accompanying school in just over a decade, and the parish had tripled in size from 1,500 parishioners in 1858 to 4,500 in 1867.[191] Unfortunately, he did not have much time to savor his achievements. In the following year, the priest, who was just fifty-three, suddenly took ill and died of "a hemorrhage of the lungs" right before Christmas. The *Mercury* published a lengthy account of the funeral Mass—listing the names of the more than forty priests who assisted Bishop McFarland— and the procession with its forty-eight carriages that slowly wound its way through the streets and into Saint Mary's Cemetery. The correspondent concluded his report with a stirring tribute:

> Thus lived and thus died and was buried, the Very Rev. Wm. O'Reilly, a foreigner by birth and a priest of what is by many considered a foreign religion; and, yet, who had, during thirteen years residence here, by his urbanity and integrity, so won upon our regards, that, at his death, there were not wanting many of our citizens of all creeds, who were willing and anxious to honor his memory, by their presence at the church and at the grave.[192]

The *Providence Journal*'s Newport correspondent seemed equally affected. Reporting on the eve of the funeral, the reporter noted, "A truly just and good man has passed to his rest. . . . The church over which he has long presided, is being draped in mourning. . . . A universal feeling of sorrow pervades all classes in our community at the sad event."[193]

To replace O'Reilly, Bishop McFarland would need to find an able administrator, capable of running a large parish and a school. He would also want a pastor who would be able to get along with a wide variety of civic and religious leaders. Newport was different from what it had been when O'Reilly arrived. The city was becoming a center of Gilded Age society. The genteel southern summer colonists were gone, replaced by brash, rich New Yorkers eager to flaunt their wealth. O'Reilly's successor would need to be able to relate to these people as well.

Chapter 7

ACCEPTED AND YET APART

Newport's Catholics at the Dawn of the Gilded Age

The Very Rev. Philip Grace, pastor of St. Mary's church in this
city, celebrated upon a recent Sunday the third anniversary of
his present pastor-ship. . . . With a parish of nearly five thousand
souls to care for, besides schools to look after, he has developed the
work of his parish with energy and ability. Although we of course
hold to Protestant opinions, we are yet capable of appreciating
the work of a clergyman of another faith; and therefore, when his
Holiness, Pius the ninth, has another bishop to make in this part
of his jurisdiction we respectfully suggest the name, as that of an
accomplished scholar, and able clergyman, of Father Grace!

—*Newport Mercury*, January 11, 1873

In the years following the Civil War, Newport grew ever more popular
as a summer destination for the wealthy. Southern visitors, who had
been pillars of the city's antebellum summer colony, did not return, but
their places were filled by New Yorkers and other northerners. Most of
these well-heeled vacationers were unimpressed by the city's hotels and
chose to build, buy, or rent private homes. The historian Jon Sterngass
notes that the new mansions required even more staff than the hotels did,
and the owners wanted their butlers, cooks, and maids to be of "European
descent."[1] As a result, with ever more job opportunities, Newport's Irish
population continued to grow. The 1875 Rhode Island census lists 2,000
Irish-born Newporters and 3,800 second-generation Irish; together, they
formed 41 percent of the city's 14,000 residents.[2]

Around the United States, enterprising Irish were beginning to enter the
middle class.[3] In Newport, they prospered by catering to the summer clien-
tele's changing needs. Some, such as Thomas Galvin, Jr., and Michael Butler,

ran nurseries or floral businesses; others, such as Michael McCormick and Patrick Horgan, were builders.[4] Like other middle-class Newporters, the Irish joined a variety of clubs and societies and supported worthy causes such as temperance, aid to the needy, and the promotion of good literature. However, they generally chose to go their own way rather than join existing Protestant-founded groups, establishing Catholic charitable organizations, temperance societies, and literary clubs. While they were accepted by the mainstream, Newport's Irish Catholics tended to avoid it, concerned that they might become too assimilated and lose their identity.[5]

Newport's Postwar Prosperity

When the Civil War ended, the Naval Academy cadets and their teachers left the Atlantic House and returned to Annapolis, and the Portsmouth Grove military hospital closed.[6] Now, with the military presence gone and a new railroad connection to Fall River (established in 1864), Newport was more accessible than ever to summer visitors.[7] The city still retained some industry—three functioning textile mills, a naval torpedo station established in 1869, and a brass and iron foundry opened in 1871—but Newporters were staking their hopes on tourism.[8] As the editor of the *Newport Mercury* bluntly admitted, "We are almost solely dependent on this business for our prosperity."[9] Yet in the first few summers after the war, business remained sluggish. In 1868, the editor of the *Mercury* noted that, since 1865, there had been "a falling off of our summer patronage," which he blamed on a cholera outbreak and unusually wet weather.[10] However, he was confident that things would improve.

He was right: many more visitors came to Newport in the summer of 1868. But the *Providence Journal*'s correspondent noted in July that the city's hotels had vacancies, and he observed "a growing preference for cottage life, being more exclusive and comfortable."[11] The *Newport Mercury*'s editor was more sanguine about the hotels. While noting that 115 cottages had been rented for the season, he predicted that, by August, when "the season is at its height . . . we may be certain that the hotels will be filled."[12] By the end of September, a writer for a New York newspaper judged the season to be a "complete success," pointing out that "hotels have been filled, boarding-houses crowded and more cottages rented than ever before."[13]

The summer of 1869 proved to be even more "brilliant."[14] Along with wealthy visitors, Newport drew some of the nation's notables. Vice President Schuyler Colfax came up for a visit in June, and President Ulysses S. Grant followed in August.[15] Grant met with prominent Republicans such as Levi Morton, who owned a home on Bellevue Avenue, and Edwin Morgan, the former governor of New York.[16] Grant and Colfax both made a point of meeting Ida Lewis, the intrepid young lighthouse keeper at Lime Rock, who had gained national fame for rescuing two soldiers whose boat had capsized on the way to Fort Adams.[17]

In July, Elizabeth Cady Stanton and Susan B. Anthony had launched the New York Woman Suffrage Association in Saratoga Springs, which had attracted a wealthy summer crowd much like Newport's.[18] So at the end of August, they held a women's suffrage convention in Newport, hoping to draw more "fashionable" women into the movement.[19] Stanton and Anthony held forth at Newport's Academy of Music for two days and attracted sizable crowds though few, if any, benefactors.[20] Other prominent speakers, including Frederick Douglass, would appear at the Newport Opera House, an elegant 1,000-seat theater and music hall, which opened in 1867.[21]

Changing Shepherds

While the city as a whole was thriving, its Catholic population was unsettled. In the months following Father O'Reilly's death, one of Saint Mary's assistant pastors, Father Edmund O'Connor, took charge of the parish. An able administrator, he organized an elaborate memorial service for O'Reilly in May 1869, leading nearly six hundred students from Saint Mary's School to the church cemetery on Warner Street, where they placed flowers on O'Reilly's grave. The *Newport Mercury* gave special notice to a "magnificent cross of the choicest flowers from the floral conservatory of Messrs. Galvin and Garrity."[22]

O'Connor was described as the pastor of Saint Mary's in the local press and was well regarded in the community.[23] So Bishop McFarland created a stir when he announced in September that he was transferring O'Connor to New London, Connecticut, to become pastor of Saint Patrick's parish.[24] The new pastor of Saint Mary's would be Father Philip Grace, a thirty-one-year-old Irishman who had studied at the University of Notre

REV. PHILIP GRACE, D. D.

FIGURE 12. Portrait of Dr. Philip Grace, undated. Grace served as pastor of Saint Mary's Church from 1869 until his death in 1898. From *St. Mary's Golden Jubilee* (n.p., 1902), held by the Redwood Library and Atheneum, Newport, RI. Gift of Reverend W. B. Meenan. Reprinted by permission.

Dame and was then serving as pastor of the New London parish.[25] The *Mercury*'s editor was careful not to criticize the bishop but could not hide his disappointment. He noted that O'Connor had "faithfully discharged the duties of his position, and gained the friendship of his congregation, and it is evident that the change was not desired by the Curate [O'Connor] or his charge." The editor also printed a letter to O'Connor from two Saint Mary's parishioners, James Dowling and James McKeown, declaring their "heartfelt sorrow for being obliged to part with you." Along with an address, the pair presented O'Connor with a gift of $1,600.[26]

Having switched the two priests, McFarland left Providence for New York, then set sail for Rome to take part in Pope Pius IX's First Vatican Council, which would address questions of papal authority.[27] The bishop would be absent for almost a year. In the meantime, Father Grace arrived in Newport to take up his new assignment. It would be a challenge to replace the popular O'Connor and win over the congregation, but a more pressing problem would be erasing the church's $60,000 debt, incurred in the construction of Saint Mary's School.[28]

Grace set to work right away. In the spring of 1870, he invited the Passionist fathers to come up from Hoboken, New Jersey, for a two-week parish mission.[29] In their missions, the Passionists preached about the importance of weekly Mass attendance and regular confession, delivered stern warnings about the dangers of intemperance, and emphasized the "Four Last Things" awaiting everyone—death, judgment, heaven, and hell.[30] During the summer, Grace walked all around the city, visiting parishioners and asking for donations to eliminate the debt. By September 1870, he was pleased to report that he had raised $10,000.[31]

Dividing the Diocese Once More

Bishop McFarland returned from Rome in August 1870, just a month before Italian nationalists stormed the city and brought an end to the Papal States. At the council, he had been a leading "inopportunist," arguing that a proclamation of papal infallibility would be unwise and would antagonize many Protestants.[32] But he and his American cohort were badly outnumbered, and they decided to leave the meeting before the final vote was taken.[33]

The events in Rome were followed closely by Catholics and Protestants alike. Many Protestants were exercised about the Council's decrees, arguing that papal infallibility was an unscriptural and unsound teaching. In Newport, the Reverend J. Lewis Diman spoke at the Opera House on the "Roman Catholic question."[34] A Congregational minister, Diman held a chair in history and political economy at Brown University.[35] In Providence, a series of meetings was held to discuss the Vatican Council, led by the Episcopal bishop, Thomas Clark, and other Protestant clergy from New Haven, Boston, and Rochester, New York.[36]

Catholics, for their part, downplayed the doctrinal debates and focused instead on Pius IX, who had fled from the Quirinale Palace and declared himself a "prisoner of the Vatican." In Providence, Catholics held a meeting at Saint Patrick's Church to show their solidarity with the pope.[37] In Boston, thousands of Catholics came to a meeting organized by Bishop John Williams to "cheer the name of Pius IX," and large pro-Pius demonstrations were held in New York, Baltimore, Philadelphia, and Washington, D.C.[38]

In response, some Protestants in Boston and New York held counter-demonstrations in support of Italian unification. *Harper's Weekly* published a cartoon by the illustrator Thomas Nast lampooning Irish Americans for their support of Pius IX, and Julia Ward Howe, famous for composing "The Battle Hymn of the Republic" during the Civil War, composed another hymn to mark Italy's unification. The Reverend Asa Smith, a Presbyterian minister serving as president of Dartmouth College, remarked that "it would be sad, indeed, if the people of Italy should hear from our shores only such voices as have been strangely lifted up in certain gatherings"—namely the Catholic rallies in defense of the pope.[39]

Bishop McFarland, however, was not energized by the Council or by the controversies that followed it. Although the *Newport Mercury* reported that the bishop returned from Rome with "improved" health, he was in fact ailing and was no doubt discouraged by the results of the Council.[40] He had already been thinking of resigning his see before he left for Rome; and on his return, he felt that it was imperative to either step down or reduce the size of his diocese. At a meeting of bishops in the spring of 1871, McFarland agreed to remain in office, provided that his diocese be split. As a result, Rhode Island was separated from the Hartford diocese in 1872 and McFarland, who had resided in Providence, moved to Hartford.[41] The new Diocese of Providence encompassed all of Rhode Island as well as a portion of southeastern Massachusetts that had previously belonged to the Diocese of Boston.[42] Its first bishop was Father Thomas Hendricken, then serving as pastor of a church in Waterbury, Connecticut. Born in Ireland, Hendricken had planned to be a Jesuit missionary in China or Japan until the early 1850s, when he met Bishop Bernard O'Reilly, who convinced him that the Diocese of Hartford was also mission territory.[43] In April, Archbishop John McCloskey of New York City ordained Hendricken as bishop in the Providence cathedral.[44]

The Panic of 1873

Like Father Grace, Bishop Hendricken was a native of County Kilkenny, and he would prove a loyal friend to Newport's pastor.[45] Despite their initial disappointment at losing Father O'Connor, the local press quickly took a liking to Grace. Reporting on Saint Patrick's Day events in in 1870, the *Mercury* editor declared:

> [O]ur Irish fellow citizens had a very fine day for their celebration Thursday, and made an imposing appearance as they passed through the streets of the city. The procession was composed of the Fifth U.S. Artillery Band, Aquidneck Drum Corps, two companies of Aquidneck Rifles, and St. Mary's Catholic Benevolent Society, the whole escorting the Rev. Mssrs. Grace and O'Reilly, who rode in a barouche drawn by four horses. . . . Altogether the day was duly honored by the native born, as well as their children and children's children born in this country. Long may the memory of St. Patrick be kept green in their memories.[46]

The *Mercury* was particularly impressed by Grace's fundraising abilities, noting in January 1873 that he had raised $92,000 for the parish during his three years at Saint Mary's.[47] At this rate, Grace seemed poised to clear the church's debt quickly, but events on the national scene worked against him.

In September 1873, the nation's economy, which had been booming since the end of the Civil War, suddenly lurched downward. Excessive speculation in railroads and other industries caused numerous banks to fail and unemployment to spike. More than five years would pass before America's economy could right itself.[48] Newport, too, felt the fallout as many of its summer colonists lost their fortunes during the panic. In April 1874, the usually upbeat *Mercury* admitted that "getting ready for the summer is rather slow work this spring, and the cold weather has kept back those who are in search of homes for the season."[49] In the spring of 1875, the paper offered a more optimistic perspective. After pointing out that Newport had completed a fine new educational institution, Rogers High School, the editor declared, "The business world is beginning to take courage. The belief is general that the panic is over, and people feel easier in regard to business and money matters generally, and those who stayed home last year for economy's sake will be found at their accustomed haunts this summer."[50] Yet the *New York Times*, which followed the Newport summer scene closely, was not as positive: "The season at this watering-place is not so brilliant as many reports have pictured it. . . . Newport will continue to be the 'city of cottages,' and hotel life will continue to grow beautifully less." The correspondent noted that only two hotels, the Aquidneck and the Ocean House, were still in business.[51] The Atlantic House, which the naval cadets had occupied during the Civil War, did not open for the 1875 season and was torn down the following year.[52]

Father Mathew Men

With the economy stalled, Grace shifted his focus from fundraising for the church to supporting charities in Newport and Providence.[53] He contributed generously from his own pocket to causes such as Newport Hospital, which would open in 1873, and the new cathedral in Providence that Bishop Hendricken was planning.[54] In addition, he served as the founding president of the Newport chapter of the Saint Vincent de Paul Society and as president of the Saint Mary's Catholic Benevolent Society, both of which provided assistance to the poor in the parish and the local community.[55]

As a temperance advocate, Grace was also an ardent follower of Father Theobald Mathew—a group known as Father Mathew men. During

FIGURE 13. Postcard of Father Mathew's Hall, c. 1910. The hall on Thames Street was a place for non-drinkers to gather and socialize. Collection of Daniel P. Titus. Reprinted with permission.

the 1840s, the "Apostle of Temperance" had been celebrated in Ireland and Irish America, but enthusiasm for the cause had diminished by the time of his death in 1856.[56] Protestant support for temperance had likewise faded in the 1850s, doubtless in response to the enactment of the Maine Law of 1851, the first state law prohibiting all alcoholic beverages.[57] After the end of the Civil War, however, both Catholics and Protestants showed a renewed interest in the subject. Protestants founded the Women's Christian Temperance Union in 1874 and revived the Sons of Temperance, while Catholic men, almost exclusively of Irish descent, established the Catholic Total Abstinence Union of America in 1872.[58]

Rhode Island Catholics established a state temperance organization in 1870 and, by 1871, its various chapters were ready to hold a mass meeting.[59] In June, newspapers announced that the parish societies would converge on Newport in August. As the event approached, the *Mercury* predicted that 2,000 Catholic teetotalers from all over the state would be present.[60] On the appointed day, six hundred Catholic temperance men from Providence, Pawtucket, Valley Falls, and Woonsocket joined the local Catholic teetotalers in a "grand parade through the city's principal streets."[61] Later in the day, Father Grace and leaders of the state temperance association addressed the group at Saint Mary's Hall.

Grace continued to lecture on behalf of the cause and, in 1876, established a temperance society in his parish. In January, 125 men gathered in Saint Mary's Hall and took the pledge from him. Before administering it, he assured them that their "homes would be much more comfortable" without the presence of alcoholic beverages, which, he said, had a "tendency to stir up the evil passions of mankind."[62] Two weeks later, the new organization, known as the Father Mathew Total Abstinence Society, established a slate of officers. James Cottrell, a grocer and city councilman, was the president; Michael Butler was secretary; and Michael McCormick was a director.[63] The *Mercury* was thrilled, claiming that "the society has already largely diminished the sale of liquors in the fifth ward."[64] In March, the paper reported that the "Father Matthew [*sic*] Temperance Society numbered 140 and the [Saint Patrick's Day] parade yesterday was their first. They made a fine appearance in their new regalia"—perhaps pins or sashes featuring their insignia.[65]

Of course, not everyone in Newport's Irish community rushed to march under Father Mathew's banner. The 1876 *Boyd's Newport City*

Directory list of liquor dealers included Stephen Buckley, John Martin, Patrick Nolan, Eugene O'Neill, and Thomas Sullivan.[66] Nolan ran an advertisement in the *Directory* for his Bellevue Avenue store, which sold "ales, fine wines and segars."[67] Likewise, several Irish names were among those listed as saloonkeepers.[68]

Father Grace and "The Newport Scandal"

By 1875, Father Grace was gaining praise not only for his temperance advocacy but also for the breadth of his learning. In May, the Newport Historical Society invited him to speak at its annual meeting, held at the Redwood Library.[69] Grace took the opportunity to discuss the role of the papacy in the development of Western civilization. Afterward, he was elected a member of the society, and another member, Reverend Charles Malcolm of the Second Baptist Church, sponsored a resolution thanking Grace for his "learned and instructive address."[70]

A week later, the *Boston Pilot* reported on Grace's lecture after an unnamed Protestant minister, presumably Malcolm, sent a glowing letter about it to the paper. The *Pilot*'s publisher, Patrick Donahoe, was happy to reprint the letter in full, noting that it "speaks volumes for the liberality of the leading minds of Newport." The minister pointed out that Grace was the first Catholic to speak before the society. While he acknowledged that the priest had made a few statements from which he, as a Protestant, "might dissent," the writer considered the two-hour-long talk the best ever delivered before the society: "[Grace] showed how false is the charge of some modern sceptical scientists that the Catholic Church has opposed learning and science: and formed a valuable contribution both to the history of European civilization and to the illustration of the blessed principles of Christianity."[71]

Just a few months later, however, Grace's standing in the community plummeted. In December 1875, twelve-year-old Geneva De Fray died. Her father, Manuel, was a Portuguese-born gardener, and her mother, Anna, was an Irish immigrant. The De Frays were members of Grace's parish. However, when De Fray asked the priest to bury their child, Grace refused.[72] DeFray believed that Grace was punishing him and his wife for sending Geneva to public school rather than to Saint Mary's, though three of the other De Fray children did attend the parochial school.[73]

De Fray appealed to Bishop Hendricken for a Catholic funeral and interment for his daughter.[74] In the meantime, the story was quickly picked up by the *New York Herald*, which liked to publish sensational news.[75] The paper's publisher, James Gordon Bennett, Jr., was an avid sportsman and sailor and a frequent visitor to Newport. In October, he had purchased land on Bellevue Avenue to build himself a cottage.[76] Thus, he knew Grace and was well versed in Newport's affairs.

The *Herald* titled its first article "Priestly Intolerance" and reported that many Newporters were upset about Grace's actions.[77] The *New York Times* covered the story as well, dubbing it the "Newport Catholic Scandal."[78] The *Providence Journal* also ran a series of articles on the "So-Called Burial Scandal," and Massachusetts papers followed suit.[79] With the controversy escalating, Grace decided to take his case to the *Providence Journal*. In a letter, he responded first to the charge that he had refused to bury Geneva because she had attended a public school, decrying it as an "*infamous falsehood.*" He then took up the question of public education and offered a mixed appraisal:

> [W]hile I admire the intellectual advantages of the public school system, and admit their goodness as far as they exist, I do maintain, with every respect for the opinions of others, that there is yet something wanting to give harmony and completion to the being, and that *something* is religious instruction, without whose influence the heart becomes a dreary waste.[80]

After receiving Grace's letter, the *Journal*'s editors sent a reporter to interview Bishop Hendricken on the matter. The bishop told the correspondent that he thought Grace merely wanted to reprimand De Fray for not calling a priest sooner to administer last rites; he did not believe that Grace was opposed to giving the child a Catholic burial. When asked about public schools, the bishop assured the reporter that the Catholic church "d[id] not seek to destroy the public schools, rather to improve them. We only oppose the infidelity that threatens the country."[81] Grace's letter and Hendricken's statements seemed to assuage the *Providence Journal*'s editors, who remarked, "What seems to have been a misunderstanding in the first instance, has grown to an issue quite disproportionate to its intrinsic importance."[82]

In Newport, Grace had many defenders. Even the *New York Herald* acknowledged that he was "one of the most popular men in the city."[83] As the conflict intensified, hundreds of Saint Mary's parishioners gathered in the church hall and grilled the *Herald*'s correspondent before unanimously approving resolutions expressing both their "full confidence" in Grace and their frustration over the "calumny which charges our pastor with priestly intolerance." The parishioners noted that the priest's views had been "twisted into an attack on the public schools of this city."[84] The *Boston Pilot* weighed in as well, accusing the "Protestant press" of bias in its coverage of the situation.[85]

The *Newport Mercury*, however, was deeply disappointed with Grace. The editors did take pains not to condemn him, noting that the facts surrounding the burial were in dispute and emphasizing that "it is not our business to express any opinion." Yet elsewhere in the same issue, they took issue with what they saw as his dismissive attitude toward public education:

> We confess that we do not see how any right minded Catholic who loves his child and our common country, can consent to waste the precious time of his offspring and his own hard earned money, in dwarfing the mind and in isolating the child from those with whom it must live and act when it attains the age of maturity.[86]

Shortly after Christmas, the sad episode drew to a close. Bishop Hendricken sent a public letter to De Fray assuring him that Grace would permit a Catholic burial for his daughter.[87] On January 2, the DeFrays brought their daughter's remains to the church, and Father Thomas Clinton, the assistant pastor, presided over a brief funeral service. As the family walked out of the church, 2,000 spectators lined the streets, watching the mourners return the girl's casket to the Protestant cemetery, where it had previously been interred.[88]

While the *Mercury* and some of Newport's Protestant leaders had lost a measure of confidence in Grace, the bishop continued to back him strongly. Two years later, Hendricken took a trip to Rome and was present when the new pope, Leo XIII, bestowed on Grace an honorary doctor of divinity degree in absentia. On his return, Hendricken visited Saint Mary's to give Grace the amethyst ring and doctor's cap associated with the degree.[89] Henceforward, the priest would be known as *Doctor* rather than *Father*.

Literary Pursuits

The ill feelings generated by the De Fray case situation dissipated fairly quickly. Soon after the child's reburial, local newspapers shifted their attention to the activities of the newest Catholic organization in town: the Newport Catholic Literary Society. Founded in December 1875, this men's group was intended to provide intellectual stimulation and entertainment through lectures, debates, and musical performances.[90] At this time, literary groups, reading circles, and debating clubs were springing up throughout the United States, most notably at Lake Chautauqua in western New York, where visitors interested in self-improvement could enjoy Bible studies, lectures by popular authors, and musical performances.[91] The movement had already reached Newport. In 1872, a committee that included Colonel Thomas Higginson, a well-known abolitionist and literary critic, had founded the Newport Lecture Association, which sponsored lectures and concerts at the Opera House that were open to all.[92] Among the presenters were the renowned novelist Harriet Beecher Stowe and John Gough, a "reclaimed drunkard" and temperance advocate.[93]

Higginson was also a member of a more exclusive literary group: Julia Ward Howe's Town and Country Club. Founded in 1871, the group held regular sessions during the summer, drawing together eminent Newporters like George Bancroft, founder of the U.S. Naval Academy; Alexander Agassiz, a marine biologist; and John LaFarge, who was highly regarded for his paintings and stained-glass windows. Sometimes members—or visitors such as Mark Twain and Oscar Wilde—would read scholarly papers. At other times the group would put on humorous skits.[94]

Catholic Newporters also wanted to edify and amuse themselves; but rather than join the Protestant-oriented lecture association or wait for an invitation from the Town and Country Club, they decided to set up their own organization, just as they had done with their temperance activities.[95] For their inaugural meeting in 1876, the Catholic Literary Society's founders hosted Father Joshua Bodfish, a Boston priest who had been an Episcopal minister before converting to Catholicism.[96] Highly educated converts such as Bodfish were a point of pride for Catholics, who often worried about their standing in American society. These converts made the church look more respectable and its claims seem more compelling.[97]

On the day before Bodfish's lecture, the *Newport Daily News* reported that "many tickets have been sold and the audience promises to be large."[98] The day after the address, a columnist for the *Providence Journal* commended the young men who had organized it, reporting that Bodfish had given an "interesting account" of his odyssey from a Baptist childhood, to "high church" Episcopalianism, to Catholicism.[99]

Like Howe's Town and Country Club colleagues, members of the Catholic Literary Society could be lighthearted. In August, when the archbishop of New York, Cardinal John McCloskey, was visiting Newport, its members and the town band walked to the Caldwell cottage on Kay Street, where the cardinal was staying, and proceeded to serenade him.[100] The *Mercury* reported that "the Cardinal appeared much delighted and highly complimented" the singers and musicians. Before the evening was out, the group gathered at Saint Mary's and performed for Father Grace as well.[101] Even at their regular meetings, members would occasionally feature what the *Providence Journal* called "pleasant entertainments," with Mary Galvin, Saint Mary's organist, playing the piano; Tim Sullivan, a disabled Civil War veteran, singing "The Star Spangled Banner"; and John Cottrell, brother of the alderman, reciting Edgar Allan Poe's poems.[102] The *Newport Daily News* was impressed by the society's programs, which, it said, showed that "the members of the association, instead of lounging on the streets, etc., were constantly improving themselves."[103]

Celebrating the Centennial

In the spring of 1876, many Newporters were eagerly anticipating the Centennial Exposition, America's first World's Fair, which would take place in Philadelphia from May through November. The Exposition would be sited on 450 acres in Philadelphia's Fairmount Park. At least 8 million people would attend, viewing paintings, sculptures, and the latest machines from all over the world. Outside the exhibit halls, they could wander through the park's many gardens and listen to music.[104]

Yet some Catholics thought the Exposition was marred by nativist overtones. For one thing, only Protestant ministers had been chosen to deliver the invocations at all of its major events. Moreover, in his speech during the opening ceremonies, President Grant linked his opposition to

Catholic school funding to the nation's commemoration of its centennial. Already, when speaking to Congress in December 1875, he had declared that in "this centennial year of our national existence as a free and independent people," Congress must approve a constitutional amendment "prohibiting the granting of any school funds or school taxes . . . for the benefit . . . of any religious sect or denomination."[105] An angry Bishop Hendricken had responded, "He travels far out of his way to insult the church of which we are members . . . [and his proposal would make] the schools as godless as could well be imagined."[106]

Newport's own centennial commemorations did not have any anti-immigrant or anti-Catholic overtones. In May, the *Mercury* hoped that the city fathers would not be stingy in allocating funds so as to "give the boys a chance to have a centennial celebration that will be first class. We cannot all go to Philadelphia, and therefore we must go in for a good time at home."[107] The *New York Times* fretted that the exposition would hurt Newport's summer season, noting in June that visitors "have never before been so slow about coming."[108] Nonetheless, when July 4 arrived, the city staged an elaborate series of events. According to the *Providence Evening Post*, they exhibited a "spirit and eclat worthy of the day."[109] Events began with a morning parade including troops from Fort Adams, various bands, police officers, and a carriage carrying thirty-nine schoolgirls representing every state in the Union. Catholic societies were well represented: forty-nine men marched under the aegis of the Saint Mary's Catholic Benevolent Society, sixty-three for the Father Mathew Total Abstinence Society, and twenty-five for the Catholic Literary Society. Father Grace and Father Clinton had a carriage of their own.[110] Missing from the parade was the Newport division of the Ancient Order of Hibernians. which had been established in 1875.[111] The town's Hibernians chose to march with all of the other state Hibernians in the Providence parade.[112]

The *Mercury* believed that the procession "made [as] fine an appearance as any ever seen in the streets of Newport."[113] Afterward, Mayor Henry Bedlow recited the Declaration of Independence and a former congressman, William Sheffield, delivered an address tracing Newport's development since the colonial era. At sunset, church bells rang for half an hour, and salutes were fired at Fort Adams. The night concluded with torpedoes being shot off at Goat Island.[114]

Supporting the Sisters

In these years Newport's Catholic temperance society, literary society, and charitable organizations were all-male affairs. There were not many opportunities for Catholic women to become active in their church and community, but supporting the work of the Sisters of Mercy was one open avenue. By the mid-1870s, the sisters were running an elementary school for five hundred boys and girls, and an academy for forty high schoolers, and a Sunday-school program for six hundred children.[115] They were revered in the community. Even the nativist-oriented *Providence Journal* gushed that "there is probably no order in the Roman Catholic Church that is so universally known and admired for their piety, zeal and self-sacrifice as that of the Sisters of Mercy."[116] Indeed, when one of the Newport sisters, Mary Basilia Duffy, died suddenly at the end of 1876 at the age of twenty-eight, the *Newport Mercury* ran a long, sympathetic story about her funeral, and the *Newport Daily News* published a poem in her honor.[117]

Before Dr. Grace's arrival, parish women had planned and run fairs each August to support Saint Mary's School. However, Grace did not believe in "church entertainments," so the women had to find other ways to support the sisters. In the summer of 1876, several came together to sponsor a "grand vocal and instrumental concert" at the Opera House.[118] The committee included Caroline Bonaparte, who had married Napoleon's grandnephew Jerome at Saint Mary's in 1871 and converted to Catholicism two years later; Jeanette Bennett, the sister of the *New York Herald*'s James Gordon Bennett, Jr.; Mrs. Theodore Havemeyer, the Austrian-born wife of an American financier; and Mrs. John LaFarge, a convert to Catholicism and the granddaughter of Oliver Hazard Perry, hero of the War of 1812.[119] Tickets, priced from 50 cents to $2, were available at several outlets, including Galvin's nursery on Spring and Dearborn streets.[120] The event featured Italian and German performers, and the *Mercury* judged it "one of the most entertaining and successful concerts of the season." The editor reminded readers that the "expenses were heavy," so "any further donations will probably be gratefully received by the Sisters."[121]

Six months later, the Opera House was the site of another benefit for the sisters. This time more than one hundred girls from the Sunday school at Saint Mary's performed before an enthusiastic audience of 1,200 people. The *Providence Journal*'s correspondent deemed the show a "complete success" and hoped that "the good Sisters will receive a good round sum."[122] The *Daily News* estimated that the show netted the sisters $600.[123]

These events were no doubt helpful, but they did not address the sisters' biggest challenge. With nine or ten of them cramped into a small residence that was doubling as a high school, they urgently needed new living quarters.[124] Dr. Grace was aware of the problem but did not want to seek funds for the undertaking until the economy had recovered fully from the Panic of 1873.

Newport in "Full Blast"

At the end of 1876, the *Mercury* noted that many in Newport were impatient about economic recovery:

> When will business revive? That question is asked daily by men who are disposed to take a lugubrious view of the present situation. . . . The signs of the times are the more hopeful from the fact that this improvement is gradual. We do not in a moment step back into the business activity of 1873, but we have begun at the bottom, laid a new, and we trust, a solid foundation to our financial structure.[125]

Yet by the following spring, Newport's economy still seemed to be sluggish. In April, a *New York Times* correspondent warned that the "outlook for the season of 1877 is not so bright as many of the permanent residents of the place predicted it would be a few weeks ago."[126] In July, a Massachusetts paper described the city as "quiet and dull," adding that Newporters were missing the "enlivening presence of . . . the champion polo-player and yachtsman of the New York Herald."[127] He was alluding to James Gordon Bennett, Jr., who had brought polo to America in 1876 and had attracted a large enthusiastic crowd when his team had played a match in Newport.[128]

The outlook was sunnier in the summer of 1878. To observers, Newport seemed as prosperous as it had been before the panic. In July, a Boston paper declared, "In a few days the season will be in full blast, and then there will be no lack of ways and means for enjoyment. *Ennui* is a condition entirely unknown among the summer visitors here."[129] Another Massachusetts paper noted, "Lawn tennis is to be played by the club on the polo grounds, and as Mr. Bennett is expected, his presence, with the preparations for sport, promises a lively season of that nature."[130]

The summer of 1879 was busier still. In June, a Massachusetts paper announced that "the cottagers are arriving at Newport as usual ahead of the hotel frequenters. There is already a larger demand for cottages than last year and a decided promise of a brilliant season." After noting that the financier John Jacob Astor had just purchased a cottage on Bellevue Avenue for $200,000, the correspondent wrote that "several sumptuous new villas" were under construction."[131]

In August, Bennett dared one of his English polo-playing friends, Captain Henry Candy, to ride his horse onto the porch of the Reading Room, the elite men's club on Bellevue Avenue. After Candy carried out the prank, he learned that his membership in the club had been terminated.[132] Legend has it that Bennett was so annoyed that, out of spite, he decided to build a grander club down the street: the Newport Casino. In fact, however, Bennett had been planning to build his own club for some time.[133] Indeed, just a few weeks later, a Massachusetts paper reported that he had purchased a cottage on Bellevue Avenue called Stone Villa and a four-and-a-half-acre lot nearby that was to become a "new club house."[134] Bennett commissioned the newly established firm of McKim, Mead, and White to design his club. Eventually, the casino, which would cost Bennett $100,000 to build, included space for lawn tennis and court tennis, croquet grounds, a billiard room, a theater, a restaurant, and several retail stores.[135]

With Newport flourishing again, Dr. Grace set about fundraising for the parish and improving its infrastructure. The first project was remodeling the sacristy, which Emily Havemeyer offered to fund. When it was completed in 1878, the *Providence Journal*'s correspondent gave a rave review: "A more beautiful room cannot readily be imagined."[136] Next, Grace asked Patrick Keely, who had designed the church and the school, to suggest several enhancements for the church. Although many years had passed since Keely had designed St. Mary's, he remained closely involved with the Rhode Island Catholic community. Notably, he was creating the blueprints for the bishop's majestic new cathedral in Providence.[137] Now, with the help of a local contractor, Michael McCormick, Keely turned his attention to Saint Mary's. His plans placed Gothic wooden moldings near the ceiling, added frescoes to the ceiling, and new paint to the walls.[138] He also covered the church's original cement floor with tiles from Valencia, Spain.[139] According to the *Mercury*, the new floor made a "marked improvement in the church's appearance."[140]

Dr. Grace's most pressing concern was rehousing the sisters. His plan was to move the existing convent to another site and then have an architect design a new residence. This time he did not enlist Keely but instead chose two respected locals, Dudley Newton and John Dixon Johnston.[141] A lottery was held to dispose of the old convent, which was won by Rosie Rogers, a domestic servant. She turned the house over to Michael Dealy, an Irish boilermaker, and he moved it to Lee Avenue in the Fifth Ward.[142] By December 1880, the sisters were able to move into their new convent, a three-story wooden building containing several small bedrooms, a chapel, and a classroom.[143] The *Providence Journal*'s correspondent was impressed by the building's spacious layout and noted that it cost $80,000 to complete.[144]

Suffering Ireland

While Newport was prospering, Ireland was struggling once again. Poor potato harvests were reported in County Mayo in 1877, and several more of the country's western counties were affected in 1878, leading many to fear that the Great Famine was about to recur.[145] In 1879, two of Ireland's leading nationalists, Michael Davitt and Charles Stewart Parnell, established the Irish National Land League to assist desperate tenant farmers. Davitt, the architect of the League and a former Fenian, wanted Parnell to head the organization because he had already gained acclaim for his confrontational tactics in Parliament on behalf of Irish Home Rule.[146] The two men visited County Mayo and struck a defiant tone, urging tenants "to keep a firm grip on your homesteads and lands."[147] During the next three years, western Ireland would be locked in what came to be known as the "Land War," a bitter struggle between landlords and tenants involving boycotts, vandalism, and a number of killings.[148]

Parnell set off for the United States to seek funds for both the suffering farmers and the league's operations. In January 1880, he arrived in New York City, where he was greeted by his American-born mother, Delia Stewart Parnell, and three of his sisters. On the following day, 7,000 Irish Americans attended his lecture in Madison Square Garden.[149] From New

York, Parnell headed to Philadelphia and then to Connecticut and Rhode Island, stopping in Providence but not Newport.[150] In Boston, he received a hero's welcome before heading inland to Worcester and Lawrence.[151] From Massachusetts, Parnell traveled to the Midwest and then to Washington, D.C., where he addressed a joint session of Congress. This opportunity to speak before Congress was a rare privilege, one normally afforded only to visiting heads of state. After spending a few more weeks touring the United States and Canada, he abruptly returned to Ireland to take part in a general election campaign. Before departing, Parnell met with supporters in New York to organize an American branch of the Land League.[152] After not quite three months in North America, he had raised $300,000, 80 percent of which was targeted for famine relief.[153]

Notably, James Gordon Bennett, Jr., was among those who chose not to contribute to Parnell. While he was sympathetic to the farmers' plight, Bennett wanted nothing to do with Parnell, Irish nationalism, or the league. Instead, in February 1880, he set up the Herald Fund to aid Irish farmers and made an initial donation of $100,000.[154] He then contacted his friends among the Newport summer colonists and asked for their support. John Jacob Astor contributed $1,000, while other friends made gifts of $500. Workers at the Navy's Torpedo Factory on Goat Island pooled their funds and contributed slightly more than $20, and the troops at Fort Adams sent $200.[155] Ultimately, Bennett's appeal would raise more than $325,000 for the cause.[156]

Newport's Catholics also supported Bennett's fund, though, unlike him, most probably sympathized with Parnell's goals for Ireland. On Saint Patrick's Day in 1880, many cities, including Newport, did not hold a parade. Instead, as the *Mercury* noted, "In almost every city the money usually expended for that purpose, was devoted to Irish relief funds."[157] On the evening of March 17, a grand charity ball took place at the Newport Opera House. Its sponsors, the Newport Catholic Literary Society, hoped the event would raise funds for Bennett's fund.[158]

By the end of 1880, Newport, along with scores of other cities throughout the country, had established a local branch of the Land League; and in December, the organizer, Michael Butler, convened a meeting of the league at Saint Mary's Hall. In an address that evening, Dr. Grace praised the British prime minister, William Gladstone, for his efforts to help the Irish farmers.

Grace emphasized that change in Ireland required parliamentary measures, not rebellion.[159] He was clearly trying to separate the Newport league members from the Fenians and other revolutionary factions.

In October, Delia Parnell and her daughter Fanny launched a sister organization, the Ladies Land League. Working with them was Ellen Ford, the sister of Patrick Ford, editor of the *Irish World*, a New York paper with great influence in Irish immigrant communities.[160] In February 1881, Delia Parnell and Ellen Ford traveled to Newport to establish a chapter there. At Saint Mary's Hall, they were welcomed by Dr. Grace and a crowd of well-wishers. Margaret LaFarge was chosen as the president of the local branch, which, according to the *Mercury*, began with 150 members.[161]

In Newport, the two leagues continued to meet through 1881.[162] That year there was again no Saint Patrick's Day parade, presumably so that funds could be directed to the farmers in western Ireland.[163] In August, however, the Newport Land League organized a "grand excursion" to Rocky Point, where its members could spend the day meeting and mingling with other area chapters.[164]

"The Great Collection of 1881"

Dr. Grace remained very interested in the Land League's doings and supported Parnell's and Davitt's efforts to ameliorate the situation in Ireland. But by the summer of 1881, he was focused again on paying off Saint Mary's $20,000 debt, an effort he had dropped in 1873 after the start of the panic. In July, the *Mercury* reported that Grace had obtained $10,000 in contributions from Saint Mary's summer visitors and was hoping for an additional $5,000 from them before the end of the season. He thought he could pay off the remaining $5,000 through regular church collections.[165] Apparently, however, he did not receive as much money as he had anticipated from the summer colonists because, in the fall, he undertook a parish-wide visitation to try to erase the remaining debt. When he completed his "Great Collection" in November, he drew up a list of who had and had not contributed and asked John Sanborn, the publisher of the *Newport Mercury*, to print it as a pamphlet.[166]

Dr. Grace's collection survey provides valuable information about Saint Mary's parishioners in the early 1880s: where they lived, how much they contributed to the appeal, and how active they were in the church. In general, Irish Americans were known for attending Mass regularly and providing the church with many priestly and other religious vocations, yet Newport's Irish do not appear to have been especially devout.[167] Grace opened his booklet with a preface expressing concern about three moral failings that he had noticed during his canvass of the parish. First, he lamented over the "considerable number of men who were extremely careless" about their obligation to attend Mass on Sunday. Second, as a dedicated teetotaler, he was greatly disturbed by the "vice of drunkenness," noting the malign influence a "drunken, dissipated father" could have on his family and community. Lastly, he was concerned that the church's marriage laws were often ignored. It is not clear if he thought that certain couples were cohabitating or had been civilly married, but he was convinced that they had not been joined in a Catholic ceremony.[168]

Grace did thank his parishioners for their "generous and warm response" to the appeal, singling out several people who were especially supportive.[169] Yet he also listed those who had refused to contribute, in some cases adding acerbic comments about them below their names. For Thomas Quinn of Holland Street in the Fifth Ward, he noted "no contribution" and added that he was "not remarkable for going to church." Likewise, Lawrence McNulty of Lee Avenue in the Fifth Ward "spared the church tiles with care." And it seems that Martin Burns, Jr., of West Street in the Fifth Ward, was "of no assistance whatever to the Catholic church of Newport."[170]

Grace generally had kinder words for his parishioners from Kerry Hill, on the northern side of the city. In those years, the neighborhood had a reputation for violent crime and drunkenness; the *Providence Journal* was prone to referring to "Kerry Hill ruffians." Their priest, however, was more sympathetic, at least to the women.[171] After listing contributions from Green Lane, in the center of the neighborhood, Grace added that he "observed a good spirit in the people . . . and fe[lt] confident that they would be blessed by God if the male portion of them was more punctual to receive the sacraments of the church."[172]

Dr. Grace was especially appreciative of his major donors: the thirty men and women who contributed $100 or more to his appeal. The biggest gift, a $500 donation, came from Joseph Meister, an eighty-year-old widowed Bavarian immigrant who had worked as a gardener before his retirement.[173] Several other large gifts came from men such as Michael Butler and Thomas Galvin, Jr., who were also in the gardening and floral business.[174] The pamphlet included as well a "Ladies' List" of 125 donors who had made contributions of between $5 and $10.[175] Most, such as the cook Bridget Keegan, were in domestic service, but some, such as Mary Lanigan and the German-born Bertha Muller, were single women working as dressmakers.[176] All but a handful of the people on Grace's list were Irish, and the majority resided in the Fifth Ward. About 150 households were in Kerry Hill, and a few lived on the wharves or in the Point neighborhood.

Among the wealthier donors was Colonel Jerome Napoleon, who gave $100. Dr. Horatio Storer, a well-heeled Unitarian convert, gave $50, and Margaret LaFarge contributed $20.[177] All told, Grace netted about $12,000 from his appeal.[178] In early December, he shared his financial report, noting that, during his twelve years at Saint Mary's, he had raised almost $200,000. He had used the funds to pay off the debt on the church, repair and improve the building, erect a new convent for the sisters, and purchase a new burial ground for the parish. He had increased the size of Saint Mary's Cemetery, which his predecessor, Father O'Reilly, had established. Still, a pastor's work is never done. Noting Grace's accomplishments, a *Providence Journal* reporter remarked, "As soon as the debt is paid off the congregation will have to think of *building* a new church, as the present edifice is too small."[179]

Later in December, the *Journal* reporter returned to the point. In describing Christmas services in the Newport churches, he remarked that Mass was "attended, as usual, by a very large number, the church, as usual, being uncomfortably crowded."[180] Grace was no doubt aware of this problem; but before addressing it, he wanted to take a sabbatical of sorts, a trip to Europe. Such travels were common among his colleagues: Bishop Hendricken had taken extended tours in 1873 and 1878 to raise funds, and several other priests in the Providence diocese had also taken leisurely trips around Europe.[181]

In March 1882, Grace mentioned to his parishioners that he was thinking about traveling to Rome after Easter; and in May, shortly after Easter, he carried out his plan.[182] Accompanied by his younger brother, Thomas, also a priest in the diocese, Grace set sail for France. The *Daily News*

FIGURE 14. Map of Saint Mary's Cemetery, 1883. The cemetery was established on Spruce Street (now Kingston Avenue) by Father William O'Reilly and expanded by Dr. Philip Grace. Across Warner Street, which borders the cemetery on its south side, is a section of Kerry Hill, a neighborhood largely populated by Irish Americans and African Americans. From *Atlas of Newport, Rhode Island* (Philadelphia, 1883), plate 12.

reported that many of his parishioners were "visibly affected" when he spoke of his impending departure. Before he left, a leader of the Altar Society, a women's organization in the parish, presented him with a "handsome purse of money" for his voyage, which would take him to France, Spain, Italy, Germany, England, and finally Ireland.[183] The *Mercury* noted that it would be Grace's "first trip to Europe since he left the old country for America when a lad."[184]

FIGURE 15. Photograph of the shackers, 1918. The shackers were ball boys at the Newport Casino, and most hailed from the Fifth Ward. Reprinted courtesy of the Museum at the International Tennis Hall of Fame, Newport, RI.

A Sporting Summer

While the Grace brothers trekked around Europe, the residents of Newport enjoyed an extraordinary summer. The sporting life had taken over the city. Enthusiasts could watch polo played with ponies or on skates at a rink. They could go boating or horseback riding, which, according to the *Providence Journal*, was "all the go for young damsels."[185] President Chester A. Arthur was vacationing in town; and though he had hoped for rest, he was pressed to attend a "continuous round of festivities." The *Providence Journal* assured readers that everyone was "perfectly charmed" by the president and that he thoroughly enjoyed all of his activities, including his visit to the Newport Casino.[186]

Bennett's new club sponsored a successful hop at its theater, but the main event of its season was the second annual National Lawn Tennis Championship in September 1882.[187] Great crowds came to cheer on Richard Sears, a nineteen-year-old Harvard student who had won the championship the year before. Sears was unstoppable, taking both the singles and the doubles cups.[188] Attending all of the season's tennis tournaments were the shackers, a group of scruffy local boys who seated guests in the stands and served as ball boys during the matches. Richmond Barrett, the son of the casino's superintendent, recalled the shackers as a "redoubtable gang. Most of them were Irish, highly recommended by their priests; but in spite of their impeccable standing in the parish, they looked and acted like hoodlums on the Casino turf. Their uniforms consisted of red sweaters and cocky yachting caps, furnished by their employers, and disreputable trousers and sneakers out of their own wardrobes."[189] While most aspects of the Casino were kept in impeccable order, Barrett noted that the shackers were

> the signal exception—uncombed, unwashed, their stockings coming down, their sweaters ragged after a few days' wear. . . . All attempts to improve their appearance and their manners proved futile. Woe betide a stingy tipper on the Casino courts; he might be a power on Wall Street but the shackers could soon bring him to heel.[190]

As the summer wound down, Saint Mary's parishioners eagerly awaited Dr. Grace's return. When he arrived at the city wharf at the end of September, a "large assembly" was waiting. Representatives of Saint Mary's Benevolent Society, the Father Mathew Total Abstinence Society, the Newport Irish Land League, and the Newport band greeted him and escorted him back to Saint Mary's Hall, where more well-wishers waited. Presiding over the gathering was Dr. Storer, a retired Harvard Medical School professor.[191] Storer delivered a welcome in Latin, following with an English translation. Then Grace offered a brief response, focusing on his visit to Ireland. He assured his listeners that conditions were improving there and that there was "no hunger or want."[192]

New Causes

During the early 1880s, many Saint Mary's parishioners continued to promote temperance and fundraise for Irish relief, but the Newport Catholic Literary Society seems to have fizzled out.[193] But there was a new interest in suffrage reform in Rhode Island—specifically, the drive to secure the vote for foreign-born men. The 1843 state constitution, enacted after the

Dorr Rebellion, required immigrants to possess $134 worth of property to be eligible to vote. According to Edwin Snow, who oversaw the state's census during the mid-nineteenth century, "only one in twelve or thirteen of the foreign born was a voter" in 1865.[194] During the Civil War, there were proposals to grant suffrage to foreign-born veterans, regardless of their property holdings, but voters rejected them. In the 1870s, Charles Gorman, an Irish American state representative from North Providence, promoted the cause vigorously, but it was again defeated at the polls. Although a Newport state representative, Charles Van Zandt, backed the suffrage movement during the 1860s and 1870s, most Irish Newporters do not appear to have joined the cause.[195] However, after the Equal Rights Association was founded in 1881, the Irish in Newport took note. They established a chapter in 1882 and started to hold regular meetings.[196]

Parishioners also focused on an issue closer to home: the need for a second parish in the city. Because Grace had not taken any initiative on this matter, church members, led by Dr. Storer, decided to tackle it themselves. At the end of June 1883, the *Mercury* reported on a meeting to discuss splitting the parish, noting that a committee had been chosen to "wait upon Rev. Father Grace and Bishop Hendricken and lay the matter before them." The reporter was very much in sympathy with the group. Although Saint Mary's was commonly estimated to have 6,000 parishioners, he believed that there were as many as 8,000, especially in the summer months. Many of the summer visitors were Catholic, he wrote, and a "very large majority of the servants employed in the families and the hotels are of that faith." In addition, the Naval Training Station that had just opened on Coaster's Island would add still more Catholics to the area.[197]

There was also the unspoken issue of Dr. Grace's health. Although he was only in his early forties, he had suffered a stroke in about 1880 that had impaired an arm and affected his face. John LaFarge, Jr., who was born that year, recalled his childhood memories of the priest: "[H]e was paralyzed in one arm as a result of a partial stroke, and had just the one gesture of lifting up his left hand by his right. . . . His eyes moved in contrary directions, and I was sure he always kept one eye fixed on me."[198] The historian Robert Hayman notes that Grace compensated as best he could for his disability. He continued to walk for miles each day, rain or shine, but never brought an umbrella because he could not operate one. He celebrated Mass each morning at seven and returned to visit the church each night at six, when the Angelus bell rang.[199]

The *Mercury* reporter believed that a second parish was necessary, though he recognized that it "would give pain to Father Grace to lose a portion of those who have been his care and charge so long." Still, he claimed that both Grace and Bishop Hendricken were in favor of the proposal. He shared rumors about the possible purchase of the old Unitarian church, which could be moved to a lot on Mount Vernon and Barney streets, but he emphasized that the bishop had not yet taken any definitive action.[200]

The old Unitarian church to which he was referring was located on Mill Street, just a few blocks from the Barney Street land owned by the Catholic parish. It had been dedicated by William Ellery Channing in 1836, but the Unitarians had stopped using it in 1881, after building a new church near Bellevue Avenue, an impressive granite structure that featured John LaFarge's stained-glass windows.[201] The Mill Street church seemed like a promising option for Newport's Catholic community. However, Grace was adamant that Saint Mary's would not be divided until it was consecrated, and he could not do that until the church was completely debt-free.

"St. Mary's Notable Day"

By the beginning of 1884, Dr. Grace had paid off the parish's remaining debt and was starting to plan the consecration, which would be the first in the diocese.[202] August 15 was the chosen date: it was both the Feast of the Assumption of the Virgin Mary and the anniversary of the laying of the church's cornerstone, which occcurred in 1848. Grace arranged to have Archbishop John Williams of Boston and Bishop John Conroy of New York attend the event, along with Bishop Hendricken and more than forty priests, including a noted Dominican preacher, Charles McKenna.[203] The elaborate ceremonies began at six in the morning when Hendricken, attired in resplendent vestments and accompanied by a host of acolytes, priests, and lay members of the parish societies, processed around the church three times and blessed the exterior walls. After knocking on the front door and gaining admittance to the church, the bishop solemnly blessed the main altar and the interior walls as a choir chanted Latin hymns.[204] The consecration was followed by a Pontifical High Mass, celebrated by Hendricken, and the *Mercury* noted that the church was "filled to overflowing . . . many being unable to gain admittance."[205] According to Hayman, the consecration was "perhaps the highlight of Dr. Grace's tenure in Newport."[206] The *Providence Journal* no doubt agreed. Reporting on the ceremonies, its correspondent praised Grace fulsomely:

> Every one here, be he Protestant or Catholic, recognizes the fact that without the never failing loyalty and devotion of that gentleman towards the best interests of his people, and the riddance of the financial encumbrance upon the church, it would not be possible to record today the fact that the Church of our Lady of the Isle has not a single creditor in the wide world.[207]

Still, once the impressive ceremonies were over, Grace at last had to face the prospect of dividing his parish. Dr. Storer later recalled that the priest was "very unwilling and strenuously resist[ed]" the split, but to no avail.[208] A new parish would be established on the north side of Newport and would include 1,500 parishioners within its boundaries. In January 1885, Grace announced the division from the pulpit, explaining that the "new parish will run up the north side of Long wharf and take in the west side of Broadway and the west of it."[209] Thus, Kerry Hill residents would be in the new parish, while Fifth Warders would stay in Saint Mary's.

The pastor of the new church would be Father James Coyle, then assisting at the Cathedral in Providence. When naming him to lead this "new and important parish," Hendricken had assured him that his "zeal, piety and thoroughness" had made him an ideal choice for the new position.[210] So, after preaching a final sermon at the Cathedral, Coyle traveled to Newport to the former Unitarian church that would be the initial site of his parish.[211]

Chapter 8

IRISH CHIEFTAINS AND MAYORS

Catholic Growth during Newport's Golden Summers

[If Dr. Grace, like Father Coyle, were to oppose a community of French sisters establishing themselves in Newport], I should attribute it to the fact that he too had been born in Ireland, and in part to mutual rivalry and jealousy between the two chieftains. That such exists is known to every Catholic in Newport.

—Dr. Horatio Storer, letter to Bishop Matthew Harkins,
May 30, 1887

In the mid-1880s, Newport entered a new phase of the Gilded Age as ever more elaborate cottages were erected for the Vanderbilts, the Astors, and a host of other ultra-rich colonists.[1] By now, this stratum included a few Catholics, such as Teresa (Tessie) Fair Oelrichs, Countess Annie Leary, Emily Havemeyer, and Mamie and Gwendolyn Caldwell. Although a few hotels, including the Ocean House, remained, they had lost their cachet for most visitors. Meanwhile, many Catholics in Newport's year-round community prospered by catering to the summer colonists. And thanks, in part, to state suffrage reforms, Catholics were taking a more prominent part in city government, with Patrick Boyle gaining the mayor's office in 1895. Many Catholics were willing to serve with Protestants in civic organizations and happy to receive support from them. Yet, at the same time, they were having more difficulty working with each other. The city's two parishes, Saint Mary's and Saint Joseph's, were both led by strong-willed priests who did not appear to get along well.

Newport in 1885

The colonists' cottages were getting grander year by year. Richard Morris Hunt, a renowned Paris-trained architect, had completed several projects in Newport in the 1870s, notably the remodeling and enlargement of Chateau-sur-Mer, the Wetmore estate on Bellevue Avenue. In 1883, he completed Nethercliffe, an impressive house in the Ochre Point neighborhood on the south side.[2] Other mansions were going up in Ochre Point. In 1882, Catherine Lorillard Wolfe, an unmarried heiress, decided to build Vinland, a massive Nordic-style structure fronting the Atlantic Ocean, and, a block away, James J. Van Alen, a wealthy Anglophile, erected Wakehurst, a Tudor pile that was meant to be an exact copy of an English property of the same name.[3] In 1885, Cornelius Vanderbilt II, grandson of the tycoon, arrived in the neighborhood, spending $400,000 on a twelve-and-a-half-acre waterfront estate.[4]

The city was developing in other ways, too. In the summer of 1883, after a sixty-year hiatus, Touro Synagogue was at last able to reopen. German and Russian Jews had begun moving into the area in the 1870s, and now their numbers were large enough to sustain the synagogue. The Torah scrolls that had been stored for years in a New York synagogue, Shearith Israel, were returned to Touro, which was reconsecrated and reestablished under the leadership of Rabbi Abraham P. Mendes.[5] The city's Protestants were generally flourishing as well, especially the Episcopalians, who were attracting the Vanderbilts, the Astors, and many other summer colonists to their services. A reporter for the *Boston Journal* remarked in 1870 that "Old Trinity is the most fashionable place of worship and it is crowded to its utmost every Sunday morning."[6] A generation later, May Van Rensselaer, a chronicler of the nation's elite, declared that Trinity "holds a position second to none in the hearts of the townspeople, while the summer residents are proud when they are able to associate themselves with this ancient seat of worship and buy a pew in it."[7]

Founded in 1698, Trinity had served as Newport's only Episcopal church for more than a century, but it began to branch out in the nineteenth century. It established its first mission, Zion Episcopal on Washington Square, in 1834 and its second, Emmanuel on Spring Street, in 1856.[8] In 1861, All Saints Chapel opened on Old Beach Road to cater to the summer colonists, and in 1869, Kay Chapel was built on Church Street to offer Sunday-school services to Trinity's parishioners.[9] In 1878, yet another Episcopal church opened, Saint John the Evangelist. Located on Washington Street in the Point neighborhood, it styled itself as Anglo-Catholic, a branch of Episcopalianism that is very close to Roman Catholicism.[10] Saint John's was staffed by priests rather than ministers, and in later years the parish would house a community of Anglican nuns, the Sisters of the Holy Nativity.[11]

The U.S. Navy was also expanding its presence in Newport. In 1883, it opened a Naval Training Station for teenage cadets on Coaster's Island and established the Naval War College there in 1885.[12] Led by Admiral Stephen B. Luce, the college would offer graduate-level training to officers in what Luce called "the science of war."[13] The admiral had been stationed in Newport during the Civil War, and he still thought that it was an ideal site for naval installations. The college began as a small endeavor, but would come to be known as an intellectual center once scholars such as Alfred Thayer Mahan began teaching there.[14]

Newport's New Pastor

Father James Coyle was just thirty-four years old when he arrived in Newport, but he was already well known in the diocese. Like Grace, he had been born in Ireland and when he was about ten, his family left County Longford after the Famine and settled in Cranston, Rhode Island. Like Grace, Coyle studied in Montreal for the priesthood, and he was ordained there by Bishop Hendricken in 1876.[15] The bishop sent him to the Springfield, Massachusetts, diocese for two years and then appointed him to serve in Providence's Cathedral of Saints Peter and Paul, where he gained a reputation for eloquent preaching.

In January 1885, Coyle took up his position at the new Saint Joseph's Church, located in the former Unitarian meetinghouse on Mill Street, where William Ellery Channing had once preached. While historic, the church was small, and because Coyle was only renting it, he immediately started looking for a more spacious building to buy. Fortunately, Zion Episcopal church was looking to sell its property and relocate to a smaller building. By early 1885, the parish was deeply into debt and no longer able

FIGURE 16. Photograph of Saint Joseph's Church and rectory on Washington Square, c. 1900. Originally known as Zion Episcopal Church, it was Saint Joseph's between 1885 and 1912. Reprinted courtesy of Providence Public Library Digital Collections, CC BY-SA 4.0, https://creativecommons.org/licenses /by-sa/4.0/.

to afford a pastor. According to the *Providence Journal*, a prominent but unnamed member of Zion had already declared that Newport "cannot support five Episcopal churches."[16]

Yet Zion's trustees were unwilling to dissolve. In February, they considered selling their church and land to Saint Joseph's for $15,000 but then pulled back.[17] In March, they reconsidered and accepted the proposal. The congregation planned to move uptown to a site near Newport Hospital, where they were erecting Saint George's Church, a considerably smaller structure. While that church was under construction, parishioners were allowed to worship for several months in a chapel adjoining their old church on Washington Square.[18]

In March, Saint Joseph's parishioners established themselves in their new home. In Coyle's view, this was the church's third site, for he saw the parish as the successor to the original Saint Joseph's that had operated on Barney Street in the 1830s and 1840s. The parish was comprised of the 1,500 former Saint Mary's parishioners who lived on the north side of the city and of the Catholics associated with the Navy. As many as fifty apprentices from the training station would attend Mass on Sundays, and a group of them received confirmation at the parish.[19] When the bishop visited Newport, he and Coyle would board the training ships in the harbor and meet with several of the officers.[20] Coyle also tended to the Catholics of neighboring Portsmouth, a responsibility that had fallen to Dr. Grace before the parishes were split. In 1882, Grace had constructed Saint Thomas Chapel near the Portsmouth mines, and now Coyle or another priest from Saint Joseph's would offer Mass once a month to the miners and farmers of the town.[21]

As Coyle settled in, he focused on promoting causes dear to his heart, especially temperance and Irish independence. These were Dr. Grace's favorite causes as well, but the two priests made no effort to coordinate their organizations and activities. Before moving out of the Unitarian church, Coyle organized a temperance society for Saint Joseph's. He had served as an officer in the Catholic Total Abstinence Union of Providence and thus was very focused on the cause. As an Irish nationalist, he was also interested in lauding Saint Patrick and organizing festivities in his honor. No parades were staged, but at both parishes special Masses were offered on the morning of Saint Patrick's Day and lectures were delivered in the evening. The Father Mathew Total Abstinence Society marched from its building on Thames Street to Saint Mary's Hall, where attendees heard "stirring addresses appropriate to the occasion" from Grace and the assistant pastors. Meanwhile, Coyle delivered a lecture in Saint Joseph's Church and then hosted a reception at the Park House, a small hotel on Washington Square.[22]

An Episcopal Visit

Bishop Hendricken was anxious to visit Coyle's new church, but he also wanted to raise money for the Cathedral of Saints Peter and Paul, which was then under construction. The bishop had given Patrick Keely carte blanche to design what Robert Hayman says was intended to be "one of the finest churches in the Country."[23] Keely had drawn up plans for a massive Romanesque church, and the bishop had laid the cornerstone in 1878.[24] In the intervening years, he had kept his focus on paying for the cathedral.

So when Coyle asked him to delay his Newport visit until the end of the summer, the bishop readily agreed: "As to the collection—September will do equally as well—and better as my prospects are so much the more brilliant at that time. Let it be then the 6th of September. Anything later I fear would be after the Newport season."[25] As the visit approached, the *Providence Journal* reported that Coyle had "progressed so successfully that the congregation, besides aiding their own church, will be able to help the Bishop with the new Cathedral."[26]

On September 6, the bishop dedicated the church and its adjoining chapel, which was no longer being used by Zion's congregation. After Mass, he confirmed a very large class: 268 boys and girls. He also raised $900 in his appeal for the cathedral.[27] He no doubt left Saint Joseph's convinced that Coyle was doing an excellent job. A few weeks later, he wrote to the priest, commending him for his "splendid" efforts and promoting him from "administrator" to "pastor" of the parish.[28]

Honoring the Commodore

Just a few days after the bishop's visit, Newport's population swelled with dignitaries: politicians, admirals, and scholars converged on the city to celebrate one of its most famous sons, Oliver Hazard Perry. In 1865, August Belmont had commissioned a statue of his late father-in-law, Matthew Perry, which was placed in Touro Park. While Perry was well known for his exploits in Japan, he was not as famous as his older brother Oliver. Consequently, a subscription had been started to pay for a statue to be placed in Washington Square in honor of the hero of the Battle of Lake Erie.[29] Organizers decided to hold their celebration on September 10, 1885, the anniversary of Perry's 1813 naval victory and the centennial year of his birth.

The day featured learned addresses from intellectuals such as the eminent historian George Bancroft, but the highlight was the unveiling of the statue. Two of the commodore's granddaughters, Margaret LaFarge and her cousin, Frances Pepper, pulled on silk cords to remove the sheet covering the bronze statue. The crowd cheered, though few of them knew about the stress that LaFarge was then enduring. With her artist husband usually absent, she was raising nine children mostly on her own, and she was in "considerable financial straits," as her son John later noted.[30] Still, she remained involved in community activities and a variety of Catholic and Irish organizations.

Contrasting Styles: Coyle and Grace

Coyle does not appear to have attended the unveiling, though the ceremony took place directly across the street from Saint Joseph's. However, he remained busy throughout the fall and winter months, organizing and delivering lectures. In late September, he spoke on "Self-Culture" at Saint Joseph's; in October, the *Providence Journal* reported that he was visiting Providence to enlist speakers for a series of lectures to his parish's temperance society. In November, that series began with Coyle's own talk on the "trials and triumphs of the church in each successive age."[31]

Coyle spent even more of his time promoting Irish causes. In December 1885, he staged a grand event at the Opera House honoring Charles Stewart Parnell. Jailed in 1881–82 because of his Land League agitation, Parnell had emerged from prison more influential than ever. He now controlled eighty-five seats in the British House of Commons and thus the balance of power between the Liberals and the Conservatives. Worried about being taken for granted by Prime Minister Gladstone and the Liberals, he was starting to make overtures to the Conservatives.[32]

To support Parnell and his Home Rule movement, Coyle organized a fundraiser. The keynote speaker was Thomas Conaty, a charismatic priest from Worcester, Massachusetts.[33] An Irish-born nationalist, Conaty fully endorsed Parnell, and following Parnell's line, raised doubts about Prime Minister Gladstone: "They tell us we should be grateful to Gladstone— why? He granted, simply, what . . . he saw fit to grant, and these grants were sandwiched in between coercion acts!"[34]

A sizable crowd gathered to listen to Conaty's address. Coyle had also assembled many of Newport's Catholic leaders and had seated them on a platform in the front: Michael Butler, Dr. Storer, Alderman James Cottrell, and two of Saint Mary's priests. Dr. Grace was absent, but Coyle read a supportive letter from him and noted that he had contributed $20. Coyle also gave seats of honor to Stephen Slocum, a former mayor and a member of one of Newport's leading families, and George Downing, who was probably the most prominent African American businessman and community leader in Newport.[35] By the end of the evening, Coyle was happy to report that $1,000 had been raised for Parnell's Parliamentary Fund.[36]

Grace, for his part, kept a much lower profile. He did not deliver any lectures or attend many meetings at this time. However, the *Providence Journal* noted that he and the Mercy sisters had arranged a Christmas program for the children of Saint Mary's in the parish hall. While Grace could be stern and forbidding, the *Journal*'s account of the event shows that he had a fun-loving side as well. After a Christmas carol, he announced to the children that Santa was expected at any moment,

> and even while [Grace] was speaking [Santa's] footsteps were heard and he appeared, coming from the rear of the hall. His appearance was greeted with shouts of laughter and glee by the children. He advanced to the front, dressed in his accustomed suit, was greeted by Father Grace, depositing his pack upon the platform. . . . Pretty boxes of candy were handed to the older persons and guests, and then the classes came up in order and received . . . fruit, candy and other nice things.

Coyle also had a Christmas party for the children of his parish. He put up a Christmas tree in the church and distributed "gifts of toys, popcorn, candy, apples and other sweetmeats, and presents." The *Journal*'s correspondent remarked that the children would have "good cause to remember their first Christmas in their new parish."[37]

As 1886 dawned, Irish leaders in Rhode Island began to plan for Saint Patrick's Day events. No parades had been staged in Newport since 1879 because of the famine conditions in western Ireland. But now that conditions had eased for the farmers and Parnell was wielding influence in British politics, Irish Americans were ready to celebrate their patron again. In the days leading up to the holiday, the *Mercury* reported that between six hundred and seven hundred Hibernians from the Providence area were expected to join the Newport division and march in their full regalia.[38] In a follow-up story, the *Providence Journal* hailed the parade as the "finest and most general celebration of St. Patrick's Day ever seen in Newport."[39] A reporter for the *Mercury* declared it a "most imposing procession with true military bearing." The writer was pleased to note that "not a man could be seen in line who showed signs of drink and the police report it as the quietest St. Patrick's Day . . . ever known here. This is paying a high compliment to our Catholic friends and the citizens generally, when we consider what a celebration would have meant a few years ago."[40]

After parading in the afternoon, marchers and spectators had the choice of attending one of two lectures that evening. The Father Mathew Total Abstinence Society sponsored an address at Saint Mary's Hall. With Dr. Grace and an assistant pastor on the platform, the speaker, Thomas Murphy, a retired police inspector from Dublin, launched into what the *Mercury's* writer characterized as a "scathing denunciation of British rule." The bigger event was organized by Coyle and held at the Opera House. Coyle had arranged for John Boyle O'Reilly, the editor of the *Boston Pilot*, to lecture on Ireland's troubled history. O'Reilly was a former Fenian rebel who had escaped an Australian prison and come to the United States, where he had gained fame as a poet, lecturer, and journalist.[41]

As with his Parnell fundraiser, Coyle extended free invitations to prominent members of the Newport community. Mayor John Powel, Jr., and three former mayors accepted, as did George Downing. Admiral Stephen Luce sent his regrets, as did Bishop Hendricken, who was ailing. The bishop wrote, "Sorry I cannot go. I send greetings to the Parish and pray St. Patrick to bless its pastor and noble people. May poor Ireland soon welcome back her parliament to College Green."[42] O'Reilly's lecture was well received, and the *Newport Daily News* reported that the Opera House was "crowded to its utmost capacity."[43]

A few months later, Coyle would top these triumphs by bringing to Newport an even more prominent Irishman: Michael Davitt, the architect of the Irish Land League and an ally of Parnell. He had come to America in August and had been crisscrossing the nation, trying to gain support and additional funding for the Home Rule movement.[44] Davitt lectured at the Opera House in December. The *Mercury's* writer noted that Coyle and the local Land League organizers had wanted all of the city's Irish societies to march and had planned a fireworks show before the lecture, but a snowstorm canceled those events. Still, Davitt was able to deliver a "thrilling discourse" on Home Rule's prospects to a packed house that included Councilman Boyle, Alderman Cottrell, two ex-mayors of Newport, George Downing, and an African American minister, Reverend Henry Jeter, the longtime pastor of Shiloh Baptist Church.[45]

Meanwhile, in the spring of 1886, Bishop Hendricken set out on another fundraising tour of his parishes. He had long been ill, suffering so severely from asthma and other chronic respiratory ailments that he had not been able to get a full night's sleep for four years.[46] Then, in May, he came down with a cold that he could not shake, and he died in June at age fifty-nine. Hendricken's funeral was the first Mass celebrated in the still unfinished cathedral.[47] Archbishop John Williams of Boston was the celebrant, and Bishop O'Reilly of Springfield was the homilist. According to the *Boston Globe*, the sanctuary was draped in black, and two hundred priests and 4,000 laypersons were present.[48] The *Newport Mercury* mourned that the Catholic church had lost "one of its most faithful and untiring laborers, and one who was greatly beloved by his people."[49] Hendricken's unexpected death meant that the diocese would have to wait for the Vatican to appoint a successor. In the meantime, Father Michael McCabe, the vicar general of the diocese, served as the administrator.

Prohibition and Suffrage Revisited

In the summer of 1886, Prohibition went into effect in Rhode Island for the second time. In 1851, the state had followed Maine's example in outlawing alcohol but had repealed the law during the Civil War. By the 1880s, however, with lobbies such as the Women's Christian Temperance Union gaining strength, states were once again banning or restricting the sale of alcohol. As soon as the new Rhode Island law went into effect, the *New York Times* pointed out its ill effects on Newport hotels and clubs such as the Casino:

> There is no disguising the fact that the prohibitory law is working to the injury of Newport as a Summer resort. . . . The moral tone of the local portion of the community has improved wonderfully, but this reform will not compensate the Casino Governors, hotel keepers, and others for the losses they are sustaining. Facts are stubborn things, and figures, in this case, can't lie. The losses will increase as the season advances.[50]

The *Newport Mercury* was much more positive: "[T]he disappearance of drunkenness from our streets has been very marked. People have gone home to their families sober that have not done so before for many a long day." The writer declared that there was "little, if any drunkenness"

FIGURE 17. Portrait of George Downing, c. 1885. Downing was a leading advocate for African American civil rights and immigrant voting rights. Reprinted courtesy of the Photographs and Prints Division, Schomburg Center for Research in Black Culture, New York Public Library.

during the Fourth of July celebrations.[51] The *Mercury* was not alone in expressing enthusiasm for the measure. In March, before the law went into effect, the Newport County Prohibition Union hosted John St. John, the former governor of Kansas and an 1884 Prohibition Party presidential candidate, at the Opera House. St. John was then one of the best-known prohibitionists in the nation.[52] With him on the platform were a number of Protestant ministers, including Mahlon Van Horne, the most prominent African American clergyman in the city.[53] While no priests were on hand to welcome St. John, Catholic dignitaries such as Dr. Storer, Michael Butler, and Councilman Patrick Boyle were there to greet him.[54]

Although the Newport priests had absented themselves from that event, they were willing to back the semi-prohibitionist Law and Order League, which supported the enforcement of state liquor laws, whether that entailed the complete prohibition of alcohol or the closing of bars on Sundays. In February 1886, Coyle and Father Thomas Doran of Saint Mary's attended the group's annual meeting, and Coyle "made a powerful plea for the enforcement of the laws."[55] Doran was a vice-president of the league, and Dr. Grace was also an active member.[56]

Nonetheless, most of Newport's Catholics, even those involved in temperance activities, probably did not support Prohibition.[57] Two months after its enactment, the *Providence Journal* noted that many Newporters were violating the liquor laws and that the police were cracking down in response. The *Journal* printed the names of numerous people who had been arrested for keeping or selling alcohol, and many had Irish names: John Nolan, John MacMahon, Patrick Burke, Mary Murray, Thomas Murphy, Edward Shields, Catharine Dugan, Bernard McGowan, and others.[58] Police raids were not popular, and they probably contributed to the quick demise of the law. By 1888, the state's constitutional amendment enacting Prohibition had been repealed, and Rhode Island left the decision about licensing or outlawing bars to individual cities and towns.[59]

Though Catholics were generally skeptical about efforts to ban alcohol, they were much more enthusiastic about gaining voting rights for immigrants. For twenty years, suffrage advocates had repeatedly attempted to end the $134 property requirement for foreign-born Rhode Islanders. In 1871, Assemblyman Charles Gorman had brought before the Rhode Island voters a proposed constitutional amendment, but it had failed by a wide margin. Five years later, he took a different tack, bringing forward an amendment to exempt foreign-born army and navy veterans. This came close to passing. Finally, in April 1886, Gorman at last succeeded in obtaining the vote for landless immigrant veterans.[60] Encouraged by the victory, he and his allies planned to hold an Equal Rights Convention in Newport in July. In the days leading up to the meeting, associations in various cities met and selected delegates. In Providence, Gorman and five other men were chosen. In Newport, supporters met at the Colony House to pick their slate. Michael Butler presided over the meeting and was selected as a delegate, along with James Cottrell and George Downing.[61]

When the delegates assembled in Newport, Downing was chosen as chairman.[62] He was a well-known advocate of suffrage for both African Americans and women and had also led a successful campaign to integrate Rhode Island's public schools in the 1850s and 1860s.[63] Most of the other representatives were Irish, though there were also French Canadian delegates from Central Falls and a few Germans from Providence. In his keynote address, Gorman asked the delegates to consider forming a third party, given that neither Democrats nor Republicans were supportive of their goals.[64] In the end, however, they did not have to take such a step. With the Bourn Amendment of 1888, both major parties moved to drop the property qualification, and the Rhode Island voters agreed. Yet the historian Patrick Conley argues that the legislation was not a full-fledged victory for the Irish. Many of the Republicans had long opposed suffrage for immigrants because they wanted to keep Irish power in check. They now went along with the change because they thought that French Canadian and Italian immigrants might join their party.[65] Whatever the legislators' motives, suffrage reform enabled the Irish to gain more political influence in the years to come.

Coyle's Troubles with Nuns

In August 1886, a small notice appeared in the *Newport Journal* announcing that a community of French Canadian nuns, the Religious of Jesu-Marie (RJM), had purchased Eagle Crest, a four-acre estate on Miantonomi Hill that had belonged to Rowland Hazard.[66] The sisters were hoping to establish an academy for girls on the site. The writer noted that Dr. Storer had served as the sisters' agent and that the late Bishop Hendricken had approved of the initiative. For the sisters, coming to Newport made perfect sense. Since 1877, they had been teaching at a parish in Fall River, Massachusetts, and, in 1884, had begun staffing a parochial school in Woonsocket, Rhode Island.[67] They were hoping to establish a more selective institution and believed that Newport would have a sufficient population of affluent families, both Catholic and non-Catholic, who would be interested in supporting it.

Nonetheless, Father Coyle was incensed that the sisters had decided to establish themselves in his parish without consulting him. He had already been planning to establish a girls' high school and did not want to compete with the sisters' academy. Moreover, he had reason to be wary of these particular nuns. The Fall River parish of Notre Dame, where the RJM sisters had been teaching, was the site of a bitter feud between Hendricken and a group of nationalist-minded parishioners. In 1884, after the parish's

French Canadian pastor had died, Bishop Hendricken had replaced him with an Irish American priest who had studied in Montreal and was fluent in French. Unsatisfied with the appointment, dissident parishioners protested, disrupting Masses and clamoring for a French Canadian priest. In 1885, Hendricken decided to shut down the parish as the dissidents appealed to Rome.[68] Although the sisters had probably played no part in the conflict, Coyle may have associated them with the troublemakers.

To assuage Coyle, a group of the sisters visited him, and their superior, Mother Marie St. Paul, sent him a conciliatory letter. Rather than setting up a school immediately, she asked Coyle for "permission to give a few private lessons in music, painting and the languages." She concluded, "I cannot say how grieved we were at the mistake [of not informing you] and we could not help expressing our surprise and still more our sorrow at the evident displeasure the whole affair gave you; we trust most earnestly and hope that your kind heart will lead you to forgive and forget."[69]

Coyle's response was terse and unencouraging. He told her that he had consulted with several bishops on the subject and that they were "unanimous in terming the affair an 'unparalleled outrage.' They deem this the first case on record where the Pastor had not a voice in the selection of the religious community desiring to settle in his parish."[70] He admitted, however, that the decision was not his but the bishop's, and for the moment the diocese did not have one. Thus, Coyle and the sisters would have to wait until Rome appointed a new bishop.

Several months passed before Father Matthew Harkins was appointed as Hendricken's successor. A Boston native, Harkins was pastor of the largest parish in the archdiocese and one of Archbishop Williams's most trusted advisors.[71] He was consecrated in April 1887 in the new cathedral in Providence. Just two days later, an R.J.M. sister, Mother Marie St. Cyrille, wrote to him in French, asking to meet with him about Eagle Crest.[72] Coyle had already written to Harkins, laying out his argument that the sisters' academy would compete with his own new school.[73] Harkins soon met with Mother St. Cyrille and told her that, because the diocese already had two academies for girls—Bayview, run by the Mercy sisters, and Elmhurst, run by the Madames of the Sacred Heart—"which supplied all present demands (and oversupplied them)," there was no need for another one.[74]

After learning of the bishop's decision, Dr. Storer sent him a long emotional letter offering a frank appraisal of both Coyle and the RJM issue.

Storer acknowledged Coyle's many positive qualities: his "eloquence, untiring labor . . . [and] self sacrifice," for which he was "admired and beloved. . . . That he is succeeding admirably in constructing a typical 'Irish' parish, is acknowledged by everyone." Yet Newport prided itself on being a cosmopolitan city, and Storer believed:

> [The] presence of these French ladies in the parish would have been of assistance to Fr. Coyle, in bringing him into contact with persons, the parents of children from outside Newport, who could materially aid him in his projects, and whom he would be certain otherwise not to reach. There are those within St. Joseph's parish, influential persons, the Misses Caldwell of the Catholic University for instance, who from dislike of his intense race partisanship or other similar reasons, no longer attend St. Joseph's at all, but have returned to St. Mary's.[75]

Among the sisters, the bishop's decision had been "looked for with anxiety, as definitive of your policy regarding the intensely interesting question of race. . . . The anti-French party will of course be delighted, especially as the victims are those very Fall River Sisters whom they have, as I think wrongly, confounded with the participants in the late ecclesiastical imbroglio." Storer concluded dolefully, "I am now meeting the Real Estate agent, and endeavoring to dispose of their very beautiful estate for the Sisters, at their request. To these experts it seems incomprehensible that this property . . . should now be so quickly relinquished."[76]

Storer did try to sell the estate but found no takers.[77] So, in March 1888, two of the R.J.M. sisters visited Bishop Harkins, who promised them that he would buy the property. In April, he toured Eagle Crest and, in May, purchased it for $15,000, the exact price that the sisters had paid.[78] For several years Eagle Crest mostly sat empty as the Diocese tried to find a use for it.[79] Meanwhile, the R.J.M. sisters would go on to establish well-regarded academies in Fall River and Woonsocket, and Storer continued to work to diversify what he saw as the provincial Irishness of the Catholic church in Newport.[80]

In the midst of Coyle's battle with the R.J.M. sisters, he received a note in November 1886 from Sister M. Thomasine O'Keefe of the Sisters of

Mercy informing him that the two Mercy sisters who had been teaching Sunday school for Saint Joseph's would no longer be available: "Doctor Grace says he needs the Sisters for St. Mary's Sunday School and cannot spare them any longer for St. Joseph's. Therefore they will not be with you on Sunday or hereafter."[81] In a letter to the bishop, Storer said that the sisters "were suddenly withdrawn . . . just as they were commencing to deck the Christmas trees."[82] As soon as Coyle heard the news, he contacted his friend Bishop O'Reilly of Springfield to ask that a group of Sisters of Saint Joseph be sent to his parish. The bishop assured Coyle that his application would "be attended to."[83] However, almost three years would elapse before the sisters would arrive to teach in Newport.

New Rectories

Now that the Sisters of Mercy had a new convent, Dr. Grace decided to construct a new rectory on William Street for himself and the two other priests of the parish. For the design, he again commissioned Dudley Newton, the convent's architect. In early 1887, a *Providence Journal* correspondent described the residence as "magnificent," writing that the "four [buildings: church, convent, school, and rectory] together give St. Mary's parish an equipment in the way of church property such as is possessed by few of this denomination or of any other."[84] Noting that Grace was "not in the best of health," the *reporter* gave him high praise for the project, which had been fully paid for, leaving the parish "still free from debt."[85] In his 1889 encyclopedic history of Newport, Richard Bayles declared, "This last and crowning glory renders St. Mary's parish complete in every particular."[86]

As the Saint Mary's priests were preparing to move into their new rectory, Coyle, too, decided to build a residence for himself and his assistant pastor, Father William Simmons, a well-educated Episcopalian convert.[87] The plan was to raze the old Zion chapel adjacent to the church and build a rectory on the site. Coyle entrusted the project to John Dixon Johnston, a well-regarded local architect who had helped Newton design Saint Mary's Convent. By October, the house was complete. Two and a half stories high, the rectory was linked by a passageway to the church and had a "handsome, ecclesiastical" appearance. When the priests moved in,

Coyle held an open house, welcoming more than 1,500 visitors of various religions into his new home.[88]

A Common Burial Ground

At the end of 1880s, Grace and Coyle at last joined together on a project: they would collaborate on Saint Columba's, a new cemetery for both parishes. A new burial ground was necessary. Saint Mary's Cemetery had opened in 1855, and Grace had expanded it in 1874, but it was now nearly out of room.[89] In 1888, Bishop Harkins came to Newport to look at a possible site for the new cemetery but was not impressed.[90] Then, in January 1889, the bishop and the two pastors decided to purchase a forty-acre tract in Middletown, situated close to the Old Colony railroad line and thus easily accessed. The property had previously served as a fairground for the Aquidneck Agricultural Society. In July, the bishop met with Thomas Galvin to discuss the cemetery's layout.[91] They decided to have Galvin put in pathways, divide the lands into plats for the graves, and establish a large mound in the center of the property, topped with a cross.

In October 1889, Harkins returned to Middletown to consecrate the land. He was accompanied by thirty altar boys from both parishes and several priests, including Grace and Coyle, who flanked him. The *Providence Journal*'s reporter estimated that about 1,500 people from Newport, Middletown, and Portsmouth observed the ceremonies. The procession slowly wound its way from a farmhouse on the property to the hill with the cross. There, candles were lit, and the bishop sprinkled holy water and chanted the prayers of consecration. Before departing, he gave a brief sermon, declaring that this land was "now holy ground, God's field, your portion of God's acre. I trust you will ever love and cherish it as such." He ended with a tribute to the island's two pastors: "My learned brother and honored counsellor, who has been for so many years with you, and my younger brother, who is so zealous as to rival the most active in the diocese, will have its charge."[92]

Saint Joseph's Schools

Coyle had been very busy in his first two years at Saint Joseph's. He had moved from the Mill Street meetinghouse to the Zion Episcopal Church, had remodeled it, and had built a new rectory. He did not have a school, however, and this was a pressing concern, especially in light of the Third Plenary Council, the bishops' 1884 meeting in Baltimore. The council had largely focused on Catholic education. The bishops called for a new primer on Catholic doctrine for young people—*The Baltimore Catechism*—and stressed the importance of Catholic schools. Fearing that America's public schools were becoming agents of secularism, the bishops directed all pastors to establish Catholic schools in their parishes and all Catholic parents to send their children to parochial schools.[93]

Before he could establish a school, Coyle needed a residence for the Sisters of Saint Joseph, whom he wanted to bring from Springfield. In January 1887, he purchased the Young estate on Washington Square for $28,500, almost double what he had spent for Zion Episcopal.[94] This building was located close to the church, and apparently Coyle thought it would be suitable for the sisters' convent and school. However, it was old, dating back to colonial times, and he or the sisters may have developed reservations about it. In 1888, he turned his thoughts to Eagle Crest. He began making repairs to the property and discussed with the bishop the possibility of letting the Sisters of Saint Joseph purchase it. Harkins was willing to let them live there but refused to let them run a school on the premises.[95] So Coyle turned again to the Young estate and worked to make it habitable for the sisters.

At the beginning of July 1889, Sister Mary Rose and three other Sisters of Saint Joseph moved into the Young property and prepared to open an academy for girls to study "modern languages, mathematics, music, painting, needlework."[96] One hundred students enrolled and began taking classes in September.[97] But to establish a grammar school, Coyle needed to erect a new schoolhouse and, in light of the parish's debts, was in search of a donor to help cover costs.

By 1891, Coyle had gained the funding he needed from an unlikely source: George B. Hazard, a wealthy, elderly Protestant who was well known for his litigious and quarrelsome ways. In July, the *Mercury* reported that the three-story brick building, designed by Johnston in the Gothic style and constructed by Michael McCormick, was complete. The writer called it "by far the finest one of a public nature in Newport," describing its eight classrooms and a spacious meeting hall on the top floor.[98] The *Newport Daily News* was similarly excited about its upcoming dedication.[99]

In the beginning of August, elaborate ceremonies were held to dedicate the building. Bishop John Keane, rector of the newly established Catholic University of America, came up from Washington, D.C., to deliver the keynote address. A leader of the Americanist wing of the hierarchy, Keane championed all things American and wanted Catholic immigrants to learn English and assimilate as soon as they were able.[100] He was no stranger to Rhode Island. He had come to Providence in 1889 to take part in the dedication of the Cathedral of Saints Peter and Paul, and he had stayed with Bishop Harkins on other occasions to raise funds for Catholic University.[101] He also knew the Caldwell sisters well. Young heiresses from Kentucky, they spent each summer in Newport, and the older, Gwendolyn, had given $300,000 in 1884 to help establish the university.[102] In Newport, the sisters had just completed a major building project of their own. Johnston had expanded their cottage on Kay Street, and John LaFarge was making stained-glass windows for its new chapel and music room.[103]

At the school's dedication, Father Coyle introduced Bishop Keane, who then delivered an hour-long discourse outlining a core theme of the Americanists: that parochial schools helped to form good American citizens. Afterward, Bishop Harkins rose to speak. He informed his listeners that the entire cost of the building—$50,000—had been covered by Hazard; consequently, it would be named Hazard Memorial School rather than Saint Joseph's. Hazard had also donated funds to pay for all of the students' textbooks.[104] The donor's one request was that the school be open to Protestant as well as Catholic children, and Harkins and Coyle had readily agreed. According to the *Mercury*'s reporter, audience members were shocked to learn the identity of their benefactor: "[T]o say that it was received with surprise does not begin to express the feelings of the listeners."[105] A *New York Times* correspondent wrote that Harkins's announcement "created great surprise," while the *Providence Journal*'s reporter declared it "the talk of the town."[106] A year later, a *Times* reporter explained why Newporters had been so surprised: "Up until a year ago [Hazard] was looked upon as an avaricious money grabber of very eccentric mind, always in hot water with the owners of land adjoining his properties and several times he has been brought up in police court for assault and on other charges."[107] The *Journal* corroborated this claim six months later, when it reported that Hazard had been ordered to spend a week in the Newport County Jail over a property dispute with a neighbor, William Swinburne. The correspondent wrote, "[T]his is not the first time . . . [Hazard] has been a temporary inmate of the institution under similar circumstances, and he has also spent time in state Prison, having been convicted of an assault with a dangerous weapon."[108]

Despite these controversies and legal problems, Coyle remained friendly with Hazard. To mark the successful end of the school's first year, the priest assembled, in June 1892, a group of local notables including C. C. Churchill, a retired army captain; former mayor Thomas Coggeshall; and Richard Bliss, the librarian of the Redwood and a scholarly Catholic convert.[109] He also seated Hazard on the platform and invited him to address the students. After Hazard offered some words of encouragement, Father Mortimer Downing, the assistant pastor, read a statement from Hazard declaring that he had become a Catholic and was intent on building a new stone church for the people of Saint Joseph's.[110] However, he died the next year at the age of eighty-four. Though he had been married and widowed three times, he left only small sums to his surviving relatives. He made Father Coyle the executor of his estate and bequeathed the bulk of it—valued at $150,000 or more—to Saint Joseph's.[111]

The Return of the Know Nothings and Catholics' Rising Influence

In the spring of 1893, the nation fell into another economic depression. Like the Panic of 1873, this crisis was tied to the railroads: investors had poured money into new lines that were not proving at all profitable. Yet despite ominous signs, Newport's leaders were exuding confidence. As summer approached, they predicted a banner season for the city. According to the *New York Times*, hotelkeepers were hoping that foreign visitors to the World's Fair in Chicago might stop in Newport on the way.[112] By July, it was clear that those hopes had been realized. A *Times* correspondent listed a number of fair attendees from England, France, and Germany who were now staying at the Ocean House on Bellevue Avenue.[113] Even in September, Newport's summer season was still going strong. Visitors were enjoying the horse show at the Casino or trying to master the city's newest sports craze, golf, led by the sugar magnate Theodore Havemeyer, who established the Newport Country Club on Ocean Drive and would become the first president of the United States Golf Association in 1894.[114] Havemeyer's Austrian-born wife, Emily, was active in Saint Mary's church and was a generous supporter of it.[115]

Construction in Newport continued at a brisk pace. Richard Morris Hunt was designing palace-cottages by this time—much larger and more costly than the buildings he had worked on in the early 1880s.[116] In 1892, he completed Ochre Court, a massive French Gothic mansion commissioned by Ogden Goelet, and Marble House, a multimillion-dollar birthday present from William K. Vanderbilt to his wife, Alva.[117] In 1893, Hunt took on a still grander project for Vanderbilt's older brother, Cornelius II: the Breakers. After a fire in November 1892 destroyed the original house, Vanderbilt asked the architect to design a stone replacement. Hunt drew up plans for a seventy-room Italian Renaissance mansion made of limestone. Construction began in the spring of 1893 and took two and a half years to complete.[118]

Less glamorous constructions were also underway. In 1894, the state legislature allocated funds for an armory and awarded Michael McCormick the contract. He spent six months constructing a formidable two-towered stone structure on Thames Street.[119] He also upgraded the sewers at Fort Adams, and another Irish American contractor, Jeremiah K. Sullivan, provided the fort with large quantities of sand and stone.[120]

Still, even though Newport was largely unscathed by the economic downturn, it was not spared the nativism associated with the depression. The American Protective Association (APA), a secret society founded in Iowa in 1887, established new chapters in much of the Midwest and New England during these years.[121] Staunchly anti-Catholic, the association's leaders warned members that Pope Leo XIII was trying to organize an uprising in America. They called for a boycott of Catholic-owned stores and urged supporters not to hire Catholics under any circumstances.

The *Providence Journal* took note of this "peculiar organization" in November 1893, arguing that it had much in common with the Know

Nothings of the 1850s. The reporter wrote, "[T]he A.P.A. is a name which has just got into the mouths of men here in Providence" and pointed out its rapid national growth: already it had as many as 1 million members.[122] Interest in Rhode Island advanced quickly. A few days after this article was published, a Baptist minister running for the Providence School Committee promised that he would seek to bar all Catholics from teaching in the city's public schools. In response, Bishop Harkins urged diocesan priests to run for public school committees to counter the APA's influence. Father Simmons, the former assistant pastor at Saint Joseph's, would be the first diocesan priest elected to the Providence Public School Board.[123]

The APA had a higher profile in Providence than it did in traditionally tolerant Newport, but there were some expressions of support in the town. In December 1893, Father Coyle, angered by an encounter with a drunken APA member, took aim at the group in a Sunday sermon. He urged his parishioners to shun any stores operated by APA sympathizers and named those whom he thought were partisans of the movement. Dr. Grace also denounced the association that December.[124]

The rumored papal plots never materialized, and in the months following, the APA's influence faded throughout the country.[125] According to Patrick Conley, its membership peaked at 2,700 in Rhode Island, far below its levels in Massachusetts.[126] Meanwhile, Rhode Island Catholics grew increasingly powerful, electing several mayors and state officials.[127]

In Newport, Catholics obtained seats on various town boards. In 1893, Dr. Peter Curley won a position on the school committee, Patrick Boyle was elected to the Board of Aldermen for the Fifth Ward and Michael McCormick and four other Irish Americans were among fifteen common council representatives.[128] Curley, a popular physician, would serve on the school committee until his death from kidney disease in 1900. Only thirty-nine years old, he was universally mourned. The *Mercury* described his loss as "a great blow to the people of Newport."[129] On the day of the funeral, all of the town's public schools lowered their flags to half-mast.[130]

Patrick Boyle was even more prominent. After graduating from Saint Mary's Academy, he took a job with the Newport Gas Company and soon got involved in the Democratic Party. Elected to the Common Council in 1886 when he was only in his mid-twenties, he rose to become alderman for the Fifth Ward in 1891. In 1894, he and his family moved to Mary Street in

FIGURE 18. Portrait of Patrick Boyle, c. 1900. Boyle was Newport's first Irish mayor. He took office in 1895 and served sixteen one-year terms. Reprinted courtesy of the Museum of Newport Irish History.

the Third Ward and lost his bid to represent that district. Then, in 1895, Boyle saw an opportunity when the newly elected Democratic mayor, John Waters, died in office and two Republicans vied to replace him. Unlike most of Rhode Island, which was Republican-dominated, Newport had been fairly evenly divided since the Civil War.[131] According to the *New York Times*, the Republicans were "hopelessly split" in the race, enabling the Democrat Boyle to win and become Newport's first Irish Catholic mayor in 1895.[132] He would go on to serve sixteen one-year terms over the next twenty-eight years and would be known for his ability to work with all constituencies in Newport, especially the summer colonists.[133]

Parish Developments

For twenty years, Dr. Grace had been sprucing up Saint Mary's Church. In the spring of 1893, the *Mercury* noted that he had "been quietly at work," adding an attractive set of stained-glass windows from Austria depicting Old Testament scenes.[134] In the summer, he hosted Cardinal James Gibbons for a day, after the cardinal sailed down from Providence in the company of Bishop Harkins. Gibbons, the Irish-born archbishop of Baltimore, had traveled to Providence a few days earlier to lay the cornerstone for Saint Joseph's Hospital.[135]

Grace received considerable press attention for escorting the cardinal around Newport, but usually he kept a very low profile.[136] He had his regular routines—his walks around the city, his visits to the church when the Angelus bell rang—but his energy was flagging. Since 1888, he had needed two priests to assist him in the running of the parish.[137] Some of his parishioners were so worried about him that they worked to send him on another tour of Europe, in hopes that it would be restorative. In March 1894, a Fall River newspaper reported that "Dr. Grace . . . will, if his health permits, take a trip to Europe this spring, and . . . will be accompanied by his brother, Rev. Thomas Grace of Providence, and his sister [Mary Grace Denniston]. The trip, if it is made, will be for the benefit of Dr. Grace's health."[138]

Dr. Grace and his siblings spent three months in Europe, visiting Ireland, Italy and several other countries. When he returned to Newport, his assistant pastors and parishioners were waiting when his ship docked. The Newport Band played and fireworks lit up the sky as the Hibernians and the Father Mathew men escorted him back to Saint Mary's.[139] The *Mercury* reporter wrote that "hundreds of Dr. Grace's friends availed themselves of the opportunity to congratulate him on his safe return and his improved health."[140]

Immediately, Saint Mary's parishioners began planning another celebration in his honor: his Silver Jubilee as pastor. On the first Sunday of September, they embarked on an elaborate ceremony to mark Grace's twenty-five years in the parish. Father Thomas Doran, the diocesan vicar general, attended, and soloists from New York, Boston, and Providence joined the parish choir for the Masses. The women of the parish, led by Emily Havemeyer, presented Grace with several gifts, including a new set of vestments and a golden chalice.[141] In his sermon, he fondly recalled the many parishioners who had helped him when he had first arrived at the church. He somberly noted that most had passed away and wondered if his turn were coming soon.[142]

While Grace was slowing down, Coyle was a whirlwind of activity. A sought-after speaker, he preached and lectured throughout the Northeast. In 1893, he spoke at the Newport Academy of Music on behalf of Saint Joseph's Hospital and a few months later was in Montreal presenting a bust to the archbishop who had ordained him.[143] In 1894, he was the homilist at the Mass marking the fifth anniversary of the consecration of the Providence cathedral. In 1895, he delivered a Saint Patrick's Day lecture at the Newport Opera House and, in July, was in Plattsburgh, New York, preaching at the Sunday Masses for Catholic Summer School attendees.[144] In 1896, he lectured at a parish in Brooklyn on Saint Patrick's Day, preached at the dedication of a new church in Fall River, and traveled to Springfield to preach to the new class of novices of the Sisters of Saint Joseph.[145]

Despite his travels, Coyle remained deeply involved in the workings of his parish and school. He supported the Saint Joseph Total Abstinence Society and its cadet branch for young people. He and his assistant pastor maintained their responsibility for the boys at the naval training station and for Saint Thomas Chapel in Portsmouth. When the little chapel was blown over in a storm in 1889, Coyle erected a replacement and called it Saint Clement's. The chapel now served more than the miners; it also drew an increasing number of Portuguese immigrants, most of them from the Azores.[146] Coyle occasionally sponsored events for the Portuguese community at Saint Joseph's as well. For example, in May 1896, he organized a mission and invited Father Manuel Terra to preach for two nights in Portuguese. Terra, who was Portuguese American, was then running a Portuguese parish on Cape Cod.[147]

Above all, Coyle worked to eliminate the parish's debt. Each January, he would issue a detailed report outlining the funds received and the monies spent in the prior calendar year. From the reports, it is clear that he received help from wealthy summer colonists and well-off year-round residents. One of Coyle's most generous supporters was Joseph Banigan, an Irish-born businessman who had amassed a fortune in Providence as the president of the United States Rubber Company.[148] In 1894–95, Banigan made a $200 donation, while Thomas Galvin gave $25. Mrs. Isaac Bell, Jr., who was James Gordon Bennett's sister, presented Coyle with ornate vestments from Spain; and the Caldwell sisters were said by a *New York Times* correspondent to be "warm supporters" of Saint Joseph's.[149] Still, Coyle could not draw on many of the summer visitors as most of them worshiped at Saint Mary's. The bulk of his parishioners lived in Kerry Hill. In his annual reports, Coyle listed dozens of "Young Lady Contributors"—servants—who had responded to the appeal. Some, like Katie Burke of Cranston Avenue, could only donate $1; others, like Lizzie Gill of Ayrault Street, gave $10. In his 1895 report, Coyle noted that these women together gave $471 out of the $4,500 that the parish raised in its collection.[150] He was pleased to report that, over ten years, the parish had raised $156,000 and had finally cleared all of its debts. He also stressed that "a portion of the great success has been due to people of other faiths, who have frequently rendered kind support."[151]

"Fashionable Dames . . . of the Roman Church"

While many maids and cooks contributed what they could to Saint Joseph's appeals, a much smaller group of affluent Catholic women were also active in supporting the church and serving the poor.[152] In 1894, the Notre Dame Society was established to provide clothing to the needy. Its leaders were Margaret LaFarge; Sarah Bliss, whose husband, Richard, was the director of the Redwood Library; Agnes Storer, the daughter of Dr. Horatio Storer; and Marion Cutting, the widow of Brockholst Cutting, a businessman from New York City.[153] Members sewed clothes and then donated them to the Mercy sisters at Saint Mary's or to the Charity Organization Society.[154] The latter association was comprised mostly of Protestants who sought to improve the lives of the "deserving poor" without creating a spirit of dependency among them.[155]

Annie Leary, an heiress from New York City, was also very involved in charitable works. The daughter of an Irish immigrant who had made a fortune as a haberdasher, she stayed at an imposing brick house on Mill Street, fronting Touro Park.[156] From there, Leary ran a summer sewing class, and she and her coworkers donated the clothes they made.[157]

Another initiative was Saint Anthony's Bread, established in 1896 by Marion Cutting in memory of her son F. Brockholst Cutting, who died that year at the age of thirty-five.[158] Cutting gave $3,000 to Dr. Grace and directed him to distribute it as he saw fit to any person in need, without regard to religion, race, creed, or color. Each year she and her surviving son, William, sent additional contributions to augment the fund.[159]

The Loss of Newport's "Chieftains"

In August 1896, Father Edward Sheridan, the pastor of Saint Mary's in Taunton, Massachusetts, died after serving there for twenty-five years. In September, reports appeared in the press that Father Coyle would be replacing him, and at the end of the month the bishop informed Coyle of his transfer and commended him for his service: "The zeal, energy and prudence which have characterized your almost twelve years' pastorate in Newport, have made me desirous for some time to entrust to you a larger and more important field of labor."[160] The *Newport Mercury* praised Coyle just as effusively: "[He] has endeared himself not only to the members of his church but to the citizens generally and the regret at losing him is universal. He is a good citizen and has done much during his residence here to promote good citizenship; what he has accomplished for his parish is too well known to require any reference here."[161]

Replacing Coyle at Saint Joseph's was Father Louis Deady, who had been in the same ordination class in Montreal in 1877. Like Coyle, he had been born in Ireland and had come to the United States at a young age. Soon after arriving in Newport, Deady toured the Hazard School and was impressed by it.[162] The church was another story, however. In January 1897, he announced that the existing building was no longer big enough to accommodate the parish; he planned to build a new church. To accomplish this task, he would take up quarterly collections.[163] Exactly a year later, Deady told his congregants that the parish was purchasing the Kimber estate on Broadway for $17,500. The parish would pay for the property in installments over two years and then start building. Once the new church was completed, the present church would be converted into a parish hall for meetings.[164]

Newport was busy in the spring and summer of 1898. A *New York Times* correspondent reported that many people were excited to try golf: "[T]he craze for the game is greater than ever."[165] He also claimed that the Spanish-American War, which had started in April, was benefiting the city because fewer people were choosing to travel to Europe in the

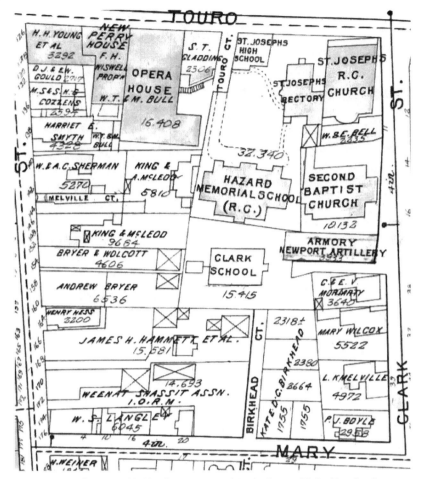

FIGURE 19. Map of Saint Joseph's Church, its rectory, and its schools, 1907. The buildings lined Washington Square in Newport's downtown. Hazard Memorial, the parish elementary school, was set back from the square. Mayor Patrick Boyle's home is visible in the lower right at the corner of Mary and Clarke Streets. Reprinted from *Atlas of the City of Newport* (Springfield, MA, 1907), plate 3.

midst of the conflict.[166] Yet, in September, as the season was drawing to a close, tragedy struck. According to the *Times*, "By 2:45 [p.m.] the most fashionable street in Newport was filled with puffing engines and a tremendous crowd of cottagers and other citizens. The fire spread with wonderful rapidity so that one hour after it was discovered every portion of the [Ocean House] hotel was in flames." The reporter mourned, "[O]ne of the largest and best known hotels on the Atlantic Coast" was gone.[167] Its destruction marked the end of the hotel era in Newport. Though they had already been fading in popularity as the cottages were multiplying, the Ocean House fire was their death blow.[168]

Two weeks later, Newport's residents were jarred by another tragedy. Dr. Grace, who, at the urging of his parishioners, had taken yet another trip to Europe in the spring of 1898, fell in New York City shortly after his return.[169] He could not recover from his injuries, and he died in late September. Grace was sixty years old and had spent twenty-nine years as pastor of Saint Mary's. Newspapers from Boston to New York announced his death. The *Providence Journal* praised the Irish-born priest as a "thorough American [promoter] . . . of positive Christian charity."[170] According to the *Newport Mercury*, he was "deeply imbued in the hearts of the residents of the city. Rich and poor, high and lowly learned to love him with equal love and trustfulness. His tender care and touching sympathy for those ailing in mind or body showed the great heart that beat beneath a somewhat austere exterior."[171] The *Journal*'s reporter predicted that the funeral would "most likely . . . be without parallel in the diocese."[172]

The correspondent was right. On the day of the funeral, parishioners crowded into Saint Mary's two hours early to get seats. Bishop Harkins presided over the Mass and was assisted by two other bishops and ninety-seven priests, including the vicar general of the diocese, Father Doran, who preached the sermon. After the two-hour ceremony, a long procession slowly wound its way to Saint Mary's Cemetery, passing many storefronts that were shuttered out of respect for Grace. Many parish organizations were represented, including the Hibernians, the Father Mathew Total Abstinence Society and the Knights of Columbus, a chapter of which had been established in Newport in the prior year.[173] The *Boston Globe* judged the funeral "one of the most memorable events in the history of Newport, the city witnessing a great outpouring of people of all classes and creeds."[174]

With Grace's death, both of Catholic Newport's chieftains had vanished from the scene. While Coyle and Grace had often been at odds with each other, they were able to accomplish a great deal for their respective parishes and contributed much to the wider Newport community. Father Deady and Grace's successor would be well positioned to build on their predecessors' accomplishments.

Chapter 9

"A TIME TO BUILD UP"

*Catholic Expansion during the Waning Days of
Newport's Gilded Age*

The golden jubilee of St. Mary's parish was successfully observed
yesterday by priests and people assisted by a very distinguished
gathering of the high dignitaries of the church. . . . Each of the
three entrances of the edifice was draped with the Papal colors,
yellow and white; over the north and south doors was the Papal
coat of arms . . . and from the belfry floated the American flag.

—*Newport Daily News,* August 18, 1902

Newport remained an extremely popular summer destination until
World War I.[1] A few Catholics, such as Tessie Oelrichs and Emily
Havemeyer, were leaders among the summer colonists and staged fabulously expensive parties for their stylish friends. Other wealthy Catholics,
including Agnes Storer and Marion Cutting, focused on charitable activities and worked to bring two more communities of nuns, the Religious
of the Cenacle and the Daughters of the Holy Ghost, to Newport. The
Sisters of Mercy also increased their presence, establishing an orphanage
called the Mercy Home and School in 1915. With the city's population
now exceeding 25,000, its two Catholic parishes needed to expand as
well.[2] Saint Joseph's moved from Washington Square to Broadway, and
its pastor laid out plans for a grand new church. Saint Mary's had to be
split again, and Saint Augustin's Church in the heavily Irish Fifth Ward
was established in 1911, with an accompanying school the following year.
However, little effort was made to accommodate Italian and Portuguese
Catholics, whose numbers in Newport reached 1,000 and 500 respectively
by 1910.[3]

Newport in the New Century

As the twentieth century began, Newport was a diminished political force in the state, clearly subordinate to Providence. Since the 1850s, the two towns had exhibited what the historian Eileen Warburton characterizes as a "sibling-like rivalry": they had served as co-capitals of the state, with legislators holding their May sessions at the Colony House and the other sessions at Providence's Old State House.[4] By the end of the century, however, Providence's population was roughly seven times larger than Newport's, and its booming economy was propelled by textile, silverware, and jewelry manufacturing.[5] As a result, the Rhode Island legislature decided to make Providence the state's sole capital. In 1891, the General Assembly solicited bids for a new state house on Smith Hill; and, by 1900, the Secretary of State was occupying the imposing but only partially completed building designed by McKim, Mead, and White.[6] In the same year, Rhode Islanders ratified the Eleventh Amendment to the state constitution, approving the change.[7]

Rosecliff - Newport. R. I.

FIGURE 20. Postcard of Rosecliff, c. 1970. One of the grand estates on Bellevue Avenue, it was built in 1901 by Teresa Fair Oelrichs, the daughter of Irish immigrants. Collection of Daniel P. Titus. Reprinted by permission.

Newport's leaders undoubtedly felt slighted by this change, and they decided to compensate by building an impressive new City Hall to replace the makeshift one that had been located in the Brick Market for fifty years. In 1898, the city asked for proposals for a new city hall but limited the entrants to Newport residents. John. D. Johnston won the bid and teamed up again with Michael McCormick to build a granite structure in the French Second Empire style on Broadway.[8]

While Newport may have faded as a political force, it had by no means lost its preeminence as the nation's leading summer resort. Construction continued apace on choice lots on Bellevue Avenue. In 1901, the Elms and Rosecliff were both completed. The owners of the Elms, Mr. and Mrs. E. J. Berwind, had demolished a house of that name on their property and replaced it with a palatial villa designed by the Philadelphia architect Horace Trumbauer and modeled on an eighteenth-century French estate, the Chateau d'Asnières.[9] Rosecliff, too, replaced a more modest building of the same name, which had belonged to the historian George Bancroft. The new owners, Mr. and Mrs. Herman Oelrichs, found that Bancroft's house was not spacious enough for entertaining, so they commissioned McKim, Mead, and White to design a much more imposing structure using the Petit Trianon at Versailles as their model. Tessie Oelrichs was often apart from her husband, who traveled frequently for business and pleasure.[10] As a result, she became fast friends with two of her neighbors, Alva Vanderbilt Belmont and Mamie Fish. Tessie's bond with Alva was further strengthened when her younger sister Virginia (known as Birdie) married Alva's son William K. Vanderbilt, Jr., in 1899.[11] Tessie, Alva, and Mamie became known as the "Great Triumvirate," the gatekeepers who decided which Newporters merited invitations to the chief celebrations of the summer season.[12] The daughter of Jim Fair, an Irish immigrant who rose to become one of Nevada's fabulously wealthy "Silver Kings," Tessie was one of the only Catholics to play a prominent part in Newport's summer elite society.[13] Her White Ball in August 1904 would be one of the costliest and most lavish parties ever staged in the city.[14]

Political Change

In 1900, Republicans decided to make a serious bid to regain the mayor's office. Patrick Boyle was then serving his sixth consecutive one-year term. To challenge Boyle, Republicans selected Frederick "Fritz" Garrettson, a well-to-do grocer whose wife, Marie, was a devout Catholic. The *Providence Journal* hoped that Garrettson and his Republican allies would unseat what the paper called "the combine" and usher in "a better state of affairs than [Newport] has had for some time."[15] The *New York Times* followed the race, too, noting that the "cottagers are taking great interest in Mr. Garrettson's candidature."[16]

In the end, the Republicans scored a big win. They captured the City Council, gaining seats in the First, Second and Third wards. Garrettson also eked out a victory over Boyle, winning by just thirty-five votes. The slate may have been helped by the Republican tide at the national level, where William McKinley and Theodore Roosevelt handily defeated William Jennings Bryan and his running mate, Adlai Stevenson.

As mayor, Garrettson stressed fiscal restraint and made a concerted effort to reach out to state officials and to the mayors of neighboring towns. This was important now that Newport was no longer a co-capital of the state. He also expressed interest in establishing a university club and a workingmen's club in the city. By the fall, however, his term was coming to an end, and he faced a rematch with Boyle. The *Providence Journal* saw the race as a simple battle between "the old combine and the advocates of good government."[17] Boyle was a formidable candidate, however. The *Boston Globe* noted that he was a gifted speaker who appealed to many Republicans. He also knew how to turn out his Irish base. Alluding to an opponent's remark that "foreign born voters could be led like sheep," Boyle declared that this was no longer the case. Yet in the Civil War, many a foreigner serving in the Union army "could be led like sheep in defence of the country of his adoption."[18] Boyle's adept campaigning helped him regain the mayor's office by the narrowest of margins.[19] He would hold it for three more terms before facing another serious challenge.

Parish Developments

Saint Mary's parishioners had to wait three months to find out who would succeed Dr. Grace as their pastor. According to the *Boston Globe*, there were "four candidates for the pulpit, which is considered a very desirable one."[20] Newspapers speculated about the choice, and at the end of December 1898 they finally reported that Father William Meenan had been selected. Born in Providence and of Irish descent, Meenan had studied for the priesthood in Montreal and had been ordained there a year after Father Coyle and Father Deady had received their orders. Meenan had established the parish of Saint John the Baptist in Pawtucket and in 1887 had been appointed to Saint Joseph's in Natick, a parish in West Warwick comprised principally of Irish American and French Canadian millworkers.[21] A Pawtucket newspaper noted that Meenan was "well known throughout the diocese for his preaching ability" and for his "amiable and tactful" personality.[22] In January 1899, he moved to Newport accompanied by his sisters Agnes and Mary, who would serve as his housekeepers.[23] Three months later, Bishop Harkins assigned him a second assistant pastor, Father Martin Reddy, who had been ordained three years earlier.[24]

Saint Joseph's Church was also in the midst of change. Father Deady was working to move the parish from Washington Square to its new property on Broadway, but he had other concerns as well. In addition to supporting the temperance societies that Coyle had organized, he now set up a branch of the Holy Name Society for the men of his parish.[25] Members promised to avoid cursing and crude language and tried to encourage other men to attend Mass regularly.[26] Deady was also focused on ministering to the increasing number of Catholics in Portsmouth, many of whom were Portuguese. In 1899, he presided over a grand Holy Ghost Festival at Saint Joseph's, placing silver crowns on the heads of thirteen Portuguese girls attired in white dresses.[27]

In 1897, twenty-four Newport men came together to form a mutual benefit society named in honor of Vasco da Gama, the famed Portuguese explorer. Members met twice a month in a hall on Thames Street and attended Saint Joseph's when a Portuguese priest was visiting the parish.[28] By now, however, about three hundred Portuguese men and women were residing in Portsmouth, and Deady wanted them to have a larger house of worship than tiny Saint Clement's Chapel.[29] In 1900, he purchased a house on East Main Road in Portsmouth to serve as the rectory.[30] In the following year, Michael McCormick built a bigger chapel next door to it.[31] Situated on the east side of Portsmouth, the buildings were close to the new trolley lines that ran from Newport up to the Stone Bridge in Tiverton.[32]

In May 1901, Deady and his assistant pastor, Father William Doran, along with Meenan and one of his assistant pastors, Father Philip Cronan, went to Portsmouth to lay the cornerstone.[33] At the ceremony, Deady announced that the chapel would be named for Saint Anthony of Padua, a Portuguese-born Franciscan friar.[34] Yet as the historian Robert Hayman notes, the chapel's mission was not limited to Portuguese Catholics but was intended to serve all Catholics in Portsmouth.[35]

Two months later, Bishop Harkins came to Portsmouth to dedicate the church as a mission of Saint Joseph's. A reporter for the *Fall River Daily Herald* wrote that the crowd was sizable and mentioned the altar flowers provided by Marie Garrettson, a parishioner of Saint Joseph's. He also described the stained-glass windows donated by Cassie Cory, Frank Silvia, and Joseph D'Arrude. The reporter approved of the site of the new church, declaring that the "chapel at the Coal Mines long since has ceased to be available, as the Catholic families which once clustered around the little chapel since the closing of the coal mines and the new families have settled away from the once busy spot." He predicted that it would attract many of Newport's Catholics in the summer "as it is but three-quarters of an hour's delightful ride from the city."[36]

Servants' Work and Recreation

At the turn of the century, many New England cities were the site of bitter conflicts between labor unions and management. Textile workers in Fall River and New Bedford and carpenters in Worcester had gone on strike for better wages and working conditions as well as reduced hours.[37] In 1902, when streetcar workers in Providence went on strike, Governor Charles Kimball declared martial law and sent in militia to keep the lines running.[38] Newport, however, had never had much industry, and its cotton plants, Perry Mill and Aquidneck Mill, were shuttered by 1885.[39] Without factories, the city was largely shielded from battles between union militants and hard-nosed owners.

Newport's labor troubles centered around its servants, who numbered about 1,000 in the summer of 1902.[40] Problems began at the Elms, owned by the coal magnate Julius Berwind. The staff was struggling to keep up with an endless round of parties and balls, which required them to work seven days a week, sixteen to eighteen hours per day. Eventually the butler, Tom Dooley, spoke to Mrs. Berwind on behalf of his co-workers.[41] She sent Dooley to her husband, who was accustomed to facing down striking miners and was not about to countenance labor unrest in his home. He

HANNAH L. (SULLIVAN) DONOVAN, COOK FOR BRADFORD NORMAN (3RD FROM RIGHT)
WITH STAFF AT "BELAIR" ON OLD BEACH RD., NEWPORT, RHODE ISLAND -1908 +/-
CHARLES DONOVAN Pic. GRAND-NEPHEW, MIKE CHRISTENSEN-2009-

FIGURE 21. Photograph of the Belair staff, 1908. The Belair estate was located on Old Beach Road. Hannah Sullivan Donovan, the cook, is third from the right. Reprinted courtesy of the Museum of Newport Irish History.

believed his employees should be grateful for the privilege of working in such beautiful surroundings, and when confronted with their concerns, he summarily dismissed them.[42] According to the *Pawtucket Times*, this meant that Mrs. Berwind "had to go out for her meals" until an employment agency could line up replacements.[43]

Trouble spread to other cottages. The butler and ten staff members at Friedham Villa on Bellevue Avenue, walked out, seeking "more pay and less work." The *Boston Globe* noted that Mr. and Mrs. Pembroke Jones, who were renting the mansion, had planned to be Newport's "principal entertainers" that summer.[44] Instead, as a reporter for the *Meriden Daily Journal* wrote, they were "almost forced to shut down."[45]

Meanwhile, James Mitchell, the butler who had replaced Dooley at the Elms, complained about Mrs. Berwind's six pet monkeys, who had the run of the house: "They were treated better than the servants and were stuck up and saucy. As long as they had their fruit and candy it did not matter whether the servants had anything."[46] Nor could he abide the domineering new house-keeper. In protest, he and four other male staff members walked out. A few days later, three servants also left Wee Bush, the summer home of Marion Cutting. The *Meriden Daily Journal* correspondent remarked, "Fashionable Newport is becoming very much alarmed."[47] Although the summer colonists appeared to win these battles, they learned some lessons and began to ease up on their employees. While Tom Dooley claimed that the Elms staff were only allowed thirty minutes off each week, Raymond Roy of the Preservation Society of Newport County notes that staff in the mansions were generally granted one afternoon and one evening off each week.[48] In their free time, many servants, especially those of Irish, English, and Scottish descent, would gather at the landing of the Forty Steps, a steep stairway adjoining the Cliff Walk, to listen to fiddle or accordion tunes. A columnist for the *Newport Daily News* recalled that "songs, dancing and general good times were the rule under star-studded skies, with cool breezes and the sound of the surf below."[49] Larry Lowenthal, who has written extensively about the Cliff Walk, notes that "the Forty Steps led to the altar on more than one occasion."[50]

Saint Mary's Jubilee Celebration

Since arriving at Saint Mary's at the end of 1898, Father Meenan had immersed himself in activity. He served as president of the Saint Mary's Catholic Benevolent Union, as chaplain to a local branch of the Hibernians, and as clergy representative to the Charity Organization Society.[51] In addition, he was state chaplain of the Knights of Columbus and traveled throughout Rhode Island to promote the organization.[52] However, his ministry to the rich and famous garnered him the most attention from the press.

When dealing with wealthy summer colonists, Meenan often had to administer the sacraments at their homes rather than at Saint Mary's because not all of the parties involved were Catholic. In the summer of 1899, he officiated at the marriage of Dora Havemeyer and Lieutenant Commander Cameron Winslow, held at the Havemeyer mansion.[53] In the following year, he married Dora's brother, Henry Havemeyer, to Charlotte Whiting at the Swanhurst estate on Pelham Street. The *Pawtucket Times* breathlessly called the latter wedding "one of the most important that has taken place here for years," and the *New York Times* emoted that "all Newport was present" for it.[54] In 1902, a *Providence Journal* story, "Millionaire Baby," reported on the baptism of Mr. and Mrs. Thomas Shaw Safe's infant son, which the priest performed at Ocean Lawn, their estate on the Cliff Walk.[55]

In the summer of 1902, Meenan received even more press attention when he organized a celebration to mark Saint Mary's Golden Anniversary. The church had been dedicated in July 1852, but he decided to hold the anniversary ceremony on August 15 so it would coincide with the Feast of the Assumption of the Virgin Mary. For the services, Meenan invited Cardinal James Gibbons of Baltimore, Bishop Harkins, and several other members of the hierarchy, including Bishop Thomas Conaty, the rector of the Catholic University of America. In addition, he asked dozens of other priests to attend.[56] Events included a Pontifical High Mass in the morning, an afternoon service for children, and evening vespers. The *New York Times* covered them in detail, noting that the church was beautifully decorated with palms and flowers, that "many of the leading Summer residents were present," and that it "was filled to overflowing."[57] A Fall River paper estimated that another 1,500 people stood outside the church to watch the lengthy procession of bishops, priests, and altar boys slowly make its way inside.[58]

Cardinal Gibbons and the other churchmen were feted by Saint Mary's parishioners. Annie Leary, recently made a papal countess in recognition of her generosity to the church, hosted an elegant dinner party at Paul Cottage.[59] She filled her house with American Beauty roses and set up tents to accommodate her many guests. The next day, the Cuttings hosted a luncheon at the Casino for the dignitaries.[60]

The golden anniversary celebrations were a major milestone for all of Newport's Catholics. Catholicism was coming of age in Newport, and its adherents were being accepted as equals by their non-Catholic neighbors. Many newspapers expressed enthusiasm and awe about the events.

FIGURE 22. Photograph of Countess Annie Leary, undated. Leary, who owned an estate on Bellevue Avenue, was made a papal countess because of her generous support of Catholic causes. From Helen Worden Erskine, *Out of This World* (New York: Putnam, 1954).

According to the *Pawtucket Times*, "[e]verybody in Newport, irrespective of creed or station in life, was deeply interested in the observances yesterday at the golden jubilee of St. Mary's. . . . which is probably one of the wealthiest churches in the country."[61]

Less than a week after Cardinal Gibbons and the bishops left Newport, President Theodore Roosevelt arrived. He had assumed office in September 1901, after McKinley was assassinated by an anarchist, and now he was making a New England tour. Roosevelt sailed into Newport to attend the baptism of Theodore Chanler, infant son of his good friends Winthrop and Margaret Chanler.[62] The couple had asked Roosevelt to be his godfather, and the Episcopal ceremony took place at the Chanlers' mansion, overlooking the Cliff Walk. It was performed by Reverend John Diman, who had recently founded Saint George's School in Middletown.[63] After the service, Roosevelt took a carriage ride through town, stopping briefly on Bellevue Avenue to visit his friend George Downing and then heading on to Massachusetts to stay at the home of Senator Henry Cabot Lodge.[64] The *Providence Journal* was thrilled by Roosevelt's brief stopover: "Newport has not been honored by a visit from the President of the United States since President Arthur's time."[65]

Dividing the Diocese Once More

By 1903, Bishop Harkins was convinced that the borders of the sprawling Providence diocese needed to be redrawn. It now served 275,000 Catholics from Woonsocket, Rhode Island, to Cape Cod in Massachusetts. His solution was to split off the Massachusetts portion and create a new Diocese of Fall River. The other New England bishops and the papal delegate in America were supportive, so the proposal went to Rome that summer. As word spread of the impending division, newspapers began speculating about whom the Vatican would appoint as the first bishop of Fall River. Father Thomas Grace's name was frequently mentioned. The brother of Dr. Grace and a former assistant pastor at Saint Mary's, he was currently serving in a parish in Providence.[66]

In the end, however, Rome selected Father William Stang to head the Fall River diocese and its 130,000 Catholics. Stang was a German-born scholar who had served as rector of the Cathedral of Saints Peter and Paul in Providence.[67] In May 1904, Bishop Harkins ordained him in the cathedral, and Stang's friend Father James Coyle traveled from Taunton to preach at the Mass.[68] When Stang arrived in Fall River a week later, 25,000 people greeted him, including 10,000 from Providence and 4,000 from Newport.[69] The *Boston Globe* reported that the demonstration "surpassed anything of the kind ever seen in this city."[70] Overcome with emotion, the new bishop asked Coyle to speak to the crowd on his behalf.

Saint Joseph's "Long Struggle"

Father Coyle was enjoying great success in his Taunton parish, but his successor at Saint Joseph's, Father Deady, was encountering difficulties in his plan to build a new church on Broadway. At first the process seemed to be going smoothly. In 1898 and 1901, he acquired plots fronting Mann Avenue and Broadway, and, by June 1904, the parish had paid off their cost and had raised $8,000 by selling another strip of land to the city as a site for the new Rogers High School.[71]

Deady announced to his parishioners that a plan had been approved for a church that would seat 1,100 people. After examining eight options, he, with the bishop's agreement, had selected the proposal of a local architect, Creighton Withers, who, with his father, had designed both Saint John's Episcopal Church in the Point neighborhood and the president's house at the Naval War College.[72] Withers envisioned a grand Italian Renaissance–style church with two towers and a dome, and Deady displayed the drawings and floor plans for all parishioners to see. The *Newport Mercury* thought it would be a "large, serviceable and showy structure," no doubt "a decided ornament to the city."[73] The *Fall River Daily Globe* estimated that the new church would cost about $100,000 to build and predicted that it would "only take two to three years to complete."[74]

In September, Deady broke ground, and construction began the following month. Meanwhile, the pastor continued to take up collections for his building fund.[75] By the spring of 1905, the basement, which had a granite exterior, was complete. Then, in June, Bishop Harkins transferred Deady to a parish in Pawtucket. The bishop was apparently worried about Deady's health and felt that the responsibilities in Newport were taking a toll.[76] In any case, he replaced him with Father James Mahon, a familiar face in the city, for in 1887–88 he had served as an assistant to Dr. Grace at Saint Mary's.[77] But as soon as he arrived, Mahon halted the construction project. It is not clear if he was concerned about costs or if he thought Withers's design was too grandiose. Contractors put a roof on the basement, and for the next five years the project sat idle.

The French Sisters Arrive

While construction on Saint Joseph's stalled, two new initiatives moved forward to strengthen the Catholic church's presence in Newport: the establishment of a convent and retreat center for the Religious of the Cenacle and the founding of a convent and a day nursery for the Daughters of the Holy Ghost.[78] Agnes Storer was the motivating force behind one of these initiatives. Like her father, she was energetic, determined, and deeply involved in the city's Catholic life. In 1904, she and her friend Marie Cisneros met with Bishop Harkins to discuss the idea of bringing the Cenacle sisters to Newport.[79] The sisters had been expelled from France in 1902 in the wake of the Dreyfus Affair and were looking to establish new foundations.[80] With the bishop's encouragement, Storer and Cisneros found a suitable property for them just a few blocks from the Storers' home on Washington Street in the Point neighborhood. The former Auchincloss estate, it was situated on about an acre of land, with many mature trees.[81]

In June 1906, four Cenacle sisters took possession of the property and moved temporarily into its old stable. They immediately began their ministries: retreats for women, French lessons, music and sewing classes, catechism for children, and Eucharistic adoration in the chapel.[82] A chaplain also lived on the property, the first of whom was the Hungarian-born Father Frederick Orosz. Because the sisters were from France and Italy, Storer had pressed for a European priest to serve as their chaplain.[83]

Unfortunately, local newspaper editors began claiming that the convent would be catering exclusively to the city's wealthiest Catholics. The *Fall River Evening Herald* reported that an eight-day silent retreat had drawn the interest of Caroline Vanderbilt, Margaret LaFarge, Teresa Oelrichs, and Countess Annie Leary.[84] The writer declared it would be "the first series of religious exercises ever arranged exclusively for the social colony at Newport. . . . The retreat will be preached by the Rev. William O'Brien Pardow, S.J., one of the best preachers in the Jesuit body, and a man agreeable to the exclusive set."[85]

The perception that the sisters were oriented toward Newport's richest residents was difficult to counter. In the winter of 1908, Bishop Harkins came to town to dedicate a new building on the sisters' property that would house a convent, a chapel, and guest quarters for up to thirty women. In its coverage, the *Newport Daily News* printed the bishop's kind words about the sisters but also mentioned the widely held view that the Cenacle was a refuge for the wealthy. The reporter did admit that the sisters found this view "particularly offensive."[86]

Despite these misconceptions, the highly educated sisters quietly continued their work. Neighbors came to pray in their chapel; others visited their library; a few took voice lessons. Their new Italian-born chaplain, Father Tomaso Fusco, who replaced Father Orosz in 1907, expended much energy on the welfare of the Italian community in Newport, and the bishop encouraged him in his efforts.[87]

Meanwhile, efforts were underway to bring another community of French nuns into the city. Father Meenan, working with the bishop and wealthy supporters such as Mr. and Mrs. Delancey Kane, Mr. and Mrs. Frederick Garrettson, and James Cottrell, was trying to establish the Daughters of the Holy Ghost—popularly known as the White Sisters— near Saint Mary's Church. Like the Cenacle sisters, they had recently been forced out of France and were establishing new foundations in New England. The sisters focused on serving the ailing poor and running day nurseries for infants and small children whose parents were both working.

In June 1908, the Kanes met with Father Meenan about the matter, and then the three approached Bishop Harkins, who did not need persuading. He was familiar with the White Sisters and had previously set up a community in Fall River in 1903, another in Pawtucket in 1905, and a third in Providence in 1906.[88] With the approval of the sisters, the Saint Clare Home corporation was established in the fall of 1908, and four sisters moved into a small house across the street from Saint Mary's in September 1909.[89] The building was meant to be a temporary dwelling. Just three months later, the corporation purchased the Francis Malbone house on Thames Street.[90] Built in 1758, the spacious and once stately Georgian structure was in need of repair. Marion Cutting provided funds, and by August 1910 the sisters were able to move in. They used part of the house as a convent and the rest as a day nursery.[91]

Italian Trials

The new communities of sisters were welcomed to Newport, but the city's rapidly growing Italian community was having a harder time gaining acceptance. In the 1890s, a cadre of Italian stonemasons had arrived to work as marble dressers for the Vanderbilts' Marble House.[92] This was a period of significant Italian emigration. During the next decade, tens of thousands of impoverished southern Italians arrived in New York City, Philadelphia, Baltimore, Boston, and Providence.[93] Of those who landed in Providence, small groups made their way to Newport, and, by 1905, the state census recorded 348 Italian immigrants living in the city.[94] Many had established themselves in small businesses. Pasquale Baccara and Alphonse Palmieri were barbers, Vito Pinto and Palo Mozella had confectionery shops, Carlo Fieri and A. G. Ferretti were fruit dealers, Anthony Marolda was a tailor, Maria della Monte and Joseph Cappuccilli operated grocery stores, and John and Peter Cappuccilli were cobblers.[95] The community was large enough to support two social organizations: the Italian

FIGURE 23. Photograph of Antonio Ferretti's fruit market on Thames Street, c. 1905. Ferretti was one of a number Italian immigrants who operated small businesses in Newport. Collection of the Newport Historical Society, P5389. Reprinted with permission.

Progressive Benefit Society and the Italian Brotherhood Benefit Society.[96] However, they had no parish to call their own.

After learning of Father Fusco's presence in Newport, Marco Russo, one of the more prominent members of the community, sent a letter to Bishop Harkins to thank him. At the same time, he mentioned that many of his compatriots did not want to pay fees for baptisms and weddings and were shocked that seat offerings were expected from those who attended Mass. According to Russo, Father Mahon of Saint Joseph's had been very condescending to the Italians in the parish, claiming that "all Italians [were] descended from Brigands." Without offering other specifics, Russo hinted, "I could say many things about Father Mahan [*sic*] if I wish to do so."[97]

Nonetheless, conditions seemed to be improving for the Italians. Under Fusco's leadership, their community appeared poised to take possession of one of the city's grand buildings: the United Congregational Church on Spring Street. Famed for its LaFarge stained-glass windows, the brownstone church was located in the heart of Newport, but the congregation was losing members and its trustees were having trouble paying the mortgage. Fusco and his associates had expressed interest in it and hoped to come to terms with the Congregationalists. By March 1908, however, the trustees had raised sufficient funds, and the president of the Newport Savings Bank informed Anthony Marolda that "there will be no sale of the property as advertised."[98] In April, a group of Italians held a fundraising ball in Newport, but efforts to buy a church then stalled after Fusco was transferred to Providence and no Italian priest was sent to take his place. According to Robert Hayman, Italian parishes had already been established in Providence and Johnston, and others would soon be set up in Bristol, Warren, and Barrington.[99] He attributes Newport's failure to Fusco, who was unable to unify the Italian residents and raise the necessary money.[100]

Although no Italian priest replaced Fusco, Italian community members did find support among the Italian sisters at the Cenacle. These nuns established the Holy Family Circle for Italian women and their children.[101] According to the historian Sister Marie Hennessy,

> The Cenacle gave real help . . . with the Italians who were numerous in . . . St. Joseph parish. . . . Sr. Luigia Testa, kind, funny and yet firm was a welcome presence for the Italian mothers especially, who

were very seldom comfortable speaking English, especially in their spiritual life. Many renewed their interest in the Church and came faithfully to their meetings.[102]

Even without a church, Newport's Italian community expressed pride in its heritage. In 1910, Italians throughout Rhode Island sponsored their first Columbus Day parades. More than 10,000 marched in Providence and watched a fireworks display over the Italian neighborhood of Federal Hill.[103] In Newport, schools and most businesses were closed, and the Italian societies staged an evening parade accompanied by the Ancient Order of Hibernians and two Newport bands.[104] In 1911, Newport's Columbus Day celebrations were even larger. The Knights of Columbus held a ball at the Masonic Hall on the evening before the holiday. On Columbus Day proper, the community hosted a big street parade, which the *Mercury* described as "an imposing affair." Taking part were three bands, two divisions of the Ancient Order of Hibernians, representatives of the Naval Training Station, members of the Knights of Columbus, Mayor Patrick Boyle and the aldermen, and three Italian organizations: the Italian Brotherhood, the Italian Brotherhood Benefit Society, and the Italian Progresso Benefit Society. In the evening a ball was held at the Music Hall on Thames Street.[105] Notably absent were the Catholic clergy, who had always played a prominent role in Newport's Saint Patrick's Day celebrations. Perhaps the tensions of the prior years with Father Mahon were still present.

Saint Mary's "Children"

Meanwhile, in 1910, Father Meenan and Bishop Harkins began discussions about dividing Saint Mary's yet again. With 6,000 parishioners, more than six hundred students in the parish school and academy, and five hundred children ready to receive their first Holy Communion, the two clergymen agreed that the existing parish was too large.[106] The new parish, to be called Saint Augustin's, would be located in the city's growing Fifth Ward and would include 1,900 of Saint Mary's former parishioners.[107]

In January 1911, Saint Mary's took up a collection to raise funds for the new parish. In February, Meenan announced that George Gordon King, a retired local banker, had donated two parcels of land adjoining property that the pastor had purchased.[108] A trustee of Trinity Episcopal

Church, King was very civic-minded. He had contributed generously to Saint Columba's Episcopal Church and to Saint George's School, both in Middletown.[109] The following year he would donate his father's house and a surrounding tract of land, which would become the new home of the city's public library.[110] Just as Father Coyle had benefited from the generosity of a non-Catholic donor when he was establishing Hazard Memorial School, Meenan and the parishioners of Saint Augustin's likewise benefited from the kindness of a supportive Protestant.

In April 1911, Bishop Harkins appointed Father Martin Reddy as Saint Augustin's first pastor. Although he was only thirty-nine years old, Reddy was a logical choice because he had been assisting Meenan at Saint Mary's since 1899.[111] He was also well known in the community, having been elected to the city's public school board in 1910. While Reddy worked with an architect on plans for the new Byzantine-style church and school, the Hibernians offered him the use of their hall on Wellington Avenue.[112] For about a year, pastor and parishioners squeezed into the hall as best they could.

The construction contract was awarded to the Charles Maguire Company of Providence, and ground was broken in August.[113] A month later, Monsignor Thomas Doran, the vicar general of the diocese, laid the cornerstone. Doran had served at Saint Mary's in the 1880s as an assistant to Dr. Grace, so this ceremony must have been especially meaningful to him.[114] Twenty area priests were also in attendance, including Father Coyle and Father William Curley, a Newport native who was serving in Fall River.[115] Before the ceremonies, several Catholic organizations staged a parade. The Hibernians, the Knights of Columbus, and the Father Mathew Total Abstinence Society were joined by the Fort Adams band in a march down Thames Street to Carroll Avenue in the Fifth Ward. The *Newport Daily News* reported that the "organizations turned out strong and made a fine appearance." Local dignitaries, including Senator George Wetmore, Mayor Boyle, former Mayor Garrettson, aldermen, and School Committee, watched from a platform.[116] The reporter called it "perhaps the largest crowd assembled in Newport in a long time. . . . [P]eople were present from all over the city and from all ranks and churches, with many who do not belong to any church."[117]

Construction moved quickly on the church and the school, and by 1912 Reddy was able to celebrate Easter Mass in the church basement. The church was completed in July, and Bishop Harkins arrived to bless it in August. Father Meenan, who preached the sermon, marveled at the

ST. AUGUSTINE CHURCH, NEWPORT, R. I.   108771

FIGURE 24. Postcard of Saint Augustin's Church, 1923. The church was established in 1912 in Newport's heavily Irish Fifth Ward. Collection of Daniel P. Titus. Reprinted by permission.

changes that had occurred in Newport during the past thirty years. In 1880, three Sunday Masses had been offered on Aquidneck Island, now there were more than twenty. He credited Saint Mary's as Newport's "mother church," and rejoiced that her two children, Saint Joseph's and Saint Augustin's, now had "fine temples of their own."[118]

Saint Augustin's School was also finished by August. In September 1912, six Mercy sisters established themselves in temporary quarters near the parish and opened it to 337 children.[119] Now that so many students had enrolled at Saint Augustin's, Saint Mary's School no longer had to worry about overcrowding.

As the new parish came into being, Saint Joseph's pastor, Father Mahon, began work on his own new church building, after a five-year hiatus. A successful fair in September 1910 had netted the parish about $13,000, enough to restart the project.[120] A team of Providence-based architects from Murphy, Hindle, and Wright was directed to scale back Withers's design. In March 1911, a reporter for the *Providence Visitor* wrote, "The original plans by Creighton Withers called for domes . . . and a structure rather too elaborate for the Church. These have been almost entirely changed and according to the new plans the people of the parish will have a large and very substantial Church that will be worthy of the long struggles that they have made."[121] Rather than use granite for the exterior, the new architects called for brick, which reduced costs.[122]

In August, Monsignor Doran laid the cornerstone for the new Saint Joseph's, just four weeks before he would return to do the same for Saint Augustin's.[123] The work moved forward, and Father Mahon was pleased to see a Celtic cross affixed to the top of the new building. But in January 1912, he died at the age of fifty-three after suffering a "paralytic shock."[124] A great crowd attended his funeral in the old Saint Joseph's Church. Bishop Harkins presided, and Mahon's old friend and classmate Father Meenan preached.[125]

Father Edward Higney, a Fall River native, was immediately appointed as Mahon's successor, and he continued to press forward with the church.[126] Over the next several months, crews worked to complete the interior. Once construction was complete, Higney brought over the altar, the statues, and the Stations of the Cross from the old church. In September 1912, Bishop Harkins came to dedicate the building, and both Father Coyle, the church's first pastor, and Father Deady, Coyle's successor, preached at the services.[127] Fifteen years had passed since Father Deady had announced his plans for a new church building, and at last they had been realized.

ST. JOSEPH'S CHURCH, NEWPORT, R. I.   108772

FIGURE 25. Postcard of Saint Joseph's Church on Broadway, c. 1912. Collection of the Newport Historical Society, 2010.10.11. Reprinted by permission.

War and the End of the Gilded Age

In the years leading up to World War I, Newport's summer set remained a hive of activity. The Great Triumvirate—Alva Belmont, Tessie Oelrichs, and Mamie Fish—were aging but still involved in the many lavish, sometimes outlandish, parties of the season. Indeed, in 1913, Fish hosted the Mother Goose Ball at Crossways, her Ocean Drive mansion, requiring each of her guests to attend dressed as a nursery-rhyme character.[128] The Casino still offered a host of activities for the colonists. In addition to the U.S. Open tennis championships, visitors could attend horse shows or listen to concerts by John Mullaly and his orchestra.[179] Yet there were warning signs before 1914 that the Gilded Age was drawing to a close. In April 1912, the *Titanic* sank off the coast of Newfoundland, claiming the lives of at least 1,500 people, including John Jacob Astor IV, whose family owned Beechwood on Bellevue Avenue. Another Newport summer colonist, Margaret Tobin Brown, was more fortunate. She survived and gained acclaim and the nickname "unsinkable" for helping row a lifeboat and seeking to rescue other passengers.[130] Long estranged from her husband, J. J. Brown, a Colorado mine owner, Margaret had started visiting Newport in the summer of 1903 at the suggestion of her friend and fellow Irish Catholic, Annie Leary.[131] After the *Titanic* tragedy, she spent more of her time in the city, renting a comfortable house on Bellevue Avenue next door to the Redwood Library and devoting her energy to worthy causes. In the summer of 1912, she led a fundraising campaign to establish a new maternity ward at Newport Hospital. She also joined forces with her friend Alva Belmont in promoting women's suffrage. The two staged a major conference on the subject at Marble House in July 1914, just days before the outbreak of war.[132]

The sinking of the *Titanic* had cast a pall over Newport's summer colonists, but the 1915 passage of the Sixteenth Amendment, establishing a federal income tax, was also worrisome.[133] While the tax was initially topped at 6 percent, Newport's wealthy must have worried that rates would increase over time.[134] Nonetheless, despite the twin calamities of death and taxes, Newport's colonists pressed on in the spring of 1914, preparing for another summer of festivities. Leading members planned elaborate parties, many with celebrity guests. By this time, several nations had established informal summer embassies in Newport, so there were a number of European dignitaries in town.[135] Mrs. Cornelius Vanderbilt III planned to showcase the German ambassador, Johann von Bernstorff, at her summer soiree at the Breakers. Mrs. Ava Astor countered, inviting to her party Grand Duke Alexander, the brother-in-law of Tsar Nicholas II. Then, in the first week of August, Europe's leading powers went to war in the wake of the assassination of the Austrian archduke, Franz Ferdinand. The Newport hostesses held their parties as scheduled but took pains to avoid discussing the political issues of the day.[136] As the season began to wind down, they shifted their energies to charity. At the end of August, Mrs. Vanderbilt held a bazaar at the Breakers that raised more than $40,000 for the International Red Cross.[137] Meanwhile, Birdie Vanderbilt set to work raising money to purchase ambulances to transport wounded Allied soldiers in France and Belgium.[138]

By this time, Newport as a whole was pivoting to a war footing. In July, the torpedo factory on Goat Island received $1 million in additional funding from the federal government, which allowed it to add to its staff of three hundred.[139] In August, President Woodrow Wilson called on all Americans to "maintain a strict and impartial neutrality," but this would prove to be a difficult proposition as the war intensified.[140]

The Sisters' Expanding Ministries

As the summer colonists lowered their profiles after the start of the war, Newport's three communities of sisters—the Religious of the Cenacle, the Sisters of Mercy, and the Daughters of the Holy Ghost—increased their presence. The Cenacle sisters continued construction on their property in the Point neighborhood. In May 1914, Monsignor Doran came down from Providence to lay the cornerstone for their new church, a small Gothic chapel designed by Maginnis and Walsh, a highly regarded Boston architectural firm.[141] The sermon that day was preached by Father Orosz, the Cenacle's first chaplain.[142] At the end of the year, Doran returned to bless the almost completed chapel and was accompanied by Father Meenan of Saint Mary's, Father Higney of Saint Joseph's, Father Reddy of Saint Augustin's, and several other local priests. The Charles McGuire Company, which had also built Saint Augustin's, had constructed the hundred-seat chapel, and the editor of the *Newport Daily News* was impressed, describing it as "a pretty little tapestry edifice" with a "neat and

FIGURE 26. Photograph of an outdoor Mass at the Mercy Home and School, 1918. The former Eagle Crest estate was transformed into an orphanage run by the Mercy sisters. Collection of the Newport Historical Society, P10612. Reprinted by permission.

cheerful" interior.[143] In the years following, finishing touches would be added: a small rose window and several stained-glass windows, an Italian marble altar, and a fresco of the Virgin Mary praying in the Cenacle.[144]

While the Cenacle sisters were encouraging prayer and contemplation, Bishop Harkins was promoting another active ministry in Newport. In 1905, he had established an orphanage in Woonsocket, and he now wanted another one in the southern part of the state.[145] In 1914, he finally decided to make use of Eagle Crest, which had been sitting empty since 1888, when the diocese had purchased it from the Religious of Jesus and Mary. What had once been envisioned as an academy for affluent girls would instead become the Mercy Home and School "for poor, neglected and indigent children," under the direction of the Sisters of Mercy.[146] In December, the Mercy provincial toured the property with the bishop and agreed to take it, provided that certain improvements were made. The bishop met with Father Higney (Father Meenan was then very ill), who agreed to oversee repairs and renovations. In July 1915, a group of nuns led by Sister M. Anacletus opened the facility to fifty-six students, whose numbers would increase in the years to come.[147]

The Daughters of the Holy Ghost were also in an expansion phase. In 1912, Marion Cutting died, leaving $150,000 to the sisters and directing them to establish a memorial to her late sons, William and Brockholst. In 1913, they considered using the bequest to erect a children's hospital on Spring Street but, in 1915, decided instead to build a new convent and chapel on the same site. Architects from the prestigious New York firm Trowbridge and Livingston designed the connected Gothic buildings. The *Providence Journal*'s correspondent considered them "very pretty," noting that sixteen sisters would be living in the new convent.[148] Bad weather slowed the project, and the sisters were not able to move into

CONVENT OF THE SISTERS OF SAINT JOSEPH
View from Washington Street

FIGURE 27. Photograph of Saint Joseph's Convent, 1922. The convent was located in Hunter House in the Point neighborhood. During the American Revolution, Admiral de Ternay resided there. Reprinted from *Souvenir Book Commemorating the Consecration of St. Joseph Church* (Newport, RI: Saint Joseph High School Alumni Association, 1922).

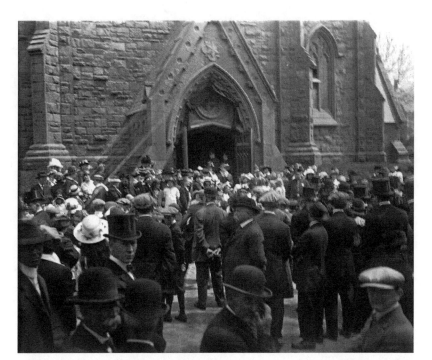

FIGURE 28. Photograph of Saint Mary's Church, 1915. The photograph was taken on the day of Father Meenan's funeral. Collection of the Newport Historical Society, P10551. Reprinted with permission.

their residence until 1918. Once they did, however, they transformed the old Malbone House on Thames Street into a home for working girls.[149]

The Sisters of Saint Joseph also moved into more spacious quarters at this time. Dr. Storer, who owned Hunter House, a colonial mansion on the Point, offered it to the fifteen sisters, who were then living next to Saint Joseph's Church.[150] He had intended to turn the house into a convalescent home for women but, in August 1917, informed the *Newport Mercury* that he was instead loaning it to Father Higney, who would turn it over to the sisters for the coming year because they had "so long and patiently endured every possible inconvenience in their overcrowded convent on Mann [A]venue."[151] The arrangement was satisfactory, and the sisters stayed in Hunter House for the next twenty-five years.[152]

Newport's Wartime Woes

In the spring of 1915, Newport suffered, in quick succession, the loss of two of its best-known residents. In April, fifty-nine-year-old Father Meenan succumbed to pneumonia. News of his death was reported in the *Boston Globe* and the *New York Times*, with the *Globe*'s correspondent claiming that he had been pastor of "one of the most fashionable and wealthy parishes in the world."[153] The bishop and numerous priests came to Saint Mary's to take part in the funeral, which was celebrated by Father Coyle, Meenan's former classmate. The city was effectively shut down on that day.[154]

More shocking was the death of thirty-eight-year-old Alfred Gwynne Vanderbilt, who had been a passenger on the *Lusitania*, which had set sail from New York to Liverpool on May 1. As the ship neared Ireland, U-20, a German submarine, torpedoed it without warning. More than half of the *Lusitania*'s 2,000 passengers and crew members were lost. Vanderbilt died heroically, helping women and children get into lifeboats as the ship sank. He had been popular in Newport because of his generosity to the city, most notably by bankrolling the Mary Street YMCA in 1908.[155] In the words of the historian Eileen Warburton, Vanderbilt's tragic death "brought home the war to Newport" and undoubtedly turned many of its residents against Germany.[156] Unlike the Irish in some American cities, who were vehemently anti-intervention and sometimes pro-German, Newport's Irish did not express opposition to the Allies.[157]

An even more disturbing event occurred in the fall of 1916, when the German submarine U-53 sailed into Newport Harbor. As the United States was still neutral at this time, officers at the Naval War College received the Germans politely. The submarine's captain appeared to be friendly; he invited the top officers and their wives on board for a tour of the vessel and offered them drinks. But the next day, U-53 torpedoed five merchant ships—three British, one Dutch, and one Norwegian—near Nantucket Island, and ships from Newport's naval base were sent to rescue roughly two hundred passengers from those ships. Newporters were enraged by the U-boat captain's duplicitous behavior.[158] In April 1917, when President Wilson called for a declaration of war against Germany and its allies, most Newport residents were very supportive.

Newport Transformed

With war declared, Newport rapidly became a military city. The Torpedo Station expanded dramatically, ultimately employing 3,300 men and women at its factory. Fort Adams was staffed with coast artillery units.[159] The most significant change was the influx of 75,000 young men, who came to Newport to train with the naval reserves.[160] Because the city had a year-round population of just 30,000 at this time, finding housing for the recruits was challenging.[161] The author Maud Howe Elliott recalled that Newporters responded generously: "Parish houses were turned into barracks; private houses were filled. Everyone who had a spare room took in a boy."[162]

FIGURE 29. Photograph of Private Michael G. Murphy, 1918. Murphy was an Irish American from Newport who was killed in combat in France in 1918. Reprinted courtesy of Patrick F. Murphy.

Local Catholics supported the war effort in any way they could. Father James Ward, who had succeeded Father Meenan at Saint Mary's, urged his parishioners to contribute generously to the United War Work fund. Saint Joseph's, which had turned its old church on Washington Square into the Lafayette, a dance hall and movie theater, opened it up often for the servicemen to use. Likewise, the Father Mathew Total Abstinence Society made its gymnasium and meeting rooms available to the soldiers.[163] The Knights of Columbus worked hard to provide entertainment for the trainees.[164] They established a hut at the Training Station where they would sponsor concerts, vaudeville shows, and dances. They also rented rooms on Thames Street for the enjoyment of the troops and sometimes made use of Saint Mary's Hall.[165]

When word reached Newport in the wee hours of November 11, 1918, that an armistice had been signed in Europe, crowds emerged into Thames Street to celebrate, lighting bonfires and performing what the *Newport Daily News* termed a "snakedance."[166] On the following day a great parade was held, featuring the Knights of Columbus and the American Legion.[167] The marchers celebrated the end of the war but also remembered the seventy-two Newporters who lost their lives.[168] Among the dead were a number of young men of Irish, Italian, and Portuguese descent, including three Sullivans, a Casey, a Silvia, a Murphy, a Shea, a Donovan, and a Cardines. In 1932, city officials erected a dozen memorials throughout the city to honor those who had died in action. Richmond Field in the Fifth Ward was renamed for Private Michael G. Murphy, who had been killed in France just days before the end of the war.[169] Several other soldiers and sailors were memorialized with markers on the Bath Road median.[170] In 1936, the city's baseball stadium was renamed in honor of an Italian-born casualty, Bernardo Cardines. All of these memorials were meant to remind Newporters of the sacrifices made by a diverse cross-section of their community.[171]

Chapter 10

IRISH, ITALIAN, AND PORTUGUESE

Catholic Prominence in Post–World War I Newport

I am here to share the enthusiasm occasioned by the 150th anniversary of American independence, but particularly to bless this tablet, which marks an epoch in religious history, especially Roman Catholic history. On this site the blessed sacrament started, not only for the sick and the wounded of the French fleet, but primarily that God's blessing might descend on the people of Newport and the universal church.

> —Bishop William Hickey, quoted in *Providence Journal*,
> July 6, 1926

After the war's end, the U.S. Navy maintained a substantial presence in Newport. The Torpedo Factory continued its work, albeit with a scaled-back pool of employees; the Naval Training Station and the War College remained in operation, and several ships from the Atlantic Fleet were moored in Newport Harbor in the summer months.[1] The colonists, however, arrived in smaller numbers and staged fewer parties, especially after the ratification of Prohibition in 1919. Some decided to sell or donate their cottages, which were becoming burdensome to maintain. The new owners were often Catholic religious communities that turned the old mansions into schools or residences for their members. Catholics, especially those of Irish descent, remained influential in local politics and sometimes turned the city's attention to Irish affairs. In general, Newporters were not concerned about nativism, which was on the rise in Providence during these years. While the city's year-round population dipped almost 10 percent in the 1920s, its three Catholic parishes—Saint

Mary's, Saint Joseph's, and Saint Augustin's—flourished and maintained bustling schools.[2] By 1926, a fourth parish, Jesus Saviour, was established in the North End to cater to the needs of the town's Portuguese population, which had grown to 1,000 by 1920.[3]

Hailing the "President of the Irish Republic"

In 1919, Patrick Boyle was no longer Newport's mayor. He had been replaced by another Irish Catholic Democrat, Jeremiah Mahoney. In his first months on the job, Mahoney faced a challenge. Eamon de Valera, a veteran of Ireland's Fenian-led Easter Rising of 1916, was coming to America.[4] The British had sentenced him to death that year for his part in the Rising but then released him. Then he was rearrested in 1918 for allegedly spying for the Germans. In 1919, an associate, Michael Collins, masterminded De Valera's escape from an English jail. Now a fugitive, he stopped in Ireland long enough for supporters to dub him "President of the Irish Republic"—a designation that the British government rejected utterly.[5] He then set sail for the United States in June and received a hero's welcome from a crowd of 8,000 in New York's Madison Square Garden.[6]

During his American tour, De Valera hoped to raise money for the Irish Republic and spoke out against the Versailles Treaty, which President Wilson had already signed and the Senate would soon vote on. In the treaty, the Allies had made no mention of Irish self-determination, so De Valera wanted the senators to reject it. However, he received a mixed reception on his travels. Dozens of governors, mayors, and other politicians embraced him, but others chose to steer clear of him.[7] In August, after Rhode Island's Republican governor, R. L. Beeckman, announced that he would welcome De Valera to Providence, a group of ten Protestant ministers from Newport advised the governor not to make him an official guest of the state.[8] Although Beeckman complied, Mayor Mahoney and Newport's aldermen did not. Instead, they decided to extend an official welcome.[9] According to the *Providence Journal*, this decision sparked "considerable ill-feeling . . . particularly among members of the summer colony."[10] One of them, Samuel Bull, penned an angry letter to the *Newport Daily News*, calling the city's decision "a direct slap in the face of our friends and allies, the people of Great Britain. . . . [The Easter Rising rebels] tried to stab England in the back . . . and should receive no recognition from any true American."[11]

FIGURE 30. Photograph of Eamon de Valera in Newport, 1919. Cornelius Moore stands at his side, with the Sullivan children in front. Reprinted courtesy of the Museum of Newport Irish History.

Despite such criticisms, De Valera's trip to Newport proceeded as scheduled. After Beeckman and Mayor Joseph Gainer welcomed De Valera and his companion, Harry Boland, to Providence, the pair sailed to Newport on the *Editha*, a luxurious yacht owned by Edith Hanan, the wife of a successful Irish-born businessman.[12] There, they were hosted by Cornelius Moore, a young Newport attorney who was active with the Friends of Irish Freedom, a leading Irish American nationalist organization. Moore brought the pair to City Hall, where they were warmly greeted by Mahoney and the aldermen and by representatives of the city's Jewish and Italian communities.[13] After lunch, De Valera and Boland were escorted to Freebody Field and a cheering crowd of 4,000 well-wishers. Seated on the platform were Father Joseph McHugh of Saint Joseph's Church and Father Bernard Redihan, Father Reddy's successor at Saint Augustin's, as well as Patrick Boyle, three aldermen, and several other notable Irish Americans. When introducing De Valera to the crowd, Mahoney made a point of referring to him as "Mr. President."

After the rally, De Valera and Boland enjoyed a leisurely ten-mile ride down Bellevue Avenue and Ocean Drive. Spectators lined the route, waiting for a glimpse of De Valera. Only at the Redwood Library and the Reading Room were there gaps in the crowd.[14] Many members of those institutions no doubt shared Samuel Bull's pro-British views.

On the next morning, Moore escorted the pair to Saint Mary's, where they met Father Ward and attended the eleven o'clock Mass. The attorney then joined them on the *Editha*, and they sailed back to Providence. De Valera and Boland would crisscross the country until December 1920, when they returned to Ireland with $5 million for the Irish Republican movement.[15]

New Life for the Mansions

Mayor Mahoney's decision to host De Valera without regard for the views of the summer colonists was a sign of their diminishing role in Newport. Fewer came to town, and their famous leaders were aging or dead. Mamie Fish had died in 1915, Tessie Oelrichs was failing physically and mentally and rarely left Rosecliff, and Alva Belmont had shuttered Marble House and now spent most of her time in France.[16] Some prominent colonists, such as the Goelets, remained but focused their energies on challenging heavy city tax burdens.[17]

As colonists died or stopped coming to Newport, their properties were often repurposed. Soon after Annie Leary's death in 1919, for instance, the Elks Club acquired her Bellevue Avenue estate, Park Gate.[18] But as the decade progressed, Catholic groups came into possession of a significant share of Newport's historic properties. In 1920, Castlewood, the luxurious home of the Hanans, became the Mercy Home and School after its directors decided to move from Eagle Crest to a larger site. The Hanans had both died that year, and their heirs wanted to sell the estate immediately.[19] A few months later, the Knights of Columbus purchased the old Unitarian church on Mill Street and renamed it Columbus Hall. Father Coyle had briefly used the building when he was organizing Saint Joseph's parish in 1885; and, in the intervening years, it had served as an auction hall and a recreation center for servicemen.[20] In 1924, a Victorian mansion on Bellevue Avenue, along with two adjoining properties, became De la Salle, a Catholic high school for boys operated by the Christian Brothers.[21]

Saint Mary's and Her "Children"

Newport's three parishes had very different experiences in the early 1920s. While two of them thrived, one suffered a terrible tragedy. On January 1921, a policeman noticed smoke rising from Saint Mary's Rectory and pulled the fire alarm. The blaze spread rapidly, and fire fighters labored hard to rescue the priests and the servants. According to the *Mercury*, the pastor, Father James Ward, and his assistants, Father Michael Ryan and Father John Henry, had "very narrow escapes."[22] They got out of the building but suffered from shock and smoke inhalation. The housekeeper, Nellie Rush, died, but her sister Norah survived; and a fireman, John Malloy, almost died of his injuries.[23]

After the fire, Sister Sainte Thérèse, the superior of the Daughters of the Holy Ghost, invited the clergy to stay at Malbone House.[24] The priests gratefully accepted and moved to Thames Street. However, Father Ward, who suffered from a heart condition, never recovered from the trauma.[25] Only fifty-five years old, he died at the end of June, having served just six years at Saint Mary's. His replacement, Father Jeremiah Baggott, moved into Malbone House, and the three priests stayed there until a new rectory was completed in 1925.[26]

Saint Mary's younger "child," Saint Augustin's, fared much better than its mother did. Led by Father Bernard Redihan, who had succeeded Father Reddy in 1915, the parish sponsored a host of activities. These included social events such as a summer bazaar, which lasted for more than a week each August and featured food, games, movies, and a sale of handmade goods.[27] The parish's drama club staged several performances each year at the parish hall, including an Irish show for Saint Patrick's Day.[28] Among these parish organizations, the Holy Name Society held pride of place. In 1920, Saint Augustin's sponsored a Holy Name rally that drew 150 new members pledged to "clean speech."[29] The parish was also well represented at the Holy Name Society's grand triennial parades in Providence, which typically drew more than 20,000 members from across the state.[30]

Redihan also arranged for missions to stir up the faith of his parishioners. In 1916, he brought in two Paulist priests to preach for two weeks—one week to the women, one to the men.[31] In 1921, he invited a band of Redemptorist priests led by Father Joseph Turner. The *Daily News* reported that Turner's "personality in the pulpit has drawn thousands night after night to listen to his eloquent discourses."[32]

Saint Mary's elder "child," Saint Joseph's, was likewise flourishing; and in the fall of 1922, its priests and parishioners staged a great celebration. Because Father Higney had swiftly paid off the $75,000 debt on the new church building, it could now be officially consecrated.[33] The ceremonies were held on Columbus Day and were led by Bishop William Hickey, who had headed the diocese since Bishop Harkins's death in 1921.[34] The *Providence Journal* noted that "thousands witness[ed] [the] spectacle," which was presided over by Hickey with the assistance of Bishop Edmund Gibbons of Albany and one hundred priests.[35] The reporter wrote that the ceremony was carried out with "the full impressive ritual of the Catholic religion." After the dedication and Mass, Father Higney hosted all of the visiting clergy at a lunch at Columbus Hall, the Knights' new property on Mill Street.

The souvenir booklet published by the parish for the occasion paid tribute to many individuals and organizations. The Ancient Order of Hibernians, the Kerrymen's Association, and the Knights of Columbus had each paid for a stained-glass window, while the Ladies' Auxiliary of the Ancient Order of Hibernians had contributed the sanctuary lamp above the tabernacle and the "French citizens of Newport" had donated the crucifix. Agnes Storer had donated the sacristy bell and some of the mosaic tiles in the Stations of the Cross. She was also probably the donor of the carved wooden pulpit, which included an inscription honoring her father.[36] Sadly, Dr. Horatio Storer, who had played a critical role in the establishment of the parish, had died just three weeks before the dedication, at the age of ninety-two.

Storer had gained a national reputation. The *Boston Globe* and the *New York Times* both lauded his significant contributions to obstetrics and his service as president of the American Medical Association.[37] Newporters knew him as a founding trustee of Saint Joseph's and as a board member of Newport Hospital and the Newport Historical Society. In a long front-page obituary, the *Newport Mercury* called him "Newport's grand old man, . . . generous in the extreme, friendly to all."[38] In addition to advocating for the Religious of Jesus and Mary and donating Hunter House to the Sisters of Saint Joseph, he had become, in his last years, an outspoken defender of civil rights for African Americans. In 1906, he persuaded Newport's libraries not to carry Thomas Dixon's *The Clansman* because it glorified the Ku Klux Klan. Nine years later, when the book became the basis for D. W. Griffith's film *The Birth of a Nation*, Storer wrote to the city's newspapers asking that the film not be shown in Newport. Given its historic involvement with the slave trade, he thought it was imperative that the city not dishonor itself or its African American residents.[39] Perhaps his efforts made a difference because the film had long runs in Fall River, Boston, and Providence but was not shown in Newport.[40]

The End of an Era

A few weeks after Dr. Storer's death, Catholic Newport lost another of its fixtures, Patrick Boyle. The mayor, aged sixty-two, had just been elected to his seventeenth term in December 1922. He had won a three-way race, defeating the incumbent, Jeremiah Mahoney, and another challenger, Assemblyman Herbert W. Smith, but he was very ill when he took office on January 1. After his death, newspapers applauded his long record of service to the city. The *Mercury* noted that, as a Democrat "in a supposedly Republican city," "his successes were remarkable."[41] The *Daily News* praised his expertise with the city's finances and for being "in touch with every class in Newport's life," adding that "in his many appointments [he] often chose members of the summer colony who were anxious to work for the community."[42]

Boyle's body lay in state at City Hall for a day, and "immense throngs" came to pay their respects. The next day his coffin was taken to Saint Joseph's for the funeral Mass offered by Father Higney and other priests. Accompanying the casket were detachments of Newport's police officers and fire fighters and representatives of the Knights of Columbus, the Hibernians, and the Robert Emmet Association.[43] Governor William S. Flynn, Providence's Mayor Gainer, and a future governor, Theodore F. Green, all attended the funeral.[44]

After Boyle's death, an alderman, Joseph Martin, stepped in as interim mayor until elections could be held. In March, another Irish Catholic Democrat, Judge Mortimer Sullivan, was elected. He beat out two other Irish Catholics, attorney Cornelius Moore and J. T. O'Connell, a prosperous young entrepreneur.[45] The new mayor was the son of Timothy Sullivan, a revered Civil War veteran who had lost an arm fighting for the Union. Sullivan would serve as mayor for the succeeding twelve years until his appointment to the state superior court.

Educational Initiatives

Bishop Harkins had been an ardent supporter of Catholic education, working to found almost three dozen new Catholic elementary and secondary schools during his episcopate. He had also served as a trustee of the Catholic University of America and played a key role in establishing Providence College in 1917.[46] When Bishop Hickey succeeded Harkins in 1921, he wanted to continue his predecessor's work, for he, too, feared that Catholic education was under siege. He was particularly alarmed by Klan-backed proposals requiring children to attend public schools through the age of sixteen. Oregon had enacted such a measure in 1922;,and while the Rhode Island legislature did not go that far, it did pass the Peck Act, which gave the state's Board of Education broad oversight over parochial schools.[47] In response, the bishop announced a new initiative in 1923: the "Million Dollar Campaign," which aimed to establish more Catholic high schools around the state. The diocese quickly reached its ambitious fundraising goal, which enabled it to establish Mount Saint Charles Academy in Woonsocket, Saint Raphael's Academy in Pawtucket, and De la Salle Academy in Newport. The funds were also used to expand Saint Francis Xavier Academy and La Salle Academy, both in Providence. Because De la Salle would be an all-boys' high school, Saint Joseph's High School, which had been coeducational since its 1891 founding, became all-girls. As a result, the Mercy sisters shut down their own girls' school, Saint Mary's Academy, and focused on their grammar school.[48]

In September 1924, the Christian Brothers opened De la Salle Academy to one hundred freshmen and twenty sophomores. The school was situated on eight acres of prime land on Bellevue Avenue, formerly the William Weld estate. With each succeeding year, the brothers added another class, and they steadily improved the campus, completing an auditorium in 1927. De la Salle soon became known for its strong sports programs, often battling Rogers High School for championships.[49] According to Eileen Warburton, Rogers–De la Salle competitions "caught up the whole city."[50]

While many Newporters were excited about their city's new Catholic high school, Franco-Americans in Woonsocket were not so pleased by the bishop's campaign. According to the lawyer and journalist Elphage Daignault, the bishop had been high-handed in requiring all parishes to support his project. Daignault and his allies also worried that the diocese would limit the teaching of French at Mount Saint Charles Academy. As a way to resist Hickey's efforts, he founded *La Sentinelle*, a French-language newspaper that alerted Franco-Americans to what Daignault perceived as the bishop's Americanizing designs. The Sentinellists' conflict with the diocese continued for five years, and Daignault unsuccessfully sought redress from the Vatican. Instead, in 1928, Pope Pius XI excommunicated more than fifty of the protesters after they attempted to sue the bishop in Superior Court.[51]

In the midst of this battle, Hickey received welcome news from Aquidneck Island: another Catholic boys' high school, Portsmouth Priory, would be opening in the fall of 1926. Although the new school had the bishop's full support, he was not the driving force behind it. Rather, it had been set up by Benedictine monks, who had come to Portsmouth in 1919 and were affiliated with a monastery in England.[52] The founding headmaster, Father J. Hugh Diman, O.S.B., was the former Episcopal clergyman who had established Saint George's School in 1896. After twenty years there, he resigned his post and began to take instruction in the Catholic faith from Father Higney and, in a less formal way, from his friends the LaFarges.[53] Shortly before Christmas 1917 he was received into the Catholic church at Saint Joseph's.[54] He then joined the Benedictines, took the name Hugh, and was ordained in 1921. In September 1926, Diman, now sixty-three, opened the Priory to eighteen boys, all boarders. The school would remain small and become known as a rigorous institution, attracting highly talented faculty such as the calligrapher John Howard Benson and the liturgical artist Ade Bethune.[55] It would also develop an athletic rivalry with Saint George's, and Diman loved to watch his two schools play against each other.[56]

Celebrating the Sesquicentennial

The year 1926 was the 150th anniversary of the signing of the Declaration of Independence, and many Newporters wanted to plan a special July 4 celebration. In April, the *Newport Mercury*'s editor fretted that "the city has made no special appropriation for the Fourth of July this year. This will be the one hundred and fiftieth anniversary of the United

States, and it seems a pity to allow this great event to pass unnoticed in Newport."[57] He seemed frustrated by the attitude of the town: elsewhere in the same issue, he asked, "What is the matter with Newport? Is there any excuse for the vacant stores on Thames Street in the heart of the business section?"[58] It is probable that officials were more focused on rebuilding City Hall, which had been badly damaged in a March 1925 fire, than in filling storefronts.[59] After the fire, city offices moved to the Levi Gale house on Washington Square and then to Father Mathew Hall on Thames Street.[60] By December, the city had collected bids for reconstruction, which was expected to take two years at a cost of $200,000. The high price may explain why city officials allocated only $500 to mark the sesquicentennial.[61]

Yet other groups organized events, and they helped give Newport a festive air. In May 1926, Fort Adams celebrated its own 150th anniversary. Coast Artillery troops headed a grand downtown parade, followed by Marines and Training Station cadets. Local military bands provided the music. Afterward, officers dined at the Hotel Viking, which had opened that week on Bellevue Avenue to great fanfare.[62] The hotel had taken two years to build and had been very much a collaborative effort, with the enterprising J. T. O'Connell taking a leading role. The Newport Chamber of Commerce spearheaded the operation, and many residents purchased shares in the corporation and helped to cover the $500,000 needed to build the brick Colonial Revival–style building.[63] The hotel's name had been chosen through a public contest that drew hundreds of submissions, and organizers hoped that the grand edifice would attract more vacationers to the city.[64] After hailing it as "a triumph for local enterprise and community spirit," the *Mercury*'s editor added, "The people of the city are hopeful that its success may be so great that outside capitalists may be inclined to build other hotels here for . . . the vast number of people who desire to come to Newport but have been kept away because of lack of adequate hotel facilities."[65]

A highlight of Independence Day was a midnight fireworks display at Easton's Beach, organized by the city. Otherwise, the *Mercury* acknowledged that "the official program for the day was a rather quiet one, sports and band concerts comprising about all that the city was able to provide for the celebration."[66] The Hibernians decided to fill this void and stage a triumphal ceremony at the Colony House, the historic building where the Declaration of Independence had been proclaimed in 1776. The Colony House had also been the site of Rhode Island's first Catholic Masses, offered by French chaplains during the American Revolution. To commemorate the day, the Hibernians commissioned a bronze tablet and organized an elaborate ceremony. A host of dignitaries attended: Michael Donahue, the national director of the Hibernians; Bishop Hickey; Senator Peter Gerry; Congressman Clark Burdick; Mayor Sullivan; Father Higney; Ellen Jolly, the former president of the Ladies' Auxiliary of the Hibernians; and the Irish Free State's ambassador, Dr. Timothy Smiddy.[67] The event drew 1,000 people to Washington Square, where they watched Hickey unveil and bless the tablet, which was then installed inside the Colony House—on the south wall, near where the French had set up their chapel. The bishop urged his listeners to "remember that monuments and tablets are not all in life, that you too contribute by showing patriotism and Christianity . . . [and by] lives of uprightness and loyalty."[68] Afterward, the Hibernians marched as a body to Trinity Church's graveyard, where the Hibernian president and the Irish ambassador laid a wreath on the grave of Admiral de Ternay, who had died in Newport in 1780 and had been buried in a Catholic ceremony.

The White Sisters Expand

Agnes Storer would surely have approved of the Hibernians' effort to commemorate Newport's first Masses, and she may have attended the ceremonies. However, her present focus was on fulfilling her late father's wishes. She knew that Dr. Storer had wanted to set up a convalescent home for women in Newport; in fact, he had once planned to use Hunter House for that purpose.[69] So, in January 1926, Storer met with Bishop Hickey to discuss her idea of donating a house in the Point, located next door to the Cenacle, for the care of elderly women. She wanted the Daughters of the Holy Ghost—the White Sisters—to oversee the new facility. Storer had already written to the community's superior, Mother Marie Similien, describing her plan and assuring the sister: "You have so readily won the complete trust of the priests in the three Newport parishes, the confidence and approval of our local physicians, both Catholic and Protestant alike, whose patients you have nursed, and also the love of all who have known you . . . making friends as well as overcoming prejudice."[70]

Mother Similien was concerned about the challenge of staffing another facility, but after meeting with the bishop, she agreed to take on the new ministry. In July, just a few days after the Colony House celebrations, the bishop returned to Newport to bless and officially open Stella Maris Home at 91 Washington Street.[71] The house, donated by Storer and formerly known as the Mayer Cottage, had been constructed in 1860 from Connecticut free stone and was roomy enough to house sixteen boarders and three White Sisters.[72] It was situated on a shady, spacious lot overlooking Newport Harbor.[73] A reporter for the *Newport Daily News* thought the location was perfect: "[The] Home will be entirely surrounded by invigorating and restful scenery."[74]

In September 1927, Bishop Hickey returned once again to Newport, this time to bless the Saint Clare's Home for Elderly Women. Since 1925, when the Saint Mary's priests had moved out of Malbone House and into their new rectory, the sisters had been thinking about how to use their reacquired space. Now, with the backing of a former mayor, Fritz Garrettson, who had recently become a Catholic, they were able to convert a portion of the mansion into a home for twenty-three older women.[75] For $10 per week, guests would receive room and board and laundry service.[76]

In 1928, the sisters decided on yet another improvement: they wanted to move their day care center out of Malbone House into a new building. The superior, Sister Rodolphe, reached out to Garrettson, who agreed to erect a brick building on Spring Street that would be named the Garrettson Memorial Day Nursery in honor of his daughter Emily, who had died the year before. The stately edifice was completed in the summer of 1930, but Garrettson did not live to see it.[77] He died in January, hailed for his many contributions to Newport.[78]

Catholics and the Klan

By 1927, Catholics were becoming more prominent on the national scene. The upcoming presidential race pitted Al Smith, the four-time Democratic governor of New York, against President Calvin Coolidge's Secretary of Commerce, Herbert Hoover. With the economy seemingly strong, Smith was facing an uphill battle. Moreover, he was also a Catholic—the first ever nominated for president—and a "wet" with regards to Prohibition.

In much of the country, these factors worked against him. Yet Smith persevered. After an attorney, Charles Marshall, raised questions in the *Atlantic Monthly* about how the candidate would reconcile his faith with his duty to uphold the Constitution, Smith replied in the subsequent issue, assuring Marshall that he believed "in the absolute separation of Church and State."[79]

Much of America was skeptical of Smith, but Rhode Island was more receptive. Locally, nativism had been on the rise, and many Rhode Islanders likely saw him as an antidote. The Ku Klux Klan was making its presence felt: crosses had been burned on the grounds of Providence College, and sizable Klan rallies had been held in rural communities such as Foster, Exeter, and Greenville.[80] Most Rhode Islanders were probably also put off by Hoover's "dry" views. With the exception of Connecticut, theirs was the only state that never ratified the Eighteenth Amendment.[81]

As Election Day neared, Smith undertook a tour of New England. After drawing massive crowds in Boston, Worcester, and Springfield, he visited Providence, Woonsocket, and Pawtucket in late October.[82] According to the *Providence Journal*, Smith "was engulfed in such an avalanche of rampant enthusiasm as has never before been accorded any political candidate in the history of the State." The reporter estimated that 40,000 people, mostly from "the middle and laboring classes," came out to cheer him. Although Smith did not visit Newport, he sent his son Walter to the city, where he was warmly greeted by Mayor Mortimer Sullivan. After a Saturday evening rally, Walter Smith attended Sunday Mass at Saint Augustin's and greeted worshipers at an "impromptu reception in front of the church."[83] Perhaps the Smiths' stops in Rhode Island made a difference. On Election Day, the state went for Smith by about 1,500 votes, a margin of slightly more than 0.5 percent. In Newport, he edged Hoover by about three hundred votes.[84] He also eked out a win in Massachusetts and took six of the southern states, but everywhere else, even in Smith's home state of New York, Hoover won easily. Nonetheless, Smith's campaign set the stage for future Democratic victories at the state and national level. Rhode Island would come under Democratic control in the 1930s, and President Franklin D. Roosevelt would draw on Smith's strength with urban ethnic groups when building his New Deal coalition.[85]

FIGURE 31. Photograph of Bishop William Hickey's dedication of the Church of Jesus Saviour, 1930. The new church was located on Broadway in the north end of Newport. Reprinted courtesy of the Church of Jesus Saviour.

Newport's New Parish

Though the nativists had made inroads into parts of Rhode Island, Newport was not affected, and its Catholics continued to expand their ministries without hindrance. At the same time, the Portuguese population was increasing in Newport and Middletown, many of the immigrants now owned their own farms or managed the greenhouses and gardens of summer colonists.[86] In 1921, a group of Portuguese men met with Bishop Hickey to discuss the idea of founding a new Catholic parish in the city's North End to minister to this growing population. They emphasized that Saint Anthony's Church, which was already serving them, was small and no longer had a Portuguese-speaking priest in residence.

In 1901, when Bishop Harkins had established Saint Anthony's, he had entrusted it to the Holy Ghost fathers, who had stationed Father Manuel Barros, a Portuguese priest from the community, at the chapel for several years. But Barros had left the parish in 1919, and his replacement was not fluent in Portuguese.[87] This put the bishop into a bind. There were very few Portuguese priests in the diocese, and Portuguese representatives in Pawtucket were also trying to form a new parish.

Finally, in 1925, he was able to send Father Antonio Lopes to Newport. A native of the Azores, Lopes had been assisting his brother, Father Jose Lopes, at Saint Francis Xavier parish in East Providence. In Newport, Father Antonio met with Father Higney, who introduced him to the Portuguese congregants of Saint Joseph. As Lopes set about creating a census of the Portuguese population, Hickey told him that the community would need to raise $25,000 to show that it could be self-sustaining. Portuguese residents responded overwhelmingly, meeting that goal in just a few days. Hickey then gave Lopes permission to look for a temporary site for the diocese's new parish, which would be called Jesus Saviour.[88] The Portuguese Beneficent Association offered him free use of the newly built Vasco da Gama Hall on Fenner Avenue.[89] On Christmas Eve in 1926, Lopes celebrated Midnight Mass at the hall, the parish's founding event.

In the following months, Lopes looked for land for the church and organized a series of bazaars and other fundraising events.[90] In 1928, a parish committee purchased land on Broadway and Vernon Avenue, and by the end of the year the diocese awarded a contract to Joseph Donatelli of Providence to construct the church for $69,000.[91] The architect was Ambrose Murphy of Murphy, Hindle, and White, who had designed several churches in Rhode Island and Massachusetts, including Holy Rosary, the first Portuguese church in the diocese. His firm had also completed Saint Joseph's Church, so Father Higney may well have recommended him to Father Lopes.

The parish continued to operate in the Fenner Avenue hall while work on the new church progressed. Masses were offered every day, and the hall also hosted First Communions, marriages, and funerals.[92] On Christmas Eve 1929, Father Lopes celebrated Midnight Mass for more than 1,000 worshippers in the new red-brick church on Broadway.[93] About six months later, Bishop Hickey formally dedicated it. Assisting him were Father Higney; Father Joseph Coleman, the pastor of Saint Augustin's; and two monks from the Portsmouth Priory. Hundreds of parishioners and well-wishers attended the ceremonies, including representatives of the Vasco da Gama Society, the Holy Name Society, the Holy Ghost Society of Jamestown, and the Portuguese-American Club of Portsmouth. The homilist was Father Jose Lopes, the pastor's brother. After the dedication, Hickey administered confirmation to 250 members of the parish, adults as well as children.[94]

A Carmel for Newport

Emilie Post, a great-granddaughter of Cornelius Vanderbilt, was a Catholic convert with a great interest in the Discalced Carmelites, especially Saint Therese of Lisieux.[95] After her husband died in 1915, she moved to France and supported the Red Cross, working as a nurse and caring for wounded soldiers. At the war's end, she spent a few years in Lisieux and became interested in bringing a Carmelite convent to Stoneleigh, her estate in Newport, located on Narragansett Avenue between Bellevue Avenue and Spring Street. On her return to America in 1927, Post contacted the Carmelite master general, who reached out to nuns across the United States to see if any wanted to undertake a new foundation. In 1929, several sisters in New Orleans agreed to establish a new house at Stoneleigh. To provide more privacy, Post raised the height of the stone wall around her mansion, and in May seven sisters moved in.[96] Post, who had become a lay Carmelite, lived with the sisters for five years and then decided to move to England.[97]

Thus, in August 1930, the bishop was back in Newport for another dedication. With the establishment of the Carmelite Monastery, the city was now home to five different communities of sisters, a total of roughly ninety nuns. The Mercy sisters were operating two parish schools and an orphanage, the Sisters of Saint Joseph were running a grammar school and a high school, the Daughters of the Holy Ghost were staffing two homes for the elderly and a day care center, the Cenacle sisters were offering retreats, and the Discalced Carmelites were a cloistered community dedicated entirely to prayer.[98] There were also ten diocesan priests serving in the city's four parishes and a group of Christian Brothers who administered De la Salle High School. For laymen and women, there was a host of religious, charitable, and cultural organizations.

EPILOGUE

Catholics in Newport had certainly come a long way since colonial times, when the townspeople were enthusiastically burning effigies of the pope on Thames Street. During the Revolutionary War, the arrival of cultured French officers and chaplains had shifted attitudes, charming Newport residents and paving the way for the Irish Catholics who would arrive early in the nineteenth century. Although the first wave of Irish came to build Fort Adams, many more soon arrived to fill service jobs in the city's thriving tourist economy. By the Gilded Age, they were mostly working for the city's wealthy summer visitors. Yet, by 1930, Catholics had become embedded in Newport's political, economic, and cultural fabric. Catholic organizations inherited and repurposed many of the summer colonists' grand properties, and that expansion continued after World War II. In 1947, the Mercy sisters acquired Ochre Court from the Goelets and established Salve Regina College. In 1957, the Sisters of Saint Joseph of Cluny acquired a portion of the Arthur Curtiss James estate and established the Cluny School.[1] Meanwhile, in nearby Portsmouth, another community of sisters, the Faithful Companions of Jesus, established Saint Philomena's School in 1953, locating it across the street from the Portsmouth Priory.[2]

In the 1960s, however, this remarkable infrastructure started to unravel. After John F. Kennedy was elected president, Catholics recognized that they had entered America's mainstream, and some began to question if they needed to maintain separate schools and hospitals any longer.[3] At the same time, the decisions of the Second Vatican Council (1962–65) were dramatically changing all aspects of Catholic life. Masses, offered in Latin for centuries, began to be celebrated in the vernacular; contemporary music often replaced Gregorian chant in the liturgies. Many nuns moved out of their convents, dropped their religious garb, and took up new work outside of the classrooms. Many sisters, priests, and brothers also embraced ecumenism, entering into sympathetic dialogues with Protestants and Jews.[4]

While some Catholics were enthusiastic about these changes, others were shaken by them. Soon fewer Catholics were attending Mass regularly, and far fewer were entering the priesthood or religious orders.[5] For Newport residents, the eroding presence of the church was compounded by the U.S. Navy's decision to move its entire Atlantic Fleet to Norfolk, Virginia, in the early 1970s.[6] The city's population dropped, and with fewer children in the community and fewer sisters and brothers available to teach them, Catholic schools and other institutions began closing.

Just as Catholics had once repurposed empty mansions to suit their needs, Newport's unused Catholic facilities have been adapted for new uses. The Cenacle is now Harbor House, a senior residence, though the liturgical artist Ade Bethune led the successful effort to preserve its 1914 Gothic chapel. Saint Mary's Convent was moved to Thames Street and is now the Admiral Fitzroy Inn; the Stella Maris Home is also an inn. De la Salle Academy and the Knights of Columbus Hall are apartment buildings, the Carmelite Monastery is a private residence, and the girls' high school is the headquarters of the Preservation Society of Newport County.[7] What had taken Catholics many decades to assemble came undone relatively quickly.

Yet much of the infrastructure remains. The city's four Catholic parishes are still operational in the city, which today has a population of just 25,000. Saint Joseph's Church has had significant renovations and now offers Sunday-evening Masses in Spanish to accommodate its increasing number of Latin American parishioners.[8] Saint Mary's Church completed a major capital campaign in 2002, and its world-class organ was restored by Canadian craftsmen in 2016.[9] Jesus Saviour Church was recently renovated, and the parish's thriving Vasco da Gama Society is well known for its annual Holy Ghost feast celebrations.[10] Saint Augustin's Church raised nearly $1 million in a 2023 capital campaign, though the parish now shares its pastor with Saint Mary's, due to a shortage of diocesan priests.[11] Saint Clare's Home was renovated by the diocese in 2013 and now houses fifty residents in its assisted-living and memory-care facility.[12]

Salve Regina, which began as a women's college, went coeducational in 1973 and achieved university status in 1991. The school's enrollment has grown from two hundred students in the 1950s to roughly 2,700 today. Praised for its careful stewardship of the Gilded Age cottages on its campus, the university completed Our Lady of Mercy Chapel in 2010. Designed by the Yale architect Robert A. M. Stern, it incorporates the LaFarge stained-glass windows that were once in the Caldwell mansion on Kay Street and bells salvaged from a shuttered church in Lawrence, Massachusetts.[13]

There are no longer any Catholic elementary or secondary schools in Newport. The Aquidneck Island grammar schools—Saint Mary's, Saint Augustin's, Hazard Memorial, Saint Anthony's in Portsmouth, and Saint Lucy's in Middletown—merged in 1971 to form the Newport County Catholic Regional School, which now is run out of Saint Lucy's. Renamed All Saints STEAM Academy in 2017, the school stresses mathematics, science, and technology.[14] Saint Philomena's School has steadily expanded and now enrolls more than four hundred students. The U.S. Department of Education has awarded it two Blue Ribbons of Excellence. Portsmouth Priory, now known as Portsmouth Abbey School, has been coeducational since 1992 and attracts students from all over the world.[15]

The Hibernian men and women remain active in Newport's Fifth Ward and always take a prominent part in the city's Saint Patrick's Day parades, which attract thousands of spectators each year. The Museum of Newport Irish History, organized in 1996, operates an Interpretive Center on Thames Street, sponsors lectures on Irish topics, and carefully maintains the Barney Street property where Father Woodley established the first Catholic parish in 1828. Perhaps those who did so much to build up Catholic Newport—the Harpers; Mother Frances Xavier Warde; Fathers Corry, Fitton, Coyle, Meenan, Higney, and Lopes; Dr. Grace; Patrick Boyle; Fritz Garrettson; George Hazard; George Downing; the Storers; Marion Cutting; Countess Leary; Emilie Post; and the several communities of sisters—would take comfort in knowing that considerable portions of it are still intact.

NOTES

ABBREVIATIONS

AAB	Archives of the Archdiocese of Boston
AAH	Archives of the Archdiocese of Hartford
BG	*Boston Globe*
BMHD	Bishop Matthew Harkins Diary, Diocese of Providence Archives
BP	*Boston Pilot*
BTFHD	Bishop Thomas Hendricken Diary, Diocese of Providence Archives
DPA	Diocese of Providence Archives
FRDG	*Fall River Daily Globe*
FRDH	*Fall River Daily Herald*
FRDN	*Fall River Daily News*
HT	*Herald of the Times*
LD	*The Literary Diary of Ezra Stiles*, 3 vols. (New Haven, CT: Yale University Press, 1901).
LEB	Land Evidence Books, Newport City Hall
MFJ	*Manufacturers and Farmers Journal*
MHC, BNC	Mercy Heritage Center, Belmont, NC
NARA-B	National Archives and Records Administration, Boston
NDN	*Newport Daily News*
NH	*Newport History*
NHS	Newport Historical Society
NM	*Newport Mercury*
NYH	*New York Herald*
NYT	*New York Times*
PAWDC	Paulist Archives, Washington, DC
PEP	*Providence Evening Press*
PESRL	Papers of Ezra Stiles, microfilm ed., Redwood Library, Newport, RI
PG	*Providence Gazette*
PJ	*Providence Journal*
PLUSCB	Hugh Nolan, ed., *Pastoral Letters of the U.S. Catholic Bishops*, 4 vols. (Washington, DC: United States Catholic Conference, 1983).

PP	*Providence Patriot*
PPo	*Providence Post*
PT	*Pawtucket Times*
PV	*Providence Visitor*
RIH	*Rhode Island History*
R-IR	*Rhode-Island Republican*
SR	*Springfield Republican*
TT	*Truth Teller*
UNDA	University of Notre Dame Archives
USC	*United States Chronicle*

INTRODUCTION

1 See, for example, *New-Bedford Mercury*, August 22, 1834; and *Liberator*, August 23, 1834.

2 *R-IR*, August 20, 1834.

3 *Jesuit*, October 18, 1834.

4 See Nancy Lusignan Schultz, *Fire and Roses: The Burning of the Charlestown Convent, 1834* (Boston: Northeastern University Press, 2000), 231–68.

5 Arthur Ross, *A Discourse, Embracing the Civil and Religious History of Newport* (Providence: Brown, 1838), 152.

6 Ray Allen Billington, *Protestant Crusade, 1800–1860: A Study of the Origins of American Nativism* (New York, 1938; reprint, Chicago: Quadrangle, 1964); George M. Potter, *To the Golden Door: The Story of the Irish in Ireland and America* (Boston: Little, Brown, 1960); John T. McGreevy, *American Jesuits and the World* (Princeton, NJ: Princeton University Press, 2016); Schultz, *Fire and Roses*; Thomas H. O'Connor, *Boston Catholics: A History of the Church and Its People* (Boston: Northeastern University Press, 1998); Timothy J. Meagher, *Inventing Irish America: Generation, Class, and Ethnic Identity in a New England City, 1880–1928* (Notre Dame, IN: University of Notre Dame Press, 2001); Evelyn Savidge Sterne, *Ballots and Bibles: Ethnic Politics and the Catholic Church in Providence* (Ithaca, NY: Cornell University Press, 2004); Robert W. Hayman, *Catholicism in Rhode Island and the Diocese of Providence*, 3 vols. (Providence: Diocese of Providence, 1982–2020); Paula M. Kane, *Separatism and Subculture: Boston Catholicism, 1900–1920* (Chapel Hill: University of North Carolina Press, 1994); Patrick T. Conley and Matthew J. Smith, *Catholicism in Rhode Island: The Formative Era* (Providence: Diocese of Providence, 1976).

7 Howard C. Rice, Jr., and Anne S. K. Brown, trans. and eds., *The American Campaign of Rochambeau's Army, 1780, 1781, 1782, 1783*, 2 vols. (Princeton, NJ: Princeton University Press, 1972), 1:245.

8 *R-IR*, August 20, 1834.

9 *NM*, July 9, 1864.

10 Jon Sterngass, *First Resorts: Pursuing Pleasure at Saratoga Springs, Newport and Coney Island* (Baltimore: Johns Hopkins University Press, 1991), 182–228.

CHAPTER 1: "WE KNOW OF NONE AMONG US"

1 Cotton Mather, *Magnalia Christi Americana*, 2 vols. (1702; reprint, New York, 1967), 2:520–21, emphasis in original. *Colluvies* means "mixture." Antinomians such as Anne Hutchinson believed that followers of Christ were not bound by God's commandments. Familists were

an ecumenical Christian sect founded in Holland. Anabaptists were Christians opposed to infant baptism. Anti-sabbatarians opposed the strict observance of the Sabbath. Arminians rejected Calvinist ideas regarding predestination. Socinians did not believe in the Trinity. Ranters were pantheists known for their outspoken preaching style.

2 Anne Hutchinson came to Portsmouth in 1638 and moved to New York in 1643 after the death of her husband, William. There she and six of her children were killed in an Indian raid. See Eve LaPlante, *American Jezebel: The Uncommon Life of Anne Hutchinson, the Woman who Defied the Puritans* (San Francisco: HarperCollins, 2004), 208–37.

3 One determined Quaker, Mary Dyer, was twice banished from Massachusetts and then hanged on Boston Common in 1660 after she returned a third time. Three Quaker men were hanged as well, and two others had their ears cut off. See Ruth Plimpton, *Mary Dyer: Biography of a Rebel Quaker* (Boston: Branden, 1994); and Richard D. Brown and Jack Tager, *Massachusetts: A Concise History* (Amherst: University of Massachusetts Press, 2000), 11–57.

4 William Pencak, *Jews and Gentiles in Early America, 1654–1800* (Ann Arbor: University of Michigan Press, 2005), 12–13, 83. For Roger Williams and the Puritan theologian John Cotton's antipathy to Judaism, see Frederic Cople Jaher, *A Scapegoat in the New Wilderness: The Origins and Rise of Anti-Semitism in America* (Cambridge, MA: Harvard University Press, 1994), 92–94.

5 Sydney V. James, *Colonial Rhode Island: A History* (New York: Scribner's, 1975), 39–47, 186–228; John Hattendorf, *Semper Eadem: A History of Trinity Church in Newport, 1698–2000* (Newport, RI: Trinity Church, 2001).

6 John M. Barry, *Roger Williams and the Creation of the American Soul* (New York: Viking, 2012), 278–312; William G. McLoughlin, *Rhode Island: A History* (New York: Norton, 1986), 28–30.

7 Patrick T. Conley and Matthew J. Smith, *Catholicism in Rhode Island: The Formative Era* (Providence: Diocese of Providence, 1976) 1–4; Edmund S. Morgan, *Roger Williams: The Church and the State* (New York: Harcourt, Brace and World, 1967), 136–37. Morgan claims that Williams would have disarmed Catholics and forced them to dress distinctively but would not have interfered with their religious practice.

8 On Charles's Catholic sympathies, see Jenny Uglow, *A Gambling Man: Charles II and the Restoration* (London: Faber and Faber, 2009), 512–25.

9 Barry, *Roger Williams*, 380–82; Plimpton, *Mary Dyer*, 195–205.

10 For the text of the Charter of 1663, see Lonang Institute, http://www.LONANG.com. See also James, *Colonial Rhode Island*, 67–70.

11 Conley and Smith, *Catholicism in Rhode Island*, 5.

12 Morris Gutstein, *The Story of the Jews of Newport* (New York: Bloch, 1936), 28, 39.

13 Mather, *Magnalia Christi Americana*, 2:520–21.

14 Gutstein, *The Story of the Jews*, 158.

15 Carl Bridenbaugh, *Fat Mutton and Liberty of Conscience: Society in Rhode Island, 1636–1690* (Providence: Brown University Press, 1974), 93–130; McLoughlin, *Rhode Island*, 25.

16 John Miller, *James II* (New Haven, CT: Yale University Press, 2000), 58–59; Robert Emmet Curran, *Papist Devils: Catholics in British America, 1574–1783* (Washington, DC: Catholic University of America Press, 2014), 126–27.

17 Brown and Tager, *Massachusetts*, 47; McLoughlin, *Rhode Island*, 48.

18 Miller, *James II*, 72–75.

19 Mary, James's daughter from his first marriage, had remained an Anglican after her father's conversion to Catholicism.

20 *Jacobite* is derived from *Jacobus*, Latin for "James."

21 Penal laws had been imposed in the early 1600s but were rescinded by Charles II. See Frank McLynn, *The Jacobites* (London: Routledge, 1988).

22 On the Irish penal laws, see Patrick J. Corish, *The Catholic Community in the Seventeenth and*

Eighteenth Centuries (Dublin: Helicon, 1981). On England's, see J. C. H. Aveling, *The Handle and the Axe: Catholic Recusants in England from the Reformation to Emancipation* (London: Blond and Briggs, 1976), 238–52; and Linda Colley, *Britons: Forging the Nation, 1707–1837* (New Haven, CT: Yale University Press, 1992), 18–19.

23 Thomas J. Curry, *The First Freedoms: Church and State in America to the Passage of the First Amendment* (New York: Oxford University Press, 1986), 47–52; Maura Jane Farrelly, *Papist Patriots: The Making of an American Catholic Identity* (New York: Oxford University Press, 2012), 193–206; Jay P. Dolan, *The American Catholic Experience* (New York: Doubleday, 1985), 84–85.

24 Steven K. Green, *Inventing a Christian America: The Myth of the Religious Founding* (New York: Oxford University Press, 2015), 33.

25 Curry, *The First Freedoms*, 59.

26 Green, *Inventing a Christian America*, 29.

27 John Tracy Ellis, *Documents of American Catholic History* (Milwaukee: Bruce, 1962), 119.

28 Thomas H. O'Connor, *Boston Catholics* (Boston: Northeastern University Press, 1998), 7–8.

29 Hattendorf, *Semper Eadem*; Delbert Tildesley, *St. Michael's Church in Bristol, Rhode Island, 1718–1983* (Bristol, RI: Saint Michael's Church, 1989); McLoughlin, *Rhode Island*, 46–47.

30 Conley and Smith, *Catholicism in Rhode Island*, 7.

31 Curry, *The First Freedoms*, 245, n. 46.

32 McLoughlin, *Rhode Island*, 74–75. He describes the statute as "a puzzle to historians" (74).

33 Mary Augustina Ray, *American Opinion of Roman Catholicism in the Eighteenth Century* (1936; reprint, New York: Octagon, 1974), 363–64; Conley and Smith, *Catholicism in Rhode Island*, 7–9.

34 C. P. B. Jefferys, *Newport: A Concise History* (Newport, RI: Newport Historical Society, 2008), 21, 16.

35 Elaine Crane, *A Dependent People: Newport, Rhode Island, in the Revolutionary Era* (New York: Fordham University Press, 1985), 20.

36 Jay Coughtry, *The Notorious Triangle: Rhode Island and the African Slave Trade, 1700–1807* (Philadelphia: Temple University Press, 1981), 36–38.

37 Christy Clark-Pujara, *Dark Work: The Business of Slavery in Rhode Island* (New York: New York University Press, 2016), 19.

38 Berkeley was appointed Anglican bishop of Cloyne in 1732.

39 George C. Mason, *Annals of the Redwood Library* (Newport, RI,: Redwood Library, 1891), 9–11; Rockwell Stensrud, *Newport: A Lively Experiment, 1639–1969* (Newport, RI: Redwood Library, 2006), 132–36.

40 Gutstein, *The Story of the Jews*, 51–52.

41 Crane, *A Dependent People*, 107.

42 George Whitefield drew crowds of up to 8,000 listeners in many of the New England cities that he visited. See Mark Noll, *The Work We Have to Do: A History of Protestants in America* (New York: Oxford University Press, 2002), 43–44.

43 George Whitefield, *A continuation of the Reverend Mr. Whitefield's Journal from Savannah, June 25. 1740. to his arrival at Rhode-Island* (Boston, 1741), 45; McLoughlin, *Rhode Island*, 77.

44 McLoughlin, *Rhode Island*, 57.

45 Stiles worried that "nothingarians" and deists were also numerous in Providence and lamented that "so greatly are they degenerated as to Religion that . . . not *one sixth* attend publick worship" in Boston. See *LD*, August 26, 1772, 1:278; September 2, 1780, 2:465. See also Elaine Crane, "Uneasy Coexistence: Religious Tensions in Eighteenth Century Newport," *NH* 53 (Summer 1980): 102–3; and *Extracts from the Itineraries and Other Miscellanies of Ezra Stiles, DD, LL.D, 1755–1794*, ed. Franklin Dexter (New Haven, CT: Yale University Press, 1916), 13, 105.

46 Curran, *Papist Devils*, 216–25; Thomas S. Kidd, *God of Liberty: A Religious History of the American Revolution* (New York: Basic Books, 2010), 16–18; Nathan O. Hatch, "The Origins

of Civil Millennialism in America: New England Clergymen, War with France, and the Revolution," *William and Mary Quarterly* 31 (July 1974): 417–22; Green, *Inventing a Christian America*, 54, 109.

47 John Burt, *The mercy of God to his people, in the vengeance he renders to their adversaries, the occasion of their abundant joy* (Newport, RI, 1759), 4. Burt is drawing on Revelation 17:4–5. On Burt, see *The First Congregational Church, Bristol, Rhode Island* (Bristol, RI, 2006), 9.

48 James Franklin, Jr., was a nephew of Benjamin Franklin.

49 There were virtually no British soldiers stationed in the port cities at the end of the French and Indian War. See Fred Anderson, *The War That Made America* (New York: Vikiing, 2005), 245–46.

50 On Howard, see Daniel Snydacker, Jr., "The Remarkable Career of Martin Howard, Esq.," *NH* 60 (Winter 1988): 2–16. Another prominent member of the Newport Junto was Peter Harrison, the architect who designed the Redwood Library and the Touro Synagogue in Newport and King's Chapel in Boston. See Carl Bridenbaugh, *Peter Harrison: First American Architect* (Chapel Hill: University of North Carolina Press, 1949).

51 [Martin Howard, Jr.], *A Letter from a Gentleman at Halifax, to His Friend in Rhode-Island* (Newport, RI, 1765), in *The American Revolution: Writings from the Pamphlet Debate, 1764–1772*, ed. Gordon S. Wood, 2 vols. (New York: Library of America, 2015), 1:159–160, emphasis in original.

52 [James Otis, Jr.], "Brief Remarks on the Defense of the Halifax Libel," in *The Collected Political Writings of James Otis*, ed. Richard Samuelson (Indianapolis: Liberty Fund, 2015), 211, emphasis in original. *Te Deum* is a Latin hymn of praise sung in Catholic churches.

53 Otis, "Brief Remarks," 211. Otis is referring to James Stuart, the son of James II. Stuart tried to gain the British crown in 1715 and continued to claim the throne until his death in 1766. See McLynn, *The Jacobites*, 190–91.

54 Edmund S. Morgan and Helen M. Morgan, *The Stamp Act Crisis: Prologue to Revolution* (New York: Collier, 1967), 161–64.

55 Robert Middlekauff, *The Glorious Cause: The American Revolution, 1763–1789* (New York: Oxford University Press, 2005), 105; Morgan and Morgan, *The Stamp Act Crisis*, 188; Stensrud, *Newport*, 184–85.

56 John Adams linked Catholics and Jacobites in his *Dissertation on the Canon and the Feudal Law*, declaring that both were "as rare as a Comet or an Earthquake." See John Adams, *Papers of John Adams*, ed. Robert J. Taylor, 19 vols. (Cambridge, MA: Harvard University Press, 1977), 1:120. He also informed his friend James Warren that there were a "few rascally Jacobites and Roman Catholics" in his hometown of Braintree, Massachusetts, in 1775. See John Adams, *Works of John Adams*, 10 vols. (Boston, 1854), 9:355.

57 *NM*, September 2, 1765.

58 Morgan and Morgan, *The Stamp Act Crisis*, 189–91; Crane, *A Dependent People*, 113–14; Snydacker, "The Remarkable Career," 14–15.

59 In Boston, the connection between the Stamp Act Riots and Pope's Day was explicit. Ebenezer McIntosh, a shoemaker, was recruited to lead the Stamp Act Riots because of his prominence in the annual Pope's Day ceremonies. See Morgan and Morgan, *The Stamp Act Crisis*, 159–61.

60 Fawkes and about a dozen other Catholic laymen attempted to kill King James I because he had refused to provide religious liberty to the recusants, the Catholic minority in England. After foiling the plot, the government then arrested and executed several Jesuits, even though none were involved in it. See Antonia Fraser, *Faith and Treason: The Story of the Gunpowder Plot* (New York: Doubleday, 1996), 15–52, 229–67. Guy Fawkes Day is still celebrated in some parts of England. See Jenny Gross, "Celebrating a Failed Revolution Can Get Crowded on Guy Fawkes Night," *Wall Street Journal*, November 6, 2013; Fraser, *Faith and Treason*, 293–94.

61 Colley, *Britons*, 19–20; Owen Stanwood, "Catholics, Protestants, and the Clash of

Civilizations in Early America," in *The First Prejudice: Religious Tolerance and Intolerance in Early America*, ed. Chris Beneke (Philadelphia: University of Pennsylvania Press, 2010), 233.

62 Francis Cogliano, *No King, No Popery: Anti-Catholicism in Revolutionary New England* (Westport, CT: Greenwood, 1995), 24. Boston's Pope's Day revelry turned deadly on at least one occasion. In 1764, a boy was run over and killed by a wagon carrying an effigy of a pope. See Morgan and Morgan, *The Stamp Act Crisis*, 159–60.

63 Peter Benes, "Night Processions: Celebrating the Gunpowder Plot in England and New England," in *New England Celebrates: Spectacle, Commemoration, and Festivity: 2000 Annual Proceedings of the Dublin Seminar for New England Folklife* (Boston: Dublin Seminar for New England Folklife, 2002), 14–17; Curran, *Papist Devils*, 216–25; Anderson, *The War That Made America*, 249.

64 "Gunpowder Treason," *NM*, January 12, 1867.

65 On Southwick's staunch opposition to the British Crown, see C. Deirdre Phelps, "Solomon Southwick, Patriotic Printer of Revolutionary Rhode Island," *NH* 77 (Fall 2008): 21–24. On his involvement in publishing, see George Champlin Mason, *Reminiscences of Newport* (Newport, RI: Hammett, 1884), 84–86.

66 Arthur J. Riley, *Catholicism in New England to 1788* (Washington, DC: Catholic University of America, 1936), 30; Charles H. Metzger, S.J., *Catholics in the American Revolution* (Chicago: Loyola University Press, 1962), 17–18; Phelps, "Solomon Southwick," 19; Kidd, *God of Liberty*, 67.

67 *NM*, June 28, 1773.

68 *NM*, October 25, 1773.

69 *NM*, November 29, 1773.

70 John O'Kelly, letter to Christopher Champlin, October 20, 1773, in *Irish Immigrants in the Land of Canaan*, ed. Kerby Miller, Arnold Schrier, Bruce D. Boling, and David N. Doyle (New York: Oxford University Press), 329–31.

71 Merrill Jensen, *The Founding of a Nation: A History of the American Revolution, 1763–1776* (New York: Oxford University Press, 1968), 461–62; David S. Lovejoy, *Rhode Island Politics and the American Revolution, 1760–1776* (Providence: Brown University Press, 1958), 166.

72 *NM*, December 27, 1773; Lovejoy, *Rhode Island Politics*, 166.

73 *NM*, January 3, 1774.

74 Jensen, *Founding of a Nation*, 464–82.

75 Middlekauff, *The Glorious Cause*, 237; Reginald Coupland, *The Quebec Act: A Study in Statesmanship* (Oxford: Clarendon, 1968), 24. Coupland estimates that Catholics outnumbered Protestants by a 350 to 1 ratio (23).

76 The text of the Quebec Act is printed in Coupland, *The Quebec Act*, 208–17.

77 *NM*, March 14, 1774, emphasis in original. See also Riley, *Catholicism in New England*, 30.

78 *NM*, July 18, 1774, August 22, 1774, September 5, 1774, September 19, 1774, October 3, 1774, December 19, 1774.

79 *NM*, August 22, 1774.

80 *NM*, October 17, 1774.

81 *LD*, August 23, 1774, 1:455. Stiles has a similar entry a week later; see *LD*, August 29, 1774, 1:455. See also Edmund S. Morgan, *Gentle Puritan: A Life of Ezra Stiles, 1727–1795* (New Haven, CT: Yale University Press, 1962), 266–67.

82 *LD*, November 5, 1774, 1:470. Lord North was the British prime minister from 1770 to 1782. Thomas Hutchinson was the Loyalist governor of Massachusetts from 1769 to1774, and Thomas Gage succeeded him as the military governor of Massachusetts from 1774 to 1775. Three years earlier, Stiles had merely noted, "Powder Plot—Pope etc. carried about" (*LD*, November 5, 1771, 1:182).

83 *LD*, November 27, 1774, 1:490. Stiles drew on Second Thessalonians, where Saint Paul

speaks of a "man of lawlessness . . . the son of perdition who . . . takes his seat in the temple of God, proclaiming himself to be God" (2:3–4).

84 *NM*, January 30, 1775, February 13, 1775, emphasis in original.

85 A couple of Portuguese Catholics settled in Newport in the 1750s; see Conley and Smith, *Catholicism in Rhode Island*, 6–7. Kerby Miller, a historian of Irish America, notes that sixty Irish came from Newfoundland to Newport in 1774, but it is not clear how many were Catholics (*Irish Immigrants in the Land of Canaan*, 329).

86 Crane, "Uneasy Coexistence," 105; *NM*, October 3, 1774.

CHAPTER 2: THE FRENCH EFFECT

1   William Ellery, letter to Ezra Stiles, August 6, 1780, *LD*, 2:454.

2   Georgia was the only colony not represented at the Congress.

3   Samuel Ward and Stephen Hopkins were archrivals battling for control of Rhode Island in the 1750s and 1760s. See William G. McLoughlin, *Rhode Island: A History* (New York: Norton, 1986), 81–83.

4   John Tracy Ellis, *Documents of American Catholic History* (Milwaukee: Bruce, 1962), 134.

5   James Hennesey, S. J., *American Catholics* (New York: Oxford University Press, 1981), 57.

6   Samuel Eliot Morison, *The Oxford History of the American People*, 3 vols. (New York: Oxford University Press, 1972), 1:279.

7   Ellis, *Documents*, 134.

8   Ellis, *Documents*, 135.

9   Charles P. Hanson, *Necessary Virtue: The Pragmatic Origins of Religious Liberty in New England* (Charlottesville: University Press of Virginia, 1998), 31–36.

10 Catholics from Maryland and Pennsylvania served in Washington's forces. See Charles H. Metzger, S. J., *Catholics in the American Revolution* (Chicago: Loyola University Press, 1962), 50; Hennesey, *American Catholics*, 59–60.

11 Ellis, *Documents*, 136. See also Thomas S. Kidd, *God of Liberty: A Religious History of the American Revolution* (New York: Basic Books, 2010), 73–74.

12 John Adams, letter to James Warren, February 18, 1775, in Annabelle M. Melville, *John Carroll of Baltimore* (New York: Scribner, 1955), 44. Just four months earlier, Adams had written to his wife Abigail about his attendance at a vespers service at Saint Mary's Church in Philadelphia: "The poor Wretches, fingering their Beads, chanting Latin, not a word of which they understood. . . . Here is every Thing which can . . . charm and bewitch the simple and the ignorant. I wonder how Luther ever broke the spell" (letter, October 9, 1774, in *Adams Family Correspondence*, ed. L. H. Butterfield, 10 vols. (Cambridge, MA: Belknap, 1963), 1:166–67.

13 Melville, *John Carroll of Baltimore*, 52–53.

14 Franklin arrived in December 1776 and joined Silas Deane, a Connecticut businessman who had been lobbying the French since the summer. See Stacy Schiff, *A Great Improvisation: Franklin, France, and the Birth of America* (New York: Holt, 2005), 1–35.

15 Richard D. Brown and Jack Tager, *Massachusetts: A Concise History* (Amherst: University of Massachusetts Press, 2000), 85–86.

16 Morison, *Oxford History*, 1:295.

17 McLoughlin, *Rhode Island*, 84.

18 David S. Lovejoy, *Rhode Island Politics and the American Revolution, 1760–1776* (Providence: Brown University Press, 1958), 169.

19 McLoughlin, *Rhode Island*, 92–94.

20 Rockwell Stensrud, *Newport: A Lively Experiment, 1639–1969* (Newport, RI: Redwood Library, 2006), 191–92.

21 Christian M. McBurney, *The Rhode Island Campaign: The First French and American Operation in the Revolutionary War* (Yardley, PA: Westholme, 2011), 2–3.

22 McLoughlin, *Rhode Island*, 94.

23 Elaine Crane, *A Dependent People: Newport, Rhode Island, in the Revolutionary Era* (New York: Fordham University Press, 1985), 126–40; Michael Hoberman, *New Israel/New England* (Amherst: University of Massachusetts Press, 2011), 188–89.

24 *LD*, February 20, 1776, 1:662; Morgan, *Gentle Puritan*, 278–80.

25 For Stiles's estimates of the number of Newporters who remained, see *LD*, December 27, 1776, January 13, 1777, 2:105, 111–12; McBurney, *The Rhode Island Campaign*, 9.

26 Donald F. Johnson, "Occupied Newport: A Revolutionary City under British Rule," *NH* 84 (Summer 2015): 5.

27 Richard M. Ketchum, *Saratoga: Turning Point of America's Revolutionary War* (New York: Holt, 1997), 428–40.

28 Ketchum, *Saratoga*, 440–48; Schiff, *A Great Improvisation*, 110–34.

29 McBurney, *The Rhode Island Campaign*, 75.

30 James Stokesbury, *A Short History of the American Revolution* (New York: Morrow, 1991), 189–90; Stensrud, *Newport*, 213.

31 Laura Auricchio, *The Marquis: Lafayette Reconsidered* (New York: Knopf, 2014), 73–75.

32 McBurney, *The Rhode Island Campaign*, 170–95.

33 McBurney, *The Rhode Island Campaign*, 208.

34 Lynne Withey, *Dearest Friend: A Life of Abigail Adams* (New York: Free Press, 1981), 102–3.

35 Robert H. Lord, John E. Sexton, and Edward T. Harrington, *History of the Archdiocese of Boston*, 3 vols. (New York: Sheed and Ward, 1944), 1:307.

36 D'Estaing battled the British in the Caribbean without much success and then took part in a failed siege of Savannah in 1779. He returned to France in 1780 and was guillotined in 1794, a victim of Maximilien Robespierre's Reign of Terror.

37 *PG*, April 17, 1779; Metzger, *Catholics in the American Revolution*, 64–65.

38 Stensrud, *Newport*, 222–23.

39 Johnson, "Occupied Newport," 7.

40 Stensrud, *Newport*, 223. The "pillaged library" was the Redwood, which had been used as an officers' club during the occupation. See also William M. Fowler, Jr., *William Ellery: A Rhode Island Politico and Lord of the Admiralty* (Metuchen, NJ: Scarecrow, 1973), 131.

41 Arnold Whitridge, *Rochambeau: America's Neglected Founding Father* (New York: Macmillan, 1965), 142. After James II's defeat at the Battle of the Boyne in 1690, considerable numbers of Irishmen left their homeland and enlisted in the French and Spanish armies. See Maurice N. Hennessy, *The Wild Geese: The Irish Soldier in Exile* (Old Greenwich, CT: Devin-Adair, 1973); Patrick Hogan, "The Role of the Irish in the French Military Service," *NH* 53 (Fall 1980): 133–58.

42 Lee Kennett, *The French Forces in America, 1780–1783* (Westport, CT: Greenwood, 1977), 48.

43 *LD*, July 26, 1780, 2:453.

44 Whitridge, *Rochambeau*, 93; Robert W. Hayman, *Catholicism in Rhode Island and the Diocese of Providence, 1780–1886* (Providence: Diocese of Providence, 1982), 3–4.

45 Allan Forbes and Paul Cadman, *France and New England*, 3 vols. (Boston: State Street Trust, 1925–29), 1:108; Second Congregational Church, records, October 1, 1780, NHS.

46 E. M. Stone, *Our French Allies* (Providence: Providence Press, 1884), 218; Patrick T. Conley and Matthew J. Smith, *Catholicism in Rhode Island* (Providence: Diocese of Providence, 1976), 11; Hayman, *Catholicism in Rhode Island and the Diocese of Providence, 1780–1886*, 4.

47 The Comte de Noailles was the brother-in-law of Lafayette.

48 Alan Simpson and Mary M. Simpson, "A New Look at How Rochambeau Quartered His Army in Newport, 1780–1781," *NH* 72–73 (Fall 2003–Spring 2004): 95; Stensrud, *Newport*, 227. Water Street, in Newport's Point neighborhood, is now Washington Street.

49 Jean-Edmond Weelen, *Rochambeau, Father and Son* (New York: Holt, 1936), 95.

50 Lord et al., *History of the Archdiocese of Boston*, 1:340. One of the Irish priests was Father Charles Whelan, a Franciscan friar who would remain in America after the war's end, ministering to Catholics in New York, Kentucky, and Maryland. See Hennesey, *American Catholics*, 75–81.

51 *LD*, October 9, 1780, 2:473. Stiles wrote to the Marquis de Chastellux a few days after the dinner to ask him to publicize in Paris the accomplishments of an American inventor whom Stiles knew. See PESRL, reel 4.

52 *LD*, March 2, 1781, 2:517–18. Stiles sent a letter to Abbé de Sepvigny on May 8, 1781. See PESRL, reel 4.

53 Forbes and Cadman, *France and New England*, 1:105; *LD*, September 30–October 19, 1780, 2: 472–74. Just two years earlier, Stiles had expressed sharp opposition to Catholicism. When the American minister in Paris, Silas Deane, urged him to hire a French professor at Yale, Stiles remarked that the study of French might encourage "popery." The Yale Corporation did not approve Deane's request. See *LD*, August 22–25, 1778, 2:296–98.

54 George Champlin Mason, *Reminiscences of Newport* (Newport, RI, 1884), 77–78.

55 Kennett, *French Forces in America*, 55.

56 Weelen, *Rochambeau, Father and Son*, 91.

57 Howard C. Rice, Jr., and Anne S. K. Brown, trans. and ed., *The American Campaign of Rochambeau's Army, 1780, 1781, 1782, 1783*, 2 vols. (Princeton, NJ: Princeton University Press, 1972), 1:121–23.

58 Conley and Smith, *Catholicism in Rhode Island*, 12; Whitridge, *Rochambeau*, 111; Stone, *Our French Allies*, 250; De B. Randolph Keim, *Rochambeau* (Washington, DC: General Printing Office, 1907), 339.

59 Marquis de Lafayette, letter to Adrienne de Lafayette, February 2, 1781, in *Lafayette in the Age of the American Revolution: Selected Letters and Papers, 1776–1790*, ed. Stanley J. Idzerda, 5 vols. (Ithaca, NY: Cornell University Press, 1977–83), 3:310. On Admiral de Ternay's unpopularity, see Eugena Poulin and Claire Quintal, *La Gazette Françoise: Revolutionary America's French Newspaper* (Lebanon, NH: University Press of New England, 2007), 61.

60 Stone, *Our French Allies*, 338.

61 Stone, *Our French Allies*, 347–48. John Hattendorf notes that, on the day preceding the funeral, de Ternay's flagship fired off a cannon every half hour; and as the funeral procession wound its way towards Trinity Church, the ship fired a fifteen-gun salute (*Semper Eadem: A History of Trinity Church in Newport, 1698–2000* [Newport: Trinity Church, 2001], 132).

62 Stone, *Our French Allies*, 348.

63 Stone, *Our French Allies*, 348.

64 Along with the apology, the Massachusetts officials promised to erect a monument in the Chevalier de Saint-Saveur's memory. No memorial was built during the war, and the promise was forgotten until 1905, when a legislator called on the state to fulfill its commitment. In May 1917—a month after America joined World War I on the side of France—a fourteen-foot monument to Saint-Saveur was dedicated with great fanfare. See John Hattendorf, *Newport, the French Navy, and American Independence* (Newport, RI: Redwood Press, 2005), 35–36; Lord et al., *History of the Archdiocese of Boston*, 1:306; Fitz-Henry Smith, Jr., *The Memorial to the Chevalier de Saint-Saveur* (Boston: Bostonian Society, 1918), 9–25.

65 O'Connor, *Boston Catholics*, 13; Lord et al., *History of the Archdiocese of Boston*, 1:303–6. At this time, King's Chapel had no minister and almost no members as most of the city's Anglicans had left with the British forces in 1776. After the Revolution, the church moved away from orthodox Anglicanism and eventually embraced Unitarianism. See Carl Scovel and Charles C. Forman, *Journey towards Independence: King's Chapel's Transition to Unitarianism* (Boston: Skinner House, 1993), 21–37.

66 William Byrne, *History of the Catholic Church in the New England States*, 2 vols. (Boston:

Hurd and Everett, 1899), 1:355. Austin Dowling, who grew up in Newport, served as a priest in the Providence diocese for twenty years before being named bishop of Des Moines in 1912 and then archbishop of St. Paul in 1919. See Marvin R. O'Connell, *Pilgrims to the Northland: The Archdiocese of St. Paul, 1840–1962* (Notre Dame, IN: University of Notre Dame Press, 2009), 389–90.

67 Byrne, *History of the Catholic Church*, 1:354–55. Eighteen French men joined the Newport Masonic Lodge in 1790. See Lord et al., *History of the Archdiocese of Boston*, 1:347.

68 Marquis de Chastellux, *Travels in North America in the Years 1780, 1781 and 1782*, trans. and ed. Howard C. Rice, Jr., 2 vols. (Chapel Hill: University of North Carolina Press, 1963), 1:6–12. One of Chastellux's top aides in Newport was Isidore Lynch, an Irishman who had been educated in France. Another officer of Irish descent, Frank-Théobald Dillon, was with Chastellux when he traveled to Virginia after the war's end. See Chastellux, *Travels in North America*, 1:248, 2:566. On Lafayette's involvement with the Freemasons, see Auricchio, *The Marquis*, 24–25.

69 Abbé Claude Robin, one of Rochambeau's chaplains, thought it likely that several officers were having affairs with married women in Newport (*New Travels through North-America* [1783; reprint, New York: Arno, 1969], 21–22). See also Whitridge, *Rochambeau*, 94; Stone, *Our French Allies*, 224–27.

70 Rice and Brown, *The American Campaign of Rochambeau's Army*, 1:22. Chastellux was also critical of the Quakers (*Travels in North America*, 1:166–67).

71 Rice and Brown, *The American Campaign of Rochambeau's Army*, 1:245. Louis Berthier later served as Napoleon Bonaparte's chief of staff.

72 Rice and Brown, *The American Campaign of Rochambeau's Army*, 1:125.

73 Whitridge, *Rochambeau*, 129–30. Maria Theresa, who ruled the Holy Roman Empire from 1740 to 1780, was the mother of Marie Antoinette.

74 According to Louis Berthier, four hundred French troops remained in Newport to protect it from British invasion. See Rice and Brown, *The American Campaigns of Rochambeau's Army*, 1:246.

75 Rice and Brown, *The American Campaign of Rochambeau's Army*, 1:245.

76 Samuel Vernon, letter to William Vernon, August 26, 1781, box 79, folder 19, NHS.

77 Jonathan Easton, letter to tax assessors, June 9, 1781, box 44, NHS.

78 Silas Cooke, letter to Christopher Ellery, January 4, 1781, box 44, NHS.

79 Stensrud claims that the French troops brought "a new and welcome gaiety to the town" (*Newport*, 230). See also John Hattendorf, "The French Connection in Newport during the American Revolution: An Overview," *NH* 72–73 (Fall 2003–Spring 2004): 5–6.

80 Admiral Barras assumed command of the fleet in Newport in May 1781.

81 John Russell Bartlett, ed., *Records of the State of Rhode Island and Providence Plantations* 10 vols. (Providence: A. Crawford Greene, 1856–65), 9:674–75.

82 Ellis, *Documents*, 137–39.

83 Lord et al., *History of the Archdiocese of Boston*, 1:320–25; O'Connor, *Boston Catholics*, 14.

84 Lord et al., *History of the Archdiocese of Boston*, 1:341; Stensrud, *Newport*, 228; Hayman, *Catholicism in Rhode Island and the Diocese of Providence, 1780–1886*, 6–7.

CHAPTER 3: SHELTER FROM THE STORM

1 The epigraph quotes from John Quincy Adams, *The Diaries of John Quincy Adams: Digital Collection*, http://masshist.org. I am indebted to Dr. John Parrillo for this reference. New York City was occupied by the British in 1776–82 but was able to recover quickly in the post-war period. See Kenneth T. Jackson and David S. Dunbar, *Empire City: New York through the Centuries* (New York: Columbia University Press, 2002), 19–21, 101–5.

2 Thomas S. Kidd, *God of Liberty: A Religious History of the American Revolution* (New York: Basic Books, 2010), 209–11.

3 Samuel Eliot Morison, *The Oxford History of the American People*, 3 vols. (New York: Oxford University Press, 1972), 1:394.

4 In 1787, a Connecticut newspaper published the following poem about Rhode Island: "Hail, realm of rogues, renowned for fraud and guile, / All hail the knaveries of yon little isle" (William G. McLoughlin, *Rhode Island: A History* [New York: Norton, 1986], 103).

5 Catherine Drinker Bowen, *Miracle at Philadelphia: The Story of the Constitutional Convention* (Boston: Little, Brown, 1986), 13.

6 Douglas Southall Freeman, *George Washington: A Biography*, 6 vols. (New York, 1954), 6:240–45; Joseph Ellis, *His Excellency: George Washington* (New York: Knopf, 2004), 195.

7 McLoughlin, *Rhode Island*, 103–4.

8 They stayed at the home of Mary Almy, who had been a secret Loyalist during the Revolution. See Donald F. Johnson, "Occupied Newport: A Revolutionary City under British Rule," *NH* 84 (Summer 2015): 7–14; and Harrison Clark, *All Cloudless Glory*, vol. 2, *The Life of George Washington* (Washington, DC: Regnery, 1996), 181–82.

9 *USC*, September 16, 1790.

10 *USC*, September 23, 1790.

11 *USC*, September 16, 1790.

12 Micah 4:4. The full text of the letter is printed in *NM*, September 13, 1790. Touro Synagogue meets each August to read and reflect upon Washington's letter (https://tourosynagogue.org).

13 Reverend John Carroll and a group of Catholic laymen from Maryland, Pennsylvania, and New York sent Washington a congratulatory letter in the fall of 1789. Washington replied in March 1790, assuring them that he had received their letter "with much satisfaction" and expressing his hope that "your fellow-citizens will not forget the patriotic part you took in the accomplishment of their Revolution . . . or the important assistance which they received from a nation in which the Roman Catholic religion is professed" (George Washington, letter to Roman Catholics in America, March 12, 1790, in John Tracy Ellis, *Documents of American Catholic History* (Milwaukee: Bruce, 1962), 171–72).

14 Thomas H. O'Connor, *Boston Catholics: A History of the Church and Its People* (Boston: Northeastern University Press, 1998), 15.

15 Robert W. Hayman, *Catholicism in Rhode Island and the Diocese of Providence, 1780–1886* (Providence: Diocese of Providence, 1982), 7–8.

16 John Thayer, *An Account of the Conversion of the Reverend John Thayer, Lately a Protestant Minister, of Boston in North-America* (Baltimore, [1788]). The book went through twenty-six editions and was translated into German, French, Spanish, Portuguese, and Latin. See Richard J. Purcell, "Father John Thayer of New England and Ireland," *Studies* (June 1942): 174, 184.

17 Robert H. Lord, John E. Sexton, and Edward T. Harrington, *History of the Archdiocese of Boston*, 3 vols. (New York: Sheed and Ward, 1944), 1:422–23. Thomas Jodziewicz notes that Thayer was not always trying to defend Catholic doctrines but was often arguing for orthodox Christian belief against the secular forces of his time ("The Catholic Missionary of Boston' Fr. John Thayer: Controversialist and Ecumenist?," *American Catholic Studies* 112 [Winter 2001]: 23–47).

18 Lord et al., *History of the Archdiocese of Boston*, 1:434.

19 John Greene, Jr., *Saint Joseph Church Reference Book* (Newport: [Saint Joseph Church], 1935), 15; Hayman, *Catholicism in Rhode Island and the Diocese of Providence, 1780–1886*, 8.

20 *LD*, April 11, 1791, 3:416; Lord et al., *History of the Archdiocese of Boston*, 1:454.

21 *LD*, April 12 and 15, 1791, 3:416.

22 Lord et al., *History of the Archdiocese of Boston*, 1:462–63. On Carroll's ambivalence about Thayer, see Thomas W. Jodziewicz, "American Catholic Apologetic Dissonance in the Early Republic? Father John Thayer and Bishop John Carroll," *Catholic Historical Review* 84 (July 1998): 455–76.

23 Greene, *Saint Joseph*, 15; Hayman, *Catholicism in Rhode Island and the Diocese of Providence, 1780–1886*, 8. When the territory gained independence from France in 1804, its leaders renamed it Haiti, which means "land of the high mountains" in Taino, the Natives' language.

24 Lord et al., *History of the Archdiocese of Boston*, 1:486–90.

25 The Austrians saw Lafayette as a dangerous republican and imprisoned him until 1797. See Simon Schama, *Citizens: A Chronicle of the French Revolution* (New York: Random House, 1989), 870–73; and Gordon S. Wood, *Empire of Liberty: A History of the Early Republic, 1789–1815* (New York: Oxford University Press, 2009), 174.

26 D'Estaing antagonized the revolutionaries by speaking out on behalf of Marie Antoinette at her 1793 trial. Rochambeau's execution was not carried out, and he lived on until 1809. See Jay Winik, *The Great Upheaval: America and the Birth of the Modern World, 1788–1800* (New York: HarperCollins, 2007), 389; Schama, *Citizens*, 870.

27 Laurent Dubois, *Avengers of the New World: The Story of the Haitian Revolution* (Cambridge, MA: Harvard University Press, 2004), 153–59; Ralph Korngold, *Citizen Toussaint* (Boston: Little, Brown, 1945), 46–93.

28 *PG*, July 13, 1793. See also *PG*, July 27, 1793; *NM*, August 6, 1793.

29 *PG*, July 13, 1793.

30 *NM*, November 5, 1793.

31 George Gibbs Channing, *Early Recollections of Newport, RI, from the Year 1793 to 1811* (Newport, RI, 1868), 165. Channing's older brother was William Ellery Channing, the founder of Unitarianism.

32 *NM*, December 28, 1802. Carpentier was still prospering in 1805; he was listed with $1,000 worth of property. See Newport tax records (1805), NHS.

33 Channing, *Early Recollections of Newport*, 136, 152. Channing said that two of his grammar-school classmates were brothers from the West Indies. As their last name was Mardenborough, they were likely of English rather than French descent (60).

34 *NM*, May 18, 1802.

35 Several hundred royalists were slaughtered in Guadeloupe in the fall of 1794, including Father Rousselot, who was guillotined. See Lord et al., *History of the Archdiocese of Boston*, 1:501–2.

36 George Champlin Mason, *Reminiscences of Newport* (Newport, RI: Hammett, 1884), 375.

37 Juan Stoughton, letter to Joseph Wiseman, November 4, 1797, Juan Stoughton Papers, New-York Historical Society.

38 Lord et al., *History of the Archdiocese of Boston*, 1:618. Cheverus arrived in Boston in 1796.

39 Peter J. Coleman, *The Transformation of Rhode Island, 1790–1860* (Providence: Brown University Press, 1963), 44–54; Kenneth Walsh, *The Economic History of Newport Rhode Island from the Colonial Era to beyond the War of 1812* (Bloomington, IN: AuthorHouse, 2014), 79–80.

40 Newport tax records (1798, 1801), NHS.

41 *NM*, July 9, 1799; Mason, *Reminiscences*, 294–96. See also Theodore L. Gatchel, "The Rock on Which the Storm Will Beat: Fort Adams and the Defenses of Narragansett Bay," *NH* 67 (Summer 1995): 10–11.

42 Lord et al., *History of the Archdiocese of Boston*, 1:542–43; Purcell, "Father John Thayer," 181–82.

43 The men demanding the bribe were listed only as "X, Y and Z" in the news reports. See Wood, *Empire of Liberty*, 240–45.

44 John Thayer, "A Discourse, Delivered at the Roman Catholic Church in Boston," in *Political Sermons of the American Founding Era, 1730–1805*, ed. Ellis Sandoz (Indianapolis: Liberty Fund, 1991), 1359–60. A number of Protestant clergymen also condemned the French Revolution at this time; however, they downplayed its anti-Catholic aspects. See Timothy

Dwight, "The Duty of Americans at the Present Crisis," in Sandoz, *Political Sermons*, 1367–94; and Wood, *Empire of Liberty*, 244.

45 Lord et al., *History of the Archdiocese of Boston* 1:543.

46 For example, on June 8, 1798, the *Albany Centinel* announced "that Mr. Thayer's sermon ranks foremost in the patriotic effusions of that day." The *Salem Gazette* noted that it was selling copies of the "Rev. Mr. Thayer's celebrated sermon on the National Fast" (July 24, 1798).

47 Greene, *Saint Joseph*, 15. Catherine was the Wisemans' third child. She would join the Ursuline convent in Charlestown, Massachusetts, in the 1820s—a community that Thayer helped to establish. See Schultz, *Fire and Roses*, 11–14.

48 Greene, *Saint Joseph*, 15; *NM*, July 3, 1798.

49 Channing, *Early Recollections of Newport*, 88–110, 235–37.

50 Channing, *Early Recollections of Newport*, 96–97.

51 Channing, *Early Recollections of Newport*, 70.

52 Mason, *Reminiscences*, 375.

53 Channing, *Early Recollections of Newport*, 256.

54 *NM*, August 3, 1805. Although the newspaper did not specify, Wiseman's funeral would probably have taken place at Trinity Church. He was interred in Newport's Common Burial Ground. See John Eylers Sterling, Barbara Austin, and Letty Champion, *Newport, RI, Colonial Burial Grounds* (Hope: Rhode Island Genealogical Society, 2009), 323.

55 Catharine Wiseman put a notice in the *Newport Mercury* indicating her interest in settling all claims on her husband's estate as soon as possible (August 31, 1805). In August, she sold a bed and some bedding for $30 to Jacob Richardson. See Joseph Wiseman Papers, box 43, folder 5, NHS; and Hayman, *Catholicism in Rhode and the Diocese of Providence, 1780–1886*, 11, n. 28.

56 Robert Hayman thinks the French refugees had started to leave as early as 1798 or 1799 (*Catholicism in Rhode Island and the Diocese of Providence, 1780–1886*, 10).

57 Hayman, *Catholicism in Rhode Island and the Diocese of Providence, 1780–1886*, 11, n. 28.

58 *NM*, October 24, 1807. The Audinets put their house in Newport up for sale in 1805. See *NM*, April 6, 1805.

59 Channing, *Early Recollections of Newport*, 156.

60 Wood, *Empire of Liberty*, 647.

61 *NM*, November 3, 1810. The coal company was backed by a congressman, a lawyer, and several of Newport's leading merchants. See Gladys Bolhouse, "Incidents through the Years at the Portsmouth Coal Mines," *NH* 40 (Winter 1967): 8.

62 *NM*, December 17, 1808.

63 James E. Garman, *A History of Portsmouth, Rhode Island* (Newport, RI: Franklin Printing House, 1978), 20–21.

64 *PG*, June 27, 1812.

65 Harvey Strum, "Rhode Island and the War of 1812," *RIH* 50 (1992): 23. On Stephen Gould, see *NM*, September 10, 1814.

66 *NM*, July 18, 1812.

67 Oliver Hazard Perry was born in South Kingstown, Rhode Island, in 1785 but was educated in Newport and married a Newport woman, Elizabeth Champlin Mason. See Patrick T. Conley, "The War of 1812 and Rhode Island: A Bicentennial Bust," *RIH* 72 (Spring 2014): 26–27. On the Battle of Lake Erie, see Walter R. Borneman, *1812: The War that Forged a Nation* (New York: HarperCollins, 2004), 119–35.

68 Daniel Walker Howe, *What Hath God Wrought: The Transformation of America, 1815–1848* (New York: Oxford University Press, 2007), 63–66. The White House was called the President's House at this time.

69 On the possibility of an assault on Rhode Island in 1814, see Walter Lord, *The Dawn's Early Light* (New York: Norton, 1972), 222, 239; and Strum, "Rhode Island and the War of 1812," 29.

70 Rockwell Stensrud, *Newport: A Lively Experiment, 1639–1969* (Newport, RI: Redwood Library, 2006), 259; Strum, "Rhode Island and the War of 1812," 28–30; Borneman, *1812*, 253–59; *Boston Daily Advertiser*, October 14, 1814.

71 Coleman, *The Transformation of Rhode Island*, 68. On the loss of the town's leading taxpayers between 1801 and 1820, see Walsh, *The Economic History of Newport*, 80–91.

72 Stensrud, *Newport*, 266.

73 John Hattendorf, *Semper Eadem: A History of Trinity Church in Newport, 1698–2000* (Newport, RI: Trinity Church, 2001), 165–77.

74 On Seixas, see *NM*, December 2, 1809.

75 *Newport Herald*, September 9, 1790, reprinted in George Champlin Mason, *Annals of the Redwood Library* (Newport, RI, 1891), 70.

76 Mason, *Annals*, 89.

77 Greene, *Saint Joseph*, 17.

CHAPTER 4: "RESPECTABLE IN THEIR VOCATIONS"

1 Epigraph quotes from Benedict Fenwick, journal, AAB.

2 Daniel Walker Howe, *What Hath God Wrought: The Transformation of America, 1815–1848* (New York: Oxford University Press, 2007), 93.

3 *Rhode-Island American*, March 14, 1817.

4 Howe, *What Hath God Wrought*, 93.

5 *NM*, July 5, 1817.

6 Harlow Unger, *The Last Founding Father: James Monroe and a Nation's Call to Greatness* (Cambridge, MA: DaCapo, 2009), 271–72.

7 Howe, *What Hath God Wrought*, 93.

8 Noble E. Cunningham, Jr., *The Presidency of James Monroe* (Lawrence: University Press of Kansas, 1996), 36.

9 John R. Weaver II, *A Legacy in Brick and Stone: American Coastal Defense Forts of the Third System, 1816–1867* (McLean, VA: Redoubt, 2001), 1–11.

10 Slater Mill, established in Pawtucket in 1790, was the first factory in the United States. See Sarah Leavitt, *Slater Mill* (Dover, NH: Arcadia, 1997). See also See Peter J. Coleman, *The Transformation of Rhode Island, 1790–1860* (Providence: Brown University Press, 1963), 77–87.

11 Coleman, *Transformation of Rhode Island*, 83.

12 William G. McLoughlin, *Rhode Island: A History* (New York: Norton, 1986), 122.

13 Coleman, *The Transformation of Rhode Island*, 21, 220, tabs.

14 Rockwell Stensrud, *Newport: A Lively Experiment, 1639–1969* (Newport, RI: Redwood Library, 2006), 255.

15 Hodgson was active in the Liverpool Anti-Slavery Society. See David Turley, *The Culture of English Antislavery, 1780–1860* (New York: Routledge, 1991).

16 Adam Hodgson, *Letters from North America, written during a tour in the United States and Canada*, 2 vols. (London: Hurst, Robinson, 1824), 1:132; Stensrud, *Newport*, 255; Coleman, *The Transformation of Rhode Island*, 69.

17 Morris Gutstein, *The Story of the Jews of Newport* (New York: Bloch Publishing Co., 1936), 214–25; Touro Synagogue, http://tourosynagogue.org.

18 George Gibbs Channing, *Early Recollections of Newport, RI, from the Year 1793 to 1811* (Newport, RI, 1868), 202–3.

19 In 1808, Rome named John Carroll archbishop of Baltimore and established four new dioceses: Boston, New York, Philadelphia, and Bardstown, Kentucky. See James Hennesey, S.J., *American Catholics* (New York: Oxford University Press, 1981), 89–90.

20 Episcopal Register, November 15, 1812, November 18, 1812, February 7, 1813, AAB.

21 Robert H. Lord, John E. Sexton, and Edward T. Harrington, *History of the Archdiocese of Boston*, 3 vols. (New York: Sheed and Ward, 1944), 1:703; Annabelle M. Melville, *Jean Lefebvre de Cheverus, 1768–1836* (Milwaukee: Bruce, 1958), 180.

22 Lord et al., *History of the Archdiocese of Boston*, 1:703.

23 The Eastern Diocese included all of New England except Connecticut.

24 Melville, *Jean Lefebvre de Cheverus*,188–89; Wilfred H. Munro, *History of Bristol, RI: The Story of the Mount Hope Lands* (Providence, 1881), 355–56.

25 Nancy Lusignan Schultz, *Fire and Roses: The Burning of the Charlestown Convent, 1834* (Boston: Northeastern University Press, 2000), 11–13.

26 Melville, *Jean Lefebvre de Cheverus*, 213.

27 Schultz, *Fire and Roses*, 14.

28 Cheverus was saddened by the death of his friend Father Matignon and frustrated by Rome's selection of bishops in America. See Lord et al., *History of the Archdiocese of Boston*, 1:780–807.

29 Laura Auricchio, *The Marquis: Lafayette Reconsidered* (New York: Knopf, 2014), 295–96.

30 Harlow Unger, *Lafayette* (Hoboken, NJ: Wiley and Sons, 2002), 349.

31 *NM*, July 24, 1824; *R-IR*, July 22, 1824.

32 *R-IR*, July 22, 1824.

33 Anne C. Loveland, "Lafayette's Farewell Tour," in *Lafayette, Hero of Two Worlds*, ed. Stanley J. Idzerda, Anne C. Loveland, and Marc H. Miller (New York: Queens Museum, 1989), 63.

34 Unger, *Lafayette*, 352.

35 Because Vernon House served as General Rochambeau's headquarters, William Vernon may have met Lafayette during the French occupation of Newport. Rogers was a scholar who had established a private school, Newport Academy.

36 *R-IR*, September 9, 1824.

37 Loveland, "Lafayette's Farewell Tour," 63–65.

38 Unger, *Lafayette*, 358–59.

39 On his visits to Providence and Pawtucket, see *PG*, August 28, 1824.

40 Out of the forty-three forts projected, Fort Adams was one of seventeen to be prioritized. See Weaver, *A Legacy in Brick and Stone*, 7–9.

41 Smaller forts were planned for Jamestown, Goat Island, and Rose Island. See Stensrud, *Newport*, 272; and Theodore L. Gatchel, "The Rock on Which the Storm Will Beat: Fort Adams and the Defenses of Narragansett Bay," *NH* 67 (Summer 1995): 15.

42 Kevin Kenny, *The American Irish: A History* (New York: Pearson Education, 2000), 64; Peter Way, *Common Labour: Workers and the Digging of North American Canals, 1780–1860* (Cambridge: Cambridge University Press, 1993), 97; Potter, *To the Golden Door* (Boston: Little, Brown, 1960), 337; George Svejda, *Irish Immigrant Participation in the Construction of the Erie Canal* (Washington, DC: National Parks Service, 1969), 19, 26, 31.

43 Charles Dickens, *American Notes for General Circulation* (1842; reprint, New York: Penguin, 1985), 129, 256.

44 Carl Wittke, *The Irish in America* (Baton Rouge: Louisiana State University Press, 1956), 33; Potter, *To the Golden Door*, 317–18; Way, *Common Labour*, 94–95; Jay P. Dolan, *The Irish Americans: A History* (New York: Bloomsbury, 2008), 43.

45 Kerby A. Miller, *Emigrants and Exiles: Ireland and the Irish Exodus to America* (New York: Oxford University Press, 1985), 26–101; Dolan, *The Irish Americans*, 35–36.

46 Potter, *To the Golden Door*, 320; Miller, *Emigrants and Exiles*, 274. Laborers on the Erie Canal were reported to drink shots every hour. See Svejda, *Irish Immigrant Participation*, 32; and

Wittke, *The Irish in America*, 36. At the Portsmouth coalmines, workers received up to a pint of whiskey per day. See Gladys Bolhouse, "Incidents through the Years at the Portsmouth Coal Mines," *NH* 40 (Winter 1967): 11–12.

47 Kenny, *The American Irish*, 65; Way, *Common Labour*, 200–202; Howe, *What Hath God Wrought*, 434.

48 See John T. Duchesneau and Kathleen Troost-Cramer, *Fort Adams: A History* (Charleston, SC: History Press, 2014), 30; *NM*, March 3, 1827.

49 *NM*, September 16, 1826; *R-IR*, September 14, 1826.

50 *NM*, October 6, 1827.

51 Gatchel, "The Rock on Which the Storm Will Beat," 16; Stensrud, *Newport*, 271.

52 *NM*, September 25, 1824.

53 *NM*, March 24, 1825. See also Alexander Macomb, letter to Joseph Totten, February 1825, RG 77, NARA-B.

54 See, for example, *NM*, August 20, 1825; *PP*, August 24, 1825.

55 One perch is equal to 16½ feet. For examples of notices, see *Rhode-Island American*, January 27, 1826, May 5, 1826; *R-IR*, July 6, 1826.

56 See *NM*, May 6, 1826, for a list of the newspapers in Rhode Island, Connecticut, Massachusetts, and New York where the notices were placed.

57 *NM*, July 8, 1826.

58 *NM*, July 8, 1826; *R-IR*, July 13, 1826. According to the Newport Historical Society, John Handy was a large landowner in Newport who died in 1828 (http://newporthistory.org).

59 Gordon S. Wood, *Friends Divided: Thomas Jefferson and John Adams* (New York: Penguin, 2017), 1–6, 426–33.

60 James Traub, *John Quincy Adams: Militant Spirit* (New York: Basic Books, 2016), 335–37.

61 John Quincy Adams, diary entry, July 16, 1826, *The Diaries of John Quincy Adams*, http://www.masshist.org.

62 Traub, *John Quincy Adams*, 316, 322–25.

63 Adams, diary entry, October 14, 1826, *The Diaries of John Quincy Adams*.

64 See John M. Daley, S.J., *Georgetown University: Origin and Early Years* (Washington, DC: Georgetown University Press, 1957), 250–54.

65 Lord et al., *History of the Archdiocese of Boston*, 2:29–31.

66 Father Byrne, a native of Kilkenny, was ordained by Cheverus in 1820. See Melville, *Jean Lefebvre de Cheverus*, 197, 217.

67 Lord et al., *History of the Archdiocese of Boston*, 2:84.

68 Fenwick, journal entry, February 2, 1827; Episcopal Register, January 30 and 31, 1827, AAB.

69 Schultz, *Fire and Roses*, 15, 41, 44.

70 Father Fitton had been ordained at the end of December, and Father Tyler would be ordained in 1829. See Lord et al., *History of the Archdiocese of Boston*, 2:48–49.

71 Fenwick, journal entry, January 4, 1828; Lord et al., *History of the Archdiocese of Boston*, 2:85.

72 Fenwick, journal entry, March 7, 1828.

73 On the founding of public schools in Newport, see Edward Peterson, *History of Rhode-Island and Newport* (New York: J.S. Taylor, 1853), 280.

74 Robert W. Hayman, *Catholicism in Rhode Island and the Diocese of Providence, 1780–1886* (Providence: Diocese of Providence, 1982), 20.

75 Fenwick, journal entry, April 12, 1828.

76 *NM*, April 12, 1828; *PP*, April 12, 1828.

77 See, for example, *NM*, May 3, 1828, June 7, 1828, March 13, 1830.

78 Benedict Fenwick, S.J., *Memoirs to Serve for the Future: Ecclesiastical History of the Diocese of Boston*, ed. Joseph M. McCarthy (Yonkers, NY: U.S. Catholic Historical Society, 1978), 245.

79 Fenwick, journal entry, November 1, 1828.

80 Fenwick, *Memoirs to Serve for the Future*, 245.

81 Fenwick, journal entry, November 2, 1828.

82 LEB, 17:434–35. On Trevett's 1828 purchase of the lot, see LEB, 17:69.

83 Fenwick refers to a "ferment" in Providence involving Woodley and his parishioners (journal entry, December 22, 1830). See also Hayman, *Catholicism in Rhode Island and the Diocese of Providence, 1780–1886*, 26.

84 Woodley served with the Jesuits in Maryland until his death in 1857. See "Newtown-Manor Appendix," *Woodstock Letters* 15 (1886): 32–33.

85 LEB, 19:333–35.

86 In an obituary for Thomas Aylward, who had once labored at Fort Adams, the *Newport Daily News* (November 17, 1887) noted that he had been one of the twenty-two "pioneers" who attended Corry's first meeting for the church. I am grateful to Steve Marino for this reference.

87 Fenwick, journal entry, December 31, 1833.

88 On the cost of the church, see Arthur Ross, *A Discourse, Embracing the Civil and Religious History of Newport* (Providence: Brown, 1838), 151.

89 John Quigley signed a contract as a laborer for $1 per day; the Museum of Newport Irish History has a copy of the contract (http://newportirishhistory.org). For estimates on the number of laborers, see *NM*, August 10, 1833.

90 *NM*, February 2, 1833.

91 *NM*, June 22, 1833.

92 Robert V. Remini, *The Life of Andrew Jackson* (New York: Harper and Row, 1988), 210–12.

93 *NM*, March 1, 1834.

94 *NM*, March 22, 1834.

95 Remini, *The Life of Andrew Jackson*, 261–71.

96 *NM*, June 28 and July 19, 1834.

97 *NM*, July 12, 1834.

98 Quotation in section heading is a phrase that the American bishops used at their 1837 meeting. See *PLUSCB*, 1:87–89.

99 Schultz, *Fire and Roses*, 37–105; Cassandra L. Yacavozzi, *Escaped Nuns: True Womanhood and the Campaign against Convents in Antebellum America* (New York: Oxford University Press, 2018), 29–40.

100 *New-Bedford Mercury*, August 22, 1834.

101 *NM*, August 16, 1834.

102 *R-IR*, August 20, 1834.

103 Schultz, *Fire and Roses*, 233.

104 *R-IR*, October 29, 1834; *PP*, November 1, 1834; *Baltimore Patriot*, October 29, 1834.

105 *The Jesuit*, October 18, 1834. I am indebted to Robert Hayman for this reference.

106 *Republican Herald*, March 25, 1835.

107 Schultz, *Fire and Roses*, 231–68.

108 *PJ*, April 4, 1835.

109 *R-IR*, January 14 and 21, 1835.

110 *United States Catholic Almanac or Laity's Directory* (Baltimore: Myers, 1837), 106.

111 *HT*, May 4, 1836.

112 *R-IR*, July 6, 1836.

113 *NM*, July 16, 1836; *PJ*, July 28, 1836.

114 Lieutenant James Mason was not impressed with Newport, either. In a letter to Edwin Morgan, a former classmate at West Point, he complained that the town was "the damnedest hole in the world." The people "are in a perfectly primitive state. The rays of civilization have as yet been unable to pierce the . . . atmosphere of puritanism by which they are surrounded" (January 18, 1837, box 123, folder 2, NHS).

115 There were at least six sizable boardinghouses on the grounds of the fort in the 1820s and

1830s. Colonel Totten tried to sell an eight-bedroom boardinghouse in 1830. See *R-IR*, March 4, 1830. I am indebted to Steven Marino for this reference. See also Richard Dow, Patricia Adams, and Gerron S. Hite, *Fort Adams—The First Season* (Providence: Rhode Island Historic Preservation Commission, 1973).

116 *PJ*, November 16, 1836; *Norfolk Advertiser* (Dedham, MA), November 19, 1836; *NM*, November 26, 1836.

117 See U.S. v. John McCarty and James Croley, U.S. Circuit Court of Rhode Island, November 1836 term, RG 21, box 81, NARA-B.

118 Richard Greene, letter to John Forsyth, March 8, 1837, RG 77, NARA-B.

119 U.S. v. John McCarty and James Croley.

120 On Corry's support for temperance, see Lord et al., *History of the Archdiocese of Boston* 2:347; Patrick T. Conley and Matthew J. Smith, *Catholicism in Rhode Island* (Providence: Diocese of Providence, 1976), 32–33; and *PJ*, October 6, 1840, February 26, 1842.

121 Fenwick, journal entry, August 20, 1837; *NM*, August 19, 1837; *R-IR*, August 16, 1837.

122 Fenwick, journal entry, August 20, 1837.

123 Lee, ordained for the Edinburgh diocese, had joined the Boston diocese in 1833. See Lord et al., *History of the Archdiocese of Boston*, 2:164–65.

124 Fenwick, journal entry, August 20, 1837.

125 Father Lee soon left Illinois for Canada, where he died in 1842. Father Corry spent five years in Little Rock and then moved to upstate New York, where he died in 1866. On Lee, see Hayman, *Catholicism in Rhode Island and the Diocese of Providence, 1780–1886*, 50. On Corry's later life, see *St. John's Church, Rensselaer, New York: Golden Jubilee* (Albany, NY: Fort Orange Press, 1902).

126 Ross, *A Discourse*, 152.

127 Ross, *A Discourse*, 152.

128 *NM*, December 10, 1836.

129 New Shoreham is on Block Island in Narragansett Bay.

130 See, for example, *R-IR*, December 20, 1831, July 6, 1836, March 6, 1839.

131 On the panics, see Howe, *What Hath God Wrought*, 502–5.

132 Several historians claim that students were let out of school in 1828 or 1829 to witness the building of a house, the first in Newport since 1814. See Antoinette F. Downing and Vincent J. Scully, Jr., *The Architectural Heritage of Newport, Rhode Island, 1640–1915*, 2nd ed. (New York: American Legacy Press, 1967), 114; and Stensrud, *Newport*, 255. On Zion Episcopal, see Hattendorf, *Semper Eadem*, 173–75; and James L. Yarnall, *Newport through Its Architecture* (Newport, RI: Salve Regina University Press, 2005), 29–30. On the Newport Artillery Company, see Walter K. Schroder, *The Artillery Company of Newport* (Berwyn Heights, MD: Heritage Books, 2014). On Alexander McGregor's home on 63 John Street, see Stensrud, *Newport*, 275.

133 Eliza Cope Harrison and Rosemary F. Carroll, "Newport's Summer Colony, 1830–1860," *NH* 74 (Fall 2005): 1–33.

134 Julia Ward, letter to Samuel Ward, August 11, 1836, in *This Was My Newport*, by Maud Howe Elliott (Cambridge, MA: Mythology Company, 1944), 53. Julia Ward married Samuel Howe in 1843 and wrote "The Battle Hymn of the Republic" in 1862.

135 Ross, *A Discourse*, 101. On the cotton mills, see Catherine W. Zipf, "Aquidneck Mill," *Coronet Chronicle* (Winter 2006): 8–17.

136 Harrison and Carroll, "Newport's Summer Colony," 3; Sterngass, *First Resorts* (Baltimore: Johns Hopkins University Press, 2001), 43–44.

137 Harrison and Carroll, "Newport's Summer Colony," 20.

138 LEB, 23:36; Harrison and Carroll, "Newport's Summer Colony," 16–17.

139 Elizabeth Ann Seton, the first American-born saint, was a widowed mother of five who converted to Catholicism in 1805 and established the Daughters of Charity in Emmitsburg,

Maryland, in 1810. The Harper children attended Seton's school, Saint Joseph Academy. On the Harpers' ties with the Setons, see Catherine O'Donnell, *Elizabeth Seton: American Saint* (Ithaca, NY: Cornell University Press, 2018), 400–430.

140 Bishop Fenwick, accompanied by Bishop John England, visited Charles Carroll at his home shortly before Carroll's death (journal entry, October 17, 1829).

141 Fenwick, journal entries, August 23, 25, 27, and 28, 1840.

CHAPTER 5: "A VALUABLE ORNAMENT TO THE TOWN"

1 *NM*, September 5, 1840; *R-IR*, September 3, 1840; *HT*, September 3, 1840.

2 Benedict Fenwick, journal entry, September 15, 1840, AAB.

3 Fenwick, journal entries, January 11, January 29, May 10, 1841, AAB.

4 Fenwick established *The Jesuit* in 1829 and sold it to a layman, Patrick Donahoe, in 1834. Donahoe renamed it *The Pilot* in 1836. See Thomas H. O'Connor, *Boston Catholics: A History of the Church and Its People* (Boston: Northeastern University Press, 1998), 58–61.

5 *BP*, June 12, 1841.

6 On James Hennessy, see *BP*, April 8, 1842.

7 Fenwick, journal entry, July 8, 1841, AAB.

8 Mary (Polly) Carroll had married an English Protestant businessman named Richard Caton. See Catherine O'Donnell, *Elizabeth Seton: American Saint* (Ithaca, NY: Cornell University Press, 2018), 219.

9 Fenwick, journal entries, July 14–16, July 31–August 7, 1841, AAB. On William Ellery Channing, see Madeline Hooke Rice, *Federal Street Pastor: The Life of William Ellery Channing* (New York: Bookman Associates, 1961), 114–15, 206–208; Jack Mendelsohn, *Channing, the Reluctant Radical* (Boston: Unitarian Universalist Association, 1971), 192–94, 211–14; and William Ellery Channing, "Letter on Catholicism," in *The Works of William Ellery Channing*, 6 vols. (Boston: James Munroe, 1845), 2:267–87.

10 William Gibbs had served as governor from 1821 to 1824. Hugh Legaré, a South Carolinian, had recently been appointed by President John Tyler. See Fenwick, journal entries, September 14–17, 1841, AAB.

11 *BP*, September 18, 1841.

12 *NM*, January 8, 1842.

13 Commissioners of the Newport Asylum, minutes, May 29, July 30, December 25, 1840, and January 12, June 10, September 24, October 1, October 22, 1841, NHS.

14 In 1840, the U.S. bishops had encouraged Catholics to join the temperance movement. See *PLUSCB*, 1:135–36. On giving the pledge, see Fenwick, journal entry, June 6, 1841, AAB. On Father Mathew, see John F. Quinn, *Father Mathew's Crusade: Temperance in Nineteenth-Century Ireland and Irish America* (Amherst: University of Massachusetts Press, 2002).

15 Fenwick, journal entries, March 7–9, 1842, AAB.

16 Father Woodley had celebrated a special Mass for Saint Patrick's Day in Newport in 1830 but did not try to organize a parade. See *NM*, March 13, 1830.

17 Dutee Pearce had served as Rhode Island's attorney general and then as a congressman. See Erik J. Chaput and Russell DeSimone, "Newport County in the 1842 Dorr Rebellion," *NH* 83 (Fall 2014): 29, n. 13.

18 *BP*, April 8, 1842; *NM*, March 19, 1842.

19 *BP*, April 8, 1842.

20 Eric J. Chaput, *The People's Martyr: Thomas Wilson Dorr and His 1842 Rhode Island Rebellion* (Lawrence: University Press of Kansas, 2013), 54; Marvin E. Gettelman, *The Dorr Rebellion: A Study in American Radicalism, 1833–1849* (New York: Random House, 1973), 40–41; *NM*, May 8, 1841.

21 Henry Duff was a prominent Irish supporter of Dorr in Providence. See Evelyn Savidge Sterne, *Ballots and Bibles: Ethnic Politics and the Catholic Church in Providence* (Ithaca. NY: Cornell University Press, 2004), 19.

22 On African American support of the Landholders, see Christy Clark-Pujara, *Dark Work: The Business of Slavery in Rhode Island* (New York: New York University Press, 2016), 134–36.

23 Peter J. Coleman, *The Transformation of Rhode Island, 1790–1860* (Providence: Brown University Press, 1963), 282.

24 On Henry Anthony, see Patrick J. Conley, *Democracy in Decline: Rhode Island's Constitutional Development, 1776–1841* (Providence: Rhode Island Historical Society, 1977), 321–22.

25 Patrick T. Conley and Matthew J. Smith, *Catholicism in Rhode Island: The Formative Era* (Providence: Diocese of Providence, 1976), 47.

26 Chaput and DeSimone, "Newport County in the 1842 Dorr Rebellion," 17.

27 Robert W. Hayman, *Catholicism in Rhode Island and the Diocese of Providence, 1780–1886* (Providence: Diocese of Providence, 1982), 46.

28 Hayman, *Catholicism in Rhode Island and the Diocese of Providence, 1780–1886*, 46; Chaput, *The People's Martyr*, 122; Sterne, *Ballots and Bibles*, 22, 24. A Catholic convert from upstate New York, Father Wiley was ordained by Fenwick in 1827. See Robert H. Lord. John E. Sexton, and Edward T. Harrington, *History of the Archdiocese of Boston*, 3 vols. (New York: Sheed and Ward, 1944) 2:42–44, 48.

29 Chaput, *The People's Martyr*, 122.

30 Chaput and DeSimone, "Newport County in the 1842 Dorr Rebellion," 19–20.

31 Chaput, *The People's Martyr*, 173–205.

32 *NM*, July 30, 1842.

33 *NM*, August 6, 1842.

34 Fenwick, journal entry, September 12, 1842, AAB.

35 *NM*, March 4, 1837.

36 *NM*, July 4, 1838.

37 *NM*, March 8, 1839.

38 Joseph Totten, letter to Benjamin Howland, February 12, 1839, transcription, Fort Adams Library, Newport, RI.

39 Colonel Totten left Newport in 1838 to assume his new position.

40 Joseph Totten, letter to James Mason, July 1840, RG 77, NARA-B.

41 Daniel Walker Howe, *What Hath God Wrought: The Transformation of America, 1815–1848* (New York: Oxford University Press, 2007), 505.

42 *HT*, October 8, 1840, emphasis in original.

43 *NM*, October 10, 1840.

44 *NM*, May 15, 1841.

45 Joseph Totten, letter to James Mason, March 12, 1841, RG 77, NARA-B.

46 Joseph Totten, letter to James Mason, August 4, 1841, RG 77, NARA-B.

47 *NM*, August 28, September 11, 1841.

48 *NM*, September 3, 1842; *PJ*, September 2, 1842.

49 Fenwick, journal entry, September 20, 1842, AAB.

50 *NM*, October 29, 1842.

51 Lawrence McCaffrey, *Daniel O'Connell and the Repeal Year* (Lexington: University of Kentucky Press, 1966).

52 Oliver MacDonagh, *The Emancipist: Daniel O'Connell, 1830–1847* (London: Weidenfeld and Nicolson, 1989), 219–36.

53 George M. Potter, *To the Golden Door: The Story of the Irish in Ireland and America* (Boston: Little, Brown, 1960), 388–92.

54 John F. Quinn, "Expecting the Impossible? Abolitionist Appeals to the Irish in Antebellum America," *New England Quarterly* 82 (December 2009): 694, 696. On the Democrats' con-

frontational stance with regard to British claims in Oregon Territory, see Howe, *What Hath God Wrought*, 715–22.

55 Angela F. Murphy, *American Slavery, Irish Freedom: Abolition, Immigrant Citizenship, and the Transatlantic Movement for Irish Repeal* (Baton Rouge: Louisiana State University Press, 2010), 54–71; Potter, *To the Golden Door*, 392–93; *TT*, February 27, 1841; January 29, February 12, 1842; and April 1, June 3, June 17, 1843.

56 For a time, there were two Repeal organizations in Providence. One was headed by an adversary of Father Corry and active Dorrite, Henry Duff, but Corry's organization eventually prevailed. See Hayman, *Catholicism in Rhode Island and the Diocese of Providence, 1780–1886*, 40–41; and Conley and Smith, *Catholicism in Rhode Island*, 33. For the Providence Repealers' activities, see *TT*, August 26, 1843, and January 13, 1844; and *PJ*, June 15, 1843.

57 Sean O'Faolain, *King of the Beggars: A Life of Daniel O'Connell* (1938; reprint, Swords, Ireland: Poolbeg, 1980), 298.

58 On Daniel O'Connell's battles with Irish Americans over slavery, see Douglas Riach, "Daniel O'Connell and American Anti-Slavery," *Irish Historical Studies* 20 (March 1976): 10–24; and Noel Ignatiev, *How the Irish Became White* (New York: Routledge, 1995), 9–30.

59 Murphy, *American Slavery, Irish Freedom*, 129–34; *TT*, August 19, 1843; *NM*, July 15, 1843.

60 One of the Philadelphia Repeal organizations offered support, and the *Catholic Telegraph* in Cincinnati was vocal in its opposition to slavery. See John F. Quinn, "The Rise and Fall of Repeal: Slavery and Irish Nationalism in Antebellum Philadelphia," *Pennsylvania Magazine of History and Biography* 130 (January 2006): 66–69; and Quinn, "Expecting the Impossible?," 678.

61 David R. Roediger, *The Wages of Whiteness: Race and the Making of the American Working Class* (New York: Verso, 1991), 146–56.

62 William Lloyd Garrison often compared Newport to southern cities. See Jon Sterngass, *First Resorts: Pursuing Pleasure at Saratoga Springs, Newport, and Coney Island* (Baltimore: Johns Hopkins University Press, 1991), 45; and *The Liberator*, September 8, 1837. For Pearce's opposition to abolition, see a letter from a Newport abolitionist (*The Liberator*, January 7, 1842) charging him with "getting up mobs which broke up our meetings, pelted the lecturers with stones . . . and showered upon them language the most abusive and obscene." Pearce was a close ally of Dorr and had been jailed briefly in 1842 because of his association with that movement. See Chaput, *The People's Martyr*, 123.

63 In the 1850s, Thomas D'Arcy McGee moved to Canada and played a part in the establishment of its confederation. See David A. Wilson, *Thomas D'Arcy McGee* (Montreal: McGill University Press, 2008).

64 *BP*, August 31, 1843; *NM*, August 5, 1843.

65 *BP*, September 23, 1843.

66 Quinn, "Rise and Fall of Repeal," 67–68; Murphy, *American Slavery, Irish Freedom*, 152–53; *TT*, September 23, 1843.

67 O'Connell's critics at the *Times* of London dubbed them "monster meetings."

68 MacDonagh, *The Emancipist*, 237–57.

69 Quinn, "Rise and Fall of Repeal," 71.

70 *TT*, July 20, July 27, August 24, 1844.

71 *BP*, September 28, 1844. See a discussion of this article at http://newportirishhistory.org.

72 After the verdict was announced, the *Boston Pilot* printed a letter from its Providence correspondent who stated, "[N]ever was a trial in this country where a worse feeling of prejudice has been shown" (April 27, 1844).

73 John Gordon was hanged in February 1845 in what is now widely agreed to have been a grave miscarriage of justice. In 2011, Rhode Island's governor, Lincoln Chafee, pardoned him. On the trial, see Charles Hoffman and Tess Hoffman, *Brotherly Love: Murder and the Politics of Prejudice in Nineteenth-Century Rhode Island* (Amherst: University of Massachusetts Press,

1993); Potter, *To the Golden Door*, 441–46; and Conley and Smith, *Catholicism in Rhode Island*, 52–55.

74 *TT*, November 23, 1844.

75 Lord et al., *History of the Archdiocese of Boston*, 2:283–84; Fenwick, journal entry, December 31, 1843, AAB.

76 Samuel Goddard v. James O'Reilly et al., Court of Common Pleas, May Term 1843, State of Rhode Island and Providence Plantations, Judicial Records Center, Pawtucket.

77 *Christian Soldier*, March 14, 1843; Robert W. Hayman, "St. Mary's, Newport," 9, unpublished manuscript, DPA.

78 Hayman, *Catholicism in Rhode Island and the Diocese of Providence, 1780–1886*, 52.

79 Benedict Fenwick, letter to Samuel Eccleston, December 2, 1841, in Lord et al., *History of the Archdiocese of Boston*, 2:293. Coadjutors automatically take office when their predecessors die or resign.

80 Peter Guilday, *A History of the Councils of Baltimore, 1791–1884* (1932; reprint, New York: Arno, 1969), 137.

81 Lord et al., *History of the Archdiocese of Boston*, 2:294.

82 After Corry departed, Fenwick sent in Fitzpatrick, Fitton, and Wiley to examine the parish's books. See Fenwick, journal entry, October 24, 1843, AAB.

83 Providence Catholics were very disappointed by Corry's departure. See *TT*, May 18, 1844.

84 Fenwick, journal entry, December 4, 1843, AAB.

85 Lord et al., *History of the Archdiocese of Boston*, 2:283–84, n. 47.

86 Fenwick, journal entry, March 17, 1844, AAB.

87 Lord et al., *History of the Archdiocese of Boston*, 2:401–2.

88 Hayman, *Catholicism in Rhode Island and Diocese of Providence, 1780–1886*, 58–59.

89 Lawrence P. McCarthy, *Sketch of the Life and Missionary Labors of Rev. James Fitton* (Boston: New England Catholic Historical Society, 1908), 20.

90 *NM*, August 31, 1844.

91 *NM*, April 11, 1846.

92 James Fitton, *Sketches of the Establishment of the Church in New England* (Boston: Donahoe, 1872), 215.

93 Lord et al., *History of the Archdiocese of Boston*, 2:170–71.

94 Robert J. Sauer, *Holy Trinity German Catholic Church of Boston, 1844–1994* (Boston: Holy Trinity German Parish, 1994), 10–11.

95 Fitton, *Sketches*, 216.

96 Fitton, *Sketches*; LEB, 17:328–30.

97 James S. Donnelly, Jr., *The Great Irish Potato Famine* (Gloucestershire, UK: Sutton, 2001); Jay P. Dolan, *The Irish Americans: A History* (New York: Bloomsbury, 2008), 67–83; Kevin Kenny, *The American Irish: A History* (New York: Pearson Education, 2000), 89–97.

98 Potter, *To the Golden Door*, 456.

99 Lord et al., *History of the Archdiocese of Boston*, 2:434. When Fenwick died, 50,000 mourners came to the cathedral to pay their respects (2:383).

100 Cecil Woodham-Smith, *The Great Hunger* (New York: Old Town Books, 1962), 241; *SR*, February 11, 1847.

101 Potter, *To the Golden Door*, 460; Helen E. Hatton, *The Largest Amount of Good: Quaker Relief in Ireland, 1654–1921* (Montreal: McGill-Queen's University Press, 1993), 113–14.

102 Stephen Puleo, *Voyage of Mercy: The USS Jamestown, the Irish Famine, and the Remarkable Story of America's First Humanitarian Mission* (New York: St. Martin's, 2020), 64–148.

103 Hatton, *The Largest Amount of Good*, 113. See also Woodham-Smith, *The Great Hunger*, 241–46.

104   Harvey Strum, "'Not Forgotten in their Affliction': Irish Famine Relief from Rhode Island, 1847," *RIH* 60 (Winter 2002): 30–32.

105   *NDN*, February 27, 1847. This paper had begun publishing in the spring of 1846.

106   *NDN*, March 4, 1847; *NM*, March 6, 1847.

107   Woodham-Smith, *The Great Hunger*, 245.

108   Famine relief accounts, Bishop William Tyler Papers, AAH; *BP*, March 6, 1847.

109   Hayman, *Catholicism in Rhode Island and the Diocese of Providence, 1780–1886*, 81.

110   *NM*, May 22, 1847.

111   The two Episcopal churches in town at this time were Trinity on Spring Street and Zion, established in 1834 on Touro Street.

112   On Catherine Harper's donation, see Hayman, *Catholicism in Rhode Island the Diocese of Providence, 1780–1886*, 108. On Patrick Charles Keely, see Francis W. Kervick, *Patrick Charles Keely, 1816–1896* (South Bend, IN, 1953).

113   Fort Adams was allocated $15,000 for work in 1847, $20,000 for 1848, and $40,000 for 1849. See *NM*, December 5, 1846, July 1, 1848, and March 17, 1849.

114   Rosecrans joined the Catholic church in January 1846. See Anne C. Rose, "Some Private Roads to Rome: The Role of Families in American Victorian Conversions to Catholicism," *Catholic Historical Review* 85 (January 1999): 41–42; William B. Kurtz, "A Singular Zeal: William S. Rosecrans's Family in Faith, Triumph, and Failure," *U.S. Catholic Historian* 35 (Spring 2017): 27–53. On the construction of Saint Mary's, see *NDN*, August 8, 1848.

115   For Rosecrans's role as a Union general during the Civil War, see William M. Lamers, *The Edge of Glory: A Biography of General William S. Rosecrans* (New York: Harcourt, Brace, 1961).

116   Father Pise, a prolific author and highly regarded public speaker, had served as chaplain to the U.S. Senate in 1832–33. See John Loughery, *Dagger John: Archbishop John Hughes and the Making of Irish America* (Ithaca, NY: Cornell University Press, 2018), 47.

117   John Fitzpatrick, journal entry, June 14, 1849, AAB.

118   Levin Street is now Memorial Boulevard.

119   *NDN*, June 15, 1849.

120   John Ross Dix, *A Handbook of Newport, and Rhode Island* (Newport, RI: Hammett, 1852), 63. See also James L. Yarnall, *Newport through Its Architecture* (Newport, RI: Salve Regina University Press, 2005), 42–43.

121   Fitzpatrick, journal entry, June 14, 1849, AAB. Sumner's older brother Charles would later become one of the most outspoken abolitionists in the U.S. Senate.

122   Fitzpatrick, journal entry, June 15, 1849, AAB.

123   This church, now known as Saint Mary's Mission, is located in West Warwick, RI.

124   *BP*, April 26, May 3, 1851.

125   James Fitton, letter to *Newport Daily News*, July 17, 1852, box 42, NHS.

126   William Byrne, *History of the Catholic Church in the New England States*, 2 vols. (Boston, 1899), 1:432.

127   *MFJ*, July 22, 1852.

128   *NDN*, July 26, July 27, 1852. See also Fitzpatrick, journal entry, July 25, 1852.

129   Quotation in section heading is from Dix, *A Handbook of Newport*, 20. See also Stensrud, *Newport: A Lively Experiment (Newport: Redwood Library, 2006)*, 311–17.

130   George Herrick, *The Origins of the Social Club in America* (Newport, RI, privately printed, 2004).

131   Sterngass, *First Resorts*, 53; Stensrud, *Newport*, 311. Newport's population was 9,963 in 1850. See Edward Peterson, *History of Rhode-Island and Newport* (New York: Peterson, 1853), 286.

132   Dix, *A Handbook of Newport*, 21.

133   Sterngass, *First Resorts*, 46.

134 The hotels were owned by two brothers, John and Joseph Weaver. See Stensrud, *Newport*, 302.

135 Downing's hotel burned down in 1860 in what may have been arson. See Myra B. Young Armstead, *"Lord, Please Don't Take Me in August": African Americans in Newport and Saratoga Springs, 1870–1930* (Urbana: University of Illinois Press, 1999), 23; and *NM*, December 22, 1860.

136 Dix, *A Handbook of Newport*, 140.

137 Roger Williams McAdam, *Floating Palaces: New England to New York on the Old Fall River Line* (Providence: Mowbray, 1972), 18–21; Edwin L. Dunbaugh, *Night Boat to New England, 1815–1900* (Westport, CT: Greenwood, 1992), 103–6.

138 Armstead, *"Lord, Please Don't Take Me in August,"* 67–69.

139 Quincy's paternal grandfather, Josiah, was mayor of Boston and later president of Harvard, and his father, Edmund, was an active abolitionist allied with Garrison. See Richard D. Brown and Jack Tager, *Massachusetts: A Concise History* (Amherst: University of Massachusetts Press, 2000), 137–40; and Clare Taylor, *British and American Abolitionists* (Edinburgh: Edinburgh University Press, 1974), 8–9.

140 Edmund Quincy, Jr., diary entry, August 18, 1852, Massachusetts Historical Society, Boston.

141 Quincy is referring to the Germania Society, a group of German musicians who performed at the hotels in the summer season. See Brian M. Knoth, "Music and Dancing at the 'Queen of Resorts': The Impact of the Germania Musical Society on Newport's Hotel Period," *NH* 89 (Summer–Fall 2018): 1–35.

142 *PJ*, August 9, 1850.

143 *NM*, August 2, 1851.

144 *NYT*, September 18, 1851; Sterngass, *First Resorts*, 46.

145 Sterngass, *First Resorts*, 46.

146 See, for example, *NYT*, May 25, 1852, and August 26, 1853.

147 George W. Curtis, "Newport—Historical and Social," *Harper's* (August 1854): 317.

148 Michael Feldberg, *The Philadelphia Riots of 1844: A Study of Ethnic Conflict* (Westport, CT: Greenwood, 1975).

149 Ray Allen Billington, *Protestant Crusade, 1800–1860: A Study of the Origins of American Nativism* (1938; reprint, Chicago: Quadrangle, 1964), 322–25.

150 Dolan, *Irish Americans*, 74.

151 David M. Emmons, *Beyond the Pale: The Irish in the West, 1845–1910* (Norman: University of Oklahoma Press, 2010).

152 Kenny, *American Irish*, 107; Roger Daniels, *Coming to America: A History of Immigration and Ethnicity in American Life*, 2nd ed. (New York: HarperCollins, 2002), 130.

153 William G. McLoughlin, *Rhode Island: A History* (New York: Norton, 1986), 140–41.

154 Billington, *The Protestant Crusade*, 326, 381.

155 James F. Connelly, *The Visit of Archbishop Gaetano Bedini to the United States of America* (Rome: Gregorian University, 1960), 1–15.

156 Pope Pius IX had been forced to flee Rome in disguise in 1848. He stayed in Naples for more than a year until Louis Napoleon's forces restored him to power.

157 David J. Endres, "Know-Nothings, Nationhood, and the Nuncio: Assessing the Visit of Archbishop Bedini," *U.S. Catholic Historian* 21 (Fall 2003): 8–9.

158 Fitzpatrick, journal entry, September 25, 1853, AAB; Lord et al., *History of the Archdiocese of Boston*, 2:661; Connelly, *The Visit of Archbishop Gaetano Bedini*, 43, 47.

159 Loughery, *Dagger John*, 228–38; Richard Shaw, *Dagger John: The Unquiet Life and Times of Archbishop John Hughes of New York* (New York: Paulist Press, 1977), 279–87.

160 John T. McGreevy, *American Jesuits and the World* (Princeton, NJ: Princeton University Press, 2016), 26–62; Billington, *Protestant Crusade*, 388, 396.

161 Newport, along with most of the rest of Rhode Island, would elect Know Nothings to the

state legislature in 1855. See Michael A. Simoncelli, "Battling the Enemies of Liberty: The Rise and Fall of the Rhode Island Know-Nothing Party," *RIH* (February 1996): 14–15.

162 Mary Teresa Austin Carroll, R.S.M., *Leaves from the Annals of the Sisters of Mercy* (New York: Catholic Publication Society, 1889), 64; Kathleen Healy, *Frances Warde: American Founder of the Sisters of Mercy* (New York: Seabury, 1973), 158.

163 Seton was a Mercy sister for forty-six years and lived to be ninety-one. See O'Donnell, *Elizabeth Seton*, 430.

164 Conley and Smith, *Catholicism in Rhode Island*, 73.

165 Frances X. Warde, R.S.M, letter to Patrick Moriarity, October 28, 1851, Bishop Bernard O'Reilly Papers, AAH.

166 *Saint Mary's Convent Chronicle*, n.d., MHC, BNC.

167 Byrne, *History of the Catholic Church*, 1:432.

168 Carroll, *Leaves from the Annals*, 409–10.

169 *Metropolitan Catholic Almanac* (Baltimore: Lucas Brothers, 1855), 157.

170 Henry Anthony was dismissive of the agitators, remarking, "Some mischievous fool . . . has placarded in the streets an invitation for a mob to assemble in front of the convent this evening" (*PJ*, March 22, 1855).

171 Hayman, *Catholicism in Rhode Island and the Diocese of Providence, 1780–1886*, 136–39.

172 *NDN*, July 11, July 12, 1855, quoted in Eugena Poulin, R.S.M., *The Paths of Mercy on Aquidneck Island* (n.p., 1979), 6–7, i–iii.

173 Lord et al., *History of the Archdiocese of Boston*, 2:510–11.

174 *NDN*, August 11, 1855. This editorial was reprinted in *HT*, August 16, 1855.

CHAPTER 6: FIGHTING FOR THE BLUE AND THE GREEN

1 William Byrne, *History of the Catholic Church in the New England States*, 2 vols. (Boston, 1899), 1:432; *BP*, September 1, 1855.

2 Bernard O'Reilly, letter to Director of Propagation of the Faith, January 17, 1856, AAH.

3 *PJ*, February 1, 1856.

4 *MFJ*, February 7, 1856.

5 *PJ*, February 8, 9, 12, 15, 18, 23, 25, 1856.

6 *PJ*, April 2, 1856.

7 *MFJ*, April 24, 1856.

8 Patrick T. Conley and Matthew J. Smith, *Catholicism in Rhode Island: The Formative Era* (Providence: Diocese of Providence, 1976), 86–87. The Mass was offered in Old Saint Patrick's Cathedral on Mott Street.

9 Robert W. Hayman, *Catholicism in Rhode Island and the Diocese of Providence, 1780–1886* (Providence: Diocese of Providence, 1982), 146.

10 *NM*, September 13, 1856; *Hampshire Gazette*, September 16, 1856.

11 Bishop McFarland may have been ambivalent about accepting the appointment. In 1857, Roman authorities offered to make him Vicar Apostolic of Florida, but he refused the position. See Hayman, *Catholicism in Rhode Island and the Diocese of Providence, 1780–1886*, 147; and Conley and Smith, *Catholicism in Rhode Island*, 89.

12 Hayman, *Catholicism in Rhode Island and the Diocese of Providence, 1780–1886*, 145–46.

13 On the Coddington Mill's closure, see *NM*, January 19, 1856. On the Perry Mill, see *NM*, June 30, 1855, and April 5, 1856.

14 Anne Sherman, *Emmanuel Church, Newport, Rhode Island* (Newport, RI: PDQ Printers, 2002), 1–6.

15 James L. Yarnall, *Newport through Its Architecture* (Newport, RI: Salve Regina University Press, 2005), 60–61; *PJ*, August 2, 1855.

16 Florence Archambault, *Forward through the Ages, In Unbroken Line: 300 Years of Congregationalism on Aquidneck Island, 1695–1995* (Middletown, RI: United Congregational Church, 1995), 27.

17 *NM*, May 3, 1856.

18 Eliza Cope Harrison and Rosemary F. Carroll, "Newport's Summer Colony, 1830–1860," *NH* 74 (Fall 2005): 25.

19 Jon Sterngass, *First Resorts: Pursuing Pleasure at Saratoga Springs, Newport, and Coney Island* (Baltimore: Johns Hopkins University Press, 1991), 186–87.

20 Sterngass, *First Resorts*, 182–228.

21 *NM*, August 2, 1856.

22 Sterngass, *First Resorts*, 115–16.

23 Robert W. Hayman, "St. Mary's, Newport," 17, unpublished manuscript, DPA.

24 *Newport City Directory* (Newport, RI: Ward, 1858), 39–69.

25 For example, thirty-one out of the thirty-six Sullivan men in the *Directory* are listed as laborers. See *Newport City Directory* (1858), 91–92.

26 Theodore L. Gatchel, "The Rock on Which the Storm Will Beat: Fort Adams and the Defenses of Narragansett Bay," *NH* 67 (Summer 1995): 17. Congress allocated $15,000 for the fort in 1857, so a small number of laborers were probably working on construction projects. See *NM*, March 7, 1857.

27 Kenneth Walsh, *The Economic History of Newport Rhode Island from the Colonial Era to beyond the War of 1812* (Bloomington, IN: AuthorHouse, 2014), 111–12.

28 *Rhode Island Census* (1865), 24, https://ancestrylibrary.com.

29 *Rhode Island Census* (1865), 23.

30 *Newport City Directory* (1858), 65, 81.

31 *Newport City Directory* (1858), 29–104. In 1994, this road was renamed Dr. Marcus Wheatland Boulevard in honor of a prominent West Indian–born physician who worked and lived in Gilded Age Newport. See Richard C. Youngken, *African Americans in Newport: An Introduction to the Heritage of African Americans in Newport, 1700–1945* (Newport, RI: Newport Historical Society, 1998), 57.

32 On Kerry Hill, see James C. Garman, "From the School-Lands to Kerry Hill: Two Centuries of Urban Development at the Northern End of Newport, Rhode Island," unpublished paper. This essay, which considered whether the neighborhood could be placed on the National Register, was submitted to the city of Newport and the Rhode Island Historic Preservation and Heritage Commission in 2002.

33 *PJ*, July 28, 1855.

34 *NDN*, August 2, 1855.

35 *NDN*, August 2, 3, 4, 1855.

36 *PJ*, August 20, 1856.

37 *PJ*, September 6, 1856.

38 *NDN*, August 15, 1857.

39 *NDN*, August 20, 21, and 22, 1857.

40 *BP*, August 29, 1857.

41 *NM*, July 10, 1858.

42 William Delany also sold books and tickets to and from Ireland in a store on Levin Street near the church. In addition, he contributed occasional pieces to the *Boston Pilot*. See Hayman, "St. Mary's," 15–16. For a sample advertisement for Delany's store, see *NDN*, October 10, 1859.

43 Francis McFarland, diary entry, August 1, 1858, AAH; Hayman, "St. Mary's," 17.

44 For Thomas Carpenter's obituary, see *PJ*, July 15, 1854. See also Hayman, *Catholicism in Rhode Island and the Diocese of Providence, 1780–1886*, 78.

45 *NM*, September 25, 1858.

46 John Calhoun married his cousin Floride Colhoun. See Sterngass, *First Resorts*, 44.

47 Sterngass, *First Resorts*, 185; Yarnall, *Newport through Its Architecture*, 39–40.

48 Harrison and Carroll, "Newport's Summer Colony," 20–21.

49 Sophia Little was a poet and close associate of William Lloyd Garrison. Charles Lenox Remond was a Black abolitionist and a friend of Frederick Douglass. See John M. Rice, "Frederick Douglass and His Abolitionist Friends in Newport and New Bedford," *NH* 97 (Summer–Fall 2022): 13–15. William Ellery Channing, the Unitarian founder, often preached about slavery, though he would not discuss it in the presence of southern visitors. Lieutenant James Mason, the supervising engineer at Fort Adams, told a friend that Channing "is an eloquent and talented man . . . [but he] was lately brandishing the torch of the incendiary to kindle sedition among the negroes of the south" (letter to Edwin Morgan, August 6, 1836, box 123, folder 2, NHS).

50 Harrison and Carroll, "Newport's Summer Colony," 22.

51 In one case, a man in southern Indiana, who had escaped from slavery nineteen years earlier, was returned to his former owner. See James McPherson, *Battle Cry of Freedom: The Civil War Era* (New York: Oxford University Press, 1988), 81.

52 McPherson, *Battle Cry of Freedom*, 119–20; Thomas O'Connor, *Civil War Boston* (Boston: Northeastern University Press, 1997), 29.

53 McPherson, *Battle Cry of Freedom*, 121.

54 McPherson, *Battle Cry of Freedom*, 149–50.

55 *NM*, May 31, 1856, emphasis in original.

56 McPherson, *Battle Cry of Freedom*, 156–62; Kenneth Stampp, *America in 1857: A Nation on the Brink* (New York: Oxford University Press, 1990), 5–6.

57 McPherson, *Battle Cry of Freedom*, 173–76; Douglas R. Egerton, *The Year of Meteors: Stephen Douglas, Abraham Lincoln, and the Election That Brought on the Civil War* (New York: Bloomsbury, 2013), 38.

58 Stampp, *America in 1857*, 102–4.

59 *NM*, March 14, 1857.

60 *PJ*, March 9, 1857.

61 Stampp, *America in 1857*, 324; McPherson, *Battle Cry of Freedom*, 188.

62 McPherson, *Battle Cry of Freedom*, 41.

63 O'Connor, *Civil War Boston*, 3.

64 *NM*, July 31, 1858; Harrison and Carroll, "Newport's Summer Colony," 25.

65 *NM*, October 29, 1859.

66 *NM*, November 26, 1859.

67 McPherson, *Battle Cry of Freedom*, 209–10; O'Connor, *Civil War Boston*, 34–35.

68 On the Providence meeting, see *PJ*, December 3, 1859.

69 *NDN*, December 9 and 13, 1859.

70 O'Connor, *Civil War Boston*, 36.

71 McPherson, *Battle Cry of Freedom*, 212.

72 Egerton, *The Year of Meteors*, 199. President Lincoln had toured New England in February and March before securing the Republican nomination. See Frank J. Williams, "A Candidate Speaks in Rhode Island: Abraham Lincoln Visits Providence and Woonsocket, 1860," *RIH* 51 (November 1993): 107–19.

73 Robert W. Johannsen, "Stephen A. Douglas' New England Campaign, 1860," *New England Quarterly* 35 (June 1962): 178; *NM*, August 4, 1860. On Rocky Point, see Sterngass, *First Resorts*, 215.

74 *NM*, August 4, 1860.

75 On Belmont's Jewish background, see Norman Lebrecht, *Genius and Anxiety: How Jews Changed the World, 1847–1947* (New York: Scribner, 2019), 40–41, 47–48. On By-the-Sea, see

Yarnall, *Newport through Its Architecture*, 67–68; and David Black, *The King of Fifth Avenue: The Fortunes of August Belmont* (New York: Dial, 1981), 192.

76 Johannsen, "Douglas' New England Campaign," 180; Egerton, *The Year of Meteors*, 198–99.

77 Lincoln edged out Douglas in Newport, 592 to 560. See Sterngass, *First Resorts*, 45.

78 Fewer than 7 percent of Irish immigrants could vote in Rhode Island in 1865. See Robert W. Hayman, "The Rhode Island Irish in the Civil War," *RIH* 74 (Spring 2016): 57; and Patrick T. Conley, "No Landless Irish Need Apply: Rhode Island's Role in the Framing and Fate of the Fifteenth Amendment," *RIH* 68 (Summer 2010): 79.

79 Edwin Snow, *Report upon the Census of Rhode Island, 1865* (Providence: Providence Press Company, 1867), 14, 46.

80 McLoughlin, *Rhode Island*, 166–67.

81 McPherson, *Battle Cry of Freedom*, 234–35.

82 Frank J. Williams, "Rhode Islanders in Conflict," in *The Rhode Island Home Front in the Civil War*, ed. Frank J. Williams and Patrick T. Conley (Nashua, NH: Taos Press, 2013), 16–17.

83 McPherson notes that many people in the four seceding states were already anxious to secede before Lincoln made his announcement (*Battle Cry of Freedom*, 276–78).

84 McPherson, *Battle Cry of Freedom*, 274, emphasis in original.

85 Black, *The King of Fifth Avenue*, 206.

86 *NM*, March 2, 1861.

87 *NM*, April 20, 1861.

88 For Rhode Island's population in 1860, see *NM*, September 9, 1860.

89 Ambrose Burnside was a West Point graduate who served in the Mexican War and then settled in Bristol to manufacture rifles that he designed. See Fred Zilian, "Rhode Island Joins March to War," *NDN*, May 26, 2012.

90 A member of the regiment, Dexter Clark, thoroughly researched the origins of each member. See Hayman, "The Rhode Island Irish and the Civil War," 66, n. 2.

91 Hayman, "The Rhode Island Irish and the Civil War," 48.

92 For a complete list of the members of Newport's Company K, see *NM*, June 22, 1861.

93 Slocum had been a captain in the Mexican War. For Sprague's departure for Washington, see *NM*, June 15, 1861.

94 Jay P. Dolan, *The Irish Americans: A History* (New York: Bloomsbury, 2008), 98.

95 In the United States, the group was known as the Fenians. See Dolan, *The Irish Americans*, 184–85.

96 Susannah Bruce, "'Remember Your Country and Keep Up Its Credit': Irish Volunteers and the Union Army," *Journal of Military History* 69 (April 2005): 333–38.

97 George Bancroft's summer home was an Italianate villa called Rosecliff. See Yarnall, *Newport through Its Architecture*, 156.

98 Sterngass, *First Resorts*, 183.

99 *NM*, June 22, July 7, 1861.

100 *NDN*, August 6, 1861.

101 *NM*, March 2, 1861.

102 *MFJ*, December 20, 1860; Conley and Smith, *Catholicism in Rhode Island*, 91.

103 *NM*, July 24, 1861.

104 McFarland, diary entry, August 4, 1861, AAH; *NM*, August 3, 1861. Father O'Reilly had started organizing the cemetery in 1855. See *S.S. Mary and Joseph's Cemetery: Rules and Regulations* (Newport, RI: Cranston and Norman's Press, 1855). Spruce is now Kingston Street. I am indebted to Steve Marino for this reference.

105 *NM*, February 23, 1861. See also obituaries in *PJ*, February 25, 1861, and *Boston Evening Transcript*, February 25, 1861.

106 For example, see *Boston Evening Transcript*, July 22, 1861, which ran the following headline: "Rebels Completely Routed."

107 *PJ*, July 23, 1861.

108 McPherson, *Battle Cry of Freedom*, 347.

109 *NDN*, July 27, 1861.

110 Wheatie King was the son of David King, a prominent physician who was the first president of the Newport Historical Society. See Jefferys, *Newport: A Concise History* (Newport, RI: Newport Historical Society, 2008), 52. See also Stensrud, *Newport: A Lively Experiment* (Newport, RI: Redwood Library, 2006), 322.

111 *NDN*, July 24, 1861.

112 *NDN*, July 27, 1861.

113 *PJ*, August 15, 1861.

114 *NDN*, July 27 and 28, 1861. John Courtney died in 1891 and is buried in Saint Mary's Cemetery in Newport. There is a marker beside his grave noting that he served in the Rhode Island Second Regiment.

115 *Adjutant General's Report (1865)*, 2 vols. (Providence: Freeman, 1895), 1:208.

116 Federal Hill, at this time, was a heavily Irish neighborhood in Providence.

117 Although Father Quinn spoke of "Gilroy," he was probably referring to Patrick Kilroy, who spent the next several months in the hospital and received a medical discharge from the army in April 1862. See *Adjutant General's Report (1865)*, 1:151.

118 Thomas Quinn, letter to Francis McFarland, [July 22, 1861], AAH. For a discussion of Quinn's letter, see Hayman, "The Rhode Island Irish and the Civil War," 51. Thomas Francis Meagher was an Irish revolutionary who would later be appointed commander of New York's Irish Brigade. See Timothy Egan, *Immortal Irishman: The Irish Revolutionary Who Became an American Hero* (Boston: Houghton Mifflin, 2016).

119 *PEP*, July 23, 1861. See also *NDN*, July 24, 1861.

120 *NDN*, July 24, 1861.

121 *NDN*, July 25, 1861. See also *NM*, July 27, 1861.

122 New York and Massachusetts had both established all-Irish regiments, but the Irish in Rhode Island were ambivalent about serving in a separate unit. See Hayman, "The Rhode Island Irish and the Civil War," 51–54.

123 Despite Governor Sprague's assurances, a law allowing immigrant veterans to vote even if they did not meet the real estate qualification was not approved until 1886. See Hayman, "The Rhode Island Irish in the Civil War," 51–54; and Patrick T. Conley, "Politics, Prejudice, Patriotism, and Perseverance: Rhode Island's Catholic Irish Confront the Civil War," in Williams and Conley, eds., *The Rhode Island Home Front in the Civil War Era*, 110–21.

124 *NDN*, September 5, 1861.

125 *PJ*, September 7, 1861.

126 *NDN*, September 5, 1861. Quinn, who was struggling with alcoholism, did not stay with the Third Regiment for long. By October or November, he resigned his position and was replaced by a Baptist minister, Reverend Frederic Denison. See Hayman, *Catholicism in Rhode Island and the Diocese of Providence, 1780–1886*, 152; and Conley and Smith, *Catholicism in Rhode Island*, 91.

127 Frank L. Grzyb, *Rhode Island's Civil War Hospital: Life and Death at Portsmouth Grove, 1862–1865* (Jefferson, NC: McFarland, 2012), 22–29; *PPo*, July 9, 1862.

128 John T. Pierce, Sr., *Historical Tracts of the Town of Portsmouth, Rhode Island* (n.p., n.d.), 73; *PPo*, August 16, 1862.

129 For a list of those who died, see Lovell General Hospital Records, NHS. For the total number of patients, see Garman, *A History of Portsmouth, Rhode Island* (Newport, RI: Franklin, 1978), 27.

130 O'Reilly had eight different assistants at Saint Mary's during his tenure there. See Hayman, "St. Mary's," 22.

131 *Sadlier's Catholic Almanac* (New York: Sadlier, 1865), 117; Pierce, *Historical Tracts*, 28.

132 William O'Reilly, letter to Francis McFarland, c. February 16, 1863, AAH.

133 Charles Carroll, *Rhode Island: Three Centuries of Democracy*, 4 vols. (New York: Lewis Historical Publishing, 1932), 2:606.

134 McPherson, *Battle Cry of Freedom*, 492.

135 Thomas Coggeshall, Jr., letter to a family member, August 13, 1862, Lovell General Hospital Records, NHS.

136 *PPo*, August 14, 1862.

137 *NM*, September 20, 1862. The Fifth Ward was 64 percent Irish or Irish American in 1865. See Snow, *Report upon the Census of Rhode Island, 1865*, 27.

138 Leonard Panaggio, "Thomas Galvin, an Early Professional Gardener," *NH* 130 (Spring 1968): 85–89; Harry J. Eudenbach, *Estate Gardeners of Newport: A Horticultural Legacy* (Newport, RI, 2010), 18–19; *NM*, June 14, 1862.

139 *NM*, October 11, 1862.

140 *Adjutant General's Report (1865)*, 1:105–6.

141 Carroll, *Rhode Island*, 2:608.

142 George C. Rable, *Fredericksburg! Fredericksburg!* (Chapel Hill: University of North Carolina Press, 2002).

143 On the Irish Brigade's losses, see Egan, *Immortal Irishman*, 225–27. See also Bruce, "'Remember Your Country and Keep Up Its Credit,'" 339–52.

144 Iver Bernstein, *The New York City Draft Riots* (New York: Oxford University Press, 1990); McPherson, *Battle Cry of Freedom*, 609–11.

145 O'Connor, *Civil War Boston*, 139–41.

146 *NM*, July 18, 1863.

147 *NM*, July 11, 1863.

148 *NDN*, July 17, 1863.

149 *NM*, July 18, 1863.

150 *PJ*, July 20, 1863.

151 *NM*, August 22, 1863.

152 *PPo*, September 10, 1863. Only 7 percent of the men whose names were called actually enlisted. See McPherson, *Battle Cry of Freedom*, 605.

153 *Adjutant General's Report (1865)*, 1:175, 208, 383.

154 *NM*, July 9, 1864.

155 David Brundage, *Irish Nationalists in America: The Politics of Exile, 1798–1998* (New York: Oxford University Press, 2016), 101–2; Leon Ó'Broin, *Fenian Fever: An Anglo-American Dilemma* (New York: New York University Press, 1971), 2–3.

156 Brundage, *Irish Nationalists in America*, 102.

157 *NM*, November 21, 1863.

158 Donal McCartney, *The Dawning of Democracy: Ireland, 1800–1870* (Dublin: Helicon, 1987), 185–88.

159 James Hennesey, S.J., *American Catholics* (New York: Oxford University Press, 1981), 163–64; William D'Arcy, O.F.M. Conv., *The Fenian Movement in the United States, 1858–1886* (PhD diss., Catholic University of America, 1947), 38–39, 49.

160 Conley and Smith, *Catholicism in Rhode Island*, 95.

161 *NDN*, July 12 and 13, 1865. The second letter is signed "An Irishman" and may have been written by Father O'Reilly.

162 *NDN*, July 18, 1865; *NYT*, July 27, 1865.

163 *PJ*, July 22, 1865.

164 *NDN*, August 7, 1865.

165 *PJ*, August 12, 1865.

166 *NDN*, September 12, 1865.

167 McFarland, diary entry, September 15, 1865, AAH.

168 W. S. Neidhardt, *Fenianism in North America* (University Park: Pennsylvania State University Press, 1975), 28–29.

169 *NDN*, March 19, 1866; *PEP*, March 19, 1866.

170 Neidhardt, *Fenianism in North America*, 43–52; D'Arcy, *The Fenian Movement in the United States*, 135–41.

171 Peter Vronsky, *Ridgeway: The American Fenian Invasion and the 1866 Battle That Made Canada* (Toronto: Allen Lane, 2011); D'Arcy, *The Fenian Movement in the United States*, 159–75.

172 Ó'Broin, *Fenian Fever*, 119–73.

173 On a Providence meeting in 1868, see Conley and Smith, *Catholicism in Rhode Island*, 94.

174 Christopher Klein, *When the Irish Invaded Canada: The Incredible True Story of the Civil War Veterans Who Fought for Ireland's Freedom* (New York: Doubleday, 2019), 193–214; Neidhardt, *Fenianism in North America*, 118–23.

175 *NM*, June 4, 1870.

176 Conley and Smith, *Catholicism in Rhode Island*, 94–96.

177 *NM*, May 13, 1865.

178 *NDN*, August 7, 1863.

179 Hayman, "St. Mary's," 18; *NM*, February 27, 1864.

180 *NM*, March 26, 1864.

181 McFarland, diary entry, April 18, 1865, AAH.

182 *NM*, April 29, 1865.

183 *NDN*, April 24, 1865.

184 William O'Reilly, letter to Francis McFarland, June 25, 1865, AAH.

185 *NM*, July 29, 1865.

186 William O'Reilly, letter to Francis McFarland, August 15, 1865, AAH.

187 McFarland, diary entry, July 17, 1866, AAH.

188 *NM*, August 15, 1866.

189 Hayman, "St. Mary's," 18; *Boyd's Newport Catholic Directory* (Newport, RI: Ward, 1867), 104.

190 *A Little Sketch of the Sisters of Mercy in Providence, Rhode Island from 1851 to 1893* (Providence: Reid, 1893), 144–50; *Boyd's Newport City Directory* (Newport, RI: Ward, 1873), 51.

191 *Sadlier's Catholic Almanac* (New York: Sadlier, 1867), 105.

192 *NM*, December 25, 1868.

193 *PJ*, December 22, 1868.

CHAPTER 7: ACCEPTED AND YET APART

1 Jon Sterngass, *First Resorts: Pursuing Pleasure at Saratoga Springs, Newport, and Coney Island* (Baltimore: Johns Hopkins University Press, 1991), 222–23. While largely excluded from the mansions, African Americans continued to staff the Fall River Line.

2 Edwin Snow, *Report upon the Census of Rhode Island, 1875* (Providence: Providence Press, 1877), xx, 14, 23.

3 In general, the Irish fared better in the cities of the Midwest and West at this time. See David M. Emmons, *Beyond the American Pale: The Irish in the West, 1845–1910* (Norman: University of Oklahoma Press, 2010); and David Brundage, *Irish Nationalists in America: The Politics of Exile, 1798–1998* (New York: Oxford University Press, 2016), 113–14.

4　Eileen Warburton, *In Living Memory: A Chronicle of Newport, Rhode Island, 1888–1988* (Newport, RI: Newport Savings and Loan Association, 1988), 25–26.

5　The Irish in other New England cities acted in much the same way at this time. For Boston, see Paula M. Kane, *Separatism and Subculture* (Chapel Hill: University of North Carolina Press, 1994). For Worcester, see Timothy J. Meagher, *Inventing Irish America: Generation, Class, and Ethnic Identity in a New England City, 1880–1928* (Notre Dame, IN: University of Notre Dame Press, 2001).

6　The hospital closed in August 1865, and the buildings were auctioned off. See Frank L. Grzyb, *Rhode Island's Civil War Hospital: Life and Death at Portsmouth Grove, 1862–1865* (Jefferson, NC: McFarland, 2012), 137, 151–52.

7　Rockwell Stensrud, *Newport: A Lively Experiment, 1639–1969* (Newport, RI: Redwood Library, 2006), 323.

8　On Newport's industry, see *Boyd's Newport City Directory 1873–1874* (Newport, RI: Ward, 1874) 51; and Richard V. Simpson, *Goat Island and the U.S. Naval Torpedo Station* (n.p., 2016).

9　*NM*, April 2, 1870.

10　*NM*, April 4, 1868.

11　*PJ*, July 11, 1868.

12　*NM*, July 18, 1868.

13　*NM*, September 26, 1868.

14　*NM*, April 2, 1870.

15　*NYT*, June 28, 1869.

16　Levi Morton would become vice president under Benjamin Harrison in 1889, and Newport's Morton Park is named for him. His home, Fairlawn, now houses Salve Regina University's Pell Center for International Affairs.

17　Ida Lewis was featured on the front page of *Harper's Weekly*, July 4, 1869.

18　*PJ*, July 29, 1869. On Saratoga Springs in this period, see Sterngass, *First Resorts*, 135, 146–81.

19　*PEP*, August 26, 1869.

20　Elizabeth C. Stevens, "'A Crisis in our Cause': The Fifteenth Amendment and the Newport Women Suffrage Convention of 1869," *The Bridge* 93 (Fall–Summer 2020): 46–71; *NM*, August 28, 1869. The Academy of Music was located on Bellevue Avenue next to the Jewish Burial Ground.

21　Frederick Douglass lectured in Newport in 1873. See Lewis Keen, "Opera House History," unpublished paper in author's possession; and *NM*, August 3, 1867, and May 1, 1869.

22　*NM*, May 8, 1869. Thomas Galvin, Jr., was at this time in a partnership with Thomas Geraghty. See Leonard Panaggio, "Thomas Galvin, an Early Professional Gardener," *NH* 130 (Spring 1968): 88.

23　On Father O'Connor as pastor, see *NM*, March 13, May 8, 1869; and *Boyd's Newport City Directory* (Newport, RI: Ward, 1869), 87.

24　Bishop McFarland's decision to move O'Connor may have been influenced by a letter from Ellen Clancy, a Saint Mary's parishioner. Having heard that he was about to be named pastor, she warned the bishop to reconsider, noting that O'Connor had treated her in a very insulting manner (June 19, 1869, AAH).

25　Robert W. Hayman, "St. Mary's, Newport," 22, unpublished manuscript, DPA.

26　*NM*, September 4, 1869.

27　*PJ*, September 3, 1869.

28　Hayman notes that the church was burdened with 7 percent interest on this debt ("St. Mary's," 23).

29　Hayman, "St. Mary's," 23.

30　On the parish missions, see Jay P. Dolan, *Catholic Revivalism: The American Experience, 1830–1900* (Notre Dame, IN: University of Notre Dame Press, 1978), 57–89.

31　Hayman, "St. Mary's," 23.

32 James Hennesey, S. J., *The First Council of the Vatican: The American Experience* (New York: Herder and Herder, 1963), 55, 101; Robert W. Hayman, *Catholicism in Rhode Island and the Diocese of Providence, 1780–1886* (Providence: Diocese of Providence, 1982), 191.

33 John W. O'Malley, S.J., *Vatican I: The Council and the Making of the Ultramontane Church* (Cambridge, MA: Harvard University Press, 2018), 132–79; Charles R. Morris, *American Catholic* (New York: Random House, 1997), 71; Hennesey, *The First Council*, 230.

34 *NDN*, February 7, 1871.

35 William Ackerman Buell, "Maker of Schools and Benedictine Monk: The Life of John Byron Diman," *NH* 43 (Fall 1970): 87–88.

36 *PJ*, January 9, 1871.

37 *NDN*, March 16, 1871.

38 Robert H. Lord, John E. Sexton, and Edward T. Harrington, *History of the Archdiocese of Boston*, 3 vols. (New York: Sheed and Ward, 1944), 3:41; Peter R. D'Agostino, *Rome in America: Transnational Catholic Ideology from the Risorgimento to Fascism* (Chapel Hill: University of North Carolina Press, 2004), 46.

39 *Harper's Weekly*, January 21, 1871; D'Agostino, *Rome in America*, 46–48.

40 *NM*, August 20, 1870. On the American bishops' difficulty in adjusting to the papal infallibility decrees, see Gerald P. Fogarty, *The Vatican and the American Hierarchy from 1870 to 1965* (Collegeville, MN: Liturgical Press, 1985), 1–9.

41 McFarland lived for only two more years after his move to Hartford. See *NDN*, October 16, 1874.

42 Hayman, *Catholicism in Rhode Island and the Diocese of Providence, 1780–1886*, 192–93; Lord et al., *History of the Archdiocese of Boston*, 3:45–46.

43 Hayman, *Catholicism in Rhode Island and the Diocese of Providence, 1780–1886*, 97; Conley and Smith, *Catholicism in Rhode Island*, 86.

44 Hayman, *Catholicism in Rhode Island and the Diocese of Providence, 1780–1886*, 197; *SR*, April 29, 1872.

45 Hayman, "St. Mary's," 25.

46 *NM*, March 19, 1870. See also *PEP*, March 18, 1870; *NM*, March 18, 1871; *NDN*, March 16, 1871; and *NM*, March 16, 1872. The young men in the Aquidneck Rifles were under the direction of Colonel William Delany, Saint Mary's sexton and schoolmaster, and were affiliated with the Rhode Island state militia. The mention of O'Reilly is likely a mistake as the assistant pastor at Saint Mary's was then Father James Finnegan. See *NM*, September 9, 1871.

47 *NM*, January 11, 1873.

48 Ron Chernow, *Grant* (New York: Penguin, 2017), 776–79; Robert H. Wiebe, *The Search for Order, 1877–1920* (New York: Hill and Wang, 1967), 5–7.

49 *NM*, April 25, 1874.

50 *NM*, April 17, 1875. The first Rogers High School was on Church Street. The building still stands and houses the Newport Boys and Girls Club.

51 *NYT*, July 26, 1875.

52 Sterngass, *First Resorts*, 183–84; *NM*, February 5, 1876.

53 Hayman, "St. Mary's," 26.

54 *NM*, October 26, 1872; Howard S. Browne, *The Newport Hospital, A History: 1873–1973* (Newport, RI: Newport Hospital, 1976), 15–30. Dr. Grace pledged $1,500 over five years to help with the cathedral's costs. See *PEP*, January 8, 1873.

55 *Rules of the Society of St. Vincent de Paul; conference at Newport, RI* (Newport, 1870). See also Daniel T. McColgan, *A Century of Charity: The First Hundred Years of the Society of St. Vincent de Paul in the United States*, 2 vols. (Milwaukee: Bruce, 1951) 1:265–68.

56 John F. Quinn, *Father Mathew's Crusade: Temperance in Nineteenth-Century Ireland and Irish America* (Amherst: University of Massachusetts Press, 2002), 172–75, 179–80.

57 Rhode Island, Massachusetts, and Vermont followed Maine's example in 1852, but popular sentiment quickly turned against the movement. See Ian R. Tyrrell, *Sobering Up: From*

Temperance to Prohibition in Antebellum America, 1800–1860 (Westport, CT: Greenwood, 1979), 290–309.

58 The definitive work on the Catholic Total Abstinence Union is Joan Bland, S.N.D., *Hibernian Crusade: The Story of the Catholic Total Abstinence Union of America* (Washington, DC: Catholic University of America Press, 1951).

59 Bland, *Hibernian Crusade*, 49; Hayman, *Catholicism in Rhode Island and the Diocese of Providence, 1780–1886*, 188.

60 *NM*, August 19, 1871.

61 *NM*, September 2, 1871. Valley Falls is now Central Falls.

62 *PJ*, January 18, 1876.

63 For Cottrell, see *Boyd's Newport City Directory* (Newport, RI: Ward, 1876), 117.

64 *NM*, February 5, 1876.

65 *NM*, March 18, 1876.

66 *Boyd's Newport City Directory* (1876), 237–38.

67 *Boyd's Newport City Directory* (1876), 88.

68 *Boyd's Newport City Directory* (1876), 242.

69 The Newport Historical Society was chartered in 1854 (https://newporthistory.org).

70 *NM*, May 22, 1875. On Charles Malcolm, see *Boyd's Newport City Directory* (Newport, RI: Ward, 1875), 50.

71 *BP*, May 29, 1875.

72 For background on the De Fray case, see Eugena Poulin, R.S.M., *The Paths of Mercy on Aquidneck Island* (n.p., 1979), 8; and Hayman, "St. Mary's," 24–25. Hayman characterizes it "one of the most painful episodes" of Grace's pastorate (24).

73 *Rhode Island State Census (1875)*, 32, http://ancestrylibrary.com. The census lists just seventeen Portuguese immigrants and thirty-six Portuguese Americans in Newport at this time. See Snow, *Report upon the Census of Rhode Island, 1875*, 14, 22, 24.

74 *PJ*, December 27, 1875.

75 James L. Crouthamel, *Bennett's New York Herald and the Rise of the Popular Press* (Syracuse, NY: Syracuse University Press, 1989), 19–42.

76 *NM*, August 28, October 16, 1875. On Bennett, see Richard O'Connor, *The Scandalous Mr. Bennett* (New York: Doubleday, 1962); and Stensrud, *Newport*, 348–50.

77 *NYH*, December 16, 1875. Additional articles on the matter were published on December 18, 23, and 30.

78 *NYT*, January 4, 1876.

79 *PJ*, December 24, 1875; *Boston Journal*, December 28, 1875; *SR*, January 3, 1876.

80 *PJ*, December 22, 1875, emphasis in original.

81 *PJ*, December 24, 1875. On Catholic concerns about secularism in this period, see Philip Gleason, *Keeping the Faith: American Catholicism Past and Present* (Notre Dame, IN: University of Notre Dame Press, 1987), 119–20, 124–29.

82 *PJ*, December 24, 1875.

83 *NYH*, December 18, 1875.

84 *PJ*, December 24, 1875. See also *NM*, December 25, 1875.

85 *BP*, January 1, 1876.

86 *NM*, December 25, 1875.

87 *NYT*, December 28, 1875.

88 *PJ*, January 3, 1876; *NYT*, January 4, 1876.

89 *NM*, October 26, 1878.

90 On the founding of the Newport Catholic Literary Society, see *Boyd's Newport City Directory* (Newport, RI: Ward, 1879), 210.

91 Donna Harrington-Lueker, *Books for Idle Hours: Nineteenth-Century Publishing and the Rise of Summer Reading* (Amherst: University of Massachusetts Press, 2019), 154–65.

92 Both Colonel Higginson and Julia Ward Howe's husband, Samuel Gridley Howe, were close associates of the radical abolitionist John Brown. On Higginson, see Howard N. Meyer, ed., *The Magnificent Activist: The Writings of Thomas Wentworth Higginson, 1823–1911* (Boston: Da Capo, 2000), 1–39; and Stensrud, *Newport*, 334–36.

93 *NM*, September 21, 1872.

94 Mary Murphy-Schlichting, "A Summer Salon: Literary and Cultural Circles in Newport, Rhode Island" (PhD diss., New York University, 1992), 22–33; Maud Howe Elliott, *This Was My Newport* (Cambridge, MA: Mythology Company, 1944), 103–14; Stensrud, *Newport*, 333–37.

95 Catholic literary societies were also being set up in some Boston and Providence parishes at this time. See Lord et al., *History of the Archdiocese of Boston*, 3:387; Hayman, *Catholicism in Rhode Island and the Diocese of Providence, 1780–1886*, 187; and Evelyne Savidge Sterne, *Ballots and Bibles* (Ithaca, NY: Cornell University Press, 2004), 121–22.

96 Father Bodfish eventually became Chancellor of the Boston Archdiocese. See Lord et al., *History of the Archdiocese of Boston*, 3:408.

97 On the importance of converts in nineteenth-century American Catholicism, see Patrick Allitt, *Catholic Converts: British and American Intellectuals Turn to Rome* (Ithaca, NY: Cornell University Press, 1997), 61–157.

98 *NDN*, March 28, 1876.

99 *PJ*, March 31, 1876.

100 John McCloskey had been appointed America's first cardinal in 1875. See John Farley, *The Life of John Cardinal McCloskey* (New York: Longmans, Green, 1918). The Caldwells were wealthy Catholic converts from Kentucky who purchased the Newport home in 1866. Both parents had died by 1874, leaving behind two young daughters, who were cared for by a guardian. See James Yarnall, "John La Farge's Windows for the Caldwell Sisters of Newport," *RIH* 64 (Summer 2006): 31, 37.

101 *NM*, August 12, 1876.

102 *PJ*, February 22, 1879; *NDN*, February 25, 1879.

103 *NDN*, February 25, 1879.

104 Dee Brown, *The Year of the Century: 1876* (New York: Scribner, 1966), 112–37; Arlene Swidler, "Catholics and the 1876 Centennial," *Catholic Historical Review* 62 (July 1976): 349.

105 Swidler, "Catholics and the 1876 Centennial," 360.

106 *PJ*, December 24, 1875. On Catholics' distrust of Ulysses S. Grant, see Lord et al., *History of the Archdiocese of Boston*, 3:66–67.

107 *NM*, May 6, 1876.

108 *NYT*, June 5, 1876.

109 *PEP*, July 6, 1876.

110 *PEP*, July 6, 1876.

111 On the Hibernians' activities in Newport, see *NM*, February 13, March 6, and June 19, 1875. When covering the Saint Patrick's Day parade in 1875, the *Mercury*'s editor reported, "The Ancient Order of Hibernians in their handsome green uniform made their first appearance as an organization on that day, and turned out to the number of nearly fifty men" (March 20, 1875).

112 *PJ*, June 29, 1876.

113 *NM*, July 8, 1876.

114 *PEP*, July 6, 1876.

115 *Boyd's Newport City Directory* (1876), 46; *NDN*, April 3, 1875. In 1871, Delany moved to Erie, Pennsylvania, to take a teaching job. After his departure, the sisters also assumed responsibility for teaching the boys. See Hayman, "St. Mary's," 23–24.

116 *PJ*, January 3, 1876.

117 Poulin, *Paths of Mercy*, iv–vi; *NM*, January 6, 1877; *BG*, January 2, 1877. When Bishop Hendricken went to meet the Mercy sisters for the first time, he listed them by name: Camillus, Stanislaus, Mary John, Mathias, Mary Edward, Genevieve, and Sebastian. See BTFHD, June 16, 1872.

118 *NM*, August 26, 1876.

119 Caroline LeRoy Edgar Bonaparte was a granddaughter of Daniel Webster. On her marriage and conversion, see *NYT*, September 10, 1871; and BTFHD, September 24, 1873. In 1878, Dr. Grace married Jeanette Bennett to Isaac Bell, Jr., a wealthy Episcopalian businessman; see *NYT*, September 22, 1878. On Margaret LaFarge, see Mary A. LaFarge and James L. Yarnall, "The Newport Life of Margaret Mason Perry LaFarge," *NH* 67 (Fall 1995): 55–105. Emily Havemeyer's father was the Austrian consul general and her husband succeeded him in that position; see *NYT*, April 4, 1914.

120 *NM*, August 26, 1876.

121 *NM*, September 2, 1876.

122 *PJ*, February 8, 1877.

123 *NDN*, February 14, 1877.

124 Hayman, "St. Mary's," 24. In the 1840s, Catherine Harper had purchased the house for the parish. See Kathleen Healy, *Frances Warde: American Founder of the Sisters of Mercy* (New York: Seabury, 1973), 239.

125 *NM*, December 18, 1876.

126 *NYT*, April 29, 1877.

127 *SR*, July 12, 1877.

128 There is some disagreement about where the first Newport match was played. Some think it was in Morton Park in Newport's Fifth Ward, but it was probably just south of there. See Stensrud, *Newport*, 386–87.

129 *Boston Journal*, July 6, 1878, emphasis in original.

130 *SR*, July 3, 1878.

131 *SR*, June 20, 1879. The house that Astor bought was named Beaulieu. See Stensrud, *Newport*, 360.

132 *Boston Journal*, August 22, 1879.

133 Stensrud, *Newport*, 348.

134 *SR*, October 6, 1879. On Stone Villa, see Paul F. Miller, *Lost Newport: Vanished Cottages of the Resort Era* (Bedford, MA: Applewood, 2008), 48–50.

135 Ron Onorato, *AIA Guide to Newport* (Providence: American Institute of Architects, 2007), 183; James L. Yarnall, *Newport through Its Architecture* (Newport, RI: Salve Regina University Press, 2005), 99–102; Sterngass, *First Resorts*, 201; Marialyn E. Riley, "The Casino Theater at Newport, Rhode Island: The Summer Colonists' Playhouse: Reality, Grandeur, Memories, 1881–1960" (PhD diss., Tufts University, 2001).

136 *PJ*, October 28, 1878.

137 Hayman, *Catholicism in Rhode Island and the Diocese of Providence, 1780–1886*, 306–8; BTFHD, August 22, 1872, December 21, 1872, and March 27, 1873.

138 *NM*, November 22, December 6, 1879.

139 George Henry Richardson Scrapbook, vol. 972, page 120, NHS; Hayman, "St. Mary's," 27; *NM*, January 7, 1880.

140 *NM*, January 17, 1880.

141 Hayman, "St. Mary's," 24. On Dudley Newton, see Onorato, *AIA Guide to Newport*, 12. On

John Dixon Johnston, see Ronald J. Onorato, "Architecture and Drawing: The Newport Career of John Dixon Johnston," *NH* 77 (Spring 2008): 1–27.

142 On Michael Dealy, see *Newport Directory* (Newport, RI: Reid, 1882), 80.

143 *NM*, July 3, 1880.

144 *PJ*, November 29, 1880.

145 Jay P. Dolan, *The Irish Americans: A History* (New York: Bloomsbury, 2008), 190–91.

146 Home Rulers wanted to reestablish a legislature in Dublin that would have control over Ireland's domestic matters.

147 Thomas N. Brown, *Irish-American Nationalism* (Philadelphia: Lippincott, 1966), 96.

148 The word *boycott* derives from the name of Captain Charles Boycott, after his tenants decided to ostracize their landlord's overseer. See Brundage, *Irish Nationalism in America*, 112.

149 Robert Kee, *The Laurel and the Ivy: The Story of Charles Stewart Parnell and Irish Nationalism* (London: Hamish Hamilton, 1993), 217–18.

150 *PJ*, January 19, 1880.

151 Kee, *The Laurel and the Ivy*, 218–19; *PJ*, January 17, 1880.

152 Dolan, *Irish Americans*, 193.

153 Brown, *Irish American Nationalism*, 103; Kee, *The Laurel and the Ivy*, 223.

154 *NM*, February 7, 1880. I am indebted to Patrick Murphy for this reference.

155 *NM*, February 14, 1880.

156 *NDN*, April 29, 1880.

157 *NM*, March 20, 1880. Fall River continued to hold Saint Patrick's Day parades.

158 *NM*, February 21, 1880.

159 *PJ*, December 28, 1880; *NDN*, December 27, 1880.

160 Jane McL. Côté, *Fanny and Anna Parnell: Ireland's Patriot Sisters* (New York: St. Martin's, 1991), 135–36; Tara M. McCarthy, *Respectability and Reform: Irish American Women's Activism, 1880–1920* (Syracuse, NY: Syracuse University Press, 2018), 65–93. On Patrick Ford, see Dolan, *Irish Americans*, 193–95.

161 *NM*, February 12, 1881.

162 On May 7, 1881, the *Daily News* reported that the league was having its "quarterly meeting."

163 *NM*, March 19, 1881.

164 *NM*, August 20, 1881.

165 *NM*, July 23, 1881.

166 A copy of the pamphlet can be found in John LaFarge, S.J. Papers, box 39, folder 1, Georgetown University Special Collections, Washington, DC.

167 On Irish Americans' close ties to Catholicism at this time, see Morris, *American Catholic*, 51; and Dolan, *The Irish Americans*, 107–11.

168 *Names of the Subscribers of the Great Collection of 1881* (Newport, RI, 1881), 3–6.

169 *Names of the Subscribers*, 6.

170 *Names of the Subscribers*, 12, 11, 14.

171 On crimes reported in Kerry Hill, see *NM*, December 2, 1882; and *PJ*, November 2, 1878, January 9, 1879, and May 9, 1882. On references to "Kerry Hill roughs" and "ruffians," see *PJ*, November 29, 1877, and May 24, 1881.

172 *Names of the Subscribers*, 22.

173 *Names of the Subscribers*, 7; *Rhode Island Census* (1875), 115; *U.S. Census* (1880), 194, https://www.ancestrylibrary.com. I am grateful to Kurt Schlichting for the last of these references.

174 *Names of the Subscribers*, 7.

175 *Names of the Subscribers*, 27–30.

176 *U.S. Census* (1880), 32, 206, 2.

177 *Names of the Subscribers*, 7, 26, 20.

178 Hayman, "St. Mary's," 26.

179 *PJ*, December 14, 1881, emphasis in original.

180 *PJ*, December 2, 1881.

181 One Providence priest, Dr. Michael Wallace, left for a year-long trip to Europe. See BTFHD, May 13, 1873, and October 31, 1875.

182 *NM*, March 18, 1882.

183 *NDN*, May 8, 1882; *NM*, May 13, 1882.

184 *NM*, May 13, 1882.

185 *PJ*, July 24, 1882.

186 *PJ*, August 26, 1882. Chester Arthur, a Republican from New York, had succeeded James Garfield a few months earlier after Garfield had succumbed to an assassin's bullet.

187 Now known as the U.S. Open, the tournament moved to New York in 1915. See Alan T. Schumacher, "The Newport Casino: Its History," *NH* 61 (Spring 1987): 67–68.

188 *NYT*, September 1, 1882; Schumacher, "The Newport Casino," 62–65.

189 Richmond Barrett, *The Good Old Summer Days: Newport, Narragansett Pier, Saratoga, Long Branch, Bar Harbor* (New York: Appleton-Century, 1941), 46–47.

190 Barrett, *The Good Old Summer Days*, 47.

191 A specialist in obstetrics and gynecology, Dr. Storer had worked closely with the American Medical Association in its campaign for more restrictive abortion laws. See Frederick N. Dyer, *The Physicians' Crusade against Abortion* (Sagamore Beach, MA: Science History Publications, 2005).

192 *NM*, September 30, 1882; *BP*, October 21, 1882.

193 On the Newport Ladies Land League, see *BP*, February 18, 1882. On an Irish relief meeting held by Newport men, see *NM*, April 21, 1883. The National Catholic Literary Society is not listed in the 1882 *Newport Directory*.

194 Conley and Smith, *Catholicism in Rhode Island*, 97.

195 Charles Van Zandt, a Republican, served as governor of Rhode Island from 1877 to 1880.

196 Hayman, *Catholicism in Rhode Island and the Diocese of Providence, 1780–1886*, 300–302; Patrick T. Conley, "No Landless Irish Need Apply: Rhode Island's Role in the Framing and Fate of the Fifteenth Amendment," *RIH* 68 (Summer 2010): 79–91. On Newport's Equal Rights Club, see *PJ*, May 4, September 27, 1882; and *NM*, April 29, May 20, 1882.

197 Rhode Island had offered Coaster's Island to the federal government in hopes of attracting a larger naval presence. See Anthony S. Nicolosi, "The Founding of the Newport Naval Training Station, 1878–1883, An Exercise in Naval Politics," *American Neptune* 49 (1989): 291–304.

198 John LaFarge, S.J., *The Manner Is Ordinary* (New York: Harcourt, Brace, 1954), 51.

199 Hayman, "St. Mary's," 31–32. The Angelus is a prayer honoring the Virgin Mary for accepting the Angel Gabriel's invitation to give birth to Jesus.

200 *NM*, June 30, 1883.

201 The Mill Street building dates back to the eighteenth century and was a Congregational meetinghouse before the Unitarians acquired it. See Florence Archambault, *"Forward through the Ages, In Unbroken Line": 300 Years of Congregationalism on Aquidneck Island* (Middletown, RI: United Congregational Church, 1995), 3–4; and *NM*, July 23, 1836. On Channing Memorial, the 1881 Unitarian church, see Yarnall, *Newport through Its Architecture*, 151–52.

202 *BG*, August 16, 1884.

203 John Conroy had been bishop of Albany from 1865 to 1877 but, in retirement, was living in New York City.

204 *BG*, August 16, 1884; *Boston Journal*, August 16, 1884; *NM*, August 16, 1884; *BP*, August 23, 1884.

205 *NM*, August 16, 1884.

206 Hayman, "St. Mary's," 26.

207 *PJ*, August 16, 1884.

208 Horatio Storer, letter to Matthew Harkins, May 5, 1887, DPA.

209 *PJ*, January 19, 1885.

210 Thomas Hendricken, letter to James Coyle, January 15, 1885, folder 1, Coyle Papers, UNDA.

211 *PJ*, January 17, 1885.

CHAPTER 8: IRISH CHIEFTAINS AND MAYORS

1 Quotation in epigraph is from DPA.

2 Paul R. Baker, *Richard Morris Hunt* (Cambridge, MA: Massachusetts Institute of Technology Press, 1980), 245–47; James L. Yarnall, *Newport through Its Architecture* (Newport, RI: Salve Regina University Press, 2005), 79; David McCullough, *The Greater Journey: Americans in Paris* (New York: Simon and Schuster, 2011), 275–77.

3 Nethercliffe, Vinland, and Wakehurst now belong to Salve Regina University. See Yarnall, *Newport through Its Architecture*, 79, 124–30. The university renamed the main Vinland building McAuley Hall and now refers to Wakehurst as Gerety Hall.

4 *SR*, September 24, 1885.

5 Eileen Warburton, *In Living Memory: A Chronicle of Newport, Rhode Island, 1888–1988* (Newport, RI: Newport Savings and Loan Association, 1988), 23–24; Morris Gutstein, *The Story of the Jews of Newport* (New York: Bloch, 1936), 256–67; *NM*, June 2, 1883; *Newport Directory* (Boston: Sampson and Davenport, 1884), 298.

6 John Hattendorf, *Semper Eadem: A History of Trinity Church in Newport, 1698–2000* (Newport, RI: Trinity Church, 2001), 214.

7 Mrs. John King Van Rensselaer, *Newport: Our Social Capital* (Philadelphia: Lippincott, 1905), 251.

8 Hattendorf, *Semper Eadem*, 187–88; Yarnall, *Newport through Its Architecture*, 45.

9 Hattendorf, *Semper Eadem*, 195–99, 212–14.

10 On Saint John's, see Lorraine Le H. Dexter, "Steps from Trinity Church to the Point: The Zabriskie Memorial Church of St. John," *NH* 48 (Fall 1975): 329–46.

11 See, for example, *Newport Directory* (Boston: Sampson and Murdock, 1919), 133. On the present-day Sisterhood of the Holy Nativity, see the Anglican Religious Life Yearbook (https://arlyb.org.uk).

12 Warburton, *In Living Memory*, 21–22; *PJ*, September 5, 1885.

13 Anthony S. Nicolosi, "The Founding of the Newport Naval Training Station, 1878–1883: An Exercise in Naval Politics," *American Neptune* 49 (1989): 304.

14 John B. Hattendorf, B. Mitchell Simpson III, and John Wadleigh, *Sailors and Scholars: The Centennial History of the Naval War College* (Newport, RI: Naval War College Press, 1984), 11–29.

15 BTFHD, December 24, 1876; *NM*, February 21, 1885.

16 *PJ*, January 19, 1885.

17 *NM*, February 14, 1885.

18 John R. McLean, *A History of St. George's Church, 1833–1933* (Newport, RI: Beans Press, 1933), 9–14; *NM*, February 28, March 14, August 8, 1885.

19 See, for example, *PV*, December 2, 1893. On the confirmation ceremonies, see *NM*, January 3, 1893.

20 BMHD, October 17, 1887. On Father Coyle visiting the apprentices, see *NM*, June 28, 1890.

21 Robert W. Hayman, *Catholicism in Rhode Island and the Diocese of Providence, 1886–1921* (Providence: Diocese of Providence, 1995), 419–20.

22 *NM*, March 21, 1885.

23 Hayman, *Catholicism in Rhode Island and the Diocese of Providence, 1780–1886* (Providence: Diocese of Providence, 1982), 306.

24 Hayman, *Catholicism in Rhode Island and the Diocese of Providence, 1780–1886*, 306–9.

25 Thomas Hendricken, letter to James Coyle, March 1885, Coyle Papers, UNDA.

26 *PJ*, September 5, 1885.

27 Thomas F. Cullen, *The Catholic Church in Rhode Island* (North Providence, RI: Franciscan Missionaries of Mary, 1936), 339; *PJ*, January 24, 1886.

28 Thomas Hendricken, letter to James Coyle, January 23, 1886, Coyle Papers, UNDA.

29 Maud Howe Elliott, *This Was My Newport* (Cambridge, MA: Mythology Company, 1944), 238.

30 John LaFarge, S.J., *The Manner Is Ordinary* (New York: Harcourt, Brace, 1954), 34; Mary A. LaFarge and James L. Yarnall, "The Newport Life of Margaret Mason Perry LaFarge," *NH* 67 (Fall 1995): 88–90.

31 *NM*, November 14, 1885.

32 Robert Kee, *The Laurel and the Ivy: The Story of Charles Stewart Parnell and Irish Nationalism* (London: Hamish Hamilton, 1993), 386–416, 479–92; *NYT*, November 23, 1885.

33 Thomas Conaty was a leading promoter of Parnell and Home Rule in Worcester in the 1880s. He was appointed rector of the Catholic University of America in 1896 and bishop of Los Angeles–Monterey in 1903. See Timothy J. Meagher, *Inventing Irish America: Generation, Class, and Ethnic Identity in a New England City, 1880–1928* (Notre Dame, IN: University of Notre Dame Press, 2001), 183–96.

34 *NM*, December 5, 1885. The Coercion Acts gave the British authorities in Ireland increased police powers to quell unrest.

35 Richard C. Youngken, *African Americans in Newport: An Introduction to the Heritage of African Americans in Newport, 1700–1945* (Newport, RI: Newport Historical Society, 1998), 52–53.

36 *NDN*, December 2, 1885; *BP*, December 12, 1885.

37 *PJ*, December 28, 1885.

38 *NM*, March 6, 1886.

39 *PJ*, March 18, 1886.

40 *NM*, March 20, 1886.

41 John Boyle O'Reilly was as popular with Boston's Protestant elite as he was with the city's Irish. In 1889, he was invited to deliver the main address at the dedication of the Pilgrim fathers monument in Plymouth. See Thomas H. O'Connor, *The Boston Irish: A Political History* (Boston: Back Bay, 1995), 134–36; and A. G. Evans, *Fanatic Heart: A Life of John Boyle O'Reilly* (Nedlands: University of Western Australia Press, 1997), 217–58.

42 Thomas Hendricken, letter to James Coyle, March 17, 1886, Coyle Papers, UNDA. The Irish had had their own parliament in College Green in Dublin in the 1780s and 1790s.

43 *NDN*, March 18, 1886.

44 Davitt had traveled around America in 1880 and 1882. The 1886 tour brought him to Chicago, San Francisco, New York, Boston, and Providence. See Ely M. Janis, *A Greater Ireland: The Land League and Transatlantic Nationalism in Gilded Age America* (Madison: University of Wisconsin Press, 2015), 60–64, 185–88; *PJ*, July 26, 1886; *SR*, September 17, 1886; and *Worcester Daily Spy*, December 6, 1886.

45 *NM*, December 11, 1886. Henry Jeter served as pastor of Shiloh Baptist Church on Mary and Division Streets from 1875 to 1916. See Richard C. Youngken, *African Americans in Newport: An Introduction to the Heritage of African Americans in Newport, 1700–1945* (Newport, RI: Newport Historical Society, 1998), 53–54.

46 Hayman, *Catholicism in Rhode Island and the Diocese of Providence, 1780–1886*, 310–11.

47 Hayman, *Catholicism in Rhode Island and the Diocese of Providence, 1780–1886*, 311.

48 *BG*, June 18 and 20, 1886.

49 *NM*, June 19, 1886.

50 *NYT*, July 17, 1886.

51 *NM*, July 10, 1886.

52 John St. John was involved in enacting Prohibition in Kansas in 1881 and then served as a spoiler in the 1884 presidential election, helping Grover Cleveland defeat James G. Blaine. See Norman H. Clark, *Deliver Us from Evil: An Interpretation of American Prohibition* (New York: Norton, 1976), 73–81.

53 Mahlon Van Horne was pastor of the Union Congregational Church and the first African American member of the Newport School Committee. In 1885, he became the first African American representative in the Rhode Island State Assembly. See Youngken, *African Americans in Newport*, 56.

54 *NM*, March 6, 1886.

55 *NM*, February 6 and 13, 1886.

56 *Newport Directory* (Boston: Sampson and Murdock, 1886), 343; Robert W. Hayman, "St. Mary's," 32, unpublished manuscript, DPA.

57 On Catholic temperance leaders' opposition to Prohibition, see Joan Bland, S.N.D., *Hibernian Crusade: The Story of the Catholic Total Abstinence Union of America* (PhD diss., Catholic University of America, 1951), 259–66; and John F. Quinn, "Father Mathew's Disciples: American Catholic Support for Temperance, 1840–1920," *Church History* 65 (December 1996): 638–40.

58 *PJ*, August 30, 1886.

59 William G. McLoughlin, *Rhode Island: A History* (New York: Norton, 1986), 159.

60 Conley and Smith, *Catholicism in Rhode Island*, 97–98.

61 *NM*, July 3, 1886.

62 On Downing's advocacy of suffrage for immigrants, see Richard M. Bayles, *A History of Newport County, Rhode Island*, 3 vols. (New York: Preston, 1889), 2:595; and S.A.M. Washington, *George Thomas Downing* (Newport, RI: Milne, 1910), 20.

63 Lawrence Grossman, "George T. Downing and the Desegregation of Newport's Schools, 1855–1866," *RIH* 36 (November 1977): 99–105; Myra B. Young Armstead, *"Lord, Please Don't Take Me in August": African Americans in Newport and Saratoga Springs, 1870–1930* (Urbana: University of Illinois Press, 1999), 32–33; Christy Clark-Pujara, *Dark Work: The Business of Slavery in Rhode Island* (New York: New York University Press, 2016), 138–44.

64 *PJ*, July 6, 1886.

65 Patrick T. Conley, "No Landless Irish Need Apply: Rhode Island's Role in the Framing and Fate of the Fifteenth Amendment," *RIH* 68 (Summer 2010): 87.

66 *Newport Journal*, August 21, 1886. This was the Saturday edition of the *Newport Daily News*. I am indebted to Sister Janice Farnham, R.J.M. for this reference and for much of what follows in this section.

67 Janice Farnham, R.J.M., *Weaving Hope: The Religious of Jesus and Mary in the United States, 1877–2017* (Eugene, OR: Wipf and Stock, 2020), 49–56, 83–88.

68 The conflict is known as the Flint Affair, after the neighborhood where Notre Dame was located. For a detailed account, see Hayman, *Catholicism in Rhode Island and the Diocese of Providence, 1886–1921*, 262–80.

69 Marie St. Paul, letter to James Coyle, August 20, 1886, collection of Sister Janice Farnham, R.J.M.

70 James Coyle, letter to Marie St. Paul, [August–September 1886], DPA.

71 Patrick T. Conley, "Bishop Matthew Harkins: A Study in Character," in *Rhode Island in Rhetoric and Reflection* (East Providence: Rhode Island Publications Society, 2002), 358–62.

72 Marie St. Cyrille, letter to Matthew Harkins, April 16, 1887, collection of Sister Janice Farnham, R.J.M.

73 James Coyle, letter to Matthew Harkins, [February–April 1887], DPA.

74 Matthew Harkins, note, [April 1887], collection of Sister Janice Farnham, R.J.M. Elmhurst

was established in Providence in 1872, and Saint Mary's–Bayview was founded in 1874 in East Providence.

75 Horatio Storer, letter to Matthew Harkins, May 5, 1887, DPA. As I mention later in the chapter, Gwendolyn Caldwell provided a major grant to help establish the Catholic University of America.

76 Storer, letter to Harkins, May 5, 1887.

77 For example, see *NDN*, October 24 and 31, 1887, for an advertisement offering the property.

78 BMHD, March 24, April 18, 1888; Hayman, *Catholicism in Rhode Island and the Diocese of Providence, 1886–1921*, 486.

79 In 1892, the diocese leased Eagle Crest to Newport officials, who considered turning it into a rest home for cholera victims but dropped the idea after neighbors raised objections. See *NYT*, September 20, 1892; *NM*, October 7, 1893.

80 Cullen, *The Catholic Church in Rhode Island*, 424–25; Hayman, *Catholicism in Rhode Island and the Diocese of Providence, 1886–1921*, 491.

81 M. Thomasine O'Keefe, R.S.M., letter to James Coyle, November 25, 1886, Coyle Papers, UNDA.

82 Storer, letter to Harkins, May 5, 1887.

83 Patrick T. O'Reilly, letter to James Coyle, November 28, 1886, Coyle Papers, UNDA.

84 *PJ*, January 3, 1887.

85 *PJ*, January 3, 1887. See also *NM*, March 12, 1887.

86 Bayles, *A History of Newport County*, 2:472.

87 Bishop Harkins would soon transfer Father Simmons to Providence, where he would erect Blessed Sacrament, one of the most ornate churches in the diocese. See Hayman, *Catholicism in Rhode Island and the Diocese of Providence, 1886–1921*, 374–78.

88 *NM*, October 15, 1887; Yarnall, *Newport through Its Architecture*, 226–27, n. 40; Bayles, *History of Newport County*, 2:473.

89 *NDN*, February 11, 1889.

90 BMHD, May 28, 1888.

91 BMHD, July 26, 1889.

92 *PJ*, October 7, 1889; BMHD, October 6, 1889.

93 Philip Gleason, *Keeping the Faith: American Catholicism Past and Present* (Notre Dame, IN: University of Notre Dame Press, 1987), 115–35.

94 Bayles, *History of Newport County*, 2:473.

95 BMHD, May 28, September 1, 1888.

96 Mary Borgia Paquin, S.S.J., *History of the Sisters of St. Joseph of Springfield* (n.p., 1972), 142; *Newport Directory* (Boston: Sampson and Murdock,1889), 279.

97 *St. Joseph's Parish: One Hundred Twenty-Five Years of Service* (Newport, RI, 2010), unpaginated.

98 *NM*, July 25, 1891.

99 *NDN*, August 1, 1891.

100 On John Keane, see Patrick H. Ahern, *The Life of John J. Keane, Educator and Archbishop* (Milwaukee: Bruce, 1955). On Americanism, see Gerald P. Fogarty, S.J., *The Vatican and the American Hierarchy from 1870–1965* (Collegeville, MN: Liturgical Press. 1985), 114–42; and Philip Gleason, *Contending with Modernity: Catholic Higher Education in the Twentieth Century* (New York: Oxford University Press, 1997), 6–12.

101 *PJ*, July 1, 1889; BMHD, July 18, 1888; Hayman, *Catholicism in Rhode Island and the Diocese of Providence, 1886–1921*, 11, 14; Scott Molloy, *Irish Titan, Irish Toilers: Joseph Banigan and Nineteenth-Century New England Labor* (Durham: University of New Hampshire Press, 2008), 156.

102 C. Joseph Nuesse, *The Catholic University of America: A Centennial History* (Washington, DC: Catholic University of America Press, 1990), 27–29; *PJ*, May 14, 1888.

103 Paul F. Miller, *Lost Newport: Vanished Cottages of the Resort Era* (Bedford, MA: Applewood, 2008), 28–29; James L. Yarnall, "John LaFarge's Windows for the Caldwell Sisters of Newport," *RIH* 64 (Summer 2006): 31–32; *NM*, December 21, 1890. The LaFarge windows are now in Salve Regina University's chapel, which was constructed in 2010.

104 Hazard Memorial was the only school in the diocese to pay for students' books. See *Boston Journal*, August 31, 1893; *NDN*, August 1, 1891.

105 *NM*, August 8, 1891; BMHD, August 2, 1891.

106 *NYT*, August 3, 1891; *PJ*, August 3, 1891. The *New York Times* referred to George Hazard as "Eccentric but Liberal."

107 *NYT*, June 24, 1892.

108 *PJ*, December 22, 1892.

109 Richard Bliss ran the Redwood Library from 1884 to 1914. See Robert H. Lord. John E. Sexton, and Edward T. Harrington, *History of the Archdiocese of Boston*, 3 vols. (New York: Sheed and Ward, 1944), 3:409; and Mary Victoria O'Connor, R.S.M., *A History of the Redwood Library and Athenaeum of Newport, Rhode Island* (MLS thesis, Catholic University of America, 1956), 62.

110 *NYT*, June 24, 1892; *NM*, June 25, 1892. Father Downing, an Irish immigrant, had replaced Simmons as the assistant pastor of Saint Joseph's. See *Newport City Directory (1889)*, 279.

111 *NM*, September 2 and 9, 1893; *PV*, September 2, 1893. Hazard's relatives tried to break the will, claiming that he had gone insane and that Coyle had exerted "undue influence" over him. The case was dropped in 1895; Coyle may have settled out of court with the plaintiffs. See *Boston Journal*, January 29, 1895; *PJ*, January 30, 1895; and *NM*, May 18, 1895.

112 *NYT*, April 2 and 23, 1893.

113 *NYT*, July 13, 1893.

114 Rockwell Stensrud, *Newport: A Lively Experiment, 1639–1969* (Newport, RI: Redwood Library, 2006), 388–90.

115 Theodore Havemeyer converted to Catholicism shortly before his death, and his funeral was held at Saint Patrick's Cathedral in New York City. See *NYT*, April 27, May 3, 1897; and *PJ*, April 27, 1897.

116 Baker, *Richard Morris Hunt*, 348.

117 Ron Onorato, *AIA Guide to Newport* (Providence: American Institute of Architects, 2007), 231–32; Yarnall, *Newport through Its Architecture*, 133–41.

118 Baker, *Richard Morris Hunt*, 364–66; Onorato, *AIA Guide to Newport*, 223–27.

119 *PJ*, April 17, 1894; FRDG, November 17, 1894; John Herzan, *The Southern Thames Street Neighborhood in Newport, Rhode Island* (Providence: Rhode Island Historical Preservation Commission, 1980), 16.

120 F. E. Hanson, letter to D. W. Lockwood, June 20, 1896; and Jeremiah K. Sullivan, letter to D. W. Lockwood, January 10, 1899; both in RG 77, NARA-B.

121 John Higham, *Strangers in the Land: Patterns of American Nativism, 1860–1925* (New Brunswick, NJ: Rutgers University Press, 1992), 81; *PJ*, November 3, 1893; *SR*, November 2, 1893.

122 *PJ*, November 12, 1893.

123 Hayman, *Catholicism in Rhode Island and the Diocese of Providence, 1886–1921*, 661.

124 *PV*, December 9, 1893.

125 Higham, *Strangers in the Land*, 85.

126 Patrick T. Conley, "The Persistence of Political Nativism in Rhode Island, 1893–1915: The APA and Beyond," in *Rhode Island in Rhetoric and Reflection* (East Providence: Rhode Island Publications Society, 2002), 467; Evelyn Savidge Sterne, *Ballots and Bibles: Ethnic Politics and the Catholic Church in Providence* (Ithaca, NY: Cornell University Press, 2004), 77–78. On the APA in Massachusetts, see Lord et al., *History of the Archdiocese of Boston*, 3:140–59.

127 For example, Charles Gorman, who had led the fight for Irish-born suffrage rights, was

elected U.S. attorney in 1893, and Edwin McGuinness was elected mayor of Providence in 1896. See Patrick T. Conley, *The Irish in Rhode Island: A Historical Appreciation* (Providence: Rhode Island Heritage Commission and Rhode Island Publications Society, 1986), 16–18; and Sterne, *Ballots and Bibles*, 75–77.

128 Dr. Curley served on the school committee until his death in 1900. See *NDN*, December 14, 1900. On the other elected officials, see *Newport Directory* (Boston: Sampson and Murdock, 1893), 291.

129 *NM*, December 15, 1900.

130 *NDN*, December 15, 1900.

131 Republicans had a lock on most state and federal positions; see McLoughlin, *Rhode Island*, 148–64. In Newport, however, two Democrats served as mayor in the last half of the nineteenth century: Stephen Slocum (1873–76, 1880–82) and John Hare Powel, Jr. (1886–88).

132 *NYT*, May 25, 1895.

133 *NDN*, January 30, 1923.

134 *NM*, April 18, 1893. Dr. Grace started replacing the clear glass windows with stained glass after the church's consecration in 1884. See Hayman, "St. Mary's," 27.

135 On James Gibbons, see John Tracy Ellis, *The Life of James Cardinal Gibbons, Archbishop of Baltimore*, 2 vols. (Milwaukee: Bruce, 1952). After Gibbons's visit, Grace then invited him to return to Newport for several weeks and assured him that he could stay at the Havemeyers' cottage on Bellevue Avenue. See *NYT*, July 16, 1893.

136 See *PJ*, July 4, 1893.

137 *Newport Directory* (Boston: Sampson and Murdock, 1888), 288.

138 *FRDG*, March 16, 1894.

139 *FRDG*, July 17, 1893; *PJ*, July 17, 1894.

140 *NM*, July 21, 1894.

141 *NM*, September 1 and 8, 1894.

142 Hayman, "St. Mary's," 33–34.

143 *PJ*, January 9, 1893; *FRDH*, May 10, 1893.

144 *NM*, March 23, 1896; *Daily Morning Journal and Courier*, June 29, 1895. On the Catholic summer school movement, see Donna Harrington-Lueker, *Books for Idle Hours: Nineteenth Century Publishing and the Rise of Summer Reading* (Amherst: University of Massachusetts Press, 2019), 166–75.

145 *FRDG*, March 11, June 8, 1896; *NDN*, August 21, 1896.

146 Hayman, *Catholicism in Rhode Island the Diocese of Providence, 1886–1921*, 419–20; *PJ*, May 19, 1889; M. Rachel Cunha, Susan A. Pacheco, and Beth Pereira Wolfson, *The Portuguese in Rhode Island: A History* (Providence: Rhode Island Publications Society and Rhode Island Heritage Commission, 1985), 7–9.

147 Hayman, *Catholicism in Rhode Island and the Diocese of Providence, 1886–1921*, 295; *NDN*, May 25, 1896.

148 On Joseph Banigan, see Molloy, *Irish Titan, Irish Toiler*.

149 *NM*, May 9, 1895; *NYT*, October 27, 1891.

150 *Tenth Annual Report and General Collection of St. Joseph's Church, Newport, R.I.* (Newport, RI: Newport Herald, 1895), Newport Churches Collection, NHS.

151 *PJ*, January 28, 1895.

152 The phrase "fashionable dames . . . of the Roman church" appears in Mrs. John King Van Rensselaer, *Newport: Our Social Capital* (Philadelphia: Lippincott, 1905), 270.

153 *NM*, April 16, 1904.

154 Hayman, "St. Mary's," 30. Agnes Storer was the society's liaison to the Charity Organization Society.

155 On the Charity Organization Society, see Stephen T. Ziliak, "Self-Reliance before the Welfare State: Evidence from the Charity Organization Movement in the United States,"

Journal of Economic History 64 (June 2004): 433–61; and Deirdre M. Moloney, *American Catholic Lay Groups and Transatlantic Reform in the Progressive Era* (Chapel Hill: University of North Carolina Press, 2002), 133–38.

156 Annie Leary's house, then known as Paul Cottage, was built in the Federal style. See Onorato, *AIA Guide to Newport*, 133.

157 *NDN*, June 21, 1889. On Leary, see Helen Worden Erskine, *Out of this World* (New York: Putnam, 1953), 100–113.

158 A correspondent for the *New York Times*, writing shortly before F. Brockholst Cutting's death, hailed him as "one of the best known clubmen and one of the most popular bachelors in society" (September 9, 1896).

159 Hayman, "St. Mary's," 33–34; *NM*, September 24, 1898.

160 Matthew Harkins, letter to James Coyle, September 28, 1896, Coyle Papers, UNDA.

161 *NM*, October 3, 1896. See also *FRDG*, September 26, 1896.

162 *FRDG*, October 10, 1896.

163 *PV*, January 9, 1898; *FRDG*, January 4, 1897.

164 *Fall River Daily Evening News*, January 4, 1898.

165 *NYT*, June 5, 1898.

166 *NYT*, May 15, 1898.

167 *NYT*, September 10, 1898.

168 Jon Sterngass, *First Resorts: Pursuing Pleasure at Saratoga Springs, Newport and Coney Island* (Baltimore: Johns Hopkins University Press, 1991), 219.

169 See *PJ*, April 30, 1898, for Grace's arrival in Ireland.

170 *PJ*, September 24, 1898.

171 *NM*, October 1, 1898.

172 *PJ*, September 24, 1898.

173 The Knights of Columbus were founded in New Haven, Connecticut, in 1882, and the Newport chapter was established in August 1897 with fifty-seven members. See *FRDG*, August 30, 1897.

174 *BG*, September 26, 1898; Hayman, "St. Mary's," 33.

CHAPTER 9: "A TIME TO BUILD UP"

1 Quotation in title is from Ecclesiastes 3:3.

2 According to the 1905 state census, Newport's population was 25,039. See *Newport Directory* (Boston: Sampson and Murdock, 1910), 71.

3 U.S. Census data for 1910 is from Steven Ruggles, Sarah Flood, Matthew Sobek, Danika Brockman, Grace Cooper, Stephanie Richards, and Megan Schouweiler, Integrated Public Use Microdata Series, version 13.0 (Minneapolis, 2023). I am grateful to Kurt Schlichting for help with this reference.

4 Eileen Warburton, *In Living Memory: A Chronicle of Newport, Rhode Island, 1888–1988* (Newport, RI: Newport Savings and Loan Association, 1988), 26.

5 William G. McLoughlin, "Providence: The Confident Years, 1890–1920," *RIH* 51 (May 1993): 39–68.

6 Leland M. Roth, *McKim, Mead and White, Architects* (New York: Harper and Row, 1983), 150–55.

7 Patrick T. Conley, *An Album of Rhode Island History, 1636–1986* (Providence: Rhode Island Publications Society, 1986), 160; McLoughlin, "Providence," 52.

8 The building suffered extensive damage in a 1925 fire and was rebuilt and expanded. See James L. Yarnall, *Newport through Its Architecture* (Newport, RI: Salve Regina University Press, 2005), 167–68.

9 Yarnall, *Newport through Its Architecture*, 154.

10 Richard O'Connor, *The Golden Summers: An Antic History of Newport* (New York: Putnam, 1974), 182–88.

11 Birdie and William Vanderbilt were married in a Catholic ceremony at Tessie Oelrichs's residence on Fifth Avenue in Manhattan. See *NYT*, April 2 and 5, 1899.

12 O'Connor, *The Golden Summers*, 175–215.

13 Jim Fair was widely viewed as greedy and unscrupulous. See Oscar Lewis, *Silver Kings: The Lives and Times of Mackay, Fair, Flood, and O'Brien, Lords of the Nevada Comstock Lode* (Reno: University of Nevada Press, 1986), 115–215.

14 Oelrichs had a dozen full-size white model ships built for the occasion. See O'Connor, *The Golden Summers*, 244–45; and *NYT*, August 20, 1904.

15 *PJ*, October 28, 1900.

16 *NYT*, October 28, 1900.

17 *PJ*, October 6, 1901.

18 *BG*, December 30, 1901.

19 *PJ*, November 6, 1901.

20 *BG*, December 31, 1898.

21 Robert W. Hayman, *Catholicism in Rhode Island and the Diocese of Providence, 1886–1921* (Providence: Diocese of Providence, 1995), 109; *FRDH*, December 31, 1898.

22 *PT*, December 31, 1898.

23 *PJ*, January 3, 1899. On the Meenan sisters, see *Newport Directory* (Boston: Sampson, Murdock, and Company, 1900), 164.

24 Hayman, *Catholicism in Rhode Island and the Diocese of Providence, 1886–1921*, 418.

25 *NM*, December 19, 1896.

26 Evelyn Savidge Sterne, *Ballots and Bibles: Ethnic Politics and the Catholic Church in Providence* (Ithaca. NY: Cornell University Press, 2004), 120–21; Hayman, *Catholicism in Rhode Island and the Diocese of Providence, 1886–1921*, 623–26.

27 *NDN*, June 12, 1899. I am grateful to Patrick Murphy for this reference.

28 See, for example, *FRDH*, August 10, 1897, and August 16, 1900.

29 *FRDH*, June 27, 1898; M. Rachel Cunha, Susan A. Pacheco, and Beth Pereira Wolfson, *The Portuguese in Rhode Island: A History* (Providence: Rhode Island Publications Society, 1985), 7.

30 *St. Anthony's Church, Portsmouth, Rhode Island, Celebrating 100 Years, 1908–2008* (n.p., 2009), 6.

31 *FRDH*, May 20, 1901.

32 The first trolley lines were laid in Newport in 1889. See Warburton, *In Living Memory*, 31–32, 45.

33 *Fall River Daily Evening News*, May 20, 1901.

34 On Saint Anthony, see Madeline Pecora Nugent, *Saint Anthony: Words of Fire, Light of Life* (Boston: Pauline Books, 1995).

35 Hayman, *Catholicism in Rhode Island and the Diocese of Providence, 1886–1921*, 327.

36 *FRDH*, July 15, 1901.

37 On Fall River and New Bedford, see Richard D. Brown and Jack Tager, *Massachusetts: A Concise History* (Amherst: University of Massachusetts Press, 2000), 206–8. On Worcester, see Timothy J. Meagher, *Inventing Irish America: Generation, Class, and Ethnic Identity in a New England City, 1880–1928* (Notre Dame, IN: University of Notre Dame Press, 2001), 211–14.

38 William G. McLoughlin, *Rhode Island: A History* (New York: Norton, 1986), 189.

39 *FRDH*, January 3, 1885: "With the sale, and conversion to other uses, of the Perry cotton mill, Newport bids good-bye to the industry of cotton manufacturing in its midst."

40 On the estimated number of servants, see Warburton, *In Living Memory*, 63.

41 *Brooklyn Eagle*, June 24, 1902.

42 *NDN*, May 30, 2012.

43 *PT*, June 26, 1902.

44 *BG*, July 9, 1902.

45 *Meriden Daily Journal*, July 12, 1902.

46 *PT*, July 12, 1902.

47 *Meriden Daily Journal*, July 12, 1902; *NYT*, July 11, 1902.

48 Raymond Roy, personal communication, February 20, 2021.

49 *NDN*, June 20, 1962. I am grateful to Patrick Murphy for the reference.

50 Larry Lowenthal, "The Cliff Walk at Newport," *NH* 61 (Fall 1988): 137. On the Forty Steps, see 120–22, 137–39.

51 *Newport Directory* (Boston: Sampson, Murdock, and Company, 1902), 369, 372.

52 On Father Meenan's ties with the Knights of Columbus, see *PJ*, September 18, 1899.

53 *NYT*, September 18, 1899.

54 *NYT*, July 12, 1900; *PT*, July 10, 1900.

55 Emily Havemeyer wanted her daughter's marriage to take place in Saint Mary's, but Bishop Harkins refused to give her a dispensation. See *PJ*, August 29, 1899.

56 Pope Leo XIII removed Bishop Keane as rector in 1896 over concerns about his Americanist sympathies. Bishop Conaty was not as outspoken. See C. Joseph Nuesse, *The Catholic University of America: A Centennial History* (Washington, DC: Catholic University of America Press, 1990), 75–78, 116–26.

57 *NYT*, August 16, 1902.

58 *FRDN*, August 18, 1902.

59 On Annie Leary's appointment as a papal countess, see *NYT*, January 12, 1902.

60 The host of the luncheon was supposed to be William F. Cutting, Jr., but he was too ill to attend so Father Meenan filled in. See *FRDN*, August 18, 1902; *NYT*, August 18, 1902.

61 *PT*, August 18, 1902.

62 President Roosevelt had traveled to Newport twice before to visit the Naval War College. See John B. Hattendorf, "Theodore Roosevelt, the Navy and Newport," in *Forging the Trident: Theodore Roosevelt and the United States Navy*, ed. John B. Hattendorf and William P. Leeman (Annapolis, MD: Naval Institute Press, 2020), 1–4.

63 On Reverend Diman's relationship with Roosevelt, see William Ackerman Buell, "Maker of Schools and Benedictine Monk: The Life of John Byron Diman," *NH* 140 (Fall 1970): 95.

64 *NYT*, August 25, 1902; *NM*, August 30, 1902.

65 *PJ*, August 2, 1902. Chester Arthur was president from 1881 to 1885.

66 Hayman, *Catholicism in Rhode Island and the Diocese of Providence, 1886–1921*, 32–35.

67 Diocese of Fall River (https://www.fallriverdiocese.org).

68 Hayman, *Catholicism in Rhode Island and the Diocese of Providence, 1886–1921*, 34; Barry W. Wall, *Bearing Fruit by Streams of Water: A History of the Diocese of Fall River* (Strasbourg, France: Éditions du Signe, 2003), 43–45.

69 Wall, *Bearing Fruit*, 46.

70 *BG*, May 9, 1904.

71 The building that became the new Rogers High School now houses Thompson Middle School.

72 Ron Onorato, *AIA Guide to Newport* (Providence: American Institute of Architects, 2007), 84; John B. Hattendorf, B. Mitchell Simpson III, and John Wadleigh, *Sailors and Scholars: The Centennial History of the Naval War College* (Newport, RI: Naval War College Press, 1984), 48–49.

73 *NM*, June 11, 1904.

74 *FRDG*, June 6, 1904.

75 *FRDG*, October 21, December 6, 1904.

76 *Souvenir Book Commemorating the Consecration of St Joseph's Church* (Newport, RI: Saint

Joseph's High School Alumni Association, 1922), 28. I am grateful to Patrick Murphy for sharing his copy of this rare pamphlet.

77 See *Newport Directory* (Boston: Sampson, Murdock, and Company, 1887), 302.

78 Agnes Storer's mother, Augusta Caroline Storer, died in Sorrento, Italy, of "Roman fever," shortly after giving birth to her daughter. See Frederick N. Dyer, *Champion of Women and the Unborn: Horatio Robinson Storer, MD* (Canton, MA: Science History Publications, 1999), 398.

79 Helen Lynch, *In the Shadow of Our Lady of the Cenacle* (New York: Paulist Press, 1954), 111–12; Hayman, *Catholicism in Rhode Island and the Diocese of Providence, 1886–1921*, 30.

80 Alfred Dreyfus, a Jewish officer in the French army, was wrongly accused of spying for Germany in 1894, and many leading French Catholics thought he was guilty. After he was pardoned in 1899, the anticlerical government took aim at the communities of priests and nuns and expelled almost all of them from France. See John McManners, *Church and State in France, 1870–1914* (New York: Harper and Row, 1972), 118–39.

81 Richard Lundgren, with Hugh Dudley Auchincloss III and Maya Lillayla Auchincloss, "Early Years of the Auchincloss Family in Newport," *NH* 83 (Fall 2014): 43–48. One member of the Auchincloss family moved across town to Hammersmith Farm on Ocean Drive.

82 For recollections of the sisters' work in the Point, see Virginia Covell, "An Early Washington Street Estate," *Green Light* 29 (August 1984): 14–16; and Erik Dahl, "Music Lessons and Lobsters: Memories of the Cenacle," *Green Light* 47 (March 2002): 8–9.

83 Walter Elliott, C.S.P. to Agnes Storer, November 14, 1906, Storer Papers, PAWDC. Father Elliott had written to Bishop Harkins in support of Father Orosz's appointment.

84 *NYT*, March 25, 1903. The former Cathleen Neilson was married to Reginald Vanderbilt, the youngest son of Alice and Cornelius Vanderbilt II. Father Meenan had officiated at a Newport mansion.

85 *Fall River Evening Herald*, August 3, 1906.

86 *NDN*, January 9, 1908. See also Hayman, *Catholicism in Rhode Island and the Diocese of Providence, 1886–1921*, 31.

87 Hayman, *Catholicism in Rhode Island and the Diocese of Providence, 1886–1921*, 194–95.

88 Hayman, *Catholicism in Rhode Island and the Diocese of Providence, 1886–1921*, 519–23.

89 *NM*, September 25, 1909.

90 Onorato, *AIA Guide to Newport*, 287–88.

91 Anita Dion, D.H.S., *By the Power of the Spirit: The Daughters of the Holy Spirit in the United States*, 3 vols. (n.p., 1986) 2:47–48; *Rhode Island Catholic*, October 8, 2009.

92 Warburton, *In Living Memory*, 26.

93 Jerre Mangione and Ben Morreale, *La Storia: Five Centuries of the Italian American Experience* (New York: HarperPerennial, 1993), 109–64.

94 Hayman, *Catholicism in Rhode Island and the Diocese of Providence, 1886–1921*, 194.

95 *Newport Directory* (Boston: Sampson and Murdock, 1907), 341–75.

96 *Newport Directory* (Boston: Sampson and Murdock, 1908), 33.

97 Marco Russo, letter to Matthew Harkins, January 11, 1908, DPA.

98 J. Truman Burdick, letter to Anthony M. Marolda, March 13, 1908, DPA. See also Florence Archambault, *Forward through the Ages, in Unbroken Line: 300 Years of Congregationalism on Aquidneck Island, 1695–1995* (Middletown, RI: United Congregational Church, 1995), 36–37.

99 Robert W. Hayman, *The Diocese of Providence, Rhode Island: A Short History, 1780–2000* (Strasbourg, France: Éditions du Signe, 2000), 68–75. See also McLoughlin, *Rhode Island*, 184–85.

100 Hayman, *Catholicism in Rhode Island and the Diocese of Providence, 1886–1921*, 195.

101 Lynch, *In the Shadow*, 117–18.

102 Marie Hennessy, r.c., unpublished paper in the author's possession.

103 *Fall River Daily Evening News*, October 13, 1910.

104 *NM*, October 10, 1910.

105 *NM*, October 14, 1911; Warburton, *In Living Memory*, 26.

106 On the number of parishioners, see *NDN*, November 7, 1910. On school enrollments, see *Newport Directory* (Boston: Sampson and Murdock, 1910), 35, 59. On the First Communicants, see *NDN*, May 3, 1911.

107 *NDN*, April 22, 1911.

108 *NDN*, February 11, 1911.

109 *NM*, October 17, 1885, and April 1, 1922.

110 The King estate was on Spring and Bowery streets. See *NYT*, December 25, 1912; and Warburton, *In Living Memory*, 49.

111 Hayman, *Catholicism in Rhode Island and the Diocese of Providence, 1886–1921*, 418–19; *NDN*, April 22, 1911.

112 *NDN*, April 22, 1911.

113 *NDN*, August 1, 1911.

114 For Doran's biography, see Hayman, *Catholicism in Rhode Island and the Diocese of Providence, 1886–1921*, 56–57.

115 Father Curley's brother Peter was a physician who served on the Newport School Committee (see chap. 8).

116 George Wetmore, a Republican, served as governor of Rhode Island and then as U.S. senator from 1895 to 1913. He inherited the Chateau-sur-Mer estate upon the death of his father in 1862.

117 *NDN*, September 25, 1911. See also *NM*, September 30, 1911.

118 *NDN*, August 5, 1912.

119 *Newport Directory* (Boston: Sampson and Murdock, 1913), 60; Hayman, *Catholicism in Rhode Island and the Diocese of Providence, 1886–1921*, 419.

120 *NM*, September 24, 1910.

121 *PV*, March 24, 1911.

122 *Souvenir Book*, 30.

123 *NM*, August 19, 1911.

124 *Souvenir Book*, 30; *Fall River Evening Herald*, January 15, 1912.

125 *BG*, January 16, 1912.

126 Father Higney was a graduate of the College of the Holy Cross and studied for the priesthood at the North American College in Rome. See *NDN*, September 17, 1962.

127 *Souvenir Book*, 32; *Fall River Evening News*, September 9, 1912.

128 O'Connor, *The Golden Summers*, 246–49.

129 The U.S. Open was moved to Forest Hills, New York, in 1915 because the organizers wanted a larger and more accessible venue. However, an invitational tournament took its place in Newport. See Alan T. Schumacher, "The Newport Casino: Its History," *NH* 61 (Spring 1987): 67–69.

130 *NYT*, October 27, 1932.

131 Kristen Iversen, *Molly Brown: Unraveling the Myth* (Boulder, CO: Johnson, 1999), 139–40.

132 Iversen, *Molly Brown*, 181, 200–203; Howard S. Browne, *The Newport Hospital, A History: 1873–1973* (Newport, RI: Newport Hospital, 1976), 57; Sylvia D. Hoffert, *Alva Vanderbilt Belmont: Unlikely Champion of Women's Rights* (Bloomington: Indiana University Press, 2012), 102–3.

133 Stensrud, *Newport: A Lively Experiment, 1639–1969* (Newport, RI: Redwood Library, 2006), 412; O'Connor, *The Golden Summers*, 287–289.

134 On the Sixteenth Amendment, see John Morton Blum, *Woodrow Wilson and the Politics of Morality* (Boston: Little, Brown, 1956), 69–71.

135 The Russians rented James Gordon Bennett, Jr.'s Stone Villa for their summer legation. See Paul F. Miller, *Lost Newport: Vanished Cottages of the Resort Era* (Bedford, MA: Applewood,

2008), 49. For references to German, Swiss, English, and Spanish legations in Newport, see *NYT*, July 22, 1899, and June 29, 1913; *PJ*, September 15, 1910; and *SR*, March 16, 1914.

136 O'Connor, *The Golden Summers*, 301–5.

137 *NDN*, August 27 and September 19, 1914.

138 Stensrud, *Newport*, 416.

139 *NM*, July 25, 1914.

140 For Wilson's declaration, see *NYT*, August 5, 1914.

141 Maginnis and Walsh designed many of the Catholic churches in and around Boston and would be awarded the contract for the National Shrine of the Immaculate Conception in Washington, D.C., in 1919.

142 *FRDG*, May 5, 1914. Father Orosz was then the chaplain at Elmhurst Academy, a girls' school in Providence.

143 *NDN*, December 7, 1914.

144 Erik Dahl, "History of the Harbor House Property," *Green Light* 47 (March 2002): 10.

145 The diocese's first orphanage, Saint Aloysius, was founded in Providence in 1858.

146 *PT*, July 10, 1915.

147 *PJ*, July 11, 1915. Hayman, *Catholicism in Rhode Island and the Diocese of Providence, 1886–1921*, 487.

148 *PJ*, March 24, 1917.

149 Dion, *By the Power of the Spirit*, 2:50.

150 *Newport Directory* (Boston: Sampson and Murdock, 1917), 58.

151 *NM*, August 10, 1917.

152 Sister Marion Hurley, S.S.J., fondly recalled swimming off the boardwalk when she lived at Hunter House. She also remembered that two taxis picked up the sisters each morning and shuttled them to their schools (reminiscences, Sisters of Saint Joseph Archives, Holyoke, MA).

153 *NYT*, April 25, 1915; *BG*, April 24, 25, 27, 1915.

154 *Fall River Daily Evening News*, April 28, 1915.

155 Yarnall, *Newport through Its Architecture*, 170–71.

156 Warburton, *In Living Memory*, 54.

157 On Irish opposition to the Allies, see John Patrick Buckley, *The New York Irish: Their View of American Foreign Policy, 1914–1921* (New York: Arno, 1976), 1–119; and Sterne, *Ballots and Bibles*, 154. In Worcester, Timothy Meagher found no neutralist sentiment among the Irish (*Inventing Irish America*, 298).

158 Fred Zilian, "Courtesy during Wartime," *NDN*, October 7, 2016.

159 John T. Duchesneau and Kathleen Troost-Cramer, *Fort Adams: A History* (Charleston, SC: History Press, 2014), 79–81.

160 Warburton, *In Living Memory*, 57.

161 *Newport Directory* (1917), 23.

162 Maud Howe Elliott, *This Was My Newport* (Cambridge, MA: Mythology Company, 1944), 255.

163 Warburton, *In Living Memory*, 58.

164 Knights of Columbus chapters throughout the nation made it their mission to provide wholesome recreation for soldiers and sailors, without respect to race or creed. See Christopher Kauffman, *Faith and Fraternalism: The History of the Knights of Columbus, 1882–1982* (New York: Harper and Row, 1982), 192–207.

165 On Knights of Columbus activities, see *NM*, April 12, June 7, July 5, July 19, 1918.

166 *NDN*, November 11, 1918.

167 *NDN*, November 13, 1918.

168 Stensrud, *Newport*, 420.

169 Patrick F. Murphy, "Private Michael George Murphy and Newport's Great War Memorials," *Rhode Island Roots* 40 (March 2014): 45–48.

170 Bath Road is now Memorial Boulevard.

171 On Bernardo Cardines, see Newport Historical Society (https://newporthistory.org); and *NDN*, October 7, 1936. I'm grateful to John Rok for this reference.

CHAPTER 10: IRISH, ITALIAN AND PORTUGUESE

1 Eileen Warburton, *In Living Memory: A Chronicle of Newport, Rhode Island, 1888–1988* (Newport, RI: Newport Savings and Loan Association, 1988), 42–43, 61–64.

2 In 1920, Newport's population was 30,255, but by 1925 it had fallen to 27,757. See *Newport Directory* (Boston: Sampson and Murdock, 1926), 8.

3 U.S. Census data for 1920 from Steven Ruggles, Sarah Flood, Matthew Sobek, Danika Brockman, Grace Cooper, Stephanie Richards, and Megan Schouweiler, Integrated Public Use Microdata Series, version 13.0 (Minneapolis, 2023). I am grateful to Michael Quinn for his help with this dataset.

4 On the Easter Rising, see Alan J. Ward, *The Easter Rising: Revolution and Irish Nationalism* (Wheeling, IL: Harland Davidson, 2003).

5 Diarmaid Ferriter, *Judging Dev: A Reassessment of the Life and Legacy of Eamon De Valera* (Dublin: Royal Irish Academy, 2007), 25–34.

6 John Patrick Buckley, *The New York Irish: Their View of American Foreign Policy* (New York: Arno, 1979), 303–4.

7 For example, the city of New Bedford voted not to invite De Valera to visit. See *FRDG*, September 25, 1919.

8 *PJ*, August 14, 1919.

9 *PT*, August 15, 1919; *NDN*, September 13, 1919.

10 *PJ*, Sept 12, 1919. On local opposition, see also Dave Hannigan, *De Valera in America: The Rebel President and the Making of Irish Independence* (New York: Palgrave, 2010), 68.

11 *NDN*, September 12, 1919; *PJ*, September 12, 1919.

12 Joseph Gainer was an Irish Catholic Democrat. See Evelyn Savidge Sterne, *Ballots and Bibles: Ethnic Politics and the Catholic Church in Providence* (Ithaca, NY: Cornell University Press, 2004), 138.

13 *NDN*, September 15, 1919.

14 *NDN*, September 15, 1919.

15 Jay P. Dolan, *The Irish Americans: A History* (New York: Bloomsbury, 2008), 203.

16 *NM*, November 20, 1926; Cleveland Amory, *The Last Resorts* (New York: Harper and Brothers, 1952), 207–29; Richard O'Connor, *The Golden Summers: An Antic History of Newport* (New York: Putnam, 1974), 307–9.

17 *PJ*, February 3, 1923.

18 For Annie Leary's obituary, see *NYT*, April 27, 1919. She had moved from the Paul Cottage on Mill Street to Park Gate in 1903; see *Newport Directory* (Boston: Sampson and Murdock, 1903), 403. For the Elks Club's acquisition of Park Gate, see *NM*, July 10 and August 21, 1920.

19 For the Hanan obituaries, see *NYT*, January 12 and August 26, 1920. For the sale of Castlewood, see *NM*, December 18, 1920.

20 For the building's history, see *NDN*, July 18, 1969.

21 For the Weld house, see James L. Yarnall, *Newport through Its Architecture* (Newport, RI: Salve Regina University Press, 2005), 126.

22 *NM*, January 8, 1921.

23 *NDN*, January 7, 1921.

24 Anita Dion, D.H.S., *By the Power of the Spirit: The Daughters of the Holy Spirit in the United States*, 3 vols. (n.p., 1986), 2:50–51.

25 *NM*, July 2, 1921.

26 Dion, *By the Power of the Spirit*, 2:50–51, 3:173.

27 See, for example, *NDN*, August 13, 1918, August 9, 1919, and August 10, 1920. I am grateful to Patrick Murphy for several references related to Saint Augustin's.

28 *NDN*, March 20, 1918, November 18, 1919, November 17, 1920, and March 11, 1922.

29 *NDN*, April 19, 1920.

30 *NDN*, September 25, 1916, October 6, 1919, and October 2, 1922. See also Sterne, *Ballots and Bibles*, 207–8; and Robert W. Hayman, *Catholicism in Rhode Island and the Diocese of Providence, 1886–1921* (Providence: Diocese of Providence, 1995), 623–26.

31 *NDN*, November 21 and December 4, 1916.

32 *NDN*, October 17, 1921. The Redemptorists sought to promote devotion to the Virgin Mary. See Jay P. Dolan, *Catholic Revivalism: The American Experience, 1830–1900* (Notre Dame, IN: University of Notre Dame Press, 1978), 64.

33 Father Higney paid off the debt during a remarkable ten-day parish canvass in 1918. See *Souvenir Book Commemorating the Consecration of St Joseph's Church* (Newport, RI: Saint Joseph's High School Alumni Association, 1922), 34.

34 Bishop Harkins died at age seventy-five after a long illness, and Hickey had been coadjutor bishop since 1919.

35 *PJ*, October 13, 1922. Bishop Gibbons was a Fall River native and had been a classmate of Father Higney.

36 *Souvenir Book*, 60, 62.

37 *NYT*, September 19, 1922; *BG*, September 19, 1922.

38 *NM*, September 23, 1922.

39 Frederick N. Dyer, *Champion of Women and the Unborn* (Canton, MA: Science History Publications, 1999), 474, 492. In Washington, D.C., Father Walter Elliott, C.S.P. heard of Dr. Storer's actions and wrote to commend him for his "wholehearted defence of the Negroes. I applaud your public spirit in expressing them in the papers" (September 11, 1915, Storer Papers, PAWDC).

40 *FRDG*, July 28, 1915; *BG*, June 27, 1915; *PJ*, August 15, 1915. Providence had initially blocked the film but later permitted its showing.

41 *NM*, February 3, 1923.

42 *NDN*, January 31, 1923.

43 A young Irish revolutionary, Robert Emmet, had led an uprising in 1803 and was executed by the British. See Marianne Elliott, *Robert Emmet: The Legend* (London: Profile, 2003).

44 *NM*, February 3, 1923.

45 *NM*, March 21, 1923.

46 Patrick T. Conley, "Bishop Matthew Harkins: A Study in Character," in *Rhode Island in Rhetoric and Reflection* (East Providence: Rhode Island Publications Society, 2002), 77–88.

47 In 1925, the U.S. Supreme Court struck down the Oregon law in a unanimous decision. See James Hennesey, S.J., *American Catholics* (New York: Oxford University Press, 1981), 247–48. On the Peck Act, which was repealed in 1925, see Sterne, *Ballots and Bibles*, 218–23; and Hayman, *Catholicism in Rhode Island the Diocese of Providence, 1921–1948* (Providence: Diocese of Providence, 2020), 16–21.

48 Saint Mary's Academy, Newport Records, MHC, BNC.

49 See, for example, *NM*, January 13, 1933, March 3, 1933, and November 9, 1934.

50 Warburton, *In Living Memory*, 74.

51 The excommunications were lifted in 1929. See Hayman, *Catholicism in Rhode Island and the Diocese of Providence, 1921–1948*, 101–238; Sterne, *Ballots and Bibles*, 228–30; and Richard S. Sorrell, "Sentinelle Affair (1924–1929)—Religion and Militant Survivance in Woonsocket, Rhode Island," *RIH* 36 (August 1977): 67–79.

52 Portsmouth Priory was founded by Father Leonard Sargent, a former Episcopal minister. See Hayman, *Catholicism in Rhode Island and the Diocese of Providence, 1886–1921*, 28–30; and Robert H. Lord, John E. Sexton, and Edward T. Harrington, *History of the Archdiocese of Boston*, 3 vols. (New York: Sheed and Ward, 1944), 3:760.

53 John LaFarge recalled that Diman visited him when he was a seminarian, and LaFarge believed that this meeting helped persuade Diman to become a Catholic. See John LaFarge,

S. J., *The Manner Is Ordinary* (New York: Harcourt, Brace, 1954), 136–37. On reactions to Diman's departure from Saint George's, see Gilbert Y. Taverner, *St. George's School: A History* (Newport, RI: The School, 1987), 55–65.

54   William Ackerman Buell, "Maker of Schools and Benedictine Monk: The Life of John Byron Diman," *NH* 140 (Fall 1970): 112–13; *BG*, December 28, 1917.

55   Buell, "Maker of Schools,"120.

56   Buell, "Maker of Schools," 121–22; Amity Gaige, ed., *Portsmouth Abbey School: Seventy-Five Years, 1926–2001* (Portsmouth, RI: Narragansett Graphics, 2001), 58.

57   *NM*, April 17, 1926.

58   *NM*, April 17, 1926.

59   Captain John Malloy, who had been injured in the Saint Mary's fire, died while fighting the city hall blaze.

60   *NM*, September 5, 1925. Gale House is now the community center for Touro Synagogue.

61   *NM*, July 3, 1926.

62   *NM*, May 29, 1926.

63   Warburton, *In Living Memory*, 64.

64   Yarnall, *Newport through Its Architecture*, 172.

65   *NM*, May 29, 1926.

66   *NM*, July 10, 1926.

67   On Dr. Smiddy, see Troy D. Davis, "Diplomacy as Propaganda: The Appointment of T. A. Smiddy as Irish Free State Minister to the United States," *Éire-Ireland* 31 (1996): 117–29.

68   *PJ*, July 6, 1926; *NYT*, July 6, 1926.

69   In 1916, Dr. Storer had set up a home he called Shore Haven at Hunter House, but a year later he gave the building to Saint Joseph's parish. See *Newport Directory* (Boston: Sampson and Murdock, 1917), 58.

70   Agnes Storer, letter to Marie Similien, D.H.S., December 25, 1925, in Dion, *By the Power of the Spirit*, 3:11.

71   *NDN*, July 16, 1926; *NM*, July 17, 1926.

72   Esther Fisher Benson, "Stella Maris," *Green Light* 31 (December 1986): 9–10.

73   Hayman, *Catholicism in Rhode Island and the Diocese of Providence, 1921–1948*, 256.

74   *NDN*, July 10, 1926.

75   Fritz Garrettson became a Catholic in February 1925 after recovering from a serious illness. He considered Sister Rodolphe, a Daughter of the Holy Ghost, to be his honorary godmother. See Dion, *By the Power of the Spirit*, 2:52, 3:177.

76   Dion, *By the Power of the Spirit*, 3:174.

77   Dion, *By the Power of the Spirit*, 3:175–79.

78   Bishop Hickey presided at Garrettson's funeral at Saint Mary's Church. See *NM*, January 17, 1930; and *NYT*, January 10, 1930.

79   Hennesey, *American Catholics*, 252.

80   Hayman, *Catholicism in Rhode Island and the Diocese of Providence, 1921–1948*, 347–54; Sterne, *Ballots and Bibles*, 224–27.

81   William G. McLoughlin, *Rhode Island: A History* (New York: Norton, 1986), 159–60.

82   Christopher M. Finan, *Alfred E. Smith: The Happy Warrior* (New York: Hill and Wang, 2002), 221–23; *NYT*, October 25, 1928.

83   *NM*, October 26, 1928.

84   *NM*, November 9, 1928.

85   On Rhode Island's "bloodless revolution," see McLoughlin, *Rhode Island*, 200–203. On Smith's role in President Roosevelt's victories, see Oscar Handlin, *Al Smith and His America* (Boston: Little, Brown, 1958), 134.

86   Warburton, *In Living Memory*, 71–73.

87   Hayman, *Catholicism in Rhode Island and the Diocese of Providence, 1921–1948*, 274–79.

88   The other Portuguese parishes were Holy Rosary in Providence (founded in 1885), Saint

Elizabeth in Bristol (1913), Saint Francis Xavier in East Providence (1915), and Saint Anthony's in Pawtucket (1925).

89 *Jesus Saviour Parish, 1926–2001* (n.p., 2001), 11. The hall had been constructed in 1920.

90 On bazaars, see *NM*, August 23, 1929.

91 *Jesus Saviour Parish*, 11–12; *PJ*, December 28, 1928.

92 See, for example, *NM*, May 24 and September 6, 1929.

93 Hayman, *Catholicism in Rhode Island and the Diocese of Providence, 1921–1948*, 292.

94 *NM*, July 18, 1930; *PJ*, July 12, 1930.

95 Saint Thérèse's autobiography, *The Story of a Soul* (Chicago: Carmelite Press, 1900), influenced millions of Catholics worldwide.

96 Hayman, *Catholicism in Rhode Island and the Diocese of Providence, 1921–1948*, 332; *NDN*, May 17, 1930.

97 Emilie Post died in 1948. See Vilma Seelaus, O.C.D., "Notes on the History of the Carmel," undated, DPA; and Hayman, *Catholicism in Rhode Island and the Diocese of Providence, 1921–1948*, 332.

98 *Newport Directory* (Boston: Sampson and Murdock, 1930), 40–44.

EPILOGUE

1 The Goelets donated Ochre Court to Bishop Francis Keough of Providence, who immediately turned it over to the sisters. See Mary Jean Tobin R.S.M. and Mary Eloise Tobin, R.S.M., *With Courage and Compassion: A Reflection on the History of Salve Regina University in Light of the Spirit Which Engendered and Sustains It* (Newport, RI: Salve Regina University, 1993). On the Cluny School, see *PJ*, May 27, 1962.

2 On Saint Philomena's School, see its website (https://www.saintphilomena.org).

3 See, for example, Mary Ryan, *Are Catholic Schools the Answer?* (New York: Holt, Rinehart, and Winston, 1964), which argues that the time for Catholic schools has passed.

4 For a vivid account of the changes, see Garry Wills, *Bare Ruined Choirs: Doubt, Prophecy, and Radical Religion* (New York: Dell, 1972), 79–138.

5 The Catholic historian Philip Gleason claims that American Catholics entered into a "crisis of faith" in the years following the Second Vatican Council (*Keeping the Faith: American Catholicism Past and Present* [Notre Dame, IN: University of Notre Dame Press, 1987], 171–77). For a more sanguine view, see Jay P. Dolan, *The American Catholic Experience* (New York: Doubleday, 1985), 421–45.

6 C.P.B. Jefferys, *Newport: A Concise History* (Newport, RI: Newport Historical Society, 2008), 83–86.

7 Saint Catherine's Academy operated from 1940 to 1971 and was under the direction of the Sisters of Saint Joseph.

8 *NDN*, December 22, 2022.

9 *NDN*, October 7, 2016.

10 *NDN*, June 10, 2017.

11 See https://www.staugustinnewport.org/; and *NDN*, April 30, 2015.

12 *NDN*, August 7, 2013.

13 *PJ*, August 16, 2014.

14 See https://allsaintsacademy.org. Newport's other two Catholic elementary schools, Jesus Saviour and the Cluny School, closed in 1988 and 2017 respectively.

15 As the monastery grew in size, the priory became an abbey in 1969.

INDEX

NOTE: Page references in *italics* refer to illustrations and photos.

JOHN F. QUINN is professor of history at Salve Regina University in Newport, Rhode Island and author of *Father Mathew's Crusade: Temperance in Nineteenth-Century Ireland and Irish America* (University of Massachusetts Press, 2002).